CompTIA A+ Certification: Practical Application

Instructor's Edition

2009 Edition

CompTIA A+ Certification: Practical Application, 2009 Edition

President, Axzo Press:	Jon Winder
Vice President, Product Development:	Charles G. Blum
Vice President, Operations:	Josh Pincus
Director of Publishing Systems Development:	Dan Quackenbush
Writer:	Andy LaPage
Copyeditor:	Catherine Oliver
Keytester:	Cliff Coryea

COPYRIGHT © 2009 Axzo Press. All rights reserved.

No part of this work may be reproduced, transcribed, or used in any form or by any means—graphic, electronic, or mechanical, including photocopying, recording, taping, Web distribution, or information storage and retrieval systems—without the prior written permission of the publisher.

For more information, go to www.axzopress.com.

Trademarks

ILT Series is a trademark of Axzo Press.

Some of the product names and company names used in this book have been used for identification purposes only and may be trademarks or registered trademarks of their respective manufacturers and sellers.

Disclaimers

We reserve the right to revise this publication and make changes from time to time in its content without notice.

The logo of the CompTIA Authorized Quality Curriculum (CAQC) program and the status of this or other training material as "Authorized" under the CompTIA Authorized Quality Curriculum program signifies that, in CompTIA's opinion, such training material covers the content of CompTIA's related certification exam.

The contents of this training material were created for the CompTIA A+ Practical Application exam, 2009 Edition (220-702), covering CompTIA certification objectives that were current as of August 2009.

ISBN 10: 1-4260-1779-0
ISBN 13: 978-1-4260-1779-7

Printed in the United States of America

2 3 4 5 6 7 8 9 10 GL 12 11 10

Contents

Introduction   iii
Topic A: About the manual iv
Topic B: Setting student expectations ix
Topic C: Classroom setup xiii
Topic D: Support xxviii

Power systems   1-1
Topic A: Power supplies 1-2
Topic B: Power supply troubleshooting 1-19
Unit summary: Power systems 1-25

CPUs and motherboards   2-1
Topic A: CPU and motherboard installation 2-2
Topic B: Motherboard troubleshooting 2-30
Unit summary: CPUs and motherboards 2-39

Memory systems   3-1
Topic A: RAM installation 3-2
Topic B: Memory troubleshooting 3-12
Unit summary: Memory systems 3-15

Expansion cards   4-1
Topic A: Host system interaction 4-2
Topic B: Expansion card installation 4-13
Topic C: Expansion card troubleshooting 4-21
Topic D: Port, cable, and connector troubleshooting 4-25
Unit summary: Expansion cards 4-31

Data storage devices   5-1
Topic A: Hard drives 5-2
Topic B: Optical drives 5-18
Topic C: Removable storage devices 5-23
Topic D: Storage device troubleshooting 5-29
Unit summary: Data storage devices 5-42

Printers and scanners   6-1
Topic A: Maintenance 6-2
Topic B: Troubleshooting 6-9
Unit summary: Printers and scanners 6-24

Mobile computing   7-1
Topic A: Configuration 7-2
Topic B: Component replacement and troubleshooting 7-8
Unit summary: Mobile computing 7-24

Windows management   8-1
Topic A: Directory and file management 8-2

Topic B: Resource management 8-21
Topic C: Remote management 8-43
Unit summary: Windows management 8-50

Windows maintenance 9-1
Topic A: Monitoring 9-2
Topic B: Maintenance 9-28
Topic C: Task Scheduler 9-39
Topic D: Troubleshooting 9-44
Unit summary: Windows maintenance 9-61

SOHO networking 10-1
Topic A: Networking basics 10-2
Topic B: Installing a wireless network 10-26
Unit summary: SOHO networking 10-33

Network troubleshooting 11-1
Topic A: Troubleshooting basics 11-2
Topic B: Troubleshooting the network 11-6
Unit summary: Network troubleshooting 11-35

Security 12-1
Topic A: Common security threats 12-2
Topic B: Implementing and troubleshooting security 12-22
Unit summary: Security 12-54

Binary, octal, and hexadecimal numbering A-1
Topic A: Count like a computer A-2

CompTIA A+ acronyms B-1
Topic A: Acronym list B-2

Certification exam objectives map C-1
Topic A: Comprehensive exam objectives C-2

Course summary S-1
Topic A: Course summary S-2
Topic B: Continued learning after class S-4

Glossary G-1

Index I-1

Introduction

After reading this introduction, you will know how to:

A Use ILT Series manuals in general.

B Use prerequisites, a target student description, course objectives, and a skills inventory to properly set students' expectations for the course.

C Set up a classroom to teach this course.

D Get support for setting up and teaching this course.

Topic A: About the manual

ILT Series philosophy

Our goal is to make you, the instructor, as successful as possible. To that end, our manuals facilitate students' learning by providing structured interaction with the software itself. While we provide text to help you explain difficult concepts, the hands-on activities are the focus of our courses. Leading the students through these activities will teach the skills and concepts effectively.

We believe strongly in the instructor-led class. For many students, having a thinking, feeling instructor in front of them will always be the most comfortable way to learn. Because the students' focus should be on you, our manuals are designed and written to facilitate your interaction with the students, and not to call attention to manuals themselves.

We believe in the basic approach of setting expectations, then teaching, and providing summary and review afterwards. For this reason, lessons begin with objectives and end with summaries. We also provide overall course objectives and a course summary to provide both an introduction to and closure on the entire course.

Our goal is your success. We encourage your feedback in helping us to continually improve our manuals to meet your needs.

Manual components

The manuals contain these major components:
- Table of contents
- Introduction
- Units
- Appendices
- Course summary
- Glossary
- Index

Each element is described below.

Table of contents

The table of contents acts as a learning roadmap for you and the students.

Introduction

The introduction contains information about our training philosophy and our manual components, features, and conventions. It contains target student, prerequisite, objective, and setup information for the specific course. Finally, the introduction contains support information.

Units

Units are the largest structural component of the actual course content. A unit begins with a title page that lists objectives for each major subdivision, or topic, within the unit. Within each topic, conceptual and explanatory information alternates with hands-on activities. Units conclude with a summary comprising one paragraph for each topic, and an independent practice activity that gives students an opportunity to practice the skills they've learned.

The conceptual information takes the form of text paragraphs, exhibits, lists, and tables. The activities are structured in two columns, one telling students what to do, the other providing explanations, descriptions, and graphics. Throughout a unit, instructor notes are found in the left margin.

Appendices

An appendix is similar to a unit in that it contains objectives and conceptual explanations. However, an appendix does not include hands-on activities, a summary, or an independent practice activity.

Course summary

This section provides a text summary of the entire course. It is useful for providing closure at the end of the course. The course summary also indicates the next course in this series, if there is one, and lists additional resources students might find useful as they continue to learn about the software.

Glossary

The glossary provides definitions for all of the key terms used in this course.

Index

The index at the end of this manual makes it easy for you and your students to find information about a particular software component, feature, or concept.

Manual conventions

We've tried to keep the number of elements and the types of formatting to a minimum in the manuals. We think this aids in clarity and makes the manuals more classically elegant looking. But there are some conventions and icons you should know about.

Item	Description
Italic text	In conceptual text, indicates a new term or feature.
Bold text	In unit summaries, indicates a key term or concept. In an independent practice activity, indicates an explicit item that you select, choose, or type.
`Code font`	Indicates code or syntax.
`Longer strings of ▶ code will look ▶ like this.`	In the hands-on activities, any code that's too long to fit on a single line is divided into segments by one or more continuation characters (▶). This code should be entered as a continuous string of text.
	In the left margin, provide tips, hints, and warnings for the instructor.
Select **bold item**	In the left column of hands-on activities, bold sans-serif text indicates an explicit item that you select, choose, or type.
Keycaps like ⏎ ENTER	Indicate a key on the keyboard you must press.
⚠ *Warning icon.*	Warnings prepare instructors for potential classroom management problems.
Tip icon.	Tips give extra information the instructor can share with students.
Setup icon.	Setup notes provide a realistic business context for instructors to share with students, or indicate additional setup steps required for the current activity.
Projector icon.	Projector notes indicate that there is a PowerPoint slide for the adjacent content.

Instructor note/icon

Instructor notes.

Hands-on activities

The hands-on activities are the most important parts of our manuals. They are divided into two primary columns. The "Here's how" column gives short directions to the students. The "Here's why" column provides explanations, graphics, and clarifications. To the left, instructor notes provide tips, warnings, setups, and other information for the instructor only. Here's a sample:

Do it!

A-1: Creating a commission formula

Take the time to make sure your students understand this worksheet. We'll be here a while.

Here's how	Here's why
1 Open Sales	This is an oversimplified sales compensation worksheet. It shows sales totals, commissions, and incentives for five sales reps.
2 Observe the contents of cell F4	F4 = =E4*C_Rate The commission rate formulas use the name "C_Rate" instead of a value for the commission rate.

For these activities, we have provided a collection of data files designed to help students learn each skill in a real-world business context. As students work through the activities, they will modify and update these files. Of course, students might make a mistake and therefore want to re-key the activity starting from scratch. To make it easy to start over, students will rename each data file at the end of the first activity in which the file is modified. Our convention for renaming files is to add the word "My" to the beginning of the file name. In the above activity, for example, students are using a file called "Sales" for the first time. At the end of this activity, they would save the file as "My sales," thus leaving the "Sales" file unchanged. If students make mistakes, they can start over using the original "Sales" file.

In some activities, however, it might not be practical to rename the data file. Such exceptions are indicated with an instructor note. If students want to retry one of these activities, you will need to provide a fresh copy of the original data file.

PowerPoint presentations

Each unit in this course has an accompanying PowerPoint presentation. These slide shows are designed to support your classroom instruction while providing students with a visual focus. Each presentation begins with a list of unit objectives and ends with a unit summary slide. We strongly recommend that you run these presentations from the instructor's station as you teach this course. A copy of PowerPoint Viewer is included, so it is not necessary to have PowerPoint installed on your computer.

The ILT Series PowerPoint add-in

The CD also contains a PowerPoint add-in that enables you to do two things:

- Create slide notes for the class
- Display a control panel for the Flash movies embedded in the presentations

To load the PowerPoint add-in:

1. Copy the Course_ILT.ppa file to a convenient location on your hard drive.
2. Start PowerPoint.
3. Choose Tools, Macro, Security to open the Security dialog box. On the Security Level tab, select Medium (if necessary), and then click OK.
4. Choose Tools, Add-Ins to open the Add-Ins dialog box. Then, click Add New.
5. Browse to and double-click the Course_ILT.ppa file, and then click OK. A message box will appear, warning you that macros can contain viruses.
6. Click Enable Macros. The Course_ILT add-in should now appear in the Available Add-Ins list (in the Add-Ins dialog box). The "x" in front of Course_ILT indicates that the add-in is loaded.
7. Click Close to close the Add-Ins dialog box.

After you complete this procedure, a new toolbar will be available at the top of the PowerPoint window. This toolbar contains a single button labeled "Create SlideNotes." Click this button to generate slide-notes files in both text (.txt) and Excel (.xls) format. By default, these files will be saved to the folder that contains the presentation. If the PowerPoint file is on a CD-ROM or in some other location to which the slide-notes files cannot be saved, you will be prompted to save the presentation to your hard drive and try again.

When you run a presentation and come to a slide that contains a Flash movie, you will see a small control panel in the lower-left corner of the screen. You can use this panel to start, stop, and rewind the movie, or to play it again.

Topic B: Setting student expectations

Properly setting students' expectations is essential to your success. This topic will help you do that by providing:

- Prerequisites for this course
- A description of the target student
- A list of the objectives for the course
- A skills assessment for the course

Course prerequisites

Students taking this course should be familiar with personal computers and the use of a keyboard and a mouse. Furthermore, this course assumes that students have completed the following course or have equivalent experience:

- *CompTIA Certification: A+ Essentials, 2009 Edition*

Target student

This course will prepare students for the CompTIA A+ 220-702 certification exam (2009 objectives). It is designed for students who have passed the CompTIA A+ Essentials exam and are seeking to become entry-level IT professionals. Students will gain the skills and knowledge necessary to perform the following tasks on personal computer hardware and operating systems:

- Install, maintain, troubleshoot, and replace computer hardware and peripherals
- Maintain and troubleshoot the Windows operating system
- Install a small-office/home-office network, and troubleshoot network connections
- Secure personal computers

Course objectives

You should share these overall course objectives with your students at the beginning of the day. This will give students an idea about what to expect, and it will help you identify students who might be misplaced. Students are considered misplaced when they lack the prerequisite knowledge or when they already know most of the subject matter to be covered.

After completing this course, students will know how to:

- Install and troubleshoot power supplies.
- Install and troubleshoot CPUs and motherboards.
- Install and troubleshoot memory.
- Install and troubleshoot expansion cards.
- Install and troubleshoot data storage devices.
- Maintain and troubleshoot printers and scanners.
- Configure and troubleshoot mobile computer devices.
- Manage files and directories, manage resources, and manage Windows remotely.
- Monitor, maintain, and troubleshoot the operating system.
- Implement a SOHO network.
- Troubleshoot client-side connectivity.
- Implement security on Windows computers.

Skills inventory

Use the following form to gauge students' skill levels entering the class (students have copies in the introductions of their student manuals). For each skill listed, have students rate their familiarity from 1 to 5, with five being the most familiar. Emphasize that this is not a test. Rather, it is intended to provide students with an idea of where they're starting from at the beginning of class. If a student is wholly unfamiliar with all the skills, he or she might not be ready for the class. A student who seems to understand all of the skills, on the other hand, might need to move on to the next course in the series.

Skill	1	2	3	4	5
Installing power supplies					
Troubleshooting power supplies					
Installing a CPU					
Installing a motherboard					
Replacing a cooling fan					
Installing memory					
Troubleshooting memory					
Identifying system resources					
Installing an expansion card					
Troubleshooting expansion cards					
Troubleshooting ports, cables, and connectors					
Installing a hard drive					
Installing an optical drive					
Installing removable media drives					
Maintaining and troubleshooting hard drives, optical drives, and removable media drives					
Performing routine printer and scanner maintenance tasks					
Troubleshooting printers and scanners					
Configuring a mobile computer					
Troubleshooting and replacing notebook computer components					
Managing directories and files					
Managing the Windows operating system					
Participating in a Remote Assistance session					

Skill	1	2	3	4	5
Connecting to another computer via Remote Desktop					
Monitoring the Windows operating system					
Maintaining the Windows operating system					
Scheduling tasks					
Troubleshooting operating system problems					
Describing basic networking components					
Installing and configuring a SOHO network					
Preparing a network troubleshooting toolkit					
Troubleshooting client-side connectivity issues					
Recognizing and mitigating common security threats					
Implementing and troubleshooting security measures					

Topic C: Classroom setup

All our courses assume that each student has a personal computer to use during the class. Our hands-on approach to learning requires that they do. This topic provides information on how to set up the classroom to teach this course. It includes minimum requirements for the students' personal computers, setup information for the first time you teach the class, and setup information for each time you teach after the first time you set up the classroom.

This course is hardware intensive. It contains activities that require students to assemble a computer and install hardware and software. Due to the amount of hardware required for this course, we recommend that you create the following classroom configuration:

1 Designate an **Instructor PC** to be used for class activities and demonstration purposes.

2 Assign a personal computer (designated as a **Student PC**) to each student for Internet access and for the software installation and configuration activities.

3 Assign an additional PC (designated as a **Group PC**) to each group of two to four students for the hardware installation and configuration activities. If you don't have enough hardware for each student to complete an activity on his or her own student PC, have students complete the activity in small groups at the Group PC.

Note: If you have enough equipment (listed under "Additional equipment for class and independent practice activities") for each student to complete all activities on his or her own Student PC, you don't need to set up the Group PCs as described in the setup section.

4 Connect all PCs to a **single classroom hub**, which, in turn, is connected to the institution's backbone to allow for Internet connectivity and dynamic IP address assignment.

Instructor PC hardware requirements

Initial configuration

The hardware requirements for the Instructor PC are as follows:
- 800 MHz processor (1 GHz recommended)
- At least 1 GB RAM
- SuperVGA monitor; DirectX 9 support; Windows Display Driver Model (WDDM); 128 MB graphics memory; Pixel Shader 2.0 (hardware); 32 bits per pixel recommended
- Keyboard and mouse
- 10/100 Mbps network interface card (NIC), plus associated cabling to attach to a network (RJ-45 connectors)
- 40 GB hard drive
- CD-ROM/DVD drive supported by Windows Vista
- Overhead projector connected to the Instructor PC

Additional equipment to show students during lectures
- Computer toolkit (including nonmagnetic Phillips-head screwdriver)
- Assorted screwdrivers
- Grounding strap
- Grounding mat
- Multimeter
- A variety of examples of the equipment described in this course

Instructor PC software requirements

You will need to install the following operating system on the Instructor PC. Installation instructions are provided in the section titled "First-time setup instructions."
- Windows Vista Business or Windows Vista Ultimate

In addition, you will need to install the following software:
- Latest service pack for Windows
- Sample device drivers for demonstration purposes
- Device drivers for the following installed hardware:
    - CD-ROM drive (including MSCDEX.exe)
    - Sound Blaster–compatible sound card
    - Extra NIC
- Class presentation files (included on the accompanying CD)
- Microsoft PowerPoint Viewer (included on the accompanying CD)

Student PC hardware requirements

The hardware requirements for the Student PC are as follows:

- 800 MHz processor (1 GHz recommended)
- At least 1 GB RAM
- SuperVGA monitor; DirectX 9 support; Windows Display Driver Model (WDDM); 128 MB graphics memory; Pixel Shader 2.0 (hardware); 32 bits per pixel recommended
- Keyboard and mouse
- 10/100 Mbps network interface card (NIC), plus associated cabling to attach to a network (RJ-45 connectors)
- 40 GB hard drive
- CD-ROM/DVD drive supported by Windows Vista

Student PC software requirements

You will need to install Windows Vista Business or Windows Vista Ultimate on each Student PC. Installation instructions are provided in the section titled "First-time setup instructions."

Note: You will need to have the Windows installation DVD available during class.

In addition, you will need to install the following software:

- Latest service pack for Windows
- Sound card drivers
- A copy of the avast! antivirus software. An evaluation copy is suitable and is available at www.avast.com.

Optional software:

- DVD decoder software

You should have the installers for these applications available on CD or on a network share that students can access.

Group PC hardware requirements

The hardware requirements for the Group PC are as follows:

- 800 MHz processor (1 GHz recommended)
- At least 1 GB RAM
- SuperVGA monitor; DirectX 9 support; Windows Display Driver Model (WDDM); 128 MB graphics memory; Pixel Shader 2.0 (hardware); 32 bits per pixel recommended
- Keyboard and mouse
- 10/100 Mbps network interface card (NIC), plus associated cabling to attach to a network (RJ-45 connectors)
- 40 GB hard drive
- CD-ROM/DVD drive supported by Windows Vista

Group PC software requirements

You will need to install Windows Vista Business or Windows Vista Ultimate on each Group PC. Installation instructions are provided in the section titled "First-time setup instructions."

Note: You will need to have the Windows installation DVD available during class.

In addition, you will need to install the following software:

- Latest service packs for Windows
- Sound card drivers
- A copy of the avast! antivirus software. An evaluation copy is suitable and is available at www.avast.com.

Optional software:

- DVD decoder software

You should have the installers for these applications available on CD or on a network share that students can access.

Additional equipment

You will need this additional equipment for each student. If you don't have enough hardware for each student to complete an activity on his or her own Student PC, have students complete the activity and independent practice activities in small groups at a Group PC.

- Cable tester
- Compressed-air canister
- Antistatic vacuum cleaner for computers
- Blank CD-R disc
- Music CD
- Cleaning solution for external computer and monitor cases
- Cleaning supplies to clean computer components, including scanners
- CMOS battery
- Computer toolkit with assorted screwdrivers (including nonmagnetic Phillips-head screwdriver)
- CPU (optional)
- 3.5" floppy drive and cables
- 3.5" floppy disk
- Old, defective floppy disk to dismantle
- Grounding mat
- Grounding strap
- A second hard drive for each student PC, with related media and cables
- IEEE 1394 device to connect to the PC
- A mix of IEEE 1394 (FireWire 400) and IEEE 1394b (FireWire 800) cables and devices for students to view
- Inkjet printer or laser printer, drivers, and ink cartridge
- Internal modem and drivers
- Variety of internal notebook components to replace as outlined in the exam objectives
- Compatible memory card for each PDA
- Compatible memory module for each notebook computer
- Compatible memory module for each student PC
- Mini-PCI card
- Motherboard (optional)
- A variety of multimedia devices
- Multimeter
- Network/throughput analyzer
- Notebook computer and its documentation
- Optical drive for each student PC, with related media and cables
- One or more parallel cables
- Parallel device and cable
- PC Card

- PDA for each student, or devices students can share
- Variety of peripheral devices to connect to notebook computers
- Picture to scan, or a test chart
- Variety of good and bad power devices, such as batteries and power adapters
- Printer cleaning materials and maintenance kits for both laser and inkjet printers
- Printer paper and other consumables, such as toner and inkjet cartridges
- A selection of PCs, keyboards, and mice that have poorly labeled PS/2 ports, as well as better-labeled versions for students to view
- Scanner (flatbed, sheet-feed, handheld) and associated software
- SCSI tape drive and compatible tape
- One or more serial cables, both straight-through and null modem
- Serial device and cable
- Internal Sound Blaster–compatible sound card with drivers
- Speakers
- Static shielding bag
- System fan
- UPS device and associated management software
- A mix of USB 1.1 and 2.0 Type A and Type B cables, hubs, and devices for students to view
- USB device, preferably a driverless device such as a USB mouse, to connect to the PC
- USB flash drive
- Variety of USB devices, cables, and drivers if necessary
- Variety of video cards (ISA, PCI, AGP, PCIe) with video drivers
- Variety of hot-swappable and non-hot-swappable devices to connect to the notebook computers
- Variety of internal notebook components to replace
- Wireless access point
- Network cable (RJ-45 connectors)
- Nonworking versions of any of the equipment that can be used for troubleshooting activities (Refer to the "Troubleshooting lab setup suggestions" section.)

Make sure you have both UPS and USB devices.

Network requirements

The following network components and connectivity are also required for this course:

- Internet access, for the following purposes:
    - Completing activities in many units that require drivers or software to be downloaded from the Internet (if they're not available on disk in the classroom)
    - Downloading the Student Data files from www.axzopress.com (if necessary)

First-time setup instructions

Instructor, student, group, and notebook computer setup

The first time you teach this course, you will need to perform the following steps to set up the instructor's computer, each student's computer, each group computer, and each notebook computer.

1. Use a third-party disk management utility to configure the hard disk as follows:
   - A 30 GB partition for the installation of Windows Vista, with drive letter C:
   - A 6 GB partition, with drive letter D:
   - Leave the remaining as free space
2. Install Windows Vista on the C: drive according to the software manufacturer's instructions, but following these additional steps:
   a. If prompted, click the button specifying to go online and get the latest updates (unless you don't have an active Internet connection).
   b. When prompted, create a user account named **PAADMIN##** with the password **!pass1234** (an exclamation point followed by "pass1234").
   c. Name the computers in the classroom **PAVISTA01**, **PAVISTA02**, **PAVISTA03**, and so on. Students will need to know the names of their computers, so you might want to put a card with this information on it next to each computer.
   d. On the "Help protect Windows automatically" screen, choose Use Recommended Settings. (Optionally, you can turn off automatic updates.)
   e. Select the appropriate time zone and verify that the clock time is correct.
   f. On the Windows networking screen, select Work.
3. Log on as **PAADMIN##**.
4. If necessary, install drivers for the network adapter and verify that the computer is receiving IP addressing information from the institution's DHCP server. The computer must be able to connect to the Internet.
5. Create a folder named **Student Data** at the root of the hard drive. For a standard hard drive setup, this will be C:\Student Data.
6. Copy the data files to the Student Data folder. If you don't have the data CD that came with this manual, download the Student Data files for the course. You can download the data directly to student machines, to a central location on your own network, or to a disk.
   a. Connect to www.axzopress.com.
   b. Under Downloads, click Instructor-Led Training.
   c. Browse the subject categories to locate your course. Then click the course title to display a list of available downloads. (You can also access these downloads through our Catalog listings.)
   d. Click the link(s) for downloading the Student Data files, and follow the instructions that appear on your screen.
7. Turn on file sharing and public folder sharing.
   a. Click Start, right-click Network, and choose Properties.
   b. Next to File sharing, click Off.
   c. Select "Turn on file sharing" and click Apply. Click Continue.

d Next to Public folder sharing, click Off. Select "Turn on sharing so anyone with network access can open, change, and create files." Click Apply. Click Continue.

e Close the Network and Sharing Center.

8 Log out and log back in. Configure the Welcome Center window to not run at startup.

9 Log out.

Setup instructions for every class

Because students completely alter hardware and software configurations in class, you must go back and complete all steps for the student and group computers under "First-time setup instructions."

Troubleshooting lab setup suggestions

Many of the units in this course include troubleshooting activities. In each of these activities, students are asked to solve problems related to the material in that unit. The following sections present ideas for problems you can implement.

We suggest two possible means for implementing these problems. In the first, you would send students off on a break while you induced these problems in their computers. In the second scenario, you would divide students into two groups. Each group would implement problems in a set of computers. The groups would then switch places and solve the problems that the other group created.

When determining which problems to implement, make sure you consider the technical proficiency of your students.

Unit 1: Power systems

For the Topic B activity entitled "Troubleshooting power supply problems," you can implement one or more of these problems:

- Unplug the computer from the wall outlet.
- Plug the computer into a non-functioning UPS device or surge protector.
- Disconnect the power supply from the motherboard.
- Disconnect the hard disk from the power supply.
- Replace the power supply with a non-functioning power supply.

Unit 2: CPUs and motherboards

For the Topic B activity entitled "Troubleshooting BIOS and POST problems," you can implement one or more of these problems:

- Switch the keyboard and mouse cables so that each one is plugged into the other's port.
- Substitute a keyboard with a stuck key or some other defect that would cause the POST to fail.
- Replace the CMOS battery with a dead battery, or simply remove the battery from the motherboard.

- Reset one or more BIOS setup values that would leave the computer unbootable or unusable. For example, change the boot drive order, disable the hard drive controller (if it's the boot device), or configure the on-board video controller to an extremely low-resolution display.
- Install a defective memory module so that the POST fails when it tests memory.
- (Advanced) Flash the BIOS with an incorrect or outdated version.

Unit 3: Memory systems

For the Topic B activity entitled "Troubleshooting memory," you can implement one or more of these problems:

- Replace one or more memory modules with a defective memory module.
- Loosen a module in its socket so that its pins don't make proper connections.
- Reconfigure the BIOS with an incorrect quantity of memory.
- Install the incorrect type of module for the computer—install modules that are too slow, implement parity when the motherboard doesn't, or don't implement parity when the motherboard does, and so forth.
- Install modules of different size or speed within a single bank.
- Remove one of the modules from a bank.

Unit 4: Expansion cards

For the Topic C activity entitled "Troubleshooting expansion card problems," you can implement one or more of these problems:

- Set the video mode to a mode that the monitor cannot support.
- Set the video refresh rate to a value that the monitor cannot support.
- Install a failing monitor that is blurry or displays an unsteady image.
- Install an out-of-date and buggy version of the video driver.
- Install the wrong video driver for the video adapter.
- Mute the sound.
- Disconnect the speaker's power cord.
- Loosen the adapter card in its slot so that its connectors do not make full contact.
- Disconnect the CD-to-sound-card audio cable.
- Turn off all Windows sounds in the Control Panel.
- Disconnect the phone cable from the modem.
- Use a bad phone cable to connect the modem to the jack.
- Configure the modem to use incorrect connection parameters (stop bits, parity, etc.).
- After the modem is installed, change COM port configurations so that the modem can't access the ports.
- Change the COM port configurations in the BIOS to values that the modem card doesn't support.
- Give students a voice or fax number to dial into instead of another modem line.
- Install damaged or nonfunctioning adapter cards, such as video cards, modem cards, and sound cards.
- (Advanced) Put tape over the adapter's edge connector or paint some of the connector's pins with nail polish so that they cannot make contact.

For the Topic D activity entitled "Troubleshooting port, cable, and connector problems," you can implement one or more of these problems:

- Connect the keyboard to the mouse port and vice versa.
- Disable the serial port in the BIOS.
- Disable the parallel port in the BIOS.
- Within the BIOS, assign nonstandard system resources that are likely to conflict with other devices in the system.
- Cut one of the wires in the serial, parallel, USB, or FireWire cable.
- Substitute a null modem cable for a straight-through cable.
- Provide students with a USB device that requires external power, but don't give them the power adapter.
- Install too many unpowered devices on the USB bus.
- Provide students with a USB 2.0–only device to go with their USB 1.1 systems.
- Disable the infrared port in the BIOS.
- Provide students with a nonfunctioning external modem.
- Bend one of the pins in the male serial or parallel connector so that it cannot make contact.
- Provide students with a defective or nonfunctioning mouse or keyboard (for example, one that has been dropped or had liquid spilled on it).
- Configure the external modem to use nonstandard connection parameters, such as a very slow port speed, mark or space parity, hardware flow control, and so forth.
- Provide students with a printer that supports just one parallel port mode (bi-directional, EPP, and so forth), but configure the BIOS to implement a different port mode.
- Provide students with a nonfunctioning printer.
- Tell students to connect to a remote PC with their modems, but give them a voice number to dial into (such as an automated weather line or some other line not likely to be answered by a person, who would get annoyed by the data calls).
- Cover the infrared window on the PC or device with tape, dirt, or something like nail polish that will attenuate the infrared signal without being too obviously present.
- Disconnect or remove the antenna from the radio wireless device.
- (Advanced) Provide students with an 802.11a hub and 802.11g wireless networking cards.
- (Advanced) Within the system case, disconnect the ribbon cable that runs from the serial, parallel, or USB port connector to the motherboard.

Unit 5: Data storage devices

For the Topic D activity entitled "Troubleshooting data storage devices," you can implement one or more of these problems:

- Provide students with a damaged floppy disk. (You could scratch the disk surface, poke a pinhole in it, wrinkle it, or jam the spindle so that the disk won't turn.)
- Remove the twist from the floppy drive cable.
- Configure the BIOS so that floppy drive A: is addressed as B: and vice versa.
- Disable the floppy drive in the BIOS.
- Disconnect the power cable from the floppy drive.
- Install the floppy drive cable's connector backward (force the connector backward into the socket).
- Configure the BIOS so that the system will not boot from the floppy drive.
- Install a damaged, failing, or dead hard drive.
- Install the hard drive cable's connector backward (force the connector backward into the socket).
- Install the hard drive's cable backward (connect the motherboard connector to the drive, and connect the master drive connector to the motherboard).
- Install a bad hard drive cable.
- Bend one of the pins in the hard drive's connector so that the cable cannot make full contact with all of the conductors.
  Warning: Doing this may permanently damage the drive. Bent pins can break, leaving the drive unusable.
- Configure the IDE drive identification incorrectly (for example, configure the drive as a slave when it's actually the only drive in the system).
- Configure SCSI IDs incorrectly so that there's a conflict on the bus.
- Remove termination from one or both ends of the bus, or install extra terminators within the chain.
- Disconnect the power cable from the hard drive.
- In the BIOS, configure the boot order so that it does not include the primary hard drive.
- Delete all partitions on the hard drive to leave the system unbootable.
  Warning: Doing this will destroy all information on the hard drive.
- Remove the "active" designation from the primary hard drive so that the system won't boot.
- Install a new drive that is partitioned, but not formatted, so that the system cannot boot from that drive.
- Install, or provide students with, an extremely large hard drive (160 GB or larger) in a system that cannot support it.
- With an older, slower drive, configure the BIOS to speed the boot process to the point where the drive cannot spin up and be ready by the time the startup process accesses it.
- Use a scratched CD for the CD or DVD.
- Use a burned DVD or CD.
- Provide a DVD in place of a CD for use with a CD drive.

- Plug the speakers into the MIC jack.
- Disconnect or loosely connect the cable from the CD drive to the sound card.
- Remove the driver for the CD drive.
- Set the SCSI ID on a SCSI CD drive to a duplicate ID used by another SCSI device.
- Remove (or add) termination to the SCSI CD drive.
- Change the CD drive to the master drive (or as slave if it's already a master) on an IDE channel.
- Disconnect or loosely connect the power or data cable from the CD drive.
- For an external CD drive, disconnect or loosely connect the power or data cable.
- Use an audio DVD for the audio CD (if it is a CD drive rather than a DVD drive).
- Change or remove the driver for the CD player.
- Install a damaged CD drive that no longer works.
- If you're using an external CD drive, plug the drive into a power strip, but turn the power strip off.
- Install the CD drive cable's connector backward (force the connector backward into the socket).
- Install the CD drive cable backward (connect the motherboard connector to the drive, and connect the master drive connector to the motherboard).
- Install a bad CD drive cable.
- Bend one of the pins in the CD drive's connector so that the cable cannot make full contact with all of the conductors.
  Warning: Doing this may permanently damage the drive. Bent pins can break, leaving the drive unusable.
- Disable the use of flash drives on the system.
- Use a drive that has been damaged.
- Password-protect the flash drive, but don't tell students the password (until they ask later when they figure out that this is the problem).
- Use a damaged drive that no longer works.
- Use a damaged tape.
- Provide the wrong drivers for the drive.
- Use a controller card that is incompatible with the tape drive.
- Use a damaged power and/or data cable.
- Plug the drive into a power strip, but turn the power strip off.

Unit 6: Printers and scanners

For the Topic B activity, entitled "Troubleshooting printer problems," you can implement one or more of these problems:

- Replace the ink cartridges with empty ones or ones that produce poor output.
- Install a printer that prints stray marks on output.
- Disconnect or loosely connect the interface cable.
- Disconnect or loosely connect the power cord.
- Leave the cover or door open, off, or slightly ajar.
- Plug the printer into the power strip, but turn off the strip.
- Create a paper jam.
- Remove the printer driver.
- Install the wrong printer driver.
- Remove the ink cartridge(s).
- Turn the printer off midway through a cleaning cycle or while printing.
- Provide the wrong interface cable, power cord, and/or drivers.
- In the BIOS, disable the port to which the printer connects.
- Add paper that is either very static-laden or humid (to produce poor images and possibly printer jams).
- Replace the toner cartridge with an empty one or one that produces poor output.
- Remove the toner cartridge.
- If the printer requires setup on the printer, change the settings to use a different interface, or other settings. (For example, on a LaserJet printer, use the menu on the printer to specify that it's connected via the serial port, while it is actually connected via parallel port.)

For the Topic B activity entitled "Troubleshooting scanner and multifunction device problems," you can implement one or more of these problems:

- Install a defective scanner.
- Provide the wrong interface cable, power cord, and/or drivers.
- Install the wrong scanner driver.
- Disconnect or loosely connect the interface cable.
- Disconnect or loosely connect the power cord.

For the independent practice activity, choose from any of the problems above, or come up with additional ones as appropriate to students' levels of understanding of the troubleshooting process and the equipment.

Unit 7: Mobile computing

For the Topic B activity entitled "Troubleshooting portable-computer problems," you can implement one or more of these problems:

- Install an uncharged battery.
- Install a battery that won't keep a charge.
- Disconnect or loosely connect the power cord.
- Plug the power cord into a power strip, but turn off the power strip.
- Connect the notebook to an external keyboard and boot it. Then disconnect the external keyboard without pressing the Fn key combination to switch back to the notebook keyboard. (Often this results in the keyboard having the numeric keypad enabled on the letter keys.)
- Connect the notebook to an external monitor, switch to the external monitor, and then disconnect the monitor.
- Remove the hard drive.
- Remove any PC Cards.
- Install a nonworking PC Card.
- Remove a memory module.
- Remove the hard drive.
- Install additional memory, but don't configure the system to recognize it.
- Don't fully seat a memory module.
- Remove the drivers for any PC Cards that are installed.
- Set the power options so that the monitor and hard drive are turned off after one minute of inactivity.
- Plug in an external monitor and/or keyboard, leave the notebook open, and place the external components behind the notebook and facing the other direction so that it's not obvious that they're connected to the notebook.
- Loosely connect peripheral cables.
- Disconnect the network cable.
- Remove the battery, power cable, and hard drive. Provide the wrong power cable, battery, and hard drive to each student.
- If the power cord comes apart in the middle, where the transformer is, disconnect or loosely connect this connection.
- Plug the notebook into a power strip that is turned off, and remove the battery or install a dead battery.

For the Topic B activity entitled "Identifying power problems," you can implement one or more of these problems:

- Install an uncharged battery.
- Install a battery that won't keep a charge.
- Disconnect or loosely connect the power cord.
- Substitute a broken power cord.

Unit 11: Network troubleshooting

For the independent practice activity, you can implement one or more of these problems:

- Disconnect or loosely connect the network cable on either the NIC end or the hub end of the connection.
- Change the IP address to an invalid address for the network.
- Change the subnet mask.
- If a wireless connection was unsecured previously, require WEP or WAP security access.
- Replace the network cable with a crossover Ethernet cable.
- Replace the network cable with a broken network cable.
- Disable the network card.
- Install the wrong driver for the network card.
- If using a modem, switch the phone cables for the phone line and the data line.
- If using a modem, use a broken phone line.
- Replace the NIC with a nonworking NIC.
- Replace the modem with a nonworking modem.
- If using a cable connection, remove the power cord from the transceiver.
- If using a cable connection, disconnect or loosely connect the cable line to the transceiver.
- If using a notebook with a power switch for the wireless network card, turn that switch off.

Choose from any of the problems above, or come up with additional ones as appropriate to students' levels of understanding of the troubleshooting process and the equipment.

CertBlaster software

CertBlaster pre- and post-assessment software is available for this course. To download and install this free software, students should complete the following steps:

1. Go to www.axzopress.com.
2. Under Downloads, click CertBlaster.
3. Click the link for **CompTIA A+ Practical Application**.
4. Save the .EXE file to a folder on your hard drive. (**Note:** If you skip this step, the CertBlaster software will not install correctly.)
5. Click Start and choose Run.
6. Click Browse and then navigate to the folder that contains the .EXE file.
7. Select the .EXE file and click Open.
8. Click OK and follow the on-screen instructions. When prompted for the password, enter **c_a+pracapp**.

Topic D: Support

Your success is our primary concern. If you need help setting up this class or teaching a particular unit, topic, or activity, please don't hesitate to get in touch with us.

Contacting us

Please contact us through our Web site, www.axzopress.com. You will need to provide the name of the course, and be as specific as possible about the kind of help you need.

Instructor's tools

Our Web site provides several instructor's tools for each course, including course outlines and answers to frequently asked questions. To download these files, go to www.axzopress.com. Then, under Downloads, click Instructor-Led Training and browse our subject categories.

Unit 1
Power systems

Unit time: 120 minutes

Complete this unit, and you'll know how to:

A Install a new power supply in a PC.

B Troubleshoot faulty power supplies.

Topic A: Power supplies

This topic covers the following CompTIA A+ 220-702 exam objectives.

#	Objective

1.1	Given a scenario, install, configure, and maintain personal computer components
	• Power supplies
	   – Wattages and capacity
	   – Connector types and quantity
	   – Output voltage

1.4	Given a scenario, select and use the following tools • Antistatic pad and wrist strap

Characteristics of electricity

Explanation

Electricity is the flow of electrons, which are one of the fundamental building blocks of all matter. In some materials, electrons flow easily, while in others, electrons are tightly bound to their atoms and hardly flow at all.

A *conductor* is a material that permits the flow of electricity. An *insulator* is a material that inhibits the flow of electricity. Most metals, some plastics, and some liquids are conductors. Most ceramics, plastics, and gases are insulators.

Voltage

Voltage is analogous to water pressure.

Voltage is the force of electricity caused by a difference in charge, or electrical potential, at two locations. This value, measured in *volts*, is also called the *potential* or *potential difference*. The abbreviation for volts is officially an uppercase "V," but a lowercase "v" is commonly used.

Electricity flows to equalize potential. More electricity flows when there's a greater difference in potential than when there's a smaller difference in potential. Thus, more energy can be drawn from a high-voltage system than from a low-voltage system.

In the United States, electrical systems in typical buildings operate at 110 volts (actually, within a range of 90–135 V). Household devices, such as light bulbs, are designed to work at this power level. Sensitive electronics inside computers, televisions, and other devices use a much lower voltage. Computer components use either 5 V or 12 V.

Current

Current is a measure of the flow of electrons past a given point—essentially measuring the speed of the electrons through the conductor. It is measured in amps, or amperes.

For current to flow, there must be a complete *circuit*, or path, from the source, through any intervening devices, and back to ground. A complete circuit is called *closed;* an incomplete circuit is called *open*.

Any interruption in the circuit causes the current to stop. This is the principle behind a switch, which is simply a device with which you can open a circuit to stop the flow of current.

Alternating and direct current

Current that flows in a single direction at a constant voltage through a circuit is called *direct current* (DC). Batteries provide this sort of current, and it's the type required by most electronic components. (Especially in non-technical usage, "component" is sometimes used to mean a whole device, such as an MP3 player, monitor, and so forth. In this context, however, components are circuit boards, chips, and other internal devices.)

Current that flows repeatedly back and forth through the circuit at a constantly varying voltage level is called *alternating current* (AC). A building's electrical service is an AC system, and most household devices require AC to operate.

AC systems complete a full cycle—voltage change from zero, through maximum voltage, minimum voltage, and back to zero—many times a second. In the United States, Canada, and elsewhere, AC operates at 60 cycles per second (60 *hertz*, or Hz). Europe and other countries use 50 Hz AC electricity.

Resistance and impedance

Resistance is a force that opposes the flow of DC through a conductor. *Impedance* is like resistance, but applies to AC instead. When resistance (or impedance) is present, electrical energy is converted to heat or some other form of energy. All conductors possess some resistance (or impedance), though considerably less than that possessed by insulators.

Resistance and impedance are measured in *ohms*. This quantity is written using the Greek letter omega (Ω). One ohm (1Ω) is defined as the resistance of a system in which 1 volt maintains a current of 1 amp.

Electrical power and energy

Electrical power, measured in *watts* (W), is a derived quantity that you can calculate by multiplying the voltage by the current. It's a measure of the energy delivered by the flow of electricity.

Consumption estimate from the U.S. National Renewable Energy Laboratory (www.nrel.gov).

Power supplies are rated according to the watts of electrical power they can supply. A power supply rated at "450 W" promises to deliver 450 watts of power (though, in practice, it might deliver a bit more or less than that value).

Electrical energy is electrical power delivered over time. For example, one *kilowatt-hour* (kWh) is the flow of one kilowatt (1000 W) delivered for a one-hour period. The average home in the U.S. consumes about 800 kWh of electrical energy per month.

Do it!

A-1: Examining the characteristics of electricity

Questions and answers

1 Which delivers more power: a 500 W power supply or a 1 kilowatt power supply?

   1 kilowatt equals 1000 watts, so it's the more powerful power supply.

2 Why might you be concerned about the output power rating of a power supply?

   Power supplies with a higher power rating can supply power to more components and peripherals than power supplies with lower ratings can.

3 Of the various properties of electricity, which will you be concerned with as a PC technician?

   You might be concerned with any of them at one time or another. Certainly, you will work with volts when you connect components inside the PC, so you can connect devices to the correct power supply connectors. You will encounter watts as a power supply rating.

4 Given what you've learned about electricity (particularly voltage and current), speculate on the purpose of a PC's power supply.

   A power supply converts the 110 V AC electricity delivered at the outlet to the 5 V and 12 V DC electricity required by the computer's components.

PC power supplies

Explanation

A PC's power supply, shown in Exhibit 1-1, is the internal component that converts wall voltage (110 V or 220 V) to the various DC voltages used by the computer's other components. Power supplies have a fan to cool their components and sometimes to help cool the other components inside the PC. Typically, a power supply provides some conditioning functions and can maintain DC supplies during very brief drops and outages of supply voltage.

Exhibit 1-1: A PC power supply

Selecting a power supply

Power supplies are rated according to the number of watts of DC power they output. Modern power supplies typically offer at least 300 watts, and often more, to power the PC and its internal components. Older power supplies typically offered 200 watts or less.

The power supply's rating isn't necessarily an indicator of the amount of power that the unit draws from the outlet. A 350 W power supply might not use more electricity than a 200 W model. Power supplies draw only as much power as is needed to run the internal components. If your system needs less than the power supply's full capability, the power supply draws enough electricity to run the PC and no more. When selecting a power supply for a computer, make sure it delivers enough power for all the computer's internal components.

Standard outputs

Most power supplies provide three output voltage levels at various amperage ratings to supply power to the internal components. The following table lists these voltage levels and the typical devices that use them.

Output	Amperage	Typical device that uses this output
+3.3 V	14 A	AGP video cards, motherboard. (This output level isn't produced by older, AT-class power supplies.)
-5 V	0.3 A	ISA bus (AT bus) adapter cards.
+5 V	30 A	Motherboard, optical (CD and DVD) drives, hard drives, PCI adapter cards, Pentium III and earlier processors.
+5 V	0.85 A	The "soft power" switch, which maintains the system in a ready-to-start state.
-12 V	1 A	Some older network adapters and serial ports.
+12 V	12 A	Optical drives, hard drives, Pentium 4 and Athlon processors, motherboard.

More devices draw power at the +12 V level than at any of the other ranges. When you replace a power supply, make sure it has sufficient +12 V connectors to meet your needs. It's better to use an oversized power supply because it will be more efficient when run below its maximum output rating.

Power connectors

Standard connectors are used to connect the power supply's output to the various devices. Separate standards exist for the following connectors:

- Drive power connectors
- Motherboard power connectors

Standards for drive power connectors

Hard drives, optical drives, and floppy drives use power connectors that are standardized in size and shape, as well as in the placement of and voltage carried by the wires connected through them. There are three common power connectors: the peripheral, floppy, and *serial ATA (SATA)* power connectors.

- The peripheral connector, shown in Exhibit 1-2, is sometimes called a *Molex connector*, after one of the manufacturers of this style of connector. Peripheral connectors are typically used to connect hard drives and optical drives to the power supply.
- The floppy connector, shown in Exhibit 1-3, is a 4-pin *Berg connector*. It's smaller than a Molex connector and is used to connect the floppy drive to the computer's power supply unit.
- New SATA (serial ATA) drives use the third type of power connector, which is shown in Exhibit 1-4.

Power systems 1-7

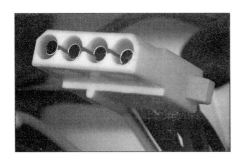

Exhibit 1-2: A peripheral power connector, also called a Molex connector

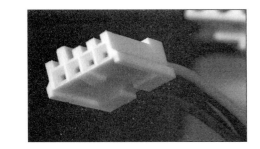

Exhibit 1-3: A floppy power connector, also called a Berg connector

Exhibit 1-4: A serial ATA (SATA) power connector

Due to their shapes, these connectors can be inserted into drives in only one orientation. They are said to be "keyed," which ensures that you connect the appropriate power input wires to the correct points on the device.

Standards for motherboard power connectors

The motherboard and its components must get power from the power supply. The motherboard is connected to the power supply with either one or two connectors. Newer, single motherboard connectors are keyed; you can't insert them incorrectly (unless you force them in backwards).

Exhibit 1-5: Single power connector on a motherboard

The older standard for motherboard power connectors is the two-connector system. These older connectors weren't keyed, so they could be inserted in either direction. Not only could you connect one of the pair to the wrong motherboard connector, but you could also connect the plugs backwards. Such a misconnection could damage the motherboard.

Exhibit 1-6: Dual power connectors on an older motherboard

Static electricity

Static electricity—or electrostatic discharge (ESD)—is a phenomenon that occurs when the charges on separated objects are unequal. From the perspective of a PC technician, the most interesting (and dangerous) aspect of static electricity happens when statically charged objects are brought near each other. When that happens, a current can flow between them to balance their charges. This current flow is characterized by a high voltage, but low amperage.

Static discharge isn't typically a problem when the computer case is closed. The static current is dissipated through the computer's metal case to ground or is otherwise dampened before reaching sensitive components. (Of course, you should still avoid discharging static through the case.) The biggest problems with static arise when you have the computer's case open and are working with its internal components.

Static dangers

Static discharges aren't dangerous to humans, even though the voltage in the system can measure in the thousands of volts. However, such discharges are potentially harmful to electronics. Electronics can be damaged by a 1000-volt discharge or less—a third or less than the minimum discharge you can feel.

The microscopic wires and components that make up chips and other devices are very sensitive to even small amounts of current. A static spark can melt such components, rendering them useless. Smaller discharges can alter the data stored in chips or otherwise upset their operation without causing physical damage.

Preventing problems with static charges

There are two ways to prevent problems from static electricity:

- Prevent the buildup of static charges.
    - Don't shuffle your feet as you walk.
    - Increase the humidity in the room or building.
    - Keep yourself grounded as you work and move around. Use the tools found in a typical ESD kit, such as wrist straps (see Exhibit 1-7) and mats.

        An ESD toolkit includes tools you can use to prevent the buildup of charge differentials and to equalize them safely if they do build up. You should purchase and use a good ESD toolkit. You and the components you're servicing can remain connected to ground so that charges can't build up.
    - Wear cotton clothing, which is less likely to generate static charges than are many synthetic materials.
    - Remove carpeting from rooms where you service computers and from computer rooms.
    - Use an air ionization system to build up an opposite charge in the air and thereby neutralize the discharge.

- Prevent discharges, or discharge them safely.
  - Equalize the charge safely. Unplug the computer, and then touch a metal portion of its chassis.
  - If you must move around as you work, keep yourself grounded with an antistatic wrist strap, like the one shown in Exhibit 1-7, so that charges can't build up.

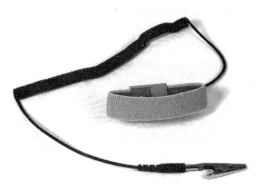

Exhibit 1-7: An antistatic wrist strap

Tell students that while some guides recommend leaving the computer plugged in, doing so is a dangerous practice they shouldn't follow.

To prevent a damaging discharge from occurring, you need to be at equal charge potential with the device you're servicing (not at equal charge with ground). Do not leave the computer plugged in while servicing it.

If there's a fault in the building's wiring system, full wall current could be flowing through the ground wire. You could be injured or killed if you came into contact with the ground.

Safety precautions

You should always follow common-sense safety precautions to avoid electric shock. These precautions include the following:

- Don't touch exposed electrical contacts with any part of your skin.
- Touch only insulated handles and parts of tools, probes, cords, etc.
- Leave covers on equipment unless you need to access internal components.
- Work one-handed. If you use only one hand, electricity is less likely to flow through your body (specifically, through your heart or head) and cause injury or death.
- Never insert anything other than a power cord into a wall outlet.
- Remove jewelry when working around electricity. Rings, watches, and jewelry can cause unintended contact with electrified components. Furthermore, these metallic items can increase the surface area that's in contact with an electrical source and thus lower your body's resistance.
- Keep your hands clean and dry.
- Don't work with electricity in wet surroundings, especially on wet floors.

Do it!

A-2: Identifying your computer's power supply

Here's how	Here's why
1 Follow safety precautions to avoid electrical shock and use the tools in your ESD toolkit	Place your antistatic mat under the area you are working in and wear your antistatic wrist strap.
2 Disconnect the power cord from the computer	
3 Disconnect any other cables from the computer	Such as those from the monitor, network, keyboard, mouse, and other peripheral devices.
4 Release the restraining mechanisms securing the case side that exposes the internal components If you opened the side covering the underside of the main circuit board, open the other side	The restraining mechanisms can be screws, slides, or push-buttons.
5 Touch the metal frame of the computer and count slowly to three	To discharge any static charges present on your body or on the computer.
6 Remove the front cover	
7 Identify the power supply in your computer	
8 Identify your power supply's rating and output voltages	This information is normally listed on a label on the power supply.
9 Locate a peripheral's power connector and examine its shape	
10 Locate a floppy drive power connector and examine its shape	
11 Determine if your computer has a SATA power connector	The power supplies in newer computers provide these connectors. You can purchase adapters for older power supplies.
12 Locate the motherboard's power connector Do you have a single or paired power connector?	*Answers will vary. Most new motherboards will have a single, keyed connector.*

Power supply installation and replacement

Explanation

You might need to replace or install a power supply if:

- The power supply in your system doesn't provide sufficient power for the components that are installed.
- An older power supply has failed.
- You're building a new computer from components.

To install or replace a power supply, follow these general steps:

1. Shut down the computer.
2. Unplug the computer.
3. Remove the cover from the computer. You might need to remove both sides or both the top and bottom to access all of the retaining screws for the power supply.
4. Disconnect all of the power wires from the various components, including the motherboard.
5. Remove any retaining screws that secure the power supply to the case.
6. Remove the power supply.
7. Install the new power supply and screw it into place.
8. Connect power wires to the various components as needed, including the motherboard. Take care to attach the connectors in the proper orientation.
9. Replace the cover or covers.
10. Plug the computer into the outlet and boot the system to test your work.

Warning: Don't open the cover of the power supply itself. Components within the power supply retain a high-voltage charge even after the unit has been unplugged for a long period of time. Shock or death could result if you were to touch these components.

Voltage selection

When installing a power supply unit, you can often adjust the power supply to run on either 110 V or 220 V wall voltage. To make this adjustment, with the computer off, you slide a small switch to the appropriate voltage. This switch is normally next to the electrical cord port on the back of the PC, as shown in Exhibit 1-8.

Exhibit 1-8: Voltage selection switch near the electrical cord port

Power systems **1–13**

Do it!

A-3: Installing a new power supply

> ⚠ *Make sure students have unplugged the computer before they perform this step.*

Students' computers should already be shut down, unplugged, and open.

If you don't have spare power supplies for students, they can simply re-install the one they removed, or if you use consistent equipment, you can have them install a power supply from another computer in the room.

Here's how	Here's why
1 Carefully disconnect all of the power wires from the various components	Your computer is already shut down and unplugged, and the case is open. You're using your ESD tools and following safety precautions to avoid electrical shock.
2 Remove any retaining screws that secure the power supply to the case	
3 Remove the power supply and set it aside	
4 Install the power supply provided by your instructor	
5 Connect the power cables to the motherboard and other internal components	Make sure to attach connectors in the appropriate orientation.
6 Replace the cover or covers	
7 Plug the computer into the outlet and reconnect all of the peripherals	
8 Boot the computer	To verify that you have installed the power supply correctly.

Why power conditioning is needed

Explanation

In an ideal situation, an AC electric signal would be steady and consistent, and the power would never go out. In reality, AC electricity is a "noisy" signal with many variations. Some of these variations can interrupt service long enough to shut down your computer. Other signal problems can damage your equipment.

AC signal problems

An ideal AC signal is a sine wave in which the voltage varies smoothly and steadily from a consistent positive voltage level to a negative voltage level. Such a wave is illustrated in Exhibit 1-9.

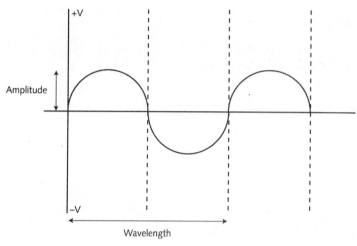

Exhibit 1-9: An ideal AC signal

The AC signal rarely matches the ideal. The following table lists some typical power problems and their causes.

Problem	Description	Cause
Blackout	A total loss of power	Accidents that knock down or cut wires, blown circuit breakers (or fuses), and transformer damage can cause localized blackouts. Natural disasters can cause widespread blackouts.
Brownout	A brief decrease in voltage level; also called a *sag*	Motors, compressors, and other devices can use so much power when starting that they can decrease the voltage available to other devices on the circuit. Demand that's greater than supply, such as when too many people run air conditioners on extra-hot days, can cause longer-term brownout conditions.
Noise	A disruption of the smoothly varying AC signal	Lighting, industrial equipment, arc-welding equipment, generators, and radio transmitters can all introduce noise into the line.
Spike	A very brief increase in voltage	Lightning strikes are the major cause. Spikes also occur when power is first returned after a blackout.
Surge	A brief increase in voltage (longer duration than spikes)	Extra voltage is dissipated through the circuit after motors, compressors, and other high-use devices are switched off.

According to the APC Web site, brownouts account for 87% of all power problems. For details, see www.apc.com/power/power_event.cfm.

Power conditioning

Power conditioning is the process of restoring a problematic AC signal to a high-quality smooth signal that's safe for your computer and other electronic devices. Power conditioning equipment includes:

- Surge protectors
- Battery backup devices
- Generators

Surge protection

You can add a surge protector to a circuit to filter out spikes and surges. Typically, plug strips include surge protection circuitry. However, you can also wire in this sort of protection by using surge-protecting circuit breakers or other devices.

Surge protectors don't protect against noise, brownouts, or blackouts.

Battery backup

You can use a battery backup unit, often called an *uninterruptible power supply* (UPS), to condition the power signal. (See Exhibit 1-10.) During normal power conditions, a small portion of electricity is used to charge a battery in the UPS. During a blackout, battery power is converted from DC to AC by an *inverter* and is supplied to the computer or other devices.

Exhibit 1-10: A UPS that provides battery-protected and surge-protected outlets

Some UPSs also protect against brownout conditions. When voltage levels drop below a preset range, battery power is used to supplement the voltage from the electrical service.

UPSs are either standby or continuous. A *standby UPS* does not use power from the battery during normal operations. During a power problem, such as a sag, the UPS quickly supplements the power. The UPS switches between wall voltage and battery voltage so quickly that power to your computer appears to be continuous, even though it isn't.

Continuous UPSs constantly draw some or all power from the battery. Wall voltage is used to charge the batteries. Voltage to power devices is drawn from the battery even when the electrical service is operating normally. There's no need to switch between sources during a power incident.

Thus, continuous UPSs are better suited to very sensitive electronics that can't tolerate the switching time associated with a standby UPS.

Most UPSs include a voltage regulator that keeps voltage output levels within a predefined range. With a voltage regulator and the surge protection features also commonly provided, a UPS can provide a continuous and clean AC electric signal that's well suited to powering computers and other sensitive electronics.

UPS software

If a power failure occurs, the battery in a UPS can provide power for only a short time. Once its battery is exhausted, the UPS won't be able to supply power to your computer anymore. In essence, the UPS simply delays a blackout.

Many UPSs include software and a method to send battery-level information to your computer. Together, these components enable the UPS to signal your computer that the battery is nearing empty and that the computer should shut down.

Exhibit 1-11: APC's PowerChute software, indicating the UPS's remaining battery life

Some versions of Windows, as well as other operating systems, include built-in UPS monitoring software. If the UPS vendor provides software, you should use it instead. It provides more features and is designed specifically to work with the UPS hardware.

Exhibit 1-12: PowerChute software when running off of the UPS's batteries

Generators

The battery in even the best UPS eventually runs out. You can use a generator to provide power for extended periods of time or when utility service is simply not available. Generators use motors, powered by gasoline, diesel fuel, natural gas, or other fuels, to produce electric power. As long as you have fuel, you can produce electricity.

Home generators—the type designed to provide power in the event of a winter storm or other disaster—generally produce noisy and inconsistent AC signals. Power from these generators can damage computers, televisions, and other electronic devices.

Computer-grade generators produce clean and consistent AC signals by including features often provided by UPSs, including voltage regulators and battery backup components. Large companies often install computer-grade generators to keep their computer centers operating during power outages and brownouts.

Do it!

A-4: Discussing power conditioning equipment

Here's how	Here's why
1 How much protection does a surge protector offer?	Your computer is protected from spikes and surges. However, it is still susceptible to brownouts, blackouts, and noise.
2 What types of systems should be protected by a UPS?	Given that UPSs are available for as little as $40, most computers should be protected by a UPS. You might also consider protecting TVs, stereos, and other home electronics with a UPS.
3 Shut down your computer and install the power conditioning equipment provided by your instructor	Your instructor might provide surge protectors and UPSs for you to install.
4 If you installed a UPS, boot your computer Log on as **PAADMIN##** with a password of **!pass1234** Unplug the UPS from the wall	To simulate a blackout condition. Your computer should continue running.
5 Plug the UPS back into the outlet	

Provide students with a mix of surge protectors and UPSs.

⚠ *For this step to work, the battery in the UPS must be charged before class!*

Topic B: Power supply troubleshooting

This topic covers the following CompTIA A+ 220-702 exam objectives.

#	Objective

1.2	Given a scenario, detect problems, troubleshoot, and repair/replace personal computer components
	• Power supplies
	  – Wattages and capacity
	  – Connector types and quantity
	  – Output voltage

1.4	Given a scenario, select and use the following tools • Multimeter • Power supply tester • Specialty hardware / tools

Electrical measurements

Explanation

When troubleshooting, you might be called upon to measure some aspect of electricity, such as the voltage level output from a power supply or other computer component, such as a printer or scanner. You measure these values with a *multimeter*. Multimeters are available in digital and analog models.

- Digital multimeters output discrete numeric values on an LED or LCD display.
- Analog multimeters, the older type, display their output with a needle and dial.

Students used multimeters in the prerequisite course, CompTIA A+ Certification: Essentials.

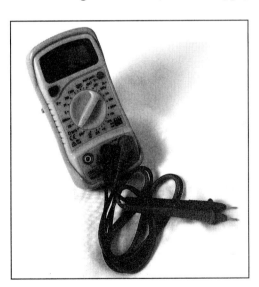

Exhibit 1-13: A digital multimeter

Exhibit 1-14: An analog multimeter

Using a multimeter

Before taking a measurement with a multimeter, you must set options with a dial, button, or other means to indicate what you're about to measure. For example, if you were using a digital meter, as shown in Exhibit 1-13, you'd press the appropriate buttons to indicate which electrical property you were going to read.

Measuring resistance

To measure resistance:

1. Turn off the device you're measuring and disconnect it from its power source. You can damage your meter if you leave the device connected to the power source.
2. You might need to disconnect the device from its circuit. If it remains connected and multiple paths through the circuit exist, you'll get misleading readings. These readings can be high or low depending on the circuit.
3. Set the multimeter to read resistance. On most meters, you must indicate the resistance range that you expect to be reading.
4. Touch the two leads of the multimeter together. The meter "zeros out" and provides an indication that it's functioning properly in the resistance mode.
5. Touch the black and red probes to either side of the circuit to be measured, and read the resistance from the meter's display.

Note: If you're using an analog meter and the needle moves very little or moves all the way to its maximum, you need to choose another resistance scale. Full scale deflection could indicate a short.

Measuring voltage

⚠ *You must exercise care when taking voltage readings as the computer is powered up.*

To measure voltage:
1. The power supply must be on.
2. Set your multimeter to read either DC or AC voltage. On most meters, you must also indicate the voltage range you expect to be reading.
3. Touch the black probe to the ground, and touch the red probe to the spot where you want to measure the voltage.

   If you're using an analog meter, the needle might attempt to swing backward. This indicates that you have the red probe on the ground. Reverse your contact points to take the reading. A digital meter will indicate a negative voltage, for example –55 V.

Note: The device must be connected to its power source and turned on while you measure voltage.

Measuring current

To measure current, you must break the circuit and insert the meter in the break. The current in the circuit then flows through the meter, which should offer little disruption and not change the reading appreciably.

A device specifically made for measuring current is called an *ammeter*. A special form of ammeter, called a clamp-on ammeter, clamps around a single wire to measure the current flow. Such a meter doesn't require you to break the circuit. Clamp ammeters are often used by electricians to measure current flow in 110 V and higher circuits.

Measuring continuity

You can determine whether a fuse is good or a wire is whole by measuring continuity. You might also use this technique to determine which pins on one end of a cable are connected to which pins on the other end.

To measure continuity, you can set your multimeter to display resistance (ohms) and look for circuits with zero resistance, or if your multimeter includes a continuity mode, you can use that. In this mode, the multimeter sounds a tone whenever it detects a closed (unbroken) circuit.

Measurements you might need to take

You probably won't be called on to measure current. But you might need to measure voltage, resistance, or continuity.

You might need to check the output voltage of a power supply at various leads to verify that a component is getting the power it requires. You might also need to verify that appropriate input wall voltage is available.

You measure resistance most often when determining if a cable is whole or if a break exists. You might also need to determine if the appropriate size resistor (the correct value in ohms or wattage) is being used for an application.

You should have your meter calibrated periodically by an approved source to ensure that it meets proper working and safety conditions.

Do it!

B-1: Measuring electrical values

⚠ *Make sure students follow electrical safety rules during this activity.*

Provide students with batteries, power adapters, good and bad network cables, and so forth to measure.

Here's how	Here's why
1 Using a multimeter, determine the voltage being output by the various devices provided by your instructor	Your instructor will provide you with devices, such as a battery or power adapter, that you can use to determine output voltages.
2 Determine the resistance of the various components provided by your instructor	Your instructor will provide you with cables and other components for you to measure.

Troubleshooting power supplies

Explanation

Power supply failures and electrical service outages can cause a variety of problems. As a PC technician, you should be familiar with the most common symptoms, probable causes, and suggested "first try" solutions for power supply problems.

Troubleshooting models were covered in the prerequisite course.

You might encounter problems not listed in the following table, but it provides a few scenarios to consider when you're troubleshooting.

Symptom	Probable cause	Suggested solution
Computer fails to boot when powered on, but boots after you press Ctrl+Alt+Del	Power_Good signal from the power supply isn't present, is at the wrong voltage, or is being sent at the wrong time.	Replace the power supply with a better-engineered model.
Computer intermittently stops working or reboots	Electrical service supply is causing problems, such as brownouts or blackouts.	Add a UPS or contact an electrician to check your building's wiring. Confirm that UPSs, surge protectors, or generators are working correctly.
There are not enough power connectors for all the devices you want to install in the computer	Power supply is undersized for your needs. Less expensive power supplies sometimes come with just a few connectors.	Replace the power supply if it's undersized. If it's rated to handle your selection of devices, use a Y-adapter to split the connectors and make more available.
Computer fails to boot at all, with no lights or beeps; fans don't start	Computer is not plugged in. "Hard" power switch is turned off. Power supply has failed. Outlet or power cord is bad. No electrical service due to blackout or other outage. Power switch has failed.	Make sure the computer is plugged in. Use a multimeter to test the power source and cords. Make sure the 110/220 V switch on the power supply is set appropriately.
Computer fails to boot, but fans start	Power connector to motherboard is not hooked up. Computer component other than the power supply has failed.	Confirm internal power connections. Troubleshoot to discover other failed devices.

The Power_Good signal

Insufficient power or a disrupted and noisy electrical connection could damage the power supply or the PC's internal components. Modern power supplies provide some monitoring of the quality of the electrical signal. Specifically, they test the voltage levels of the power and send a signal to the motherboard indicating whether the power is sufficiently good.

The *Power_Good signal* (also called the Power Good, PowerGood, Power_OK, or PWR_OK signal) is a +5 V voltage that is supplied over a specific wire in the connector that sends power from the power supply to the motherboard. If the signal isn't sent because the electrical power is insufficient, the computer won't boot.

Sometimes a system doesn't boot when you press its power button, but finishes booting after you press Ctrl+Alt+Del. This situation indicates a problem with the Power_Good signal and is a sign of a poorly designed power supply. The Power_Good signal might not be arriving when the motherboard expects it, or it might not be at the proper voltage. You can replace the power supply to fix this problem.

Do it!

B-2: Troubleshooting power supply problems

Questions and answers

> *You must set up this lab according to the "Troubleshooting Labs Setup" section of the Course Setup instructions.*

1 The customer reports that pressing the power button does nothing, and the computer fails to start. You press the button and indeed, nothing happens. What's the first thing you should check? What else might you check?

Make sure the computer is plugged in. Then use a meter to confirm that suitable voltage is present at the outlet. Try using a different power cord. Check the internal power connections.

2 You're working on a computer that beeps and shows drive activity when you press the power button. The monitor's power light comes on, but no image is displayed. You try a different monitor and it works just fine. Do these conditions indicate a problem with the PC's power supply?

No. The monitor has its own power supply.

3 Your computer shuts itself down shortly after you boot it. You've had power-related problems in the past and have even installed a UPS with software monitoring functions. Because of the past problems, you suspect a power problem. What should you investigate?

Try disabling the UPS's monitoring software. If the UPS is disconnected, its battery has failed, or the communications with it have been lost. The software might be erroneously shutting down the PC.

Try running without the UPS. Perhaps it has failed. Check power cords and test the wall voltage. Try plugging the PC into a different outlet on a different circuit.

4 One or more power supply problems have been introduced into your lab computer. Troubleshoot these problems to determine their causes.

5 Correct the problems you have found in your PC to return it to a working state. Solving one problem might reveal the presence of another problem. Troubleshoot and fix all problems that arise.

6 Document the problem(s) you find:

7 Document the steps you take to fix the problem(s):

Power systems **1–25**

Unit summary: Power systems

Topic A In this topic, you learned how to select, replace, and install a **power supply**. You also learned how to follow proper **ESD precautions** while working in a computer. Then, you learned about surge protectors, **UPSs**, and generators that can condition a poor AC signal.

Topic B In this topic, you learned about some common symptoms related to **power supply failures**. You also learned the associated probable causes and suggested solutions to the problems. You learned how to use a **multimeter** to measure electricity.

Review questions

1 List the voltage levels output by an AT power supply.

   +5 V, -5 V, +12 V, and -12 V

2 What's the purpose of the Power_Good signal?

   It signals the CPU that the power supply has stabilized and is producing clean, usable power levels. After receiving this signal, the system can proceed with booting.

3 List at least four electrical safety precautions you should follow when working with electronic equipment.

   Answers might include:

   - *Never touch exposed electrical contacts.*
   - *Touch only insulated handles and parts of tools.*
   - *Leave covers on equipment unless you need to access their internal components.*
   - *Remove rings, watches, and so forth to prevent unintended contact with electrified components.*
   - *Never insert anything into a wall outlet other than a plug meant for that outlet.*
   - *Don't work in wet surroundings.*
   - *Keep your hands clean and dry.*

4 Which provides greater power conditioning and protection: a surge protector or a UPS?

   A UPS (uninterruptible power supply) provides better power conditioning, because it provides line conditioning, surge protection, blackout protection, and often brownout protection. A surge protector simply blocks spikes and surges.

5 What multimeter modes can you use to determine if a wire is whole or broken?

   You can use the resistance mode to look for a circuit with zero resistance (0 Ω), or use the continuity setting and listen for the tone indicating a complete circuit.

6 List at least three ways to prevent static buildup.

Answers might include:
- *Don't shuffle your feet.*
- *Increase the humidity in the room.*
- *Keep yourself grounded as you work.*
- *Wear cotton clothing.*
- *Remove carpeting from computer service areas.*
- *Use an air ionization system.*

7 You're about to open a PC's case. To limit the likelihood of a static discharge, you plan to touch the PC's chassis to dissipate any built-up static charges. Should you unplug the computer from the wall outlet or leave it plugged in?

Always unplug the computer from the outlet. You need to be at equal potential with the computer, not with the building's electrical ground. A fault in the building wiring could send wall voltage back through ground, and you, if you leave the computer plugged in.

8 How many ohms does a multimeter read for a closed circuit, such as a good fuse or good wire?

Zero

9 Which are more common: brownouts or blackouts?

Brownouts are the most common power problem.

10 What is a PC power supply?

The component that converts wall voltage to the required DC voltages used by the computer's other components. It's an internal component.

11 Which internal PC component generally uses the most power?

Typically, the CPU uses the most power.

Independent practice activity

In this activity, you'll practice replacing a power supply in your PC.

1 Open your computer by removing both sides of the case and its front cover while following proper electrical and ESD safety precautions.

    a Remove the power supply.

    b Re-install the power supply.

    c Test that you installed the power supply correctly.

Unit 2
CPUs and motherboards

Unit time: 150 minutes

Complete this unit, and you'll know how to:

A Configure the BIOS, replace a system fan, install a CPU onto a motherboard, and install a motherboard into a case.

B Identify the symptoms of, probable causes of, and potential solutions to problems with motherboards and CPUs.

Topic A: CPU and motherboard installation

This topic covers the following CompTIA A+ 220-702 exam objectives.

#	Objective

1.1	**Given a scenario, install, configure, and maintain personal computer components**
	• Motherboards
	  – Jumper settings
	  – CMOS battery
	  – Advanced BIOS settings
	  – Bus speeds
	  – Chipsets
	  – Firmware updates
	  – Socket types
	  – Expansion slots
	  – Memory slots
	  – Front panel connectors
	  – I/O ports
	    • Sound, video, USB 1.1, USB 2.0, serial, IEEE 1394 / FireWire, parallel, NIC, modem, PS/2
	• Processors
	  – Socket types
	  – Speed
	  – Number of cores
	  – Power consumption
	  – Cache
	  – Front side bus
	  – 32bit vs. 64bit
	• Cooling systems
	  – Heat sinks
	  – Thermal compound
	  – CPU fans
	  – Case fans

1.2	**Given a scenario, detect problems, troubleshoot, and repair/replace personal computer components**
	• Cooling systems
	  – Heat sinks
	  – Thermal compound
	  – CPU fans
	  – Case fans

#	Objective

4.2	Implement security and troubleshoot common issues
	• System
	   – BIOS security
	      • Passwords
	      • Intrusion detection

Firmware

Explanation

Firmware straddles a gray area between hardware and software. *Firmware* is software written permanently or semi-permanently on a computer chip. Firmware is used to control electronic devices, such as remote controls, calculators, and digital cameras. In a computer, firmware is implemented using the BIOS and CMOS.

The BIOS

The *BIOS* (Basic Input/Output System) is the computer's firmware—a set of software instructions stored on a chip on the motherboard. The BIOS instructions enable basic computer functions, such as getting input from the keyboard and mouse, serial ports, and so on. Without the BIOS, your computer would be a useless collection of wires and electronic components.

AMD (Advanced Micro Devices), AMI (American Megatrends Inc.), Award, MR BIOS (Microid Research Inc.), and Phoenix are some common BIOS manufacturers. A motherboard manufacturer selects a BIOS and integrates it into the design.

At startup, many computers copy the contents of the BIOS into standard memory to improve performance. This technique is called *shadowing* because the contents in memory are like a shadow of those on the BIOS chip.

CMOS

CMOS is an area of memory that stores BIOS configuration information. A battery, typically on the motherboard as shown in Exhibit 2-1, provides power to the CMOS chip so that its contents are maintained when the computer is turned off or unplugged.

CMOS (complementary metal oxide semiconductor) is actually a type of computer chip. This type of chip can maintain information without a supply of power. The most common use of CMOS chips is to store BIOS configuration data. The term "CMOS" is frequently used to refer to the storage location of the BIOS configuration information, rather than the chip technology.

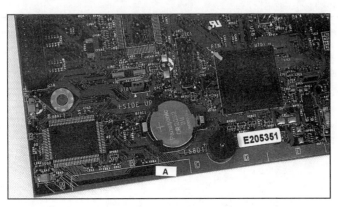

Exhibit 2-1: A CMOS backup battery

CMOS configuration

To configure the values stored in CMOS, you use a system setup utility provided by your computer's manufacturer (or by the BIOS maker). This utility is often built into the BIOS itself. Sometimes the utility is stored on a special hidden portion of your hard disk (on a separate partition) or an optical disc.

CMOS utility access

BIOS manufacturers provide various ways to access the system setup utility. The following table describes some of the more common methods. The alternative key combinations represent the methods you use with various computer models from these vendors (rather than alternative options for a single model). Consult your system's documentation to determine the exact procedure you need to follow.

Maker	Key combination	When to press the keys
ALR	F2 or Ctrl+Alt+Esc	During text mode portion of boot.
AMD	F1	During text mode portion of boot.
AMI	Delete	During text mode portion of boot.
Award	Delete or Ctrl+Alt+Esc	During text mode portion of boot.
Compaq	F10	During text mode (black background, white text) portions of boot process, when the underline cursor jumps to the upper-right corner of the screen.
Dell	F1, Delete, or Ctrl+Alt+Enter (on some systems, you must press the reset button twice)	During text mode portion of boot.
Gateway	F1	During text mode portion of boot.
HP	F1	During text mode portion of boot.
IBM	Insert or F1 (early ThinkPads used Ctrl+Alt+Insert)	During text mode portion of boot. (This method works only if the PC is configured with a reference partition. Otherwise, you need to use the system setup diskette.)

Maker	Key combination	When to press the keys
Phoenix	F1, Ctrl+Alt+Esc, Ctrl+Alt+S, or Ctrl+Alt+Insert	During text mode portion of boot.
Toshiba	F1 or Esc	During text mode portion of boot.

At the time of this writing, a more comprehensive list of CMOS access key combinations was available at:

    http://murfsgarage.cybertechhelp.com/cmossetup.htm

Configuring BIOS settings

Setting BIOS configuration values is normally a "set and forget" operation. On most systems, you won't need to configure anything; the settings from the manufacturer have been configured to meet the needs of the system. However, you might need to configure the BIOS when you set up the computer for the first time or when you add new hardware. Other than that, you typically don't need to modify the BIOS configuration.

Typical BIOS configuration settings include:

- **Date and time** — Set the system date and time.
- **CPU options** — Specify the type of CPU installed in the system, and configure speed and voltage options.
- **Optical drive options** — Specify which CD and DVD drives the system should boot from, and in what order. You can also typically enable, disable, and configure optical drive options.
- **Floppy drive options** — Specify which floppy drives the system should boot from, and in what order. You can also typically enable, disable, and configure floppy drive options.
- **Hard drive options** — Specify the hard drive's type, size, and geometry, and enable or disable on-board hard drive controllers.
- **Serial port options** — Set configuration options, such as device addresses and communication modes.
- **Parallel port options** — Specify whether to enable unidirectional or bidirectional printing, and configure ECP (Extended Capabilities Parallel port) and EPP (Enhanced Parallel Port) settings.
- **Integrated devices** — Enable or disable integrated devices, such as video adapter or network adapter functionality.
- **Plug and Play** — Enable or disable hardware support for Plug and Play features.
- **Power management options** — Specify whether to enable hardware-based power management features. Typically, you must choose a set of supported power management standards, such as APM (Advanced Power Management) or ACPI (Advanced Configuration and Power Interface), as well as "wake up" options, such as whether to wake up the computer when the modem rings.
- **Intrusion and virus detection** — Enable or disable hardware-based virus and intrusion detection.
- **Boot password** — Enable or disable hardware-based passwords, and set the password.

These steps assume that the setup utility is built into and accessible directly from the BIOS, and not from a disk location.

To configure the BIOS:

1 If necessary, shut down your PC.
2 From a powered-off state, boot your PC.
3 At the appropriate time in the boot sequence, press the key combination that opens the BIOS setup utility on your system.
4 Follow the on-screen prompts or menu system to configure your system.
5 Follow the on-screen prompts or menu system to save the new configuration data to CMOS memory.

Do it!

A-1: Changing your computer's BIOS settings

Here's how	Here's why
1 If necessary, shut down your PC	Don't put the computer in hibernate or sleep mode. You must turn it all the way off.
2 Turn on the computer	
3 At the appropriate time in the boot sequence, press the key combination that opens the BIOS setup utility on your system	
4 Follow the on-screen instructions or use the menus to set the date and time	If they're already correctly set, set them back an hour or so and then reset them to the current time.
5 Explore your computer system's setup utility	To determine its capabilities. Each BIOS manufacturer provides similar setup options.
6 Exit and save your configuration changes	Your system automatically restarts when you're done.

CPUs inside the case

Explanation

Hardware designers must include many functions to create a complete working computer. CPUs must be connected to the motherboard circuitry in order to function. In addition, processors generate a lot of heat during their operation and require some means to keep cool, or their internal wiring can melt. In this topic, you'll examine:

- Chipsets
- CPU packaging
- Slots
- Cooling techniques

Chipsets

A *chipset* is one or more chips, packaged into a single unit and sold together, that perform a set of functions in a computer. The term is used most often to describe the core features of a computer, which often include:

- Memory control
- System bus functions
- Audio functions
- Video display functions
- System management functions

The chipset doesn't actually include the CPU. However, each chipset is designed to support a select few CPUs.

Sometimes the term "chipset" is used with video adapter cards. In those cases, the video chipset combines what used to be separate video chips into a single chip or unit.

Northbridge and Southbridge chips

Two of the most important components of a PC chipset are the Northbridge and Southbridge chips. Together with the CPU, these chips define the characteristics and capabilities of the computer.

The Northbridge chip controls interactions between the CPU, memory, AGP video control circuitry, and the Southbridge. The Southbridge controls interactions between buses and devices not controlled by the Northbridge, including the standard PCI expansion bus, the floppy drive controller, and the serial, parallel, and PS/2 keyboard and mouse ports.

CPU packaging

Any type of microchip is made up of microscopic wires, transistors, and other components. This plain chip is called the *die*. To be useful, it must be connected to the rest of the circuitry of the computer. Due to the size differences between the wires on the die and the circuit boards in the computer, the die can't be connected directly to the circuit board.

Instead, the die is built into a package. A *package* is a case made from plastic, ceramic, glass, metal, or other material, plus the wires and connectors that bridge the microscopic connections on the die with the external circuitry. A package might also include support function chips, memory, and cooling-related components.

Exhibit 2-2: A PDIP (plastic dual inline package) memory chip

Older package types, such as the PDIP pictured in Exhibit 2-2, used connectors that were large compared to the die. Newer packages use ever smaller connectors, packing more connections into a smaller area. The *pin grid array* (PGA) package, shown in Exhibit 2-3, provides many more connections in an area not much larger than the die.

Exhibit 2-3: The underside of an 80486DX2 CPU, showing the pins of its PGA package

Even though newer packages use smaller connectors, overall package size has grown as functionality has grown. Newer packages include support chips, cache memory, and features that enhance the cooling of the processor. One such larger package is shown in Exhibit 2-4.

Exhibit 2-4: The Single Edge Contact Cartridge package

CPU packages

The following table lists some current and historical CPU packages used with desktop computers. Manufacturers can vary these with updated lines, so be sure to check the technical specifications for your particular CPU on the manufacturer's Web site.

Package	Full name	Description	Processors
PDIP	Plastic dual inline package	The die is encased in plastic (or another material). Large, flat, metal pins are inserted into a socket that's soldered to the motherboard.	8080, 8086, 8088
PGA	Pin grid array	Rows of pins extend from the bottom of the package. A nickel-plated copper slug sits atop the die to improve thermal conductivity. The pins are arranged so that the chip can be inserted in just one way.	80286 (68 pins), 80386 (132 pins), 80486 (168), and Xeon (603 pins)
CPGA	Ceramic pin grid array	A package that uses a ceramic substrate with pins arranged in a pin grid array.	AMD Socket A Athlons and the Duron
SPGA	Staggered pin grid array	Similar to PGA, but pins are staggered to fit more pins in a given area.	Pentium, Pentium MMX, Pentium Pro with 387 pins
PPGA	Plastic pin grid array	An updated version of the SPGA package.	Pentium Pro, early Celeron processors, and Pentium III with 370 pins
FC-PGA	Flip chip pin grid array	Similar to PGA, but the die is exposed on top. This design enhances heat transfer and cooling options.	Pentium III and Celeron with 370 pins; the 423-pin version is used with Pentium 4 processors
FC-PGA2	Flip chip pin grid array 2	Similar to FC-PGA, but with an integrated heat sink, which is connected to the die during manufacturing.	Pentium III and Celeron with 370 pins; the 478-pin version is used with Pentium 4 processors; 469 version used with AMD Athlon Thunderbird processors

Package	Full name	Description	Processors
OOI	OLGA On Interpreter	The die is mounted face down, as with the FC-PGA package, for better cooling, but uses a different pin arrangement.	423-pin Pentium 4
OPGA	Organic pin grid array	The silicon die is attached to an organic plastic plate (fiber glass), which is pierced by an array of pins to make the connections to the socket. This package is cheaper, thinner, and lighter than the ceramic package. It also reduces electrical impedance.	AMD Athlon XP
SECC	Single Edge Contact Cartridge	Rather than mounting horizontally, this package mounts the CPU vertically on the motherboard. Rather than pins, this package uses an edge connector similar to an adapter card's. The die is covered with a metal case. A metal thermal plate mounted to the back of the cartridge acts as a heat sink.	Pentium II processors with 242 contacts, and Pentium II Xeon and Pentium III Xeon processors with 330 contacts
SECC2	Single Edge Contact Cartridge 2	Similar to SECC, but without the thermal plate.	Later versions of the Pentium II and Pentium III processor with 242 contacts; AMD Athlon K7
SEP	Single Edge Processor	Similar to SECC without the metal case.	Early Celeron processors with 242 contacts
FCBGA	Flip chip ball grid array	Similar to FC-PGA, but uses balls rather than pins for contacts. The balls can't be bent as the pins can.	Xeon, plus many support chips in current Pentium-class computers
LGA	Land grid array	Has small raised contacts instead of pins. The corresponding socket has pins that meet the contacts. This is a very high-density package.	Celeron D, Pentium 4, Pentium 4 D, Pentium Extreme Edition, Core2 Duo, Core2 Extreme

Sockets and slots

The processor packages listed in the preceding table must be inserted into a socket or slot on the motherboard. The following table lists common desktop computer sockets and slots. As with packages, manufacturers can vary sockets and slots with updated lines, so check the technical specifications for your CPU on the manufacturer's Web site. Exhibit 2-5 shows a desktop processor and its associated socket.

Type	Supports these packages	Processors	Notes
Slot A	AMD's Card Module package	AMD Athlon	This wasn't a popular design and didn't last very long on the market.
Socket A (also called Socket 462)	SPGA with 462 pins	AMD Athlon and Duron	Eleven holes in this socket were plugged to ensure that packages were installed correctly.
Socket 5	PGA, SPGA with 320 pins	Pentium	
Socket 7	PGA, SPGA with 321 pins, and PGA, SPGA, and FC-PGA with 296 pins	AMD K5 and K6, Cyrix 6x86, Pentium, and Pentium MMX	First socket to support dual voltage inputs, which support the various core and I/O voltages introduced with the Pentium MMX processors. Socket 7 has one more hole than Socket 5, but it isn't electrically connected. It simply prevents a new CPU from being plugged into a Socket 5 socket.
Socket 8	387-pin PGA, SPGA, and FC-PGA	Pentium Pro	A short-lived socket used primarily with the Pentium Pro.
Socket 423	423-pin SPGA and FC-PGA, OOI	Pentium 4	A short-lived socket design used for early Pentium 4 processors.
Socket 478	FC-PGA2	Celeron, Pentium 4, Pentium D, and Pentium Extreme Edition	The current general-purpose socket for Pentium-class processors.
Socket 370	SPGA and PPGA with 370 pins	Celeron, Celeron II, Pentium III	Similar to the Socket 7 design, with six staggered rows of pins rather than five.
Slot 1	SECC, SECC2, SEP with 242 contacts	Pentium II, early Celeron, and Pentium III	Edge connector slot developed specifically for the SECC, SECC2, and SEP packages.
Slot 2	SECC, SECC2, SEP with 330 contacts	Pentium II and Xeon	Similar to Slot 1, but the CPU can communicate with the Level II cache at full CPU speed, rather than the half-speed supported through Slot 1.
LGA775 (also called Socket T)	LGA	Celeron D, Pentium 4, Pentium D, Pentium Extreme Edition, Core2 Duo, and Core 2 Duo Extreme	Designed to work specifically with the new high-density LGA package. This is Intel's current high-end socket.

Exhibit 2-5: A Pentium with MMX CPU atop its associated Socket 7 socket

CPU performance

You can determine the performance of a processor by examining the number of instructions it can perform in a second. With microprocessors, this number is usually rated in *millions of instructions per second (MIPS)*.

CPUs are often rated according to their clock speed. In a PC, the clock circuit keeps the CPU and other chips synchronized so that they can work together.

Modern processors perform many instructions in a single cycle. In fact, the clock speed is no longer a good indicator of the performance of a modern CPU. By using the techniques listed in the following table, a modern CPU can perform more than one instruction per clock cycle and even perform multiple instructions at the same time.

Ultimately, many factors control the actual speed (performance) of a CPU. The following table describes some of these factors.

These are listed in alphabetical order, not in order of their contribution to performance.

Design	Relation to CPU performance
Addressable RAM	The total amount of memory that's accessible to the processor.
Branch prediction	A technique by which the processor anticipates the code that will be used next and loads that code to try to "get ahead" of the program. When the processor guesses correctly, the program speeds up. Otherwise, performance slows while the correct instruction is retrieved.
Bus, address	The bus (pathway) that connects the processor to main memory. The wider the address bus, the more memory can be accessed. Data isn't transferred over this bus.
Bus, data	The number of bits of data or instructions that can be transferred in a single operation. The larger the data bus, the more data that can be moved and thus the faster the processor can operate.
Bus, internal	The bus that determines how many bits of information the processor can work with at once. If the internal bus is smaller than the data bus, data and instructions must be manipulated in parts. For example, a processor with a 32-bit internal bus and a 64-bit data bus must deal with data in two halves.

Design	Relation to CPU performance
Cache	High-speed memory contained within or directly coupled to the processor. Accessing data from cache is considerably faster than accessing it from main memory. Processors use levels 1, 2, and 3 caching, where level 1 cache is the fastest and most closely coupled to the processor, level 2 less so, and level 3 even less (yet still much faster than normal system memory). Processors save instructions, the data to be processed, and the results in the caches.
Clock speed	The number of cycles per second of the computer's synchronization clock, measured in hertz (Hz), millions of cycles per second (megahertz or MHz), or billions of cycles per second (gigahertz or GHz). A modern processor performs more than one instruction during every clock cycle. Older processors performed one or fewer. Normally, a clock speed rating refers to the internal or core speed of the processor, rather than to the actual speed of the computer's synchronizing clock chip.
Dual Independent Bus (DIB)	A processor architecture that includes two buses: one to the main system memory, and another to the level 2 cache. The processor can access both buses simultaneously for improved performance.
Front-side bus speed	The speed at which the processor interacts with the rest of the system. A processor's internal core speed can be many times higher than its front-side bus speed. If the core speed is too much higher than the front-side bus speed, the processor can sit idle, waiting for data to be moved in or out and made available for processing.
Hyperthreading	An Intel technology that enables a single processor to execute two streams of instructions at the same time, as if it were two processors.
Multimedia extensions (MMX)	An expanded set of instructions supported by a processor that provides multimedia-specific functions. Without MMX, a programmer might have to implement multiple low-level commands to perform a multimedia operation. With MMX, the same function would involve a single instruction.
Multiprocessing	The use of more than one processor within a system to speed program execution. Operating systems and applications need to be written to support multiprocessing, or no speed benefits are realized.
Out-of-order completion	A technique by which instructions can be executed out of order when order isn't important and the processor determines a more efficient sequence.
Overclocking	Running the CPU at a higher speed than it was rated to run at. Overclocking increases performance, but also increases the potential for errors. Also, more heat is generated by an overclocked CPU.
Pipelining	The overlapping of the steps involved in processing instructions. Instructions are normally fetched, decoded, and executed, and the results are written out to memory. Modern processors overlap these steps to speed overall execution. While one instruction is being executed, another is being decoded, and a third is being fetched.
Register renaming	A technique by which modern processors can rename registers so that instructions can access their own set of registers and not interfere with other instructions. When multiple instructions are running at the same time, there's a chance that two will attempt to read or write to the same register simultaneously. Register renaming prevents this.
Single Instruction Multiple Data (SIMD)	A technique by which a single instruction can be applied to more than one piece of data. For example, with SIMD, five numbers might be moved into the processor along with the single command to add them up in one operation. The next operation would carry out that instruction. Without SIMD, the numbers would be added together one by one in a longer sequence of instructions.

Design	Relation to CPU performance
Speculative execution	A technique by which a processor executes an instruction in the expectation that the result is needed. This technique can improve performance when the program branches, as in an "if this condition is met, do that operation" situation. The processor can begin performing the operation before the condition is fully evaluated, in the expectation that it will be met.
Superpipelining	An improvement over pipelining. Superpipelining uses a larger number of shorter stages and support for a higher clock rate to improve performance.
Superscalar	A technique that enables a processor to execute more than one instruction in a single clock cycle.
Throttling	A technique by which the speed of the processor is scaled back so that it uses less power and creates less heat. Throttling reduces performance. It's most useful with portable computers, for which low power consumption and low heat production are critical design factors.

Multiple-processor support

Some computers come with two processors. However, in order to take advantage of the increased performance gained with two processors, the operating system and applications you run must include *symmetric multiprocessing code*. Windows 2000 Professional, Windows XP Professional, and Windows Vista Business, Ultimate, and Enterprise include symmetric multiprocessing code. Windows XP Home and Media Center Editions and Windows Vista Home Basic and Home Premium don't. You can get the Linux operating system and all of its compatible applications in symmetric multiprocessing versions.

Processor specifications

There are several manufacturers of CPUs. Probably the two most recognizable in the personal computer realm are Intel and AMD (Advanced Micro Devices). These two companies have the largest market share. Other manufacturers include Motorola, IBM, SIS (Silicon Integrated Systems), VIA (VIA Technologies Inc.), and Cyrix.

CPUs can be compared according to many specifications, including:

- **Primary specifications** — Clock speed, front-side bus speed, addressable RAM, and cache sizes.
- **Bus width specifications** — The width, or number of bits, that can pass at one time over the processor's internal bus and data bus, plus the address bus width, which determines the maximum addressable memory.
- **Internal specifications** — The internal and external voltages used by the chips, the number of transistors that make up the processor, and whether it includes an integrated FPU (floating point unit).

The following tables detail the primary specifications, bus width specifications, and internal specifications of various processors.

Primary specifications

It isn't necessary to go over the primary specifications for each processor in class. Refer students to this table for review.

Processor	Clock speed (core speed)	Front side bus speed	Maximum RAM	L1 cache	L2 cache
8088	4.77–8 MHz	4.77–8 MHz	1 MB	-	-
8086	4.77–10 MHz	4.77–10 MHz	1 MB	-	-
80286	6–12 MHz	6–12 MHz	16 MB	-	-
80386DX	16–40 MHz	16–33 MHz	4 GB	-	-
80386SX	16–33 MHz	16–33 MHz	16 MB	-	-
80486DX	25–100 MHz	25–33 MHz	4 GB	8 KB	-
80486SX	16–50 MHz	16–25 MHz	4 GB	8 KB	-
80486DX2	50–80 MHz	25–33 MHz	4 GB	8 KB	-
80486DX4	75–120 MHz	33 MHz	4 GB	16 KB	-
AMD 5x86	133 MHz	33 MHz	4 GB	16 KB	-
Cyrix 5x86	100 MHz	33 MHz	4 GB	16 KB	-
Pentium	60–200 MHz	60–66 MHz	4 GB	16 KB	-
Pentium MMX	133–233 MHz	66 MHz	4 GB	32 KB	-
Cyrix 6x86	80–133 MHz	40–66 MHz	4 GB	16 KB	-
AMD K5	75–133 MHz	66 MHz	4 GB	24 KB	-
Pentium Pro	150–200 MHz	60–66 MHz	4 GB	16 KB	128–256 KB
Pentium II	233–400 MHz	66–100 MHz	4 GB	32 KB	512 KB
AMD K6	166–266 MHz	66 MHz	4 GB	64 KB	-
Cyrix 6x86 MX	133–188 MHz	66 75 MHz	4 GB	64 KB	-
Celeron	266 MHz–1.3 GHz	66–400 MHz	4 GB or 64 GB	32 KB	0–256 KB
Pentium II Xeon	400–450 MHz	100 MHz	64 GB	32 KB	1 MB
Pentium III	450 MHz–1 GHz	100–133 MHz	64 GB	32 KB	256–512 KB
Pentium III Xeon	600 MHz–1 GHz	100–133 MHz	64 GB	32 KB	256 KB
Duron	600 MHz–1.8 GHz	100–133 MHz	4 GB	64 KB	64 KB

	Processor	Clock speed (core speed)	Front side bus speed	Maximum RAM	L1 cache	L2 cache
	Pentium 4	1.3–2.8 GHz	400–533 MHz	4–16 GB	20 KB (8 KB data, 12 KB instruction)	256 KB–2 MB
Uses the 64-bit instruction set, even though most Semprons are 32-bit CPUs.	Sempron	1.5–2 GHz	166–333 MHz	4–16 GB	256 KB	128 KB
TB is terabyte or 1,024 GB.	Itanium	1–1.6 GHz	400–533 MHz (128-bit wide)	16 TB	32 KB	256 KB
	AMD Athlon	900 MHz–2.13 GHz	100–133 MHz	8 TB	64–128 KB	256–512 KB
The HT stands for hyperthreading.	Pentium 4 HT	3.8 GHz	800 MHz	1 TB	16 KB data plus 12 KB instruction	512 KB– 2 MB, plus 2 MB level 3 cache
	AMD Athlon 64	1.8–2.4 GHz	1.6–2 GHz	16 TB	128 KB	1 MB
The D is nearly identical to the Extreme Edition, but with hyperthreading disabled.	Pentium 4D	3.2 GHz	800 MHz	16 TB	2×16 KB data, plus 2×12 KB instruction	2×1 MB
	Pentium Extreme Edition	3.73 GHz	1,066 MHz	16 TB	2×16 KB data, plus 2×12 KB instruction	2×1 MB, plus 2 MB level 3 cache
	Core2 Duo	1.86–2.66 GHz	1,066 MHz	1 TB	64 KB (One 32 KB cache per core)	4 MB (One 2 MB cache per core)
	Core2 Extreme & Extreme Quad	2.66–2.93 GHz	1,066 MHz	1 TB	64–128KB	4–8 MB

Bus width specifications

It isn't necessary to go over the bus width specifications for each processor in class. Refer students to this table for review.

Processor	Internal bus (bits)	Data bus (bits)	Address bus (bits)
8086	16	16	20
8088	16	8	20
80286	16	16	24
80386DX	32	32	32
80386SX	16	16	24
80486DX	32	32	32
80486SX	32	32	32
80486DX2	32	32	32
80486DX4	32	32	32
AMD 5x86	32	32	32
Cyrix 5x86	32	32	32
Pentium	32	64	32
Pentium MMX	32	64	32
Cyrix 6x86	32	64	32
AMD K5	32	64	32
Pentium Pro	32	64	36
Pentium II	32	64	36
AMD K6	32	64	32
Cyrix 6x86 MX	32	64	32
Celeron	32	64	32 or 36
Pentium II Xeon	32	64	36
Pentium III	32	64	36
Pentium III Xeon	32	64	36
Duron	32	64	13
Pentium 4	32	64	32
Sempron	64	64	13

Processor	Internal bus (bits)	Data bus (bits)	Address bus (bits)
Pentium 4 HT	64	64	64
Itanium	64	64	44
AMD Athlon	32	64	43
AMT Athlon 64	64	64	64
Pentium 4D	64	64	64
Pentium Extreme Edition	64	64	64
Core2 Duo	64	64	64
Core2 Extreme & Extreme Quad	64	64	64

Internal specifications

The internal specifications of processors refer to the way the CPU's circuits are constructed. The *core voltage* value describes the voltage level required by the core processing components of the CPU. The *I/O voltage* value, sometimes called the external voltage, is the level required by the CPU's input and output circuitry. In modern processors, the core and I/O voltage values typically differ.

In modern processors, one or more *voltage ID* (VID) pins send a signal containing the exact voltage requirements to the *voltage regulator module* (VRM) on the motherboard. The VRM then supplies that specific power to the CPU. Not all motherboards include a VRM. On a few motherboards, you must set jumpers or switches to match the voltage supplied to the CPU with the amount it requires. If you supply the wrong voltage, you can ruin the CPU.

The number of transistors is simply a count of the transistors (electronic switches) that make up the CPU. This count provides a rough estimate of the size and complexity of the chip.

Older processors didn't include an integrated floating point unit (FPU). Modern CPUs all include this feature. The following table lists the internal specifications of various processors.

It isn't necessary to go over the internal specifications for each processor in class. Refer students to this table for review.

Processor	Core voltage	I/O voltage	Number of transistors (millions)	Integrated FPU?
8086	5 V	5 V	0.029	No
8088	5 V	5 V	0.029	No
80286	5 V	5 V	0.120	No
80386DX	5 V	5 V	0.275	No
80386SX	5 V	5 V	0.275	No
80486DX	5 V	5 V	1.2	Yes
80486SX	5 V	5 V	1.2	No
Intel 80486DX2	5 V	5 V	1.2	Yes
AMD and Cyrix 80486DX2	3.3 V	3.3 V	1.2	Yes
80486DX4	3.3 V	3.3 V	1.4	Yes
AMD 5x86	3.45 V	3.45 V	1.6	Yes
Cyrix 5x86	3.45 V	3.45 V	2	Yes
Pentium	3.3 or 3.52 V	3.3 or 3.52 V	3.1	Yes
Pentium MMX	2.8 V	3.3 V	4.5	Yes
Cyrix 6x86	3.3 V	3.3 V	3	Yes
AMD K5	3.52 V	3.52 V	4.3	Yes
Pentium Pro	3.1 V	3.1 V	5.5	Yes
Pentium II	2.0, 2.8, or 3.3 V	3.3 V	7.5	Yes
AMD K6	2.9 or 3.2 V	3.3 V	8.8	Yes
Cyrix 6x86 MX	2.9 V	3.3 V	6	Yes
Celeron	2.0 or 1.5 V	3.3 V	7.5	Yes
Pentium II Xeon	1.3–1.6 V	3.3 V	7.5	Yes
Pentium III	1.65 V	3.3 V	24	Yes
Pentium III Xeon	1.5–2.8 V	3.3 V	28	Yes
Duron	1.5–1.75 V	3.3 V	25–37	Yes
Pentium 4	1.4–1.75 V	3.3 V	42	Yes
Sempron	1.4–1.6 V	3.3 V	22–37	Yes

Newer Celerons use the lower core voltage.

Processor	Core voltage	I/O voltage	Number of transistors (millions)	Integrated FPU?
Pentium 4 HT	1.2–1.4 V	3.3 V	125	Yes
Itanium	1.1–1.5 V	3.3 V	220	Yes
AMD Athlon	1.6 V	3.3 V	37.5–54.3	Yes
AMT Athlon 64	1.55 V	3.3 V	68.5–114	Yes
Pentium 4D	1.2–1.4 V	3.3 V	230	Yes
Pentium Extreme Edition	1.2–1.4 V	3.3 V	230	Yes
Core2 Duo	0.85–1.3625 V	1.20–1.33V	151	Yes
Core2 Extreme & Extreme Quad	0.850–1.372V	1.20–1.350V	528	Yes

Do it!

A-2: Identifying the socket and package type of your CPU

Here's how	Here's why
1 Turn off and unplug your computer, and then open your system case	Make sure you follow proper electrical safety and ESD precautions.
2 Examine your CPU and record the socket and package type	Package: _____ Socket: _____
3 Identify the chipset chip on your motherboard	It's typically a very large chip placed near the CPU socket.

Explanation

Cooling techniques

CPUs and the other components in a computer are designed to operate within a range of temperatures. Temperatures outside that range can damage components. In particular, too much heat can cause logic errors, in which data within the chips and wires is altered, or circuit damage, by which components can melt!

To keep CPU and other computer components within an appropriate temperature range, PC designers include various features to cool the case and processor. If one of the cooling systems fails, you need to replace it. In addition, if you upgrade an older component, such as the CPU, the new component might generate more heat than the current cooling system can handle.

Fans

Older CPUs generated so little heat that a simple fan (typically part of the power supply) and a few openings in the case were all it took to maintain permitted operating temperatures. Modern cases include multiple openings through which air can flow. Some cases include multiple fans, in addition to the power supply fan, to move air. Some CPUs have their own dedicated fan.

Fans have both mechanical and electrical components that can fail. You can purchase replacement fans to fit in particular system cases.

Heat sinks and cooling fins

A *heat sink* is a device that absorbs and dissipates heat produced by electrical components. The most common type of heat sink used with CPUs has *cooling fins*. Fins increase the surface area that can transfer heat away from the CPU. Hardware designers began adding cooling fins to CPUs before the Pentium era.

Exhibit 2-6: Cooling fins on an older 80486DX2 CPU

The fins are normally connected directly to the die or to an integrated metal plate on the CPU, depending on its packaging design. A *thermal compound*—basically a glue that transmits heat well—is used between the parts to improve heat flow. Because of this, you can't replace the cooling fins on a CPU.

A heat sink relies on convection—warm air rises away from the fins, while cooler air flows in from below. After a certain point, heat can't dissipate quickly enough on its own. Thermal engineers can add fans to the cooling fins to forcibly improve convection. If the fan that sits atop the CPU cooling fins fails, you might be able to purchase a replacement from the manufacturer.

Exhibit 2-7: Cooling fins and a fan on a Pentium processor

Heat pipes

Heat pipes are small tubes, typically built into cooling fins, filled with a small amount of fluid. Heat vaporizes the fluid, which expands and rises to another area of the piping. There, heat is transferred away and condenses, flowing back toward the CPU and heat source. You won't be able to replace the heat pipes in cooling fins.

Water pumps

For systems that generate too much heat for fins and heat pipes to cool, designers can turn to more exotic cooling systems. One such system is a pumped water system. Like heat pipes, tubes carry water past the CPU to pick up heat. The heated water is transported away from the CPU, often outside the computer's case, where it passes through cooling fins to transfer the heat away.

Some computer-game aficionados and others who work their PCs hard go even further. They run the water cooling pipes through an ice-water bath or put the cooling fins outside their windows during the winter. Typical office computer use rarely requires such extreme cooling methods.

Peltier coolers

Pronounced "PELT-ee-āy".

A *Peltier* device is an electronic component that gets colder when a voltage is applied. Peltier coolers for CPUs provide cooling when convective methods won't work, such as in factories and other environments where the ambient room temperature can be very hot.

A Peltier device is connected directly to the CPU. Devices that can drop the temperature of a CPU by 70° C are available. If more cooling is needed, you can combine Peltier devices with water coolers.

CPUs and motherboards **2–23**

Do it!

A-3: Replacing a system fan

Here's how	Here's why
1 Locate the system fan	
Disconnect the system fan cable from the motherboard	
2 If your system fan is covered by an air baffle, remove the air baffle	
3 Remove the system fan from the system case by releasing its retaining mechanism	Some fans are held in place by clips; others might be held in with screws.
4 Insert the new system fan and secure it to the system case	
If necessary, replace the air baffle	
5 Reconnect the system fan cable to the motherboard	
6 Close your system case and reconnect the power cable	
7 Boot the PC to confirm that the fan is functional	
Log on to Windows Vista as: User name: **PAADMIN##**	
Password: **!pass1234**	

If you don't have extra system fans, students can reinstall the one they just removed.

CPU installation

Explanation

Identifying the different types of CPUs is covered in the prerequisite course, CompTIA A+ Certification: Essentials.

CPUs themselves rarely fail. Furthermore, you typically won't upgrade a PC by replacing the CPU. Instead, you'll probably either replace the whole motherboard (including the CPU) or replace the whole computer.

You might have the opportunity to install a CPU if you purchase all of your computer components separately to build a computer from parts. Some motherboards support multiple processors. In such a situation, you might need to install an additional CPU in a computer.

Regardless of why you might install a CPU, you must match the CPU to the motherboard. The CPU's packaging must match the slots or sockets available on the motherboard. Furthermore, the motherboard must supply sufficient power and be rated for the speed of CPU you plan to install. If you purchase components as a set, your vendor will have selected a matching CPU. If you purchase components separately, make sure to match your CPU and motherboard.

CPU packages are held in their sockets by retaining clips or other mechanisms. Older PGA packages are held in place by a locking lever. Newer slot and socket designs use retaining clips to keep the processor package in place. Retaining clips are shown in Exhibit 2-8.

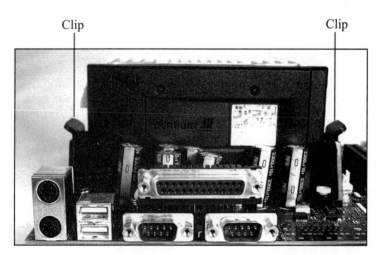

Exhibit 2-8: Retaining clips for a SECC CPU package

To install a CPU:
1. Unplug the computer and open the case while observing general electrical and ESD safety precautions.
2. If necessary, remove the old CPU by releasing its retaining mechanisms and lifting the package from its socket.
3. Store the old CPU in an appropriate, static-safe bag or box.
4. Insert the new CPU package into its socket and secure it with the retaining mechanism.
5. Close the case, reconnect cables, and boot the PC.

If you're installing a new motherboard and CPU at the same time, install the CPU on the motherboard before you install the motherboard in the case.

Do it!

This is an optional activity.

A-4: Replacing a CPU (optional)

Here's how	Here's why
1 Using the PC provided by your instructor, unplug the PC and then open the case while following electrical and ESD safety precautions	Your instructor might have a different computer into which you can install a new or additional CPU.
2 If necessary, remove the old CPU	
3 Place the old CPU in a static-safe bag or box	
4 Install the new CPU	
5 Close the case and reconnect cables	
6 Boot the PC to confirm that you've installed the CPU correctly	
Log on to Windows as: User name: **PAADMIN##** Password: **!pass1234**	

Motherboards

Explanation

The *motherboard* is the main circuit board in a personal computer. It's made up of various components, including the CPU and other electronic devices, wires, adapter sockets to which additional circuit boards and devices can be attached, and front and back panel connectors. Exhibit 2-9 shows a motherboard with some of its primary components labeled.

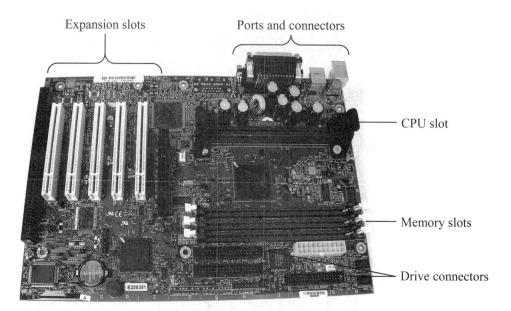

Exhibit 2-9: A motherboard with primary components labeled

The following table describes the primary components on a motherboard.

Component	Function
CPU	The chip that processes instructions, manipulates data, and controls the interactions of the other circuits in your computer.
Expansion slots	Slots into which you can plug additional circuit boards to expand the capabilities of a computer. For example, you can add a sound card for better sound and music reproduction.
Graphics adapter slot	A slot into which you can plug a graphics adapter card, which produces the output displayed on the monitor.
Hard drive interface connectors	Slots into which you can plug cables to connect hard drives, CD drives, and DVD drives to the system.
Floppy drive interface connector	A slot into which you can plug the cable to connect a floppy drive to the system.
Power connector	The connector to which you attach the output of the power supply to provide electrical power to the motherboard. Older systems have a pair of slots rather than a single connector.
Memory slots	Slots into which you insert memory modules to add system memory to a PC.
PS/2 mouse and keyboard ports	Ports into which you can plug PS/2-style keyboard and mouse cables.

Component	Function
USB port	One or more ports into which you can plug cables to connect USB 1.1 and USB 2.0 devices to a PC.
IEEE 1394 / FireWire port	One or more ports into which you can plug cables to connect FireWire devices to a PC.
Serial port	One or more ports into which you can plug cables to connect serial devices, such as modems or mice, to a PC.
Parallel port	One or more ports into which you can plug cables to connect parallel devices, such as printers, to a PC.
Battery	A battery to provide power for maintaining system configuration information while your PC is turned off or disconnected from the outlet.
Network interface and modem	Network interface and modem circuitry built into the motherboard to enable connections to a network without an add-on adapter or modem card.
Video connectors	Video circuitry built into the motherboard so that an add-on adapter card is unnecessary. Such motherboards include a video connector on the back of the system case.

The motherboard is sometimes called the *system board* or *main board*. However, the latter term is typically used to describe the main circuit board in non-PC devices, such as alarm systems, televisions, and so forth.

Motherboard installation

Motherboards occasionally fail, often due to manufacturing defects or rough handling. If failure occurs, you might need to install a new motherboard. You might also need to install a motherboard when upgrading a PC or building one from scratch.

Motherboards are typically held in the case by screws, but occasionally plastic clips are used. Most often, you need to open both sides of the system case to access these screws or clips. Additionally, you need to remove any wires, cables, connectors, and perhaps even other system components, such as the power supply and drives, to remove the motherboard.

To install a motherboard:

1. Unplug the computer and open the case while observing general electrical and ESD safety precautions.
2. Disconnect any wires, cables, and connectors from the old motherboard.
3. If necessary, remove the power supply and drives from the system. In some cases, these items are in the way and prevent you from removing the motherboard.
4. Remove the old motherboard by unscrewing it from the case or by releasing the retaining clips that secure it.
5. Store the old motherboard in an appropriate, static-safe bag or box.
6. Install the new motherboard and secure it with the retaining mechanism (screws or clips).
7. If necessary, reinstall the power supply and drives.
8. Connect the necessary wires, cables, and connectors.
9. Close the case, reconnect cables, and boot the PC.

Windows activation requirements

With Windows XP, Microsoft introduced product activation for its Windows operating system. *Product activation* is a type of cataloging process by which the software product (in this case, Windows), its product key, and the hardware signature of your computer are entered into a Microsoft database. Microsoft assures users that the process of activation is completely anonymous, yet specific enough to prevent the same product key from being reused on a different computer.

Commercial versions of Windows XP and Windows Vista have a 30-day grace period, after which activation is mandatory. After the grace period expires, Windows basically functions only enough to allow you to complete the activation process, although Windows Vista provides some additional functionality above that offered by Windows XP after the activation deadline. Every few days, Windows uses a pop-up window to remind you about activation until you successfully complete the process.

You can activate Windows over the Internet or by telephone. The Internet option is usually completed in seconds. The phone option can take several minutes while you exchange unique numbers with the customer service representative.

If you attempt to activate a copy of Windows that uses the same product key as an already activated system, Internet and automatic activation will fail. You will then be forced to perform telephone-based activation. This is a security measure to prevent piracy. If you've simply upgraded your hardware, Microsoft will allow the new system to be activated, but the activation of the old system will be voided in Microsoft's database.

Activation might be unnecessary for some new computer systems on which Windows is already installed. Also, some of the volume licenses purchased by large companies use special product keys for Windows that do not require individual system activation.

Activation has both benefits and drawbacks. One benefit is that it ensures that you've purchased a fully licensed and valid product and did not inadvertently obtain a pirated copy. Unfortunately, it can have one large drawback. If you make a significant change in your hardware—such as replacing the motherboard or replacing multiple system components simultaneously—your activation can be invalidated.

Do it!

This is an optional activity.

A-5: Replacing a motherboard (optional)

Here's how	Here's why
1 Using the PC provided by your instructor, unplug the PC and then open the case while following electrical and ESD safety precautions	Your instructor might have a different computer into which you can install a new or replacement motherboard.
2 Disconnect any cables, wires, and connectors from the motherboard	
3 If necessary, remove the power supply and drives	To access the motherboard. You might not have to remove these components.
4 Remove the old motherboard	
5 Place the old motherboard in a static-safe bag or box	
6 Install the new motherboard	
7 If necessary, reinstall the power supply and drives	
8 Connect any cables, wires, and connectors from the motherboard	
9 Close the case and reconnect cables	
10 Boot the PC to confirm that you have installed the motherboard correctly Log on to Windows as: User name: **PAADMIN##** Password: **!pass1234**	

Tell students that if the new motherboard is of a different model than the original, they might need to perform a repair installation of Windows.

Topic B: Motherboard troubleshooting

This topic covers the following CompTIA A+ 220-702 exam objectives.

#	Objective
1.2	Given a scenario, detect problems, troubleshoot, and repair/replace personal computer components • Motherboards 　– Jumper settings 　– CMOS battery 　– Advanced BIOS settings 　– Bus speeds 　– Chipsets 　– Firmware updates 　– Socket types 　– Expansion slots 　– Memory slots 　– Front panel connectors 　– I/O ports 　　• Sound, video, USB 1.1, USB 2.0, serial, IEEE 1394 / FireWire, parallel, NIC, modem, PS/2 • Processors 　– Socket types 　– Speed 　– Number of cores 　– Power consumption 　– Cache 　– Front side bus 　– 32bit vs. 64bit

The CMOS battery

Explanation

Configuration data is stored in the CMOS chip. This chip retains its data when the PC is off, thanks to a battery connected to the motherboard. In older PCs, the battery was soldered in place and wasn't replaceable. Nowadays, the battery is inserted into a socket and is held in place with retaining clips.

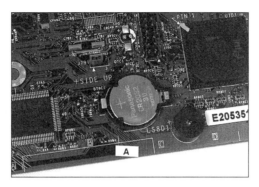

Exhibit 2-10: A CMOS backup battery

Do it!

B-1: Replacing the CMOS battery

Here's how	Here's why
1 Shut down your PC and unplug it from the electrical outlet	
2 Following electrical and ESD safety precautions, open the case	
3 Locate the CMOS battery on the motherboard	
4 Remove or release the retaining clip, and slide the battery out of its holder	
5 Install the new battery, securing it with the retaining clips	
6 Close the system case	
7 Restart the computer	
8 If necessary, use the BIOS setup utility to set the correct date, time, and device options	These values will probably be lost when you remove the battery.
Log on to Windows as: User name: **PAADMIN##** Password: **!pass1234**	

If you don't have spare batteries for students, they can reinstall the batteries they remove.

BIOS-related problems and causes

Explanation

As a PC technician, you should be familiar with the most common symptoms, probable causes, and suggested "first try" solutions for BIOS-related problems. You might encounter problems not listed in the following table, but it provides some scenarios to consider when you're troubleshooting problems.

Symptom	Probable cause	Suggested solution
Devices misidentified	The BIOS is configured incorrectly.	Use the BIOS setup utility to reconfigure device options in the BIOS.
Wrong memory size reported during POST or available after booting	The BIOS is configured incorrectly.	Use the BIOS setup utility to configure the correct memory size.
Hard drive inaccessible	The geometry parameters are set incorrectly in the BIOS (older hard drives). The hard drive might be disabled in the BIOS (newer hard drives).	Use the BIOS setup utility to reconfigure the hard drive settings.
System won't boot from hard drive	The boot drive order is incorrect. Hard drive configuration data in CMOS doesn't match the hard drive's actual geometry. The hard drive is disabled in CMOS.	Use the BIOS setup utility to reconfigure device options in the BIOS.
System boots from the wrong device	The BIOS boot order is set incorrectly, or the drive isn't bootable.	Use the BIOS setup utility to configure the boot order. If that doesn't solve the problem, the device isn't bootable; see a hard-drive troubleshooting reference.
Date and time incorrect or reset after the computer is turned off	Most likely, the CMOS battery is dead and needs replacing. However, the BIOS date could be set wrong.	Try resetting the correct date and time in the BIOS; then shut down and unplug the computer. Wait five minutes or so, and then plug in and start the computer. If the date is still incorrect, replace the CMOS battery.

BIOS updates

The BIOS is provided in the form of a memory chip that doesn't lose its contents when the power is turned off. The BIOS can be implemented either in ROM (read-only memory) or flash memory (a type of electronically reprogrammable memory chip).

- ROM-based BIOS is programmed at the factory. You can't change this kind of BIOS without replacing the chip itself.
- Using a special program provided by the computer (or BIOS) manufacturer, you can update a flash-memory-based BIOS without changing the BIOS chip. This updating is often called *flashing* the BIOS.

CPUs and motherboards **2–33**

Usually, the BIOS version that ships with your PC is all you will ever need. However, you might need to upgrade your BIOS in the following situations:

- There are device problems or other bugs that the PC manufacturer identifies as being caused by BIOS problems.
- There are device problems that you can attribute to no other cause than the BIOS. Additionally, you have exhausted all other troubleshooting avenues in trying to fix the problems.
- You need to use new hardware options that, while supported by your motherboard, aren't supported by the BIOS.

BIOS update sources

AMI, Award, and the other BIOS manufacturers don't provide BIOS updates directly to consumers. Instead, these companies provide the BIOS to computer manufacturers, who build it into their computers.

The BIOS manufacturers give the BIOS to PC manufacturers in an incomplete state. The PC manufacturers make final modifications to tailor the BIOS to their exact hardware. This tailored BIOS is what's shipped to you in your new PC. For this reason, BIOS updates must come from your PC's manufacturer, not from the original equipment manufacturer.

Flashing the BIOS

To update the BIOS in your system:

1 Use the System Information tool to determine your current BIOS version.
2 Visit your PC manufacturer's Web site and navigate to its support pages to locate the BIOS update files. Compare the version number and release date with the information reported by the System Information tool to determine if a new BIOS version is available.
3 Download the installation file for the new BIOS version. Make sure you choose the version that matches your PC model.
4 If it's not part of the BIOS installation file, download the appropriate BIOS flashing utility from your PC manufacturer's Web site. Make sure you choose the version that matches your PC model and operating system.
5 Close all open applications.
6 Open the flashing utility and follow the instructions it provides to update your BIOS.
7 Restart your PC when prompted.

Exhibit 2-11: The Phoenix BIOS flash utility's startup screen

BIOS update failures

BIOS updates can fail, and when they do, you can be left with an unbootable and useless computer. To minimize the risks of a failed update, follow these guidelines:

- Don't update your BIOS unless you must. Usually, the BIOS version that shipped with your PC is sufficient for the entire operating life of the computer.
- Never turn off the computer during a BIOS update, and make sure power doesn't go off during an update (connect the PC to a UPS). Don't press Ctrl+Alt+Delete during the operation.
- Make sure you use the correct BIOS flash utility. The utility is specific to your brand of computer, model, BIOS chip, and operating system. Contact your PC's manufacturer or visit its Web site to obtain the correct flash utility.
- Follow the flash utility's instructions exactly. Make sure you run the utility under the correct operating system. Flash utilities are typically compatible with a single version of Windows or other operating system.
- Most flash utilities offer the option of backing up your old BIOS before updating it. Perform this backup. You might be able to use it to recover if the update fails.

Recovering from a failed BIOS update

You have a few basic options for recovering from a failed BIOS update:

- Use the BIOS backup created by the flash utility to try to restore the previous version.
- Many modern BIOSs include a small area that's never overwritten during an upgrade. This "boot block" section has sufficient support to boot your PC from a floppy disk. You need to provide a floppy disk containing the correct BIOS and flash utility. The contents of this floppy vary depending on your BIOS manufacturer. No video is displayed during this operation. After the PC has booted from this floppy and copied the correct BIOS over the corrupt version, you reboot the PC.
- Some Intel motherboards include a flash-recovery jumper switch. You set this jumper switch to the recovery position, insert the system upgrade floppy disk into the drive, and boot the PC. The system boots from the disk and copies the original BIOS over the corrupted BIOS. No video is displayed during this operation. When the drive light on the floppy drive goes off, the procedure is done. Reset the recovery jumper to its normal position and reboot the PC again.
- If the preceding methods don't work for you, you might need to get a new BIOS chip from your motherboard or PC's manufacturer. You need to replace the damaged BIOS chip with the new one.

POST-related problems and causes

The following table lists some common *power-on self-test* (POST)–related symptoms that you might encounter, along with probable causes and solutions.

Symptom	Probable cause	Suggested solution
There's no video; instead, the computer emits eight short beeps.	Most likely due to failed memory on the video adapter. If the system uses integrated video circuitry, this error could also indicate a failure of main system memory.	Replace the memory modules on the video adapter. If that's not possible, swap the video adapter with a known working adapter. If you have an integrated video adapter, try replacing the main system memory modules.
The system emits three long beeps.	A keyboard error: a key is stuck, or the keyboard is plugged into the mouse port.	Attach a different keyboard and try booting again. Confirm that the keyboard and mouse are plugged into the correct ports.
The system emits one long and three short beeps.	A memory problem.	Replace the main system memory modules.
POST code 162 is displayed.	Configuration data stored in CMOS doesn't match the PC's actual hardware.	Run the BIOS setup utility to confirm the proper configuration values.
POST code 164 is displayed.	PC has more or less memory than the amount listed in the CMOS settings.	You can often press a key (your screen tells you which one) to automatically update the CMOS with the correct amount of memory and continue booting. If that's not an option, run the BIOS setup utility to configure the correct value.

CMOS-related problems and causes

The following table lists some common CMOS-related symptoms you might encounter, along with probable causes and solutions.

Symptom	Probable cause	Suggested solution
Error message "Non-system disk or disk error"	The BIOS can't find the master boot record on the boot drive.	You might have specified the wrong drive as the boot drive in the CMOS settings. Use the setup utility to confirm and reconfigure, if necessary. Alternatively, your boot drive might not be bootable, meaning that it doesn't have the files needed to boot the system.
Error message "Display type mismatch"	The video settings in the CMOS don't match the monitor attached to the system.	Connect the correct type of monitor.
Error message "Memory size mismatch"	The amount of memory listed in the CMOS settings is different from the amount actually installed in the system.	Run the BIOS setup utility to correct the information.
Error message "CMOS checksum failure"	The BIOS has detected a memory problem in the CMOS. This could be a sign that your CMOS chip has failed. More likely, it means that the CMOS battery is dead.	Try replacing the CMOS battery. If that doesn't correct the problem, the CMOS chip is probably bad. This isn't typically a replaceable component. You probably need a new motherboard to correct the error.
	Boot block virus	Replace the motherboard. Use boot-block virus removal or repair software to recover the boot block.

Do it!

You must set up this lab according to the "Troubleshooting Labs Setup" section of the Course Setup instructions.

B-2: Troubleshooting BIOS and POST problems

Here's how

1 One or more BIOS- and POST-related problems have been introduced into your lab computer. Troubleshoot these problems to determine their causes.

2 Correct the problems you've found in your PC to return it to a working state. Solving one problem might reveal the presence of another problem. Troubleshoot and fix all problems that arise.

3 Document the problem(s) you find:

4 Document the steps you take to fix the problem(s):

Motherboard and CPU failures

Explanation

Motherboards and CPUs can fail for various reasons. One of the most common causes of failure is a large electric spike, such as that caused by a nearby lightning strike. Often, a motherboard or CPU failure shows up in one of two ways: a complete system failure occurs (nothing happens when you turn the computer on); or unusual problems occur, perhaps sporadically.

As a PC technician, you should be familiar with the most common symptoms, probable causes, and suggested "first try" solutions for motherboard- and CPU-related problems. You might encounter problems not listed in the following table, but it will give you a few scenarios to consider when troubleshooting motherboard and CPU problems.

Symptom	Probable cause	Suggested solution
The system fails to boot.	Power problems are the most likely cause. If those aren't the cause, a motherboard component could have failed.	Replace the motherboard.
A burning or foul odor or smoke comes out of the case.	Components, including the CPU, are overheated or burning.	Unplug the computer immediately and try to identify the failed component. If it can be replaced, do so. Otherwise, try replacing the motherboard.
Fans come on and power lights indicate that power is present, but the system fails to boot.	Power-control circuitry on the motherboard could have failed.	Replace the motherboard.
Video display problems occur on a system with an integrated display adapter.	Video circuitry has failed.	Replace the motherboard. In some computers, you can disable the on-board video circuitry and then install a separate video adapter.
Intermittent problems occur that can't be traced to the failure of another component.	The motherboard might be faulty.	Replace the motherboard.

For a motherboard and CPU troubleshooting flow chart, see
www.fonerbooks.com/cpu_ram.htm.

Do it!

B-3: Troubleshooting motherboard and CPU problems

Questions and answers

1. You are troubleshooting a computer. When it boots, you hear a slow, single beep, but nothing appears on screen. The power light on the monitor is amber. The computer won't begin the POST. What do you suspect is the problem?

   A bad or failing CPU can cause a slow, single beep or unrecognized beep code accompanied by a blank display. The power LED on your monitor remains amber or red and the system will not perform a POST.

2. What should you try first to resolve this issue?

   The easiest way to test a processor is to try it on a known good motherboard.

3. You are troubleshooting a computer that's unstable (it hangs, gets BSODs and memory errors, spontaneously reboots, etc.). The user states that the symptoms have gotten more frequent. What do you suspect is the problem?

   As the capacitors on a motherboard age, their ability to collect a charge of electricity decreases while their impedance increases. The capacitors can no longer filter the DC voltages on the motherboard, so the system becomes unstable. System hangs, BSODs, memory errors, spontaneous reboots are some common symptoms of motherboard failures.

Unit summary: CPUs and motherboards

Topic A In this topic, you learned how to **install a CPU** on a motherboard, and how to **install a motherboard** into a PC's case. You learned that the **BIOS** is a set of programs that control the most basic hardware interactions within a PC, and you learned how to configure BIOS settings. You also learned that CPUs generate an enormous amount of heat and require active **cooling mechanisms** to prevent overheating, and you replaced a cooling unit on a CPU.

Topic B In this topic, you learned that motherboards and CPUs **fail** for various reasons, particularly lightning strikes and electrical spikes. You learned about common symptoms of such failures, their probable causes, and suggested solutions. You also learned how to replace the CMOS battery in a PC.

Review questions

1 List at least three settings commonly configurable through the BIOS setup utility.

Answers might include: System date and time, Drive boot order, Memory quantity, Hard drive type and size, Serial and parallel port configuration options, The state (enabled or disabled) of integrated devices

2 What's one symptom of a failed CMOS battery?

The clock is reset to the system's default date (often January 1, 1970).

3 True or false? BIOS and CMOS are the same thing.

False. BIOS is a set of instructions that control the low-level hardware functions of a computer. CMOS usually refers to memory that stores hardware configuration data and is backed up by a battery.

4 What does "POST" stand for?

Power-on self-test

5 You hear one short beep when you first turn on your computer. What problem does that beep code indicate?

One short beep usually means that no problems were found.

6 How do you cold-boot a computer?

Turn it on from a powered-off state.

7 What is the best source for BIOS updates?

The PC manufacturer's Web site

8 A BIOS update failure usually results in:

An unbootable computer

9 What does a beep code error of three long beeps indicate?

A keyboard error: the keyboard isn't plugged in, the keyboard has failed or has a stuck key, or the mouse is plugged into the keyboard port.

10 You receive the CMOS error message "CMOS checksum failure." What does that indicate?

A CMOS memory error has been detected. It could mean that the CMOS chip is bad, but this error is more likely to occur when the CMOS battery has died.

11 Why does your computer use beep codes to indicate an error, rather than simply displaying a message on the monitor?

Beep codes are sounded during the portion of the boot process before the video subsystem has been initialized. Thus, the system can't yet display anything on the screen. The system's only output option is to emit a beep through the system speaker.

12 True or false? Every BIOS manufacturer uses the same flashing utility.

False. Flashing utilities are proprietary to the BIOS manufacturer, and you should always use the correct version for your BIOS.

13 You see "164 – Memory Size Mismatch" on your screen as you boot your PC. What does this BIOS error indicate?

Your PC has more or less memory than the amount listed in the CMOS settings.

14 True or false? Thermal compound is basically a glue used between the CPU and its heat sink or cooling fins.

True. The compound improves heat flow by closely mating the CPU die to the heat sink or fan.

15 You open your PC and look at the CPU. How can you tell if it uses active or passive cooling?

If there is just a heat sink on the CPU, it uses passive cooling. If there's a fan attached to the CPU, it uses active cooling.

16 What is the best source for BIOS updates?

Your PC's manufacturer—in particular, its support Web site.

17 Before the Pentium CPU was introduced, what was the most common CPU cooling mechanism?

A simple fan, typically part of the power supply, was all that was used with the 80286 and 80386 CPUs. Some 80386 and most 80486 CPUs also used cooling fins.

18 True or false? CPUs of the same class are interchangeable. For example, you can replace any Pentium 4 CPU on a motherboard with any other Pentium 4–class CPU.

False. You must match the physical, electronic, and performance characteristics of a CPU to the motherboard.

Independent practice activity

In this activity, you'll practice replacing the CPU and motherboard components of a PC.

1 Remove the motherboard from your computer.

2 Remove the CPU from your motherboard.

3 Reinstall the CPU.

4 Reinstall the motherboard.

5 Boot your computer and log on to Windows as PAADMIN## to confirm that you've performed all the steps correctly.

Unit 3
Memory systems

Unit time: 90 minutes

Complete this unit, and you'll know how to:

A Install RAM into a system while handling it properly and meeting your PC's installation requirements.

B Troubleshoot memory problems.

Topic A: RAM installation

This topic covers the following CompTIA A+ 220-702 exam objectives.

#	Objective
1.1	**Given a scenario, install, configure, and maintain personal computer components** • Memory
1.3	**Given a scenario, install, configure, detect problems, troubleshoot, and repair/replace laptop components** • Hard drive and memory

Memory modules

Explanation

You install memory modules by inserting them into slots on the computer's motherboard. To do so, you must consider these factors:

- Banking requirements
- Proper handling techniques
- Slot insertion techniques
- Safe storage
- BIOS configuration

Banking requirements

You physically install memory modules into slots on the motherboard, and those slots are arranged in groups called *banks*. Depending on the computer's design, a bank might include one, two, or four slots. When you install new memory, you must fill every slot in a bank. For example, if your computer uses two-slot banks, then you must install memory modules in pairs. Many modern computers and notebooks use single-slot banks. With this type of bank, you have to install only one module.

With many motherboards, you must use the same type and speed of memory in every slot in a bank. In a few situations, you must use the same type and speed of memory in every memory slot in your computer, even across different banks.

In most computers, you simply leave empty any extra banks. However, in computers that use DRDRAM (Rambus memory), you must fill empty slots with a *continuity module*, which is a small circuit board designed to complete the electrical circuit but not add RAM to your system.

Your owner's manual tells you whether you must install RAM in banks. Additionally, markings on the motherboard—either text labels or outlines—identify the banks, if present.

Proper handling

Memory modules are extremely sensitive to static and you can easily damage them. Carefully follow static-safe work procedures, including these precautions:

- As always, unplug the computer before opening it.
- With the computer unplugged, touch the power supply's metal case or the computer's metal frame for at least three seconds.
- Once you've discharged any static potential, try to move as little as possible. The movement of your clothing or shoes on the floor could generate new charges.
- While the module is still in its static-safe packaging, place it on the computer's power supply. This helps safely discharge any electrical potential differences between the computer and the module.
- Always handle modules by their edges, without touching the pins, components, or traces (the wires embedded in the surface of the circuit board).

Inserting the modules

Memory modules include notches or are shaped in such a way that you can insert them into the slots in only the correct orientation. Don't force a module to fit if you can't insert it easily.

With most modules, follow these steps to insert a module into a slot:

1. Gently insert the module into the slot at about a 45-degree angle.
2. Firmly, but gently, push the module into its slot while moving the module to the fully vertical (or horizontal) position. As you do this, the metal or plastic retaining clips engage to hold the module.

To remove a module:

1. Gently release the retaining clips at both ends of the module.
2. With the clips released, you should be able to move the module easily to a 45-degree angle.
3. Remove the module.

Storage

You should store memory modules in their original packaging. If you don't have the packaging, store them in a static-safe bag. These bags, made of a metal-coated plastic, are conductive enough to transmit static charges slowly so that electronic components within won't be damaged.

CMOS configuration

The BIOS checks the memory in a computer when you boot it. The BIOS compares the amount of memory in the computer with the amount listed in the CMOS setup data. If there's a discrepancy, the computer displays an error message.

With most modern computers, you simply press a key to automatically change the value for the CMOS memory amount without using the BIOS setup program. In some computers, especially older computers, you must run the BIOS setup utility. Depending on the utility, you might be able to select the amount of installed memory or you might be prompted to enter the correct amount.

Package types

In the very early days of PC computing, you purchased individual DRAM chips and installed them into sockets on the motherboard. Now, however, DRAM chips are installed at the factory onto a small circuit board, called a *package*. You install the package, more commonly called a *module*, into a slot in the computer. The following table lists the most common types of memory packages (modules).

Package	Pins	Used in	Description
SIMM	30	386-class desktops, early Macintosh computers	Single inline memory module. A notch on one end ensures that you insert this module in the correct orientation. About 3.5" long by 5/8" high.
SIMM	72	486 and early Pentium desktops	One notch in the middle and another notch at one end ensure that you insert this module in the correct orientation. About 4.25" by 1".
DIMM	100	Printers	Dual inline memory module. Has 50 pins on the front and 50 pins on the back. Two notches, one centered and the other off-center, ensure correct installation. About 3.5" by 1.25".
DIMM	168	Pentium and Athlon systems	Has 84 pins on the front and 84 pins on the back. Two notches, one centered and the other off-center, ensure correct installation. About 5.25" by 1".
DIMM	184	DDR SDRAM in desktops	Has 92 pins in front and 92 pins in back. Two notches, one centered and the other off-center, ensure correct installation. About 5.25" by 1".
DIMM	240	DDR2 SDRAM in desktops	Supports 64-bit memory and processors. Has 120 front pins and 120 back pins. Two notches, one centered and the other off-center, ensure correct installation. About 5.25" by 1.18".
DIMM	240	DDR3 SDRAM in desktops	Uses the JEDEC standard fly-by technology, in which signals are routed to each component in serial-like fashion, and times to memory devices are skewed. Compare this to DDR2 technology, in which the signals are routed to arrive at the same time for all of the memory components on the DIMM. Fly-by technology improves signal integrity, but requires additional complexity for the controller. Has 120 front pins and 120 back pins. About 5.25" by 1.18" (heights can vary).
RIMM	184	Intel Pentium III Xeon and Pentium 4 systems	Used with RDRAM chips and trademarked by Rambus. Has 184 edge connector pads with 1 mm pad spacing. RIMM is sometimes incorrectly used as an acronym for "Rambus inline memory module."
MICRODIMM	144	Subnotebook computers	Micro dual inline memory module. Has 72 front pins and 72 back pins. A single notch at one end ensures correct installation. About 1.545" by 1".
SODIMM	144	Laptop and notebook computers	Small outline dual inline memory module. Has 72 front pins and 72 back pins. A single off-center notch ensures correct installation. About 2.625" by 1".

Memory systems **3–5**

Package	Pins	Used in	Description
SODIMM	200	DDR memory for laptops and notebooks	Has 100 front pins and 100 back pins. A single off-center notch ensures correct installation. About 2.625" by 1". DDR SODIMMs use PC2100, PC2700, and PC3200 SDRAM.
SODIMM	200	DDR2 memory for laptops and notebooks	Has 100 front pins and 100 back pins. A single off-center notch ensures correct installation. About 2.625" by 1". DDR2 SODIMMs use PC2-4200 SDRAM.
SODIMM	204	DDR3 memory for laptops and notebooks	Has 102 front pins and 102 back pins. About 2.6" by 1.75" (heights can vary slightly).

Consult your owner's manual to determine the exact type of memory module or modules that are compatible with your computer. Two common memory modules are shown in Exhibit 3-1.

Exhibit 3-1: PC2100 SODIMM (left) and 168-pin DIMM (right) memory modules

Do it!

A-1: Adding memory to a desktop computer

Here's how

1 Consult your PC's owner's manual to determine the PC's memory banking requirements

2 Determine the type of memory module required by your PC

You need to supply working memory modules appropriate for your classroom PCs.

3 Obtain suitable modules from your instructor

4 Install the modules into your PC

5 Boot the computer, and if necessary, reconfigure the CMOS to support the new memory

6 Continue the boot process to confirm that you've successfully installed the new memory

7 Log on as your PAADMIN## user

8 If directed by your instructor, remove the additional memory from your PC

Notebook memory

Explanation

The location where you install memory in a notebook or laptop computer varies greatly. In some notebooks, you unscrew a compartment cover on the underside of the case. In others, you have to remove the keyboard from the case to access the memory area.

Refer to the documentation for your notebook to determine exactly how to install memory into it. Memory shouldn't be installed until you shut down the computer, unplug the power cord, and remove the battery. You don't want to get shocked by voltage from the battery or wall socket. You also don't want to turn on the computer accidentally while you're installing or replacing memory.

Shared video memory

Shared video memory is typically used in lower-cost notebooks.

In some notebook computers, some of the main system memory is shared with the video circuitry. Such systems have no dedicated video memory. Reduced cost is the primary benefit of this design, though there are also some savings in power consumption and heat generation.

The downside of shared video memory is that some of your computer's RAM is dedicated to video operations and is thus inaccessible to the operating system and applications. For example, in a notebook computer with 512 MB of memory and running at 1024×768, 16-bit color display resolution, about 12 MB of RAM is used for normal video options. That's not all that bad. However, 3D, texture mapping, and shading operations can use many times that amount of memory. Even without considering the needs of gaming applications, your system might use as much as 128 MB of memory for video operations, leaving just 384 MB for operating system and application use.

Another big downside of shared video memory is that system memory is much slower than dedicated video memory. Notebooks with shared video memory perform more slowly than those with dedicated video memory.

If your notebook uses shared video memory, adding more system memory can offer more of a performance boost than you'd get from adding memory to a system with dedicated video memory. Not only does the extra memory provide more space for your applications, but it also reduces the impact that video operations have on available memory. It's critical for these systems that you use the highest performing memory modules that are supported by your notebook.

Do it!

A-2: Adding memory to a notebook computer

Here's how	Here's why
1 Shut down the computer	You'll remove and replace the memory in a notebook computer.
Unplug the computer	From the electrical outlet.
Remove the battery	From the battery compartment.
2 Remove the cover over the memory	Refer to the documentation for your notebook for instructions on accessing the memory.

Memory systems **3–7**

If you have new modules for students to install, hand them out now.

	Here's how	Here's why
3	Remove the memory module from the computer	Follow the directions in the notebook's documentation.
4	Install the memory module	Again, refer to the documentation for your notebook.
5	Replace the memory module cover	
6	Start the computer Log on as your **PAADMIN##** user	To verify that it successfully boots.
7	Click **Start**, right-click **Computer**, and choose **Properties**	To verify that the correct amount of memory is found.
8	Close all open windows	
9	How can you determine if your system uses shared video memory?	*Consult the owner's manual for your notebook.*

Handheld computer memory

Explanation

Some handheld computers can't be expanded. In those, there's no way to install additional memory. However, many of the newer handhelds, particularly the more expensive models, offer ways to add more memory.

Some expandable handhelds use memory modules similar to those in a notebook computer. However, most expandable handhelds use memory cards like those used in digital cameras. These handheld computers have a slot into which you can insert the flash memory card without removing the PDA's case. Follow the instructions in your PDA's manual.

Do it!

A-3: Adding memory to a handheld computer

Provide students with memory cards compatible with the handhelds they're working with.

	Here's how	Here's why
1	Determine if your PDA has a memory expansion slot	You'll add memory to your PDA if it supports this capability.
2	Locate a memory card that's compatible with your PDA	Most PDAs expand memory through the use of flash memory cards.
3	Install the memory card	If necessary, check the PDA's documentation for information on how to perform this step.

Memory usage monitoring

Explanation

One of the primary tools for monitoring memory usage on a PC is the Performance tab in Task Manager. (See Exhibit 3-2.) The performance indicators are described in the following table.

Indicator	Description
CPU Usage	Shows the percentage of time the processor is working. If your computer is running slowly, this graph displays a higher percentage.
CPU Usage History	Shows how busy the CPU has been over time. The value selected for Update Speed (on the View menu) determines how often this graph is updated. You can set updates to occur twice per second (High), once every two seconds (Normal), once every four seconds (Low), or not at all (Paused). You can press F5 to update a paused graph. On multiprocessor or multi-core systems, there's one graph per processor or core. On systems with a quad-core processor, Task Manager shows four graphs.
Memory (Windows Vista)	Shows, in megabytes, how much physical memory is being used at the current moment.
PF Usage (Windows XP/2000)	Shows the amount of the page file's capacity being used by the computer. If this graph shows that your page file is near the maximum, you should increase the page file's size.
Physical Memory Usage History (Windows Vista)	Shows how much physical memory has been used over the past few minutes.
Page File Usage History (Windows XP/2000)	Shows the percentage of the page file's size used over time. The value selected for Update Speed (on the View menu) determines how often this graph is updated.
System (Windows Vista) or Totals (Windows XP/2000)	Shows the dynamic totals for the number of handles, threads, and processes running. A *handle* is a unique object identifier used by a process. A *thread* is an object or process running within a larger process or program. In Windows Vista, this section also shows *up time* (the amount of time that has passed since the computer was started) and the size of the page file on the hard disk.
Physical Memory	Shows the total amount of physical memory installed on your computer. "Free" in Windows Vista (or "Available" in Windows XP and Windows 2000) is the amount of free memory available. "Cached" in Windows Vista (or "System Cache" in earlier versions of Windows) shows the amount of current physical memory being used to map pages of open files.
Commit Charge (Windows XP/2000)	Shows the amount of memory allocated to programs and the operating system. This number includes virtual memory, so the value listed under Peak might exceed the actual physical memory installed. The Total value is the same as in the Page File Usage History graph.
Kernel Memory	Shows the amount of memory being used by the operating system kernel and device drivers. "Paged" is memory that can be copied to the page file to free up physical memory for the operating system to use. "Nonpaged" is memory that won't be paged out.
Summary data	(Along the bottom of the tab.) Shows the current number of processes, the current CPU usage percentage, and the current amount of physical or commit-charge memory being used, compared to the maximum available. In Windows Vista, this value is shown as a percentage.

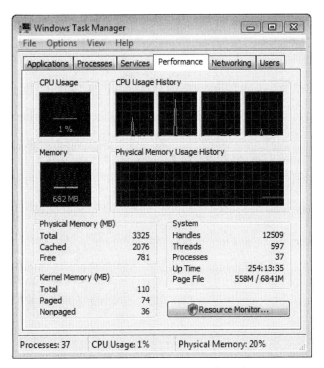

Exhibit 3-2: The Performance tab of Task Manager in Windows Vista

Do it!

A-4: Monitoring memory usage

Here's how	Here's why
1 On your PC or notebook, open Task Manager	Press Ctrl+Shift+Esc. If that doesn't work, press Ctrl+Alt+Delete; you might then need to click Task Manager.
2 Activate the Performance tab	
3 Observe the CPU Usage History graph	
4 Open **Documents**	To generate some computing activity.
Observe the CPU Usage History graph	*[CPU Usage History graph shown]* You see a spike in CPU usage as the processor carries out your request to open Documents.
5 Observe the CPU Usage box	This displays the percentage of time the processor is working.
6 If the CPU Usage box displays a high number, what does that mean?	*Your processor is being overworked.*
7 Observe the Page File value	(Under System.) This value shows the amount of the page file's capacity being used by the computer.
8 If the Page File value displays a number very close to the page file's maximum size, what should you do?	*Increase the size of the page file.*
9 Observe the Physical Memory box	This box shows the amount of RAM installed, the amount of free memory available, and the amount of current physical memory being used to map pages of open files.
10 If the Available memory was very low and the System Cache was very high, compared to the amount listed under Total, what would be your concern?	*That you don't have enough physical memory (RAM) installed. Your computer has to page too much data to the hard disk.*
11 Close Windows Task Manager and Documents	

Memory systems 3–11

Optimizing the page file

Explanation

By default, Windows places the page file on the boot partition, where the operating system is installed. The page file's size is initially determined by the amount of physical RAM installed. To provide the best performance, Windows automatically increases or decreases the size of the page file based on system memory requirements and available hard disk space. However, you can manually override these settings and establish minimum and maximum values in megabytes.

To determine the size of the page file, Microsoft recommends multiplying the amount of physical RAM by 1.5. The maximum recommended size is 4095 MB. You can also place a page file on a different hard disk from the boot partition to optimize performance. When the page file is stored on the boot partition, Windows has to perform disk input/output (I/O) processes on both the system directory and the page file. Moving the page file to a different disk allows Windows to handle multiple I/O requests more quickly.

Do it!

A-5: Changing the size of the Windows page file

Here's how	Here's why
1 Click **Start**, right-click **Computer**, and choose **Properties**	To open the System window.
In the Tasks pane, click **Advanced system settings**, and click **Continue**	To open the System Properties dialog box.
2 In the Performance section, click **Settings**	To open the Performance Options dialog box.
3 Activate the Advanced tab	If necessary.
4 In the Virtual memory section, click **Change**	To open the Virtual Memory dialog box.
Clear **Automatically manage paging file size for all drives**	
5 Select **Custom Size**	
6 In the Initial size box, enter a value that's 1000 higher than the current value	To increase the starting size of the page file.
7 In the Maximum size box, enter a value that's 2000 higher than the current value	To increase the maximum size of the page file. Clicking the Set button would enable these new values, but you'll cancel the operation instead.
8 Click **Cancel** three times	To close all dialog boxes.
9 Close the System window	

Topic B: Memory troubleshooting

This topic covers the following CompTIA A+ 220-702 exam objective.

#	Objective
1.2	Given a scenario, detect problems, troubleshoot, and repair/replace personal computer components
	• Memory

Diagnosing memory problems

Explanation

The memory-testing actions performed by the BIOS are relatively simple and not very accurate. Many memory problems aren't detected by the BIOS. To test memory fully, you should use a dedicated memory-testing utility.

Memory-testing utilities

Memory-testing utilities typically perform hundreds, if not thousands, of read and write operations in every memory location. In addition, the utilities write more than one type of value to every byte of memory to test various types of possible failures. Complete testing cycles with these utilities can take many hours, or even days, depending on the speed of the computer and the amount of RAM installed.

The following are some popular memory-testing utilities.

Utility	License	URL
Memtest86	Free, open source	www.memtest86.com
Microsoft Windows Memory Diagnostic	Free, unsupported, commercial	http://oca.microsoft.com/en/windiag.asp
DocMemory Diagnostic	Free, unsupported, commercial	www.simmtester.com/

Memtest86

Memtest86 is perhaps the most popular free memory-testing utility available. It's released under the Gnu Public License (GPL). It can test any Intel x86 computer, regardless of operating system.

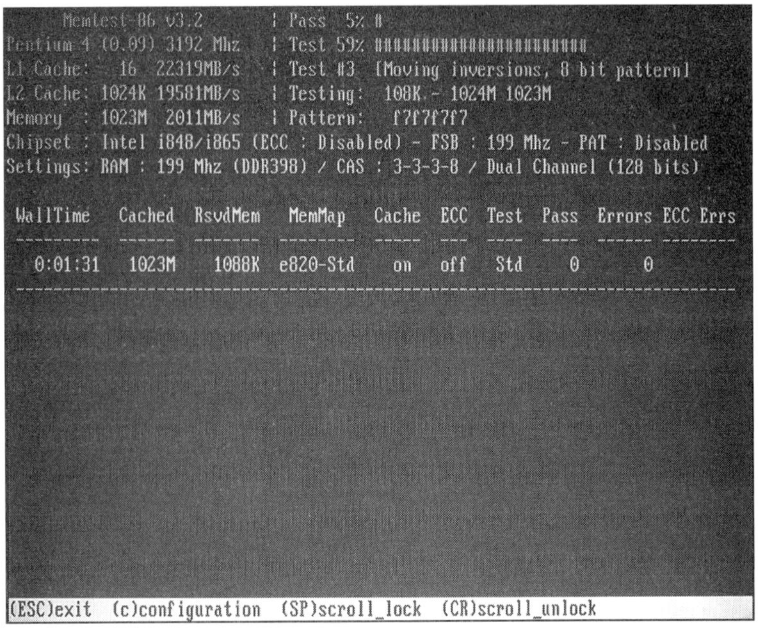

Exhibit 3-3: The Memtest86 screen, showing the default test in progress

As with nearly all such utilities, you must create a bootable floppy disk or CD that contains this utility and support files. Then you boot from that disk rather than running the utility from within Windows.

Troubleshooting

As a PC technician, you should be familiar with the most common symptoms, probable causes, and suggested "first try" solutions for memory-related problems. You might encounter problems not listed in the following table, but it provides a few scenarios to consider when you're troubleshooting memory-related problems.

Symptom	Probable cause	Suggested solution
201 BIOS error code at boot time	Bad memory location.	Test memory with a RAM-testing utility to determine which portion of memory has failed. Using the output from that program, determine which module has failed, and replace it.
Parity error message	Bad memory (in a system with parity memory).	Test memory with a RAM-testing utility to determine which portion of memory has failed. Using the output from that program, determine which module has failed, and replace it.
Computer randomly freezes (locks up) or crashes	Bad or failing memory chip; bad power supply; inconstant wall voltage.	Test memory with a RAM-testing utility to determine if memory is the cause of these symptoms. Replace modules, if appropriate.
	Using memory that's too slow for the system; mixing memory of different speeds.	Confirm that the proper type of memory is installed, according to manufacturer's specifications.

Symptom	Probable cause	Suggested solution
Wrong amount of memory reported by the BIOS	Failed memory module; less memory installed than you thought; modules not installed properly according to PC's banking requirements.	Test memory. Confirm proper BIOS configuration settings. Make sure you've installed as much memory as you think you have. Make sure you've installed memory modules according to your PC's banking requirements, such as installing equally sized DIMMs in pairs.
Windows reports General Protection Fault, Page Fault, or Exception errors	Poorly written applications (most common with Windows 9x); bad memory.	Check the application vendor's Web site for updates or patches. Test memory with a RAM-testing utility.
Random crashes, corrupted data, strange application behavior	Virus infection (more likely); bad memory.	Scan your PC for viruses. If none are found, test memory with a RAM-testing utility.

Do it!

B-1: Troubleshooting memory

You must set up this lab according to the "Troubleshooting Labs Setup" section of the Course Setup instructions.

Here's how

1 One or more memory-related problems have been introduced into your lab computer. Troubleshoot these problems to determine their cause(s).

2 Correct the problems you've found in your PC to return it to a working state. Solving one problem might reveal the presence of another one. Troubleshoot and fix all problems that arise.

3 Document the problem(s) you find:

4 Document the steps you take to fix the problem(s):

Unit summary: Memory systems

Topic A In this topic, you learned how to **install RAM** and handle modules. You also learned about banking requirements, slot insertion techniques, safe storage methods, and **BIOS configuration** requirements.

Topic B In this topic, you learned that RAM can fail for various reasons. You learned how to troubleshoot common symptoms of failures, and how to determine probable causes and implement suggested solutions.

Review questions

1 You're looking at a memory module with a row of chips on one side. You count 30 pins along its edge connector. What kind of module are you most likely looking at?

   A 30-pin SIMM. These were used in 386-class and early Macintosh computers.

2 You need to add more memory to your system. You know it has a 133 MHz system bus. How can you determine what type of memory to install?

   Consulting your owner's manual is the best way to determine the supported memory types.

3 On which Task Manager tab do you find information about a PC's memory usage?

   The Performance tab.

4 List at least two options for testing PC memory.

   Answers might include: Memtest86, Microsoft Windows Memory Diagnostic, DocMemory Diagnostic, and the POST are common and free memory testing options.

5 What types of memory packages do Pentium and Athlon-class desktop computers commonly use?

   168-pin or 184-pin DIMMs. The newest computers use 240-pin DIMMs.

6 You receive a Windows General Protection Fault message. What does this indicate?

   Typically, this error is the result of a poorly written Windows 9x program that attempts to access another program's memory space. Occasionally, this error indicates a problem with RAM.

7 When you're determining what size the page file should be, what formula should you use?

   Multiply the amount of physical RAM by 1.5.

8 When you're speaking of RAM, what is a bank?

   A group of one or more memory slots. You must fill an entire bank when installing RAM.

9 Always handle memory modules by:

   Their edges, taking care not to touch the pins, components, or traces.

10 As measured in Task Manager, what's kernel memory?

   This is the memory used by the operating system's kernel (core) and device drivers.

11 True or false? You upgrade the memory in most handhelds by opening the case and inserting memory modules similar to those used in notebook computers.

   False. You expand most handhelds with flash memory cards like those used in digital cameras.

12 True or false? The POST is sufficient to detect most memory problems.

    False. The POST is too fast and simple to catch most memory errors. You will need a dedicated memory-testing utility to find most memory problems.

13 In a Rambus system, what must you do to meet banking requirements?

    You must fill all empty slots with continuity modules.

14 What's the first step in installing memory in a computer?

    Shut down the computer. If it's already shut down, then the first step is to unplug it from the electrical outlet.

15 Where should you store unused memory modules?

    In the original packaging or in static-safe bags.

16 In Task Manager, you notice that the PF Usage value is close to the size of the Windows page file. What does that indicate?

    The computer is using most of the available page file space. You should increase the size of the page file.

17 A computer randomly freezes up. Could this be an indication of bad memory?

    Yes, random lockups can indicate bad memory. Operating system or other commands could be written to the bad memory and become corrupted. Executing those commands would cause the lockup.

Independent practice activity

In this activity, you'll practice the support tasks associated with PC memory.

1 Install an additional memory module into your computer and confirm the installation.

2 Remove a memory module from your computer and confirm that you have done so correctly.

Unit 4
Expansion cards

Unit time: 150 minutes

Complete this unit, and you'll know how to:

A Identify system resources of computer devices.

B Install a video adapter and sound card.

C Identify the symptoms, probable causes, and potential solutions for problems related to expansion cards.

D Identify the symptoms, probable causes, and potential solutions for problems related to ports, cables, and connectors.

Topic A: Host system interaction

This topic covers the following CompTIA A+ 220-702 exam objective.

#	Objective

2.3	Given a scenario, select and use system utilities / tools and evaluate the results
	• Device Manager
	  – Enable
	  – Disable
	  – Warnings
	  – Indicators
	• Task Manager
	  – Process list

Computer buses

Explanation

A PC has multiple buses to enable communications between the various components of the PC. A typical PC has the following types of buses:

- **Address bus** — The bus that transmits memory addresses between the CPU and RAM.
- **Data bus** — The bus that transfers data between the CPU and RAM.
- **Expansion bus** — The bus to which add-on adapter cards are connected to enhance the functionality of the PC.
- **Video bus** — The bus that transmits display information between the CPU and the video circuitry.

This unit is concerned primarily with the expansion and video buses.

Expansion buses

The *expansion bus* is the communications pathway through which non-core components of a computer interact with core components. You can add new hardware to a PC by installing new adapter cards into slots that connect to the expansion bus. For example, if a computer doesn't have a modem for dialing into the Internet, you can purchase a modem adapter card and plug it into the expansion bus to add this capability to the computer.

Many expansion bus standards have been used over the years, but the *PCI (Peripheral Component Interconnect) bus* is currently the predominant one. Others, such as the ISA, EISA, Micro Channel, and PC bus, are rarely found today unless you're working on an older computer.

Expansion cards **4-3**

Bus types

The following table summarizes the various expansion and video buses that are currently used or have been popular at various times during the PC's history.

ISA stands for Industry Standard Adapter.

Bus name	Type	Width (bits)	Maximum transfer rate	Plug and Play	Notes
PC/AT or ISA	Expansion	16	8 MBps (theoretical maximum); 1–2 MBps (typical actual speeds)	Some cards	Black expansion slots; sometimes white.
PCI	Expansion	32 or 64	533 MBps	Yes	White expansion slots, shorter and taller than white ISA slots.
AGP	Video	32	2 GBps	Yes	Card has hook.
PCI Express (PCIe)	Expansion	x1, x2, x4, x8, x12, x16, x32	10 GBps	Yes	Very high speed bus for video, multimedia, and gaming applications.

Interacting with the system

Hardware and adapter cards must work together to access memory and CPU resources. And they must do so in an orderly manner so they don't conflict with each other.

To avoid conflicts, hardware must perform the following functions:
- Gain the attention of the CPU.
- Access shared memory locations.
- Extend the system BIOS.
- Transfer data across the bus.

Hardware and adapter cards use the following mechanisms to perform these functions.

Interaction mechanism	Description
Interrupt	The signal sent by a device to the CPU to get its attention.
IRQ	Assigns a priority to the interrupt.
I/O address	Used to transfer data to main memory.
DMA channel	Essentially another processor chip; used to handle data transfers between devices and main memory.
Base memory address	Used by the system BIOS to locate and load BIOS extensions included with a device.

Viewing processes

To see a list of processes that the CPU is managing, use the Task Manager utility. Activate the Processes tab to see the current processes being managed by the operating system. (This list doesn't show the very-low-level tasks being handled by the CPU.) You can then identify or end any process that is causing a problem by not releasing control of the CPU.

Do it!

A-1: Examining running processes

Here's how	Here's why
1 If necessary, log on to Windows Vista	
2 Press CTRL + ALT + DELETE	
Click **Start Task Manager**	
3 Activate the Processes tab and click **Show processes from all users**	To display a list of the processes currently running on your PC.
Click **Continue**	
4 Click **CPU** twice	(The column header.) To sort the list of processes by the amount of CPU time each process is using, in descending order. The System Idle process will probably remain at the top of the list most of the time.
5 Close Task Manager	

Device Manager

Explanation

To determine which system resources have been assigned to the various devices in a computer, use the Windows Device Manager. Device Manager shows any conflicts that are occurring between devices and their system resource assignments. An exclamation point is a warning that there's a problem with the device, and a red "x" indicates that the device has been disabled.

You can enable and disable devices in Device Manager. In addition, should you need to, you can manually assign resources, overriding the default assignments made by the PnP system.

To open Device Manager in Windows Vista:
1   Click Start, right-click Computer, and choose Properties.
2   In the Tasks pane, click Device Manager.

Do it!

A-2: Examining system resources

Here's how	Here's why
1 Click **Start**, right-click **Computer**, and choose **Properties**	To open the System window. (In Windows 2000 or in Windows XP running with the Traditional theme, click Start, choose Settings, Control Panel, and double-click System.)
2 In the Tasks pane, click **Device Manager** and then click **Continue**	
3 Choose **View**, **Resources by type**	To view the system resource list.
4 Scan the list for any status indicators	All devices should be operating correctly. Note any warnings or disabled devices.

System resources by type

Explanation

System resources—interrupts, DMA channels, and so forth—have default values commonly assigned in standard Windows-based PCs. The tables in this section list common system resource assignments, arranged by resource type. The actual system resource assignments on your computer might not match the values listed here.

IRQs

When you install a new device in a PC, either you or the operating system needs to assign it a unique IRQ. With older PC designs, you had to manually configure IRQ assignments. Originally, this was done by setting DIP switches or inserting jumper blocks. *DIP switches* are small physical switches, generally rocker or slide switches. *Jumpers* are plastic blocks that enclose a metal loop. You slid these over, or removed them from a pair of metal pins protruding from the circuit board, to complete or open an electrical circuit.

With later designs, you could use software provided by an adapter card's manufacturer to configure IRQ assignments. This software eliminated the need to open the PC and change switches or jumpers. However, it left the burden of determining available IRQs to the user, so conflicts were common.

Modern operating systems calculate and assign IRQs for you. In Windows, this technology is called *Plug and Play (PnP)*. Of course, the adapters you use must support PnP. With such support, every time you start Windows, it determines which IRQs are available, which devices need IRQs assigned, and what IRQs each device can support. Then Windows dynamically assigns an IRQ to every device that's installed.

Typically, IRQs have the assignments listed in the following table.

IRQ	Priority	Common use
0	1	System timer
1	2	Keyboard
2	n/a	Cascade of IRQs 9–15
3	10	COM2
4	11	COM1
5	12	Sound cards or LPT2
6	13	Floppy disk controller
7	14	LPT1/LPT3
8	15	Real-time clock
9	3	Various
10	4	Various
11	5	Various
12	6	PS/2 mouse
13	7	Floating-point unit or math co-processor
14	8	Primary IDE (hard drive) channel
15	9	Secondary IDE (hard drive) channel

I/O addresses

Once a device has the attention of the CPU, it often needs to transfer data to main memory. It does so by sharing a section of main memory with the CPU. The CPU reads input from and writes output to this region of shared memory to transfer data between main memory and the device.

As with interrupts, devices must work together so they don't use other devices' input-output memory ranges. To ensure this, either you or PnP must configure a range of I/O addresses assigned to each device in your computer.

Typically, I/O addresses have the assignments listed in the following table.

IRQ (hex)	Common use
0000–001F	DMA controller, channels 0–3
0020–003F	Programmable interrupt controller #1
0040–005F	System timer
0060–006F	Keyboard/mouse controller
0061–0061	Speaker
0070–007F	CMOS/real-time clock
0170–0178	Secondary IDE
00C0–00DF	DMA controller, channels 4–7
01F0–01FF	Primary IDE
00A0–00AF	Programmable interrupt controller #2
0278–027F	LPT2
02E8–02EF	COM4
02F8–02FF	COM2
0378–037F	LPT1
03BC–03BF	LPT3 or sometimes LPT1
03C0–03CF	Enhanced graphics adapter (EGA) ports
03D0–03DF	Color graphics adapter (CGA) ports
03E8–03EF	COM3
03F0–03F7	Floppy disk controller
03F8–03FF	COM1

Base memory addresses

Some devices extend the system BIOS with new routines or new versions of existing routines. Display adapters are the most common type of device to do this, but IDE and SCSI adapters also use BIOS extensions. These devices include their BIOS extensions in a chip on the adapter card.

The system BIOS must locate and load these BIOS extensions. This means that the adapter BIOS must be "mapped" to memory locations that the system BIOS can find. You or PnP must configure the *base memory address* range of the device's BIOS. By setting this value, you provide a way for the operating system to access the system routines contained on these devices.

As with the other resources, each device that requires a base memory address assignment needs its own unique assignment. PnP ensures that devices are not assigned conflicting address ranges.

Typically, base memory addresses have the assignments listed in the following table.

Base memory address range (hexadecimal)	Common use
F00000–FFFFF	System BIOS
C0000–C7FFF	VGA video BIOS
C8000–CBFFF	IDE hard drive BIOS

DMA channels

The CPU must be involved in every data transfer with every device. Although the CPU is certainly powerful, this involvement with every data transfer can negatively affect performance. The DMA controller communicates with each device over a dedicated channel. Each device must have its own channel with the DMA controller. As with the other resources, you or PnP must configure the DMA channel assigned to every device.

DMA has largely been replaced by newer techniques, such as *bus mastering*. For this reason, DMA is generally used by core devices, such as the floppy disk controller, whose designs haven't changed significantly.

Typically, DMA channels have the assignments listed in the following table.

DMA channel	Common use
1	Sound card*
2	Floppy disk controller
4	DMA controller
5	Sound card*

* Most sound cards use two DMA channels: the first one is chosen from DMAs 1, 2, or 3, and the other is any other free DMA channel (selected from the less-used 5, 6, or 7).

Resources by device type

The following tables list common system resource assignments for serial and parallel ports. The actual system resource assignments on your computer might not match the values listed here. Use Device Manager to determine the actual assignments on your PC.

Serial ports

Typically, COM ports use the system resources listed in the following table.

Port	IRQ	I/O address (hex)
COM1	4	03F8–03FF
COM2	3	02F8–02FF
COM3	4	03E8–03EF
COM4	3	02E8–02EF

Parallel ports

Typically, LPT ports use the system resources listed in the following table.

Port	IRQ	I/O address (hex)
LPT1	n/a	0378–037F
LPT2	n/a	0278–027F
LPT3 or sometimes LPT1	n/a	03BC–03BF

Note: By default, Windows 2000 Professional and all versions of Windows XP and Windows Vista don't assign an IRQ to the LPT ports. However, if you need to assign an IRQ to these ports, LPT1 and LPT3 are typically assigned IRQ7, and LPT2 is typically assigned IRQ5.

Expansion cards **4–11**

Do it!

A-3: Identifying the typical usage of system resources

Here's how	Here's why
1 In Device Manager, expand **Direct memory access (DMA)**	You will determine if the default values are in use for system resources.
2 What devices are listed and which DMA channels are they using?	*Answers will vary. In general, DMA is used by older devices, such as the floppy drive controller or printer port. Newer devices typically don't use DMA. The list should at least include the direct memory access controller, which uses DMA channel 4. Other devices might also be listed.*
3 Collapse **Direct memory access (DMA)**	
4 Choose **View**, **Devices by type**	
5 Display properties for the System CMOS/real-time clock	
Which IRQ does this device use?	*The System CMOS/real-time clock is set to IRQ 8.*
Click **Cancel**	

Do it!

A-4: Identifying the system resources in use with Device Manager

Here's how	Here's why
1 Choose **View**, **Resources by type**	In Device Manager.
2 Expand **Interrupt request (IRQ)**	To view the list of IRQ assignments determined by PnP when you started your computer.

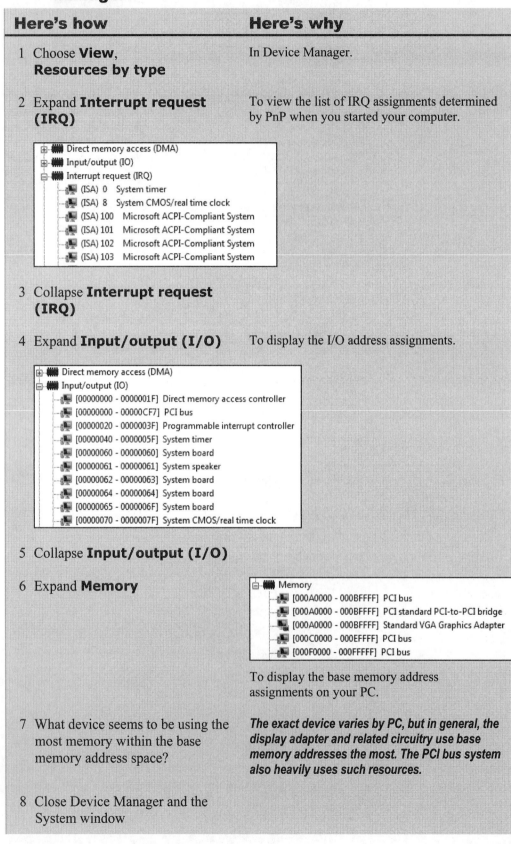

3 Collapse **Interrupt request (IRQ)**

4 Expand **Input/output (I/O)** — To display the I/O address assignments.

5 Collapse **Input/output (I/O)**

6 Expand **Memory**

To display the base memory address assignments on your PC.

7 What device seems to be using the most memory within the base memory address space?

The exact device varies by PC, but in general, the display adapter and related circuitry use base memory addresses the most. The PCI bus system also heavily uses such resources.

8 Close Device Manager and the System window

Topic B: Expansion card installation

This topic covers the following CompTIA A+ 220-702 exam objectives.

#	Objective
1.1	**Given a scenario, install, configure, and maintain personal computer components** • Adapter cards 　– Graphics cards 　– Sound cards 　– Storage controllers 　　• RAID cards (RAID array – levels 0, 1, 5) 　　• eSATA cards 　– I/O cards 　　• FireWire 　　• USB 　　• Parallel 　　• Serial • Wired and wireless network cards • Capture cards (TV, video) • Media reader

Installing expansion cards

Explanation

 Safe handling is covered in the prerequisite course. However, it's important to review this information for the safety of your students and the equipment.

To install an expansion card, you must consider how to handle the cards safely as well as how to configure the device if PnP doesn't do it for you.

Safe handling

Expansion cards are sensitive to *ESD (electrostatic discharge)*. You should always follow ESD precautions when working with these cards or any device that must be installed inside a PC's chassis. When handling expansion cards, follow these guidelines:

- Unplug the computer before opening it.
- Ground yourself to the chassis before touching internal components.
- Keep expansion cards inside static-protective bags or packaging until you're ready to install them.
- Handle cards by their edges or slot cover plates. Don't touch board components, traces, or edge-connector pins.

Drivers

Drivers are utilities that enable a device's functionality. Every expansion device or adapter card in your PC requires a driver. Some drivers are supplied with the operating system. Other devices require drivers supplied by the device manufacturer.

Device vendors often supply their drivers to Microsoft, who either includes the drivers in the operating system files or makes the drivers available on the Windows Update Web site. Sometimes, however, you need to use the drivers supplied with your expansion device, either on a CD that comes with it or on the vendor's Web site.

Inserting cards

In general, you'll follow these steps to install an expansion card in a PC. Expansion cards include graphics and video cards, sound cards, storage controllers (IDE, SCSI, SATA, eSATA, RAID), I/O cards (FireWire, USB, parallel, serial), network cards (wired and wireless), capture cards (video and TV), and media readers. Although you'll practice installing a few specific expansion cards, the installation of any expansion card will typically follow this procedure.

1. If you're not using a PnP-compatible expansion card or operating system, determine the available system resources (IRQs, I/O addresses, and so forth). Configure the DIP switches or jumpers on the card, as necessary, to assign available system resources to it.

   If you're using a PnP-compatible card and operating system, the vendor might direct you to run an installation utility before installing the device. This installation program puts the necessary drivers in a location where Windows can find them when you're done installing the device. If appropriate, run that setup program.

2. Shut down the PC, unplug it, remove peripheral cables, and open the case.

3. Locate an empty and available expansion slot of the correct type.

4. Remove the cover for that slot. These covers are generally either screwed in place or held by spring-clips.

5. If necessary, temporarily move or remove wires or other expansion cards that are in the way, so that you can access the slot.

6. If you need to connect wire assemblies to the expansion board—not to its back slot cover plate, but to the board itself—connect that end of the wire assembly before installing the card. That way, you can easily reach the connector and be sure you're installing the wire assembly in its correct orientation. Connect the other end after you've installed the card.

7. Begin inserting the end of the edge connector that's farthest from the slot cover. Then gently push the card into place in the slot. This helps you line up the connector correctly. Inserting the card at an angle is usually easier than pushing it straight into the slot.

8. Fix the card in place with screws or clips, as appropriate to the case's design.

9. Connect any wiring assemblies, including those you temporarily removed to install this card.

10. Close the case, connect peripherals, and start the system.

11. Depending on the operating system, OS version, and adapter card technology, configure the card. If you're using PnP-compatible components, PnP handles this for you.

12. If necessary, install required drivers. If you have to install drivers yourself, you most likely need to configure them to use the same hardware resources you configured the card to use.

When you're done, some devices and operating system versions will require you to restart the computer. This step fully loads the drivers and configures the operating system to support the new device.

Video adapters

Video adapters convert computer data to the signals required to produce the images you see on your screen. With the early generations of PCs, video adapters created just text output, and often monochrome output at that. Nowadays, video adapters create the signals necessary to display full color and full-motion images and video.

Due to the enormous amount of information that must be manipulated by the adapter to produce these signals, modern video adapters are almost computers in their own right. They often feature a specialized processor chip and lots of on-board memory. Perhaps even more than the type of CPU or amount of memory in your system, the video adapter is the component most responsible for the overall performance of your PC.

Video adapter slots

Specialized video buses were covered in the prerequisite course.

Some video adapters are built into the motherboard. Such integrated video cards provide all of the regular video adapter features without taking up an expansion slot. This design is common on low-end systems in which the manufacturer's main goal is to make the machine as inexpensive to the customer as possible. The BIOS often includes functions to disable the on-board video adapter. You might do this if you suspect a problem with it or if you want to use a specialized add-in adapter. For example, gamers often use very-high-performance aftermarket video adapters to speed up their games.

Other machines have three types of slots in which the video adapter might be installed. These are PCI, AGP, and PCIe slots.

PCI slot–based adapters

PCI slot–based adapters are the slowest of the three types. They have to share the PCI bus with all of the other PCI-based devices in the system. However, these adapters work well for implementing a two-monitor system, if you're using two video cards. If your motherboard doesn't have an AGP or PCIe slot, this is your only option for upgrading the video on your system.

AGP slot–based adapters

AGP is a special slot specifically designed for video adapters. The speed of an 8X AGP 3.0 slot is 2.13 GBps, assuming a clock rate of 533 MHz for the PCI bus. Older systems might use AGP 2X or 4X, running at 533 MBps on a 133 MHz PCI bus system and 1.06 GBps on a 266 MHz PCI bus system, respectively. Some AGP cards are available with two connectors to enable you to connect two monitors to the system.

There's only one AGP slot in the system. This slot can be identified by color because it's brown (PCI slots are white). An AGP video card is shown in Exhibit 4-1.

Exhibit 4-1: An AGP video card

PCIe slot–based adapters

PCI Express (PCIe) cards are designed to replace AGP video cards in new systems. Motherboards that support PCIe video cards became available in 2004. A 16x PCIe video card has a 4 GBps bandwidth in each direction. Because this is a dual-line technology, you can theoretically achieve an 8 GBps capacity with data moving upstream and downstream at the same time. The high transfer speeds make this technology an ideal solution for multimedia applications, such as gaming, photography, and videography. The PCIe card fits into a 164-pin slot on motherboards that support PCIe. A 16x PCIe video card is shown in Exhibit 4-2.

Exhibit 4-2: A PCIe video card

Expansion cards **4–17**

Do it!

B-1: Installing a video adapter card

Provide students with a variety of video adapters to install.

Here's how	Here's why
1 If specified by the adapter's manufacturer, run the adapter's setup utility	To copy the driver installation files to your hard disk, where Windows can find them.
2 If necessary, shut down your PC and open its case	Follow electrical and ESD safety precautions.
3 If a video adapter is already in an expansion slot, remove that adapter	
4 Install the video adapter	
5 Close the PC case	
6 If your PC has an integrated video adapter, boot the PC and load the system's BIOS setup program Disable the on-board video adapter and save your changes	You'll need to disable the on-board video adapter.
7 If your PC doesn't have an integrated video adapter, or after you've disabled the on-board adapter, start your PC	
8 Log on to Windows	Log on as your PAADMIN## user with a password of !pass1234.
9 If necessary, configure the driver	You'll probably have to choose a resolution and color depth at which you want the driver to operate.
10 Remove the video adapter and reinstall or re-enable the original adapter	Unless your instructor directs you to do otherwise.

Sound cards

Explanation

A sound card converts digital data into analog sound waves to produce a signal for your speakers. The sound card also converts analog sound signals into digital signals to enable you to input, or capture, audio. Many sound cards also enable you to connect a game device, such as a joystick or game paddle, and to connect MIDI (Musical Instrument Digital Interface) instruments.

To perform its functions, a typical sound card includes these components:

- A *digital signal processor* (DSP), which is like a CPU for sound processing functions.
- An *analog-to-digital converter* (ADC), which converts analog signals (such as sound waves) to digital signals.
- A *digital-to-analog converter* (DAC), which converts digital signals to analog, producing the signals needed by speakers or other analog audio devices.
- Various jacks for connecting speakers, microphones, line-input or line-output devices, game adapters (joysticks), and sometimes MIDI devices.

The sound card you use must be compatible with the expansion bus in your computer. For example, you'll need a PCI sound card if your computer has only PCI slots available. Many motherboards include integrated sound card functionality.

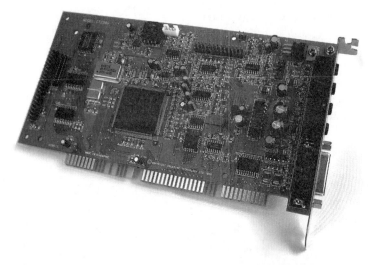

Exhibit 4-3: A sound card

CD audio connection

Internal CD drives include an audio-out cable that you can connect to your sound card. When you do so, you can play audio CDs in your CD drive and have the sound played through your PC's speakers. When you install the sound card or the CD drive, if you don't connect this cable, you won't be able to play audio CDs (no sound will come from the speakers).

Drivers

As with any add-on hardware, sound cards require device drivers. Typically, you install the drivers before installing the hardware. This process puts the driver files where Windows (specifically, Plug and Play) can find them after you install the card.

Expansion cards **4-19**

Do it!

B-2: Installing a sound card

🗔 *Provide students with a variety of sound cards to install.*

Here's how	Here's why
1 If specified by the adapter's manufacturer, run the adapter's setup utility	To copy the driver installation files to your hard disk, where Windows can find them.
2 If necessary, shut down your PC and open its case	Follow electrical and ESD safety precautions.
3 If a sound card is already in an expansion slot, remove the card	
4 Install the sound card	
5 Close the PC's case	
6 If your PC has an integrated sound card, boot the PC and load the system's BIOS setup program	You'll need to disable the on-board sound card.
Disable the on-board sound card and save your changes	
7 If your PC doesn't have an integrated sound card, or after you've disabled the on-board adapter, start the PC	
8 Log on to Windows	
9 If necessary, configure the driver	
10 Connect the external speakers and plug their power adapter into an outlet	
11 In the notification area, click 🔊	To display the volume control.
Drag the volume slider up or down and release it	The computer should play a "ding" sound through your speakers.
12 Remove the sound card and reinstall or re-enable the original card	Unless your instructor directs you to do otherwise.

Do it!

B-3: Installing an expansion card

Here's how	Here's why
1 If specified by the adapter's manufacturer, run the adapter's setup utility	
2 If necessary, shut down your PC and open its case	Follow electrical and ESD safety precautions.
3 If necessary, remove an unused adapter from its expansion slot	
4 Install the new adapter	
5 Close the PC case	
6 Start your PC	
7 Log on to Windows	Log on as your PAADMIN## user with a password of !pass1234.
8 If necessary, configure the driver, and use Device Manager to verify that the new adapter is functional	
9 If necessary, remove the new adapter and reinstall the original adapter	Unless your instructor directs you to do otherwise.

Provide students with one of the following expansion cards: storage controller and hard disk (RAID or eSATA); I/O card; network card; TV or video capture card; or media reader.

If necessary, help students select an adapter to remove so they can complete this activity.

Topic C: Expansion card troubleshooting

This topic covers the following CompTIA A+ 220-702 exam objective.

#	Objective

1.2	**Given a scenario, detect problems, troubleshoot, and repair/replace personal computer components**
	• Adapter cards
	  – Graphics cards, memory
	  – Sound cards
	  – Storage controllers
	    • RAID cards
	    • eSATA cards
	  – I/O cards
	    • FireWire
	    • USB
	    • Parallel
	    • Serial
	• Wired and wireless network cards
	• Capture cards (TV, video)
	• Media reader

Updating drivers

Explanation

Often one of the solutions to hardware problems involves obtaining and installing updated device drivers. As a device is put in use by users, the manufacturer might find that the driver needs to be changed due to conflicts or faulty code, or just to make the device function more efficiently.

Although most devices are packaged with drivers, some of them might not be the most up-to-date. In addition, Windows might not install the best drivers for your new device if it's installed with PnP. At some point, you might need to find additional drivers on the Web, most likely from the device manufacturer's Web site.

Most manufacturers offer free downloads of drivers and utilities for their devices. Just find the name of the manufacturer and visit the appropriate Web site. Look for a link that offers drivers, support, or downloads. Then download the driver (which is often zipped) to a local hard disk, from where you can install it on the appropriate computer.

After you've found an updated device driver, you can install it. In Device Manager, choose to update the driver for a device, and then point the wizard to the location of the new driver.

Do it!

Suggest a device to students. You can assign students to work in pairs.

Students can install the drivers if they're the same version or newer.

Depending on the device and manufacturer, the driver might be a self-contained install file. If it is, have students follow the on-screen instructions.

C-1: Searching for and installing updated drivers

Here's how
1 In Device Manager, pick a device you want to update (maybe one of the devices you installed or maybe a display adapter). Write down the manufacturer's name and the model of the device.
2 Visit the manufacturer's Web site. (Use a search engine if you have to.) On the Web site, find the link for support, downloads, or drivers.
3 Find the drivers for the device you chose. Download them to your computer and save them on the desktop.
4 In Device Manager, right-click the device and choose **Update Driver Software**. Don't search for a driver automatically; choose to browse your computer for driver software and navigate to the folder on your desktop. Complete the wizard, clicking **Have Disk** if prompted. Update the drivers if they're the same version or newer.
5 If necessary, restart the computer. Use Device Manager to verify that the device is working properly.

Troubleshooting expansion cards

Explanation

As a PC technician, you should be familiar with the most common symptoms, probable causes, and suggested "first try" solutions for problems related to expansion cards. You might encounter problems not listed in the tables here, but they provide a few scenarios to consider when you're troubleshooting.

The following tables list problems, probable causes, and suggested solutions for the following types of expansion cards:

- Video adapters
- Sound cards

Video cards

The following table lists video adapter problems you might encounter.

Symptom	Probable cause	Suggested solution
No video at all	Monitor is turned off or disconnected; video card failed; cable is bad; wrong video mode is used.	Make sure the monitor is connected and turned on. Attach another monitor that's capable of very high resolution modes. If video is displayed, set a lower resolution mode and then reattach the original monitor. Check for bent or broken pins in the video connector. Replace the video card.
Video scrolls, flips, wavers, is too large; doubles up lines; and so forth	Video card is set to refresh rate or resolution mode that monitor can't support.	Either replace the monitor with a better one, or reconfigure the driver to use a lower resolution mode or lower refresh rate.
Video flickers	Refresh rate is too low.	Configure the driver to use a higher refresh rate.
Video is blurry	Monitor is failing.	Replace the monitor.
Image artifacts are displayed across the screen	Software is at fault: either drivers or application software.	Update the video card drivers. Check for application updates.
System freezes during a video change, such as an image scrolling or changing	Video driver could be at fault.	Update the video card drivers.
Video is connected to DVI connector, but monitor displays message that analog connection is disconnected	Button that switches between analog and video was pressed or menu option was changed.	Reset the button or menu choice to digital connection.

Sound cards

The following table lists sound card problems you might encounter.

Symptom	Probable cause	Suggested solution
No sound	External speakers not connected or turned off; Windows configured to operate silently.	Connect the speakers or turn them on. Confirm the sound configuration in the Control Panel.
Sound is very low	Volume on speakers set too low; audio output levels set too low or muted.	Turn up the volume knob on the speakers. Click the speaker icon in the system tray and drag the volume slider up. You might need to uncheck Mute.
Sound is distorted	Volume set too high for speakers; bad driver.	Turn down the volume knob on the speakers. Click the speaker icon in the system tray and drag the volume slider down. Update the audio card drivers.
No audio captured	Microphone not connected; bad microphone; audio input levels set too low or muted.	Right-click the speaker icon in the system tray and choose Open Volume Controls. Under Line In, drag the volume slider up. You might need to uncheck Mute.
No audio from CD	CD audio volume set too low or muted; CD audio cable not connected to sound card.	Right-click the speaker icon in the system tray and choose Open Volume Controls. Under CD Audio, drag the volume slider up. You might need to uncheck Mute. Open the PC and confirm that the sound cable from the CD drive is connected to the sound card and is connected properly.

Do it!

C-2: Troubleshooting expansion card problems

You must set up this lab according to the "Troubleshooting Labs Setup" section of the Course Setup instructions.

Here's how

1. One or more expansion card–related problems have been introduced into your lab computer. Troubleshoot these problems to determine their cause(s).

2. Correct the problems you've found in your PC to return it to a working state. Solving one problem might reveal the presence of another one. Troubleshoot and fix all problems that arise.

3. Document the problem(s) you find:

4. Document the steps you take to fix the problem(s):

Topic D: Port, cable, and connector troubleshooting

This topic covers the following CompTIA A+ 220-702 exam objectives.

#	Objective

1.2	**Given a scenario, detect problems, troubleshoot, and repair/replace personal computer components**
	• Adapter cards
	   – I/O cards
	      • FireWire
	      • USB
	      • Parallel
	      • Serial

1.4	**Given a scenario, select and use the following tools** • Loopback plugs

Working with ports, cables, and connectors

Explanation

As a PC technician, you should be familiar with the most common symptoms, probable causes, and suggested "first try" solutions for port, cable, and connector problems. The following tables list problems, probable causes, and suggested solutions for the following equipment:

- Serial ports, cables, and connectors
- Parallel ports, cables, and connectors
- PS/2 ports, cables, and connectors
- USB ports, cables, and connectors
- IEEE 1394 ports, cables, and connectors
- Wireless ports
- Multimedia ports

You might encounter problems not listed in the tables that follow, but they provide a few scenarios to consider when you're troubleshooting problems.

Serial ports, cables, and connectors

The following table lists common problems you might encounter with serial ports, cables, and connectors.

Symptom	Probable cause	Suggested solution
Serial port physically present, but not listed in Device Manager	Port disabled in BIOS; system resource conflicts; external connector not plugged into motherboard.	Use the BIOS setup utility to enable the serial port. Check for device conflicts in Device Manager. Confirm that the connector is plugged into the motherboard, and if it's not, connect the cable.
Serial port inaccessible	System resource conflicts.	Check for device conflicts in Device Manager.
PC can't detect or connect to external modem	Bad serial cable; communications settings configured incorrectly; serial port disabled on motherboard.	Try using a different serial cable. Confirm the communications settings between the PC and modem. Use the BIOS setup utility to enable the serial port.

Parallel ports, cables, and connectors

The following table lists common problems you might encounter with parallel ports, cables, and connectors.

Symptom	Probable cause	Suggested solution
Parallel port physically present, but not listed in Device Manager	Port disabled in BIOS; system resource conflicts; external connector not plugged into motherboard.	Use the BIOS setup utility to enable the parallel port. Check for device conflicts in Device Manager. Confirm that the connector is plugged into the motherboard, and if it's not, connect the cable.
Parallel port inaccessible	System resource conflicts.	Check for device conflicts in Device Manager.
Can't print to printer connected to the parallel port	Printer turned off or disconnected; bad parallel cable; wrong type of parallel cable; wrong parallel port operation mode for printer; no printer drivers installed.	Confirm that the printer is plugged in and turned on. Confirm that you're using the correct type of cable; try using a different cable that you know to be working. Use the BIOS setup utility to confirm that the parallel port mode (SPP, ECP, EPP) is compatible with the printer.

PS/2 ports, cables, and connectors

The following table lists common problems you might encounter with PS/2 ports, cables, and connectors.

Symptom	Probable cause	Suggested solution
"No Keyboard Found" BIOS error	Keyboard not connected; keyboard connected to the mouse port; bad keyboard.	Confirm the keyboard and mouse connections. Try using a different keyboard.
Moving the mouse causes random characters to appear on screen, or computer emits a series of beeps	Mouse connected to the keyboard port.	Confirm the keyboard and mouse connections.
No mouse pointer, or pointer won't move when you move the mouse	Bad mouse; cable disconnected; or operating system crash.	Replace the mouse with one you know to be good. Confirm that the mouse is connected to the correct port. Restart the computer.
Mouse moves erratically	Dirt in roller mechanisms.	Clean the mouse.

USB ports, cables, and connectors

The following table lists common problems you might encounter with USB ports, cables, and connectors.

Symptom	Probable cause	Suggested solution
Can't connect to or use USB device	Cable not connected; USB cable is bad; device is powered off; USB port isn't enabled; motherboard doesn't support USB.	Confirm that the cable is connected. Try using a different USB cable. Make sure the device is powered on. Use the BIOS setup utility to confirm that the motherboard supports USB; enable that support, if necessary.
USB device not listed in Device Manager	Operating system or motherboard doesn't support USB; device is turned off or not connected.	Windows 95 OSR-2 and later supports USB, as do OS/2 and Linux. Upgrade to a newer operating system version, if necessary. Confirm that the motherboard supports USB. Confirm that the device is connected and turned on.
USB device works intermittently or not at all	Bad cable; too long a cable; insufficient power on the bus.	Try replacing the cable with a shorter cable that's known to be good. Use a powered USB hub, or connect the device directly to the PC. Unplug other USB devices to further reduce power demands.
"Unknown Device" in Device Manager	Device driver not installed; corrupted installation of driver.	Detach the USB device, install drivers for it, and re-attach it. Alternately, use Device Manager to remove the device and the USB host controller from the operating system, and then reboot. Windows will detect the host controller and re-install operating system support for it.

IEEE 1394 ports, cables, and connectors

The following table lists common problems you might encounter with IEEE 1394 ports, cables, and connectors.

Symptom	Probable cause	Suggested solution
Device doesn't appear in Device Manager or is marked with a yellow exclamation point	Device is unsupported.	If the device is a host controller, try using a comparable Windows driver. Only OpenHCI host controllers are supported by Windows. Sony CXD1947A VAIO, all Adaptec, and any other non-OpenHCI controllers require additional device drivers, which are supplied by the manufacturer.
Device disappears from Device Manager after installation	Power management feature of device has turned it off, thus removing it from the system.	Change the power management settings on the device itself.
System stops responding after you connect the device	Bus is reset due to bad hardware, unsupported hardware, or a loopback condition in which cables have been looped back to the controller.	Turn off power to the device, remove the device, verify that the cables haven't looped back to the host controller, and then turn on the power.
Device that's bus-powered isn't receiving power	Host controller that supplies the power isn't connected to power source inside the system.	Verify that power has been connected to the host controller.
	A 4-pin device being used that can't draw power from the bus.	Plug the 4-pin device into a separate power source. Verify that the 4-pin device is connected to the end of the device chain.

Wireless ports

The following table lists common problems you might encounter with wireless ports.

Symptom	Probable cause	Suggested solution
Can't connect to infrared wireless device	Out of range; obstructions blocking ports; infrared serial port disabled in BIOS or operating system.	Move closer to the device. Remove obstructions and gently clean the infrared ports' windows. Use the BIOS setup utility and Device Manager to confirm that the infrared port is enabled.
Can't connect to radio wireless device	Out of range; interference from electrical motors or equipment; drivers not installed; wireless router turned off; security settings preventing connections.	Move closer to the device, and move away from sources of interference. Use Device Manager to confirm that the wireless device is installed and that there are no conflicts. Confirm that the router is turned on. Confirm that you have sufficient permissions to connect to the wireless device.
Can't connect to Bluetooth wireless device	Out of range; interference from electrical motors or equipment; drivers not installed; security settings preventing connections.	Move closer to the device, and move away from sources of interference. Use Device Manager to confirm that the wireless device is installed and that there are no conflicts. Confirm that you have sufficient permissions to connect to the wireless device.
Wireless device not responding	Batteries run down.	If the device uses alkaline batteries, replace them. If the device uses rechargeable batteries, place the device or batteries in the charger.

A mouse with rechargeable batteries is placed in the charger; other devices might require the batteries to be removed and placed in a charger.

Multimedia ports

The following table lists common problems you might encounter with multimedia ports.

Symptom	Probable cause	Suggested solution
S/PDIF connection produces garbled data, or error messages indicate Unknown Format or Wrong Sample Rate	RCA cable used instead of digital cable.	Replace the cable with a digital 75 ohm cable.
MIDI device isn't found	Usually an application problem.	Review the MIDI sequencer application for information on how to locate and use the MIDI device.
Video problems occur when using S-Video connection	Driver problem.	Try using an older or newer driver for the video card. If you're using a tuner card, try changing the driver for it.
No sound from speakers	Speakers plugged into line-in jack; no power.	Verify that the speakers are plugged into the line-out or speaker port on the sound card. Verify that the speakers are connected to a power source.

Loopback plugs

When you're testing ports, a useful device to have in your toolkit is a *loopback plug*, also known as a loopback adapter. This device is specific to the type of port you're testing, and it plugs into the port. The loopback adapter enables you to perform a loopback test, in which a signal is sent, passes through all of the necessary circuits to complete the path, and returns to the port being tested. The returned signal is compared to the sent signal to determine if there's a problem with the port or on the path that the signal traveled.

Do it!

D-1: Troubleshooting port, cable, and connector problems

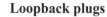 *You must set up this activity according to the "Troubleshooting Labs Setup" section of the Course Setup instructions.*

Here's how
1 One or more problems related to ports, cables, and connectors have been introduced into your lab computer. Troubleshoot these problems to determine their causes.
2 Correct the problems you've found in your PC to return it to a working state. Solving one problem might reveal the presence of another one. Troubleshoot and fix any other problems that arise.
3 Document the problem(s) you find:
4 Document the steps you take to fix the problem(s):

Unit summary: Expansion cards

Topic A In this topic, you learned how to use Device Manager to identify the system resources that are assigned to a particular device—the **IRQ**, **I/O addresses**, **DMA channels**, and **base memory addresses**. You learned that you can use Device Manager to identify resource conflicts between devices.

Topic B In this topic, you learned how to install **expansion devices**, such as video and sound cards, into desktop computer systems.

Topic C In this topic, you learned that expansion cards can fail for various reasons, and you learned how to **update** hardware device drivers and **troubleshoot** expansion cards. You also examined common symptoms of failures and the probable causes and suggested solutions.

Topic D In this topic, you learned that ports, connectors, and cables can fail for various reasons. You learned how to **troubleshoot** these components. You also examined common symptoms of failures and the probable causes and suggested solutions.

Review questions

1 Name the typical connectors on a sound card.

   Typically, sound cards provide speaker-out, line-out, microphone-in, line-in, and MIDI/game port connectors.

2 To play audio CDs through your computer's speakers, what do you have to connect to the sound card?

   You must connect the CD drive's audio-out port to the sound card's CD-in connector.

3 Name the four types of buses in a typical PC.

   Address, data, expansion, and video.

4 List the types of system resources used in PCs.

   IRQs (interrupt request lines), I/O addresses, base memory addresses, and DMA (direct memory access) channels.

5 What are the functions of the ADC and DAC components on a sound card?

   The ADC is the analog-to-digital converter, which converts analog sound signals to digital signals. The DAC is the digital-to-analog converter, which converts digital signals to analog, producing the signals needed by speakers or other analog audio devices.

6 Can you manually assign system resources to all devices?

   No. You can't manually assign system resources to many modern devices. Typically you can assign resources only to legacy devices.

7 What's the best source for driver updates?

   The device manufacturer's Web site.

8 List two popular modern bus types.

   PCI and AGP are two of the most popular bus types in current use.

9 True or false? PCIe video cards are replacing AGP cards in newer systems.

   True

10 Which type of bus transfers information between the CPU and RAM?

The data bus

11 How can you resolve a "keyboard not found" BIOS error?

Answers will include: plug the keyboard into the correct port; and replace the current keyboard with a known good keyboard.

Independent practice activity

In this activity, you'll practice completing support tasks for expansion cards.

1 Replace the video adapter in your computer, and connect your monitor to it. If necessary, install device drivers or use the Display Properties Control Panel utility to configure your screen.

Unit 5
Data storage devices

Unit time: 150 minutes

Complete this unit, and you'll know how to:

A Install hard drives into a PC.

B Describe optical data storage, and install and use optical drives and discs.

C Install, use, and safely remove USB flash drives, and install and use floppy drives.

D Identify the symptoms, probable causes, and potential solutions for drive-related problems, and maintain a hard drive by checking for errors, freeing up space, and defragging.

Topic A: Hard drives

This topic covers the following CompTIA A+ 220-702 exam objectives.

#	Objective

1.1	**Given a scenario, install, configure, and maintain personal computer components**
	• HDD
	   – SATA
	   – PATA
	   – Solid state
	• Adapter cards
	   – Storage controllers
	      • RAID cards (RAID array – levels 0, 1, 5)

2.1	**Select the appropriate commands and options to troubleshoot and resolve problems** • FORMAT

2.3	**Given a scenario, select and use system utilities / tools and evaluate the results**
	• Disk Manager
	   – Active, primary, extended, and logical partitions
	   – FAT32 and NTFS
	   – Drive status
	      • Foreign drive
	      • Healthy
	      • Formatting
	      • Active unallocated
	      • Failed
	      • Dynamic
	      • Offline
	      • Online

Physical installation

Explanation

Physically installing a hard disk drive into a PC involves a few steps, which you must perform in the following order:

1. Shut down the PC and open its case. (Observe electrical and safety precautions.)
2. Set jumpers or switches on the drive to provide drive identification.
3. If you're installing a SCSI drive, you might need to configure bus termination by setting switches or jumpers or by installing or removing terminator blocks. The bus must be terminated on both ends and cannot have extra termination installed in the middle of the chain.
4. Install the drive into the PC chassis.

5 Connect data and control cables from the drive controller to the drive.
6 Connect the power cable from the PC's power supply to the drive.

After you physically install the drive, additional preparation steps are required to make it available to the operating system.

ATA drive identification

With IDE/ATA drives, you can install one or two drives per channel. One drive must be designated as the master, or primary disk. The other is called the slave. With older drives, you set a jumper or DIP switch to specify its role: master, slave, or the only drive in the system. You also had to connect the drives to the correct location on the cable. With newer drives, you can set the switch to the cable-select position so that the drive detects where it's connected on the cable. Its position defines its role, as shown in Exhibit 5-1. Both the motherboard and drives must support cable-select. Otherwise, you'll have to configure the drives manually.

Exhibit 5-1: An ATA cable showing where to connect the master and slave drives

SCSI drive identification

You must assign a unique SCSI device ID number to every device, including the host bus adapter, on the SCSI bus. SCSI IDs begin at 0 and count upward, with higher IDs having a higher priority on the SCSI bus.

Most newer SCSI devices include switches you can use to set the device's SCSI ID. Older devices provided a block of jumpers for setting the SCSI ID. Exhibit 5-2 shows a typical switch you'd use to assign SCSI IDs.

Exhibit 5-2: A switch for assigning the SCSI ID

Chassis installation

You can typically use any available bay for a hard drive. However, one or more smaller, drive-sized bays are typically available for this precise purpose. Make sure you install the drive in a location that the data and power cables can reach from the motherboard connections.

Most modern drives work equally well mounted horizontally or vertically. Unlike older drives, there's typically no harm in mounting a drive one way and then mounting it in a different orientation later.

As always, before you open a PC's case, make sure you shut down the computer and unplug it from the outlet. Follow all of the typical static safety precautions. Don't bump or jar the drive. Hard drives are sensitive to shocks, and you can easily damage them.

Data cable connections

Most drive cables are *keyed*—that is, their connectors are molded in such a way that you can insert them only the correct way into the connector sockets. If you're using an older non-keyed cable, wire 1 in the cable is marked with a red stripe. Pin 1 on the socket is labeled, with either a number or a small triangle pointing at the pin. You need to line up the cable so that pin 1 goes into socket 1.

If you're using cable-select to set the master/slave selection for a drive, make sure you connect the IDE drive to the correct connector.

You must terminate each end of the SCSI bus. Typically, the HBA (host bus adapter) includes removable resistors. Modern devices have switch-selectable termination built in. If you need a device to provide termination, you switch on its terminators. Otherwise, you can leave its terminators turned off.

You can purchase internal or external hard disks. Internal hard disks can be connected through IDE/ATA, SCSI, Serial ATA (SATA) or Parallel ATA (PATA) interfaces. External hard disks might use SATA, eSATA, USB, or IEEE 1394 (FireWire) connections. Some external hard disks will come with a variety of ports so you can choose the one that best meets your performance needs and the connections available in the computer.

Power cable connections

Most IDE/ATA and SCSI drives use the large peripheral power connector. This connector has triangular corners so that you can insert it into the socket correctly. SATA drives use a specialized power connector that looks very different from the peripheral power connector. It's also keyed so that you're sure to connect it properly.

Solid-state drives

Some hard disk drives are *solid-state drives (SSDs)*, which use memory chips (DDR RAM or flash memory) instead of a rotating disk to read and write data. SSDs have no moving parts. Therefore, they are less fragile than magnetic hard drives and are silent. Memory-based disks require power to maintain their data, so solid-state disks include backup batteries.

SSDs are becoming increasingly available in laptops, such as ultra-mobile PCs and lightweight systems, but they are more expensive than magnetic hard drives of comparable capacity, form factor, and transfer speed. Dell and Apple computers both charge a premium of several hundred to a thousand dollars for an SSD in their laptops. In addition, current Windows products are not optimized for SSDs. Microsoft has stated that Windows 7 will be optimized for both solid-state and magnetic hard drives.

Do it!

A-1: Physically installing a hard drive

Here's how	Here's why
1 If necessary, shut down your PC and unplug it from the outlet	You'll install an additional hard drive in your system.
2 Open your PC's case	Follow all electrical and ESD precautions.
3 Set the jumpers or switches, as appropriate, to specify the drive identification	You'll need to set master, slave, single drive, or cable-select for an IDE drive, or set the SCSI ID for a SCSI drive.
4 Locate an available drive bay and install the drive	
5 Install the data ribbon cable	Install the cable in the correct orientation, and attach the drive to the correct connector on the cable.
6 Install the power cable	
7 Close the PC's case	
Don't turn on your computer yet	You have physically installed the drive, but you must prepare it for use with the operating system. You'll do that next.

Provide students with drives to install in their systems.

Students are installing a second drive in their systems.

Hard drive preparation

Explanation

Once you've physically installed a hard drive, you must prepare it for use by the operating system. With hard drives, the following steps must be performed separately:

1. If necessary, perform a low-level format.
2. Partition the drive.
3. Format the drive (with a high-level format).

Low-level formatting

Low-level formatting divides the disk into tracks and divides each track into sectors. This step must be performed when a drive is brand new. Additionally, with older drives, you occasionally had to reformat them at a low level to fix read and write errors.

In older hard drives, each track contained the same number of sectors. These hard drives used a stepper motor to move the heads into position; this motor was a less precise mechanism than modern voice coil actuators. Over time, the motor might begin to place the heads in a slightly different position than it did when it was new. When that happened, read and write errors would become more frequent. To solve these problems, you could redo the low-level format of the drive. Of course, doing so obliterated all of the data on the drive, so you had to carefully back up your data first.

Modern hard drives use complex sector arrangements such as *zoned bit recording (ZBR)*. With ZBR, more sectors are recorded in the larger outer tracks than in the smaller inner tracks. Modern voice coil actuators are precise and accurately position the heads over the tracks every time.

With modern drives, low-level formatting isn't a generic process that can be performed by the operating system. Nowadays, low-level formatting is almost always done by the hard drive manufacturer and never needs to be redone.

Partitioning

Some users like to create multiple partitions so they can store different types of data on each one. For example, they might store their data on drive D: rather than mixing it with Windows and the application files on drive C:.

If the low-level formatting is already done, your first step is to *partition* the drive. Partitioning divides the hard drive into one or more *logical drives*, also called *volumes*. Consider a 20 GB drive. You could partition it into two 10 GB drives, each of which would get its own drive letter. You'd still have one physical disk drive, but it would appear to the operating system to be two drives.

Partitioning drives was an important consideration with early hard drives and operating systems that couldn't support large volumes. Without partitioning to create additional volumes, you couldn't use all of the available space on a hard drive.

Most modern computers and operating systems support very large volumes, so you can generally use the entire space of a drive in a single volume. However, you must still partition a hard drive into at least one volume.

The master boot record (MBR)

The first sector on the bootable hard disk is called the *master boot record (MBR)*. This sector serves the same purpose as the boot sector on a floppy disk. The MBR, which is sometimes called the *master boot block* or *partition table*, contains partition information and other information used by the computer after the POST (power-on self test) has finished.

Primary and extended partitions

Primary partitions are those partitions that are directly accessed by the operating system as volumes. In DOS and Windows 9.x, you can create a single primary partition on each hard drive. In Windows NT Workstation, Windows 2000 Professional, and all versions of Windows XP and Windows Vista, you can create four primary partitions per drive. Most of the partitions you create will be primary partitions.

You can also create *extended partitions*. Each extended partition contains one or more *logical drives*, which are what the operating system accesses for file storage. With all of the PC operating systems, you can create a single extended partition, which can contain up to 23 logical drives. In general, you won't create extended partitions unless you need to create a system that boots to both DOS/Windows 9.x and Windows NT Workstation/2000 Professional/XP/Vista; for that, you need multiple volumes.

Partitioning utilities

For DOS and Windows 9x systems, you use the MS-DOS `fdisk` command to partition a hard drive. The version of `fdisk` that was included with Windows 98 could also partition drives for use with the FAT32 and NTFS file systems.

The `fdisk` command doesn't rewrite the MBR if an MBR is present. To force `fdisk` to write a new MBR, you must use the `fdisk /mbr` command.

In Windows 2000 Professional and all versions of Windows XP and Windows Vista, you can use the Disk Management component of the Computer Management console. From the Start menu, choose Administrative Tools, Computer Management; then, in the left pane, select Disk Management. You can use this utility to partition and format new disk drives, as well as to manage partition types.

The Disk Management utility is designed for adding a drive to a working Windows system. For new drives in new systems, you need a different method. Most versions of Windows since Windows NT offer you the option of partitioning the hard drive during the operating system installation.

Formatting

Formatting is the final hard-disk preparation step. This step is sometimes called *high-level formatting*. Formatting defines the type of file system that is used on a hard disk.

The *file system* is the collection mechanism that enables the operating system to access and track files stored on the hard drive. A file system defines such parameters as the minimum and maximum cluster size, the way the locations of files are tracked, and the way files and directories are stored within the clusters.

There are two broad families of file systems used with PCs. They are:
- FAT (File Allocation Table)
- NTFS

Different operating systems use different file systems. Currently, the most popular file systems for PCs include NTFS (the Windows NT file system, used also by Windows 2000 Professional and all versions of Windows XP and Windows Vista) and FAT32 (the Windows 98 file system).

File system comparison

To help you choose the appropriate operating system, the following table compares selected features of the FAT16, FAT32, and NTFS file systems.

Feature	FAT16	FAT32	NTFS
File-name length	1–8 characters	1–255 characters*	1–255 characters*
File-name extensions	0–3 characters	0–255 characters*	0–255 characters*
Maximum file size	2 GB	4 GB	Limited only by volume size
Maximum volume size	2 GB	32 GB	2 TB (2048 GB)
Maximum files per volume	Approx. 6500	Unlimited	Unlimited
Most often used with	DOS, Windows 3.1, Windows 95	Windows 9x, Windows Me	Windows NT, Workstation, Windows 2000 Professional, Windows XP, and Windows Vista**
Supports file-level security	No	No	Yes**
Supports file compression and encryption	No	No	Yes**

* FAT32 and NTFS file names are limited to 255 characters overall, which are divided between the file name and extension. For example, you could assign a 200-character file name and a 55-character file extension.

** Windows XP Home Edition and Media Center Edition don't support EFS, and they allow only limited control over Access Control Lists (ACLs) to allow simple file sharing.

The *root directory* is the highest-level folder on the disk. In the FAT16 file system, the root directory can contain a maximum of 512 files and folders. The FAT32 and NTFS file systems do not have this limitation.

Format commands

For DOS and Windows 95 systems, you use the MS-DOS format command to format a hard drive partitioned with the FAT16 file system. You can use the Windows 98/Me format command to format FAT16- and FAT32-partitioned hard drives. Windows NT Workstation, Windows 2000 Professional, Windows XP, and Windows Vista include a format command-line utility you can use to format FAT32- and NTFS-partitioned hard drives. You can also use Disk Management.

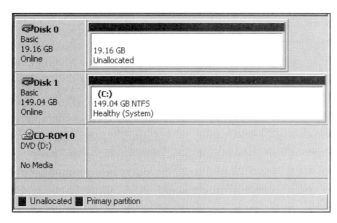

Exhibit 5-3: A new, unpartitioned disk, as shown in Windows Disk Management

The Disk Management utility

You can use the Disk Management utility in Windows 2000, Windows XP, and Windows Vista to manage hard disks and partitions. To open Disk Management, open Computer Management (right-click My Computer or Computer, and choose Management), and select Disk Management in the left pane.

As you can see in Exhibit 5-3, Disk Management displays information about all hard disks and partitions in the computer. You can format and create partitions on hard disks, and you can add and initialize new hard disks.

Depending on the status of a hard disk or partition, Disk Management will display one of the status messages listed in the following table.

Status	For	Description
Healthy	Partition/Volume	The partition/volume is available for use and functioning correctly. If the partition or volume shows "Healthy (At Risk)," it means that I/O errors have been detected.
Unallocated	Partition/Volume	The partition/volume hasn't been formatted yet.
Formatting	Partition/Volume	The partition/volume is being formatted.
Failed	Partition/Volume	The disk containing the partition/volume is likely damaged, or the file system has become corrupt.
Basic	Disk	The disk is configured as a basic disk.
Dynamic	Disk	The disk is configured as a dynamic disk.
Not initialized	Disk	The disk doesn't contain a valid signature. You will have to re-initialize the disk.
Initializing	Disk	The disk is being initialized by the operating system.
Online	Disk	The disk is accessible and functioning correctly. A disk will show "Online (Errors)" when a volume status is Healthy (At Risk).
Offline	Disk	The dynamic disk has suffered a hardware failure or has become corrupted in some way. If the status changes to Missing, the disk can no longer be located.
Unreadable	Disk	This status indicates a hardware failure or I/O errors.
Foreign	Disk	This status is displayed on a dynamic disk that's been moved from another Windows computer. You can import the foreign disk into Disk Management to access its data.

Data storage devices 5–11

Do it!

A-2: Partitioning and formatting a hard drive

📦 *To complete this activity, students must have installed an additional hard drive or have an unpartitioned drive in their systems.*

Here's how	Here's why
1 Boot your PC Log on to Windows as **PAADMIN##** with a password of **!pass1234**	
2 Right-click **Computer** and choose **Manage** Click **Continue**	To open the Computer Management console.
3 In the left pane, select **Disk Management**	To open the Disk Management utility.
4 If the new drive isn't listed in Disk Management, shut down your PC and use the BIOS setup utility to enable the drive	Depending on your system and on other drives already present, you might need to enable the drive controller or drive channel.
5 Right-click the unpartitioned drive and choose **New Simple Volume...**	To start the New Simple Volume Wizard.
6 Click **Next** If necessary, select **Primary partition** and click **Next**	To specify that you're creating a primary partition on the drive.
7 Click **Next**	To accept the default partition size, which typically fills the entire drive.
8 Click **Next**	To accept the default drive-letter assignment.

9 Configure the partition formatting options as shown
 	
Choose whether you want to format this volume, and if so, what settings you want to use.
 	
○ Do not format this volume
⦿ Format this volume with the following settings:
   File system: NTFS
   Allocation unit size: Default
   Volume label: My Drive
   ☑ Perform a quick format
   ☐ Enable file and folder compression	

10 Click **Next** and then click **Finish**	To proceed with partitioning and formatting.

11	Observe the Disk Management window	Your drive is partitioned, formatted, and ready for use.
12	Right-click **My Drive** and observe the Mark Partition as Active option	With this option, you can mark the partition as a bootable partition.
13	Record the drive letter of your new drive	Drive letter: _____
14	Don't choose the option; instead, choose **Explore**	(If necessary.) To open the drive and display its contents. The drive is empty, so no files are displayed.
15	Close the window	

Tell students not to select this option.

RAID levels

Explanation

Because hard drives are prone to failure, one of the best data security measures is to plan for disk redundancy in servers and host computers. This redundancy is accomplished in two ways: by performing regular backups and by installing RAID drives.

RAID is a set of standards for lengthening disk life, preventing data loss, and enabling relatively uninterrupted access to data. There are six basic levels of RAID (other levels exist beyond the basic levels), beginning with the use of disk striping.

The six basic RAID levels are as follows:

- **RAID level 0** — Striping with no other redundancy features. *Striping* works by spreading data equally over two or more drives. It is used to extend disk life and to improve performance. Data access on striped volumes is fast because of the way the data is divided into blocks that are quickly accessed through multiple disk reads and data paths. The disadvantage is that if one disk fails, you can expect a large data loss on all volumes.
- **RAID level 1** — Simple disk mirroring, which provides a means to duplicate the operating system files if a disk fails. *Disk mirroring* prevents data loss by duplicating data from a main disk to a backup disk, as shown in Exhibit 5-4.

Disk duplexing, shown in Exhibit 5-5, is similar to disk mirroring, but to provide greater redundancy, the backup disk is placed on a different controller or adapter than the one used by the main disk. Some administrators consider the combination of disk mirroring and duplexing to offer one of the best guarantees of data recovery when there is a disk failure.

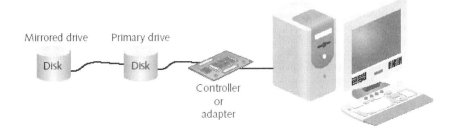

Exhibit 5-4: Disk mirroring

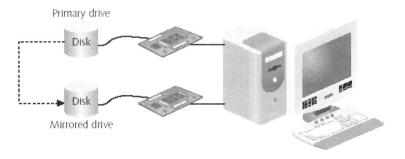

Exhibit 5-5: Disk duplexing

- **RAID level 2** — An array of disks in which the data is striped across all disks in the array. Also, in this method, all disks store error correction information that enables the array to reconstruct data from a failed disk. The advantages of level 2 are that disk wear is reduced and data can be reconstructed if a disk fails.
- **RAID level 3** — Uses disk striping and stores error correcting information (like level 2), but writes the information to only one disk in the array. If that disk fails, the array cannot rebuild its contents.
- **RAID level 4** — Stripes data and stores error correcting information on all drives, in a manner similar to level 2. An added feature is its ability to perform checksum verification. The *checksum* is a sum of bits in a file. When a file is re-created after a disk failure, the checksum previously stored for that file is checked against the actual file after it is reconstructed. If the two do not match, the file might be corrupted.

Windows server and client OSs don't support RAID levels 2 through 4.

- **RAID level 5** — Combines the best features of RAID, including striping, error correction, and checksum verification. The Windows operating systems that support dynamic disks also support RAID level 5, calling it "stripe set with parity on basic disks" or a "RAID-5 volume" (for dynamic disks), depending on the disk architecture.

    Whereas level 4 stores checksum data on only one disk, level 5 spreads both error correction and checksum data over all of the disks, so there is no single point of failure. This level uses more memory than other RAID levels, with at least 16 MB recommended as additional memory for system functions. In addition, level 5 requires at least three disks in the RAID array.

    Recovery from a failed disk provides roughly the same guarantee as with disk mirroring, but takes longer with level 5. The system can recover from a single disk failure, but if more than one drive in the array fails, all data is lost and must be restored from backup.

Considerations for using RAID

Windows server and client OSs support RAID levels 0, 1, and 5 for disk fault tolerance (each of these levels is discussed further in the sections that follow), with levels 1 and 5 recommended. RAID level 0 is not recommended in many situations because it does not really provide fault tolerance, except to help extend the life of disks while providing relatively fast access. All three RAID levels support disks formatted with FAT or NTFS.

When you decide to use RAID level 1 or RAID level 5, consider the following:
- The boot and system files can be placed on disks configured for RAID level 1, but not for RAID level 5. Thus, if you use RAID level 5, these files must be on a separate disk or in a separate disk set using RAID level 1.
- RAID level 1 uses two hard disks, and RAID level 5 uses from three to 32.
- RAID level 1 is more expensive to implement than RAID level 5, when you consider the cost per megabyte of storage. Keep in mind that in RAID level 1, half of your total disk space is used for redundancy, whereas that value is one-third or less for RAID level 5. The amount of disk space used for parity in RAID level 5 is $1/n$, where n is the number of disk drives in the array.
- RAID level 5 requires more memory than RAID level 1.

- Reading from disk is faster than write access in both RAID level 1 and RAID level 5. Read access for RAID level 1 is better than from individual drives because the system can read off any partner of the mirror.
- Because RAID level 5 involves more disks and because the read/write heads can acquire data simultaneously across striped volumes, it has much faster read access than RAID level 1.

Striped volumes (RAID 0)

The reasons for using a RAID level 0 (striped) volume are to:
- Reduce the wear on multiple disk drives by equally spreading the load.
- Increase disk performance compared to other methods of configuring dynamic disk volumes.

Although striped volumes do not provide fault tolerance, other than to extend the life of the disks, there are situations in which they might be used. Perhaps your organization maintains a "data warehouse" in which vital data is stored and updated on a mainframe. To avoid slowing down the mainframe, a copy is downloaded at regular intervals to a Windows server, which is used to create reports and provide fast lookup of information. In this instance, the goal is to provide the fastest possible access to the data. Fault tolerance isn't needed because the primary data services are on the mainframe. For this application, you might create a striped volume because it yields the fastest access.

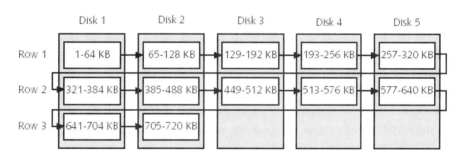

Exhibit 5-6: Disks in a striped volume

Mirrored volumes (RAID 1)

Disk mirroring involves creating a copy of data on a backup disk and is known as RAID level 1. It is one of the most guaranteed forms of disk fault tolerance because the data on a failed drive is still available on the mirrored drive (with a short downtime to make the mirrored drive accessible).

A disadvantage of mirroring is that the time needed to write information is doubled because it is written twice, once on the main disk and once on the shadow disk. (It is normally faster than writing to RAID level 5 arrays.) Also, if there are three or more volumes to be mirrored or duplexed, this solution is more expensive than the other RAID levels. A mirrored volume cannot be striped and requires two dynamic disks.

A mirrored volume is particularly well suited for situations in which data is mission-critical and must not be lost under any circumstances, as with customer files at a bank. A mirrored volume is also valuable for situations in which a computer system must not be down for long, such as for medical applications or in 24-hour manufacturing. The somewhat slower update time is offset by the assurance that data cannot be lost through disk failure, and that the system will quickly be functioning again after a disk failure.

However, if fast disk updating is the most important criterion, such as for copying files or taking orders over a telephone, then a striped volume may be a better choice than a mirrored volume.

RAID-5 volumes

A RAID-5 volume provides better fault tolerance than a striped volume and uses disk space more efficiently than a RAID-1 volume. With RAID-5, parity information, a form of error correction, is distributed on each disk so that if one disk fails, the information on it can be reconstructed. A minimum of three disk drives is required.

The parity used by Microsoft is Boolean (true/false, one/zero) logic, with information about the data contained in each row of 64 KB data blocks on the striped disks. Using the example of storing a 720 KB file across five disks, one 64 KB parity block is written on each disk. The first parity block is always written in row 1 of disk 1, the second is in row 2 of disk 2, and so on, as shown in Exhibit 5-7. (Compare Exhibit 5-7 to the striped volume shown in Exhibit 5-6.)

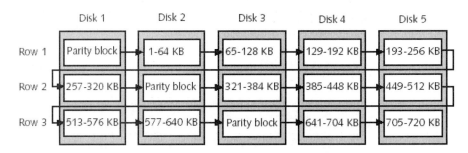

Exhibit 5-7: Disks in a RAID-5 volume

When you set up a RAID-5 volume, the performance is not as fast as with a striped volume, because it takes longer to write the data and calculate the parity block for each row. However, reading from the disk is as fast as for a striped volume.

A RAID-5 volume is a viable choice for fault tolerance with mission-critical data and applications when full mirroring is not feasible due to the expense. Also, disk arrays are compatible with RAID level 5. A RAID-5 volume is particularly useful in a client/server system that uses a separate database for queries and reports because disk read performance is fast. In applications such as a customer service database that is constantly updated with new orders, disk read performance is slower than it would be with striping without parity.

The amount of storage space used for parity information is based on the formula $1/n$, where n is the number of physical disks in the volume. For example, if there are four disks, the amount of space taken for parity information is 1/4 of the total space of all disk drives in the volume. This means you get more usable disk storage if there are more disks in the volume. A set of eight 2 GB disks yields more usable storage than a set of four 4 MB disks using RAID level 5.

Software RAID and hardware RAID

Two approaches to RAID can be implemented on a computer: software RAID and hardware RAID. Software RAID implements fault tolerance through the computer's operating system, such as by using RAID levels 0, 1, or 5 through the Disk Management tool in Windows Vista Business, Enterprise, or Ultimate. Hardware RAID is implemented through the server hardware and is independent of the operating system.

Many manufacturers implement hardware RAID on the adapter, such as a SCSI adapter, to which the disk drives are connected. The RAID logic is contained in a chip on the adapter. Also, a battery is often connected to the chip to ensure that it never loses power and has the fault tolerance to retain the RAID setup even when there is a power outage.

Hardware RAID is more expensive than software RAID, but offers many advantages over software RAID:

- Faster read and write response.
- The ability to place boot and system files on disks with different RAID levels, such as RAID levels 1 and 5.
- The ability to hot-swap a failed disk with one that works or is new, thus replacing the disk without shutting down the server. (This option can vary by manufacturer.)
- More setup options to retrieve damaged data and to combine different RAID levels within one array of disks. For example, you can mirror two disks using RAID level 1 and set up five disks for RAID level 5 in a seven-disk array. (The RAID options depend on what the manufacturer offers.)

Do it!

A-3: Exploring RAID

Questions and answers

1 How many hard disks are required to implement a RAID-5 volume at a minimum?

　A　Two

　B　Three

　C　Four

　D　Five

2 What term is used to describe disk mirroring when each drive is connected to its own hard disk controller?

　A　Disk mirroring

　B　Disk duplexing

　C　Shadowing

　D　Controller mirror

3 Which of the following RAID levels provides no fault tolerance?

　A　RAID 0

　B　RAID 1

　C　RAID 4

　D　RAID 5

Topic B: Optical drives

This topic covers the following CompTIA A+ 220-702 exam objective.

#	Objective
1.1	Given a scenario, install, configure, and maintain personal computer components • Optical drives • CD / DVD / RW / Blu-Ray

CD drives

Explanation

CD drives are standard on computer systems today. In fact, many computers no longer contain a floppy drive unless the buyer selects it as an option. CD drives come in two types: CD-ROM drives, which can only read CDs; and CD-RW drives, which can read from and write to CDs.

CD drives contain three major parts:

- The spindle spins the disc. A small motor turns the spindle.
- The laser lens and laser pickup focus on and read the disc.
- The tracking drive and tracking motor move the laser to follow the track on the CD.

Exhibit 5-8: CD drive components

Drives might also contain buttons—such as Start, Stop, Next track, and Previous track—to control the operation of the CD. The drive might also contain a headphone jack and/or a volume-control dial.

A small hole—the size of a small, straightened paperclip wire—is also usually found on the face of the drive. Inserting a wire into this hole releases the drive when the software won't release the CD and allow the drive to be opened in the usual manner. Be careful if you insert a paperclip or other item into this hole: you could damage the CD with the end of the wire.

When a CD contains computer data, the data stays in digital format. If the CD is an audio CD, a digital-to-analog converter converts the digital information into analog sound. Writable CDs are written using a process called *burning*.

CD drive speeds

The speed of a CD drive is expressed in #X, where # is the number of times faster than the rate at which an audio CD spins. A 1X CD spins from approximately 210 to 539 RPM. The rate varies depending on where on the disc the information is being read.

A 2X CD is twice as fast as a 1X CD. This power of X is accurate up to 12X. After that, to increase the access speed, various methods are used that don't actually produce speeds directly X-times faster than a 1X CD. Access time is affected by how many times the read head has to move to various locations on the CD.

DVD drives

DVD drives are becoming standard devices on computers, often replacing CD drives. DVD drives can be internal or external devices. Internal devices can be connected via IDE, Serial ATA, or SCSI. External drives are most often IEEE 1394 or USB 2.0 devices. Some external drives might also be connected via SCSI.

DVD drives use red and infrared lasers with a 650 nm (nanometer) laser beam. A DVD drive running at 1X transfers 1.38 MB per second. DVD drives are available in higher speeds, up to 16X. They come in read-only, write-once, and rewritable versions.

DVD drives are often DVD-Rewritable drives. If the drive only plays DVDs, then the computer often has a CD-RW drive, too.

To play a DVD movie, the system requires an MPEG-2 decoder. Originally, this was a separate board installed in the system. Sometimes it was incorporated into the graphics card. Current systems are powerful enough to handle decoding the content through software.

Blu-ray drives

Blu-ray discs are optical discs created with a "blue" (actually, violet) laser. Because of the violet laser's shorter wavelength, dual-layer Blu-ray discs can hold up to 50 GB of data, and single-layer Blu-ray discs can hold up to 25 GB of data. This capacity is significantly higher than a DVD's capacity.

Currently, Blu-ray discs are primarily used to store high-definition video or large amounts of data. The Blu-ray disc was developed by the Blu-ray Disc Association, a group of representatives from consumer electronics manufacturers, computer hardware manufacturers, and the motion picture industry. The Blu-ray standards were finalized in 2004.

Optical drive installation

Installing an optical drive is similar to installing other internal drives. In addition to the interface cable and power cable, an optical drive has an audio cable that connects to the sound card so you can listen to music and other audio components from the disc.

You need a horizontal 5.25" drive bay to install an internal optical drive. A drive bay with a vertical orientation can't hold the disc in place, so you must place the drive horizontally.

Verify that the interface cable and power cable can both reach the back of the optical drive. You can get extensions for the power cable if you need to, but not for the interface cable. You also need to connect the audio cable from the sound card to the optical drive.

Before installing the drive, you need to set the jumpers on an IDE drive to master, slave, or cable-select. It's much easier to set them before you install the drive into the bay. On SCSI drives, you need to set the device ID.

For most systems, the drive is installed directly into the bay and screwed in place. Along both sides of the drive are screw holes that you should be able to match up with holes in the bay. In some systems, there's a box you remove; you install the drive in the box and re-install the box in the computer. Some systems, usually older ones, use drive rails. The rails attach to both sides of the drive, and they slide into the bay to hold the drive in place.

After you've fit the drive into the bay, you should check that the door to the optical drive can open freely and that the tray can extend freely. If the drive is off-kilter and hits against the frame, you won't be able to open the drive and insert a disc in the tray.

Optical drive connections

Most optical drives use an IDE ATAPI connection, either PATA or SATA. Some internal optical drives use SCSI connections. Because computers come standard with internal optical drives now, external versions aren't as popular as they were in the past. External optical drives can be connected via SCSI, USB, IEEE 1394, or parallel ports. Optical drive connections are shown in Exhibit 5-9.

Exhibit 5-9: Optical drive connections—in this case, for a CD drive

Drivers

After you install an optical drive and restart the PC, Windows should detect the new hardware. Windows will try to identify and install the appropriate driver for the drive. If Windows can't find it, you'll be prompted to supply the driver from another source.

If the drive requires specific drivers, they should have been supplied on a disc with the drive. The drivers are usually available on the Internet as well. Hardware manufacturers maintain up-to-date drivers on their Web sites. Third-party Web sites also maintain drivers for many devices. Be aware, though, that third-party sites might not have the most current versions of drivers.

Data storage devices **5–21**

Do it!

B-1: Installing an optical drive

Here's how	Here's why
1 Turn off the computer	
Remove any external cables	
2 Open the computer case	Refer to the system documentation if necessary.
3 If you're replacing an optical drive, remove the cables from the back of the drive	
Remove the drive from the drive bay	Unscrew any screws securing it to the bay.
4 Locate pin 1 on the drive's data connector	So that you install the data interface cable correctly in a later step. It's easier to do this before installing the drive, while you can hold it up to the light, turn it over, and inspect it more closely. Pin 1 is most often located on the side nearest the power connection.
5 Set the drive for Master, Slave, or Cable Select	If it's an IDE drive.
Set the drive ID	If it's a SCSI drive.
Terminate the drive	If it's the last drive in a SCSI chain.
6 Insert the drive in the drive bay	
Mount the drive	Use the mounting method required by your computer.
Secure the drive in place	Use screws or whatever mechanism your system uses to secure the drive to the bay.
7 Verify the alignment with the case	To make sure the drive door and disc tray can open freely.
8 Connect the interface cable	It should be connected to the secondary IDE channel or to the SCSI chain, if it's a SCSI drive.
Connect the power cable	Be sure that it's properly oriented and firmly plugged in.
Connect the audio cable	If the sound card contains a wire to connect to the optical drive.
9 Reconnect the power cord and external cables	You'll listen to an audio CD.
Turn on the computer	

Students can reinstall the optical drive they just removed.

10	Observe the New Hardware bubble	A message should be displayed, stating that new hardware was found.
11	Place an audio CD in the optical drive	The "What do you want Windows to do?" prompt is displayed.
	Select **Play audio CD**	
	Click **OK**	If this is the first time you've run Windows Media Player, you're prompted to install.
12	If necessary, click **Next** twice	
	Click **Finish**	Windows Media Player opens and the first track on the CD begins playing.
13	Click the Stop button, and remove all discs from the optical drive	
14	Close Windows Media Player	

Point out that if other software is installed that can play audio CDs, there are additional options in the list.

Topic C: Removable storage devices

This topic covers the following CompTIA A+ 220-702 exam objective.

#	Objective

1.1	Given a scenario, install, configure, and maintain personal computer components
	• Storage devices
	  – FDD
	  – Removable
	• External

USB flash drives

Explanation

USB flash drives are a popular storage solution. They're about the size of an adult person's thumb (or smaller), and they weigh about as much as a car key. They come with capacities from a few megabytes to many gigabytes. Their capacity is much greater than that of a floppy disk, and many flash drives can hold more than a CD can.

USB flash drives are typically composed of:

- A controller with a USB interface
- A non-volatile memory interface connected to memory
- An LED to indicate drive activity

Optionally, flash drives might include:

- A crystal for external clock generation on high-speed drives
- A write-protect switch
- A fingerprint sensor
- An integrated MP3 player

Many flash drives come with one or more security features. These include:

- Encryption
- Password protection
- Fingerprint sensor

Students may have heard these devices referred to by brand names such as "Thumb drives" and "Jump drives."

The drivers that support USB flash drives are included in Windows Me, Windows 2000 Professional, Windows XP, and Windows Vista. They're also included in Macintosh OS 9 and OS X or later, as well as Linux kernels 2.4 and later. For Windows 98 SE and Windows NT Workstation, you need to obtain drivers from the flash drive's manufacturer.

Hot-swapping

Flash drives are designed to be *hot-swappable*, meaning that you can attach or detach the device from the computer without shutting it down and restarting it. This functionality is part of the USB specification.

When hot-swapping, be sure that the drive has finished writing before you remove it. If the drive is in the middle of a write operation when you disconnect it, the file that was being written, or even the entire directory structure, can become unreadable. An LED light on the drive typically indicates when a write operation is in progress.

It's also recommended that you use the Safely Remove Hardware icon to stop the device before removing it. Some computer makers recommend ejecting the drive instead; in Windows Explorer, right-click the USB flash drive and choose Eject.

Booting from flash drives

If your computer supports booting from flash drives, you can do so if your flash drive is bootable. If the drive is bootable, the manufacturer usually supplies a utility to make it bootable.

Do it!

C-1: Using a USB flash drive

Provide students with USB flash drives for this activity. Have students work in pairs.

Here's how	Here's why
1 Remove the cover from the flash drive, or connect the USB cable to the drive	If appropriate.
2 Connect the USB drive or its cable to an open USB port on your computer	Modern PCs include front-accessible USB ports to make it more convenient for users to connect USB drives and other similar devices. The "What do you want Windows to do?" prompt is displayed.
Select **Open folder to view files** and click **OK**	
3 Observe the files on the flash drive	The drive might be empty.
4 From the Student Data folder for this unit, copy **USB drive.txt** to the flash drive	
5 From the USB drive, open **USB drive.txt**	
Make a change in the file and save the updated file on the USB drive	
6 Close all open windows	
7 In the system tray, double-click the Safely Remove Hardware icon	To open the Stop a Hardware Device dialog box.
Select your USB drive	
Click **Stop** and click **OK**	To safely remove the USB drive from your system.
Close the dialog box	
8 Disconnect the USB drive	Unplug it or its cable from your PC.

9	Switch computers with your partner	
10	Attach your USB drive to your partner's computer	USB drives are very portable.
	From your USB drive, open **USB drive.txt**	
	Close USB drive.txt	
11	Close all open windows	
12	Double-click the Safely Remove Hardware icon	In the system tray.
	Select your USB drive	
	Click **Stop** and click **OK**	To safely remove the USB drive from your system.
	Close the dialog box	
13	Disconnect the USB drive	Unplug it or its cable from your PC.

Floppy drive controllers

Explanation

Floppy disks were the original storage medium for PCs. In early PCs, the floppy drive controller was a separate component. For at least the past decade, floppy drive controllers have been almost universally built into the motherboard. By today's standards, floppy disks hold a miniscule amount of data and are very slow to access. Many modern computers do not include a floppy drive. You'll probably never be called upon to install a floppy drive controller.

However, you might need to enable the built-in controller or configure the system resources it uses. You would do so with the BIOS setup utility. The typical resources used by the floppy controller are listed in the following table.

System resource	Typical value
IRQ	6
I/O address range	0x03F0–0x03F7
DMA channel	2

Floppy drive controllers support up to two floppy drives, which are assigned drive letters A and B.

Floppy drive cables

The typical cable used to connect a floppy drive is a 34-pin ribbon cable with either three or five connectors. One is connected to the drive controller (typically on the motherboard), and the others are for connecting to the floppy drives (up to two of them).

The 5.25" drives use a larger, pinch-type connector, whereas 3.5" drives use a smaller pin-socket connector. Because you can connect only two floppy drives to a controller, you can use either the 5.25" or the 3.5" connector for each of the drives, but not both.

The place where you connect the drive on the cable determines whether the drive is assigned letter A or B. Floppy cables have a twisted section, and the drive plugged into the connectors beyond the twist are assigned drive letter A by the BIOS. A typical floppy cable is shown in Exhibit 5-10.

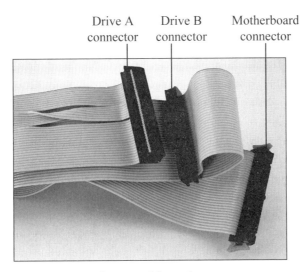

Exhibit 5-10: A floppy cable with connectors

Floppy controller connectors

The typical floppy controller connector is a 34-pin male connector soldered to the motherboard. Such a connector is shown in Exhibit 5-11.

Exhibit 5-11: A floppy controller connector on a motherboard

Do it!

C-2: Installing a floppy drive

⚠ *Make sure students turn off the computer and disconnect it from the power source.*

📦 *Supply students with internal floppy drives for this activity.*

Here's how	Here's why
1 Open your PC's case	Follow all electrical and ESD safety precautions.
2 Remove the front cover or the plate cover that closes the floppy drive bay	
3 Install the drive into the bay	Secure the drive with at least four screws. This drive receives more pressure than other drives because users push floppies in or eject them.
4 Connect the floppy cable to the motherboard	Make sure you plug the correct connector into the correct socket on the motherboard.
5 Connect the cable to the floppy drive so that this drive is drive A	
6 Connect an available power cable to the floppy drive's power socket	Modern floppies use the small peripheral power connector; older drives use the large connector.
7 Close the system case and boot your PC	
Log on to Windows as **PAADMIN##**	The password is !pass1234.
8 Open Computer	To view the floppy drive in your system. You can't access the drive because there's no diskette in it.

Topic D: Storage device troubleshooting

This topic covers the following CompTIA A+ 220-702 exam objectives.

#	Objective

1.2	Given a scenario, detect problems, troubleshoot, and repair/replace personal computer components
	• Storage devices
	  – HDD
	    • SATA
	    • PATA
	    • Solid state
	  – FDD
	  – Optical drives
	    • CD / DVD / RW / Blu-Ray
	  – Removable
	  – External

2.1	Select the appropriate commands and options to troubleshoot and resolve problems • CHKDSK (/f /r)

2.3	Given a scenario, select and use system utilities / tools and evaluate the results
	• Disk management tools
	  – DEFRAG
	  – Check Disk

Hard drive maintenance

Explanation

Common problems with hard drives include fragmentation, file system corruption, insufficient space, and damaged or deleted files.

File organization problems

Files can be divided across multiple clusters on the disk. From a speed perspective, the optimal arrangement is to have all of a file's clusters located contiguously on the disk. However, as you add, remove, and edit files, they grow or shrink. Files can become fragmented into many clusters spread across discontinuous portions of the disk.

The operating system accesses fragmented files less efficiently than contiguous files. You can use a file defragmentation utility to move file clusters and return the disk to a less fragmented state. Using such a utility is sometimes called *defragging* the disk.

Defragging

When you defrag a hard drive, software reads all of the clusters that make up the files. Then the software writes those clusters sequentially on the disk. Typically, the defragging utility must read and write files multiple times to arrange all of the various files in the most efficient physical locations on the disk.

To defrag your hard drive:
1 (Optional, but recommended) Check your drive for errors before defragging.
2 (Optional, but recommended) Free up space on your disk before defragging, so that you don't have to wait while old or temporary files are defragmented.
3 In My Computer (or Computer in Windows Vista), right-click the hard drive you want to defrag and choose Properties.
4 Activate the Tools tab.
5 Under Defragmentation, click Defragment Now.
6 Click Defragment (or Defragment now in Windows Vista). In Windows XP and Windows 2000, you can click Analyze instead to determine whether your drive needs defragmenting.

Defrag.exe

Defrag.exe is the command-line version of the Disk Defragmenter utility; this command can be used in scripts. The syntax of `defrag` is

```
defrag drive:
```

where `drive` specifies the drive you want to defragment.

Optional switches include those shown below and described in the following table:

```
defrag drive: /a /f /v
```

Switch	Description
/a	Runs the Defragmenter utility in Analyze mode.
/f	Forces the Defragmenter utility to defragment the drive even if the report indicates that defragging isn't needed.
/v	Specifies verbose output.

Do it!

D-1: Running defrag.exe

Here's how	Here's why
1 Click **Start** and choose **All Programs**, **Accessories** Right-click **Command Prompt** and choose **Run as administrator** Click **Continue**	You'll open a Command Prompt window with administrator permissions.
2 What command would you use to determine if drive C: needs to be defragmented?	`defrag c: /a`
3 What command would you use to determine if drive C: needs to be defragmented and to view the report on screen?	`defrag c: /a /v`
4 What command would you use to defragment drive C:, even if it doesn't need to be defragmented?	`defrag c: /f`
5 Analyze drive C: and then analyze it again in verbose mode Compare the information displayed by each command	In verbose mode, you can view the details of the full analysis report.

Checking a disk for errors

Explanation

Viruses or poorly written programs can break the chain of clusters that make up a file. Such a rogue application might change or remove the marker in one cluster that points to the file's next cluster.

You can use a utility like Chkdsk to test your hard drive's file system for errors. If Chkdsk finds errors that it cannot correct, you might end up with a collection of file fragments—Chkdsk creates a separate file for each lost or disconnected cluster it finds.

You should check a drive for errors if you suspect that it might be failing or that some sectors have become incapable of properly storing data. To check a hard drive for errors in Windows Vista:

1. In Computer, right-click the hard drive you want to check and choose Properties.
2. Activate the Tools tab.
3. Under Error-checking, click Check Now.
4. Optionally, check "Automatically fix file system errors" or "Scan for and attempt recovery of bad sectors" or both.
5. Click Start.

Chkdsk

You use the `chkdsk` command to search FAT and NTFS disks for file system errors. All Microsoft client operating systems—from MS-DOS through Windows Vista—ship with command-line versions of `chkdsk`. The operating systems that support NTFS have a different version from the DOS-based version used in operating systems that support only FAT.

The syntax of the `chkdsk` command is

```
chkdsk drive:
```

where *drive* is the drive letter of the volume you want to check for errors.

Optional parameters and switches include those shown below and described in the following table:

```
chkdsk drive:path\filename /f /v /r /x /i /c /l:size
```

Parameter/ switch	Description
Path\filename	Specifies a particular file to check for errors. You can use the * and ? wildcards to check multiple files.
/f	Fixes any errors it finds with the file system on the specified disk. The file system must be locked to allow chkdsk to fix errors. You're prompted to schedule chkdsk to run the next time you restart the computer.
/v	Invokes verbose mode, which displays the path and name of each file as it's checked.
/r	Locates bad sectors on the disk and recovers any data it can.
/x	Used with NTFS disks to dismount the volume before the check; includes the functionality of the /f switch. The file system must be locked for this process. You're prompted to schedule chkdsk to run the next time you restart the computer.
/i	Performs a scaled-down index check, which reduces the amount of time needed to check NTFS disks. This switch is available only in Windows NT Workstation with SP4, Windows 2000 Professional, Windows XP, and Windows Vista.
/c	Excludes the checking of cycles within the folder structure, thereby reducing the amount of time needed to check NTFS disks. This switch is available only in Windows NT Workstation with SP4, Windows 2000 Professional, Windows XP, and Windows Vista.
/l:size	Specifies the size of the log file on NTFS disks.

Windows NT Workstation, Windows 2000 Professional, Windows XP, and Windows Vista include a chkntfs command, which is similar to the chkdsk command. The chkntfs command is used at bootup on NTFS volumes. You can find out more about chkntfs at www.computerhope.com/chkntfs.htm or *http://support.microsoft.com/kb/160963*.

Third-party utilities, such as Norton Disk Doctor, are sometimes better at determining which disconnected clusters belong to which files. You can use these utilities to scan a disk for errors and correct them.

Do it!

The Command Prompt window is open.

D-2: Running chkdsk.exe

Here's how	Here's why
1 What command would you use to check drive C: for file system errors (without fixing them) and to perform a scaled-down index check?	`chkdsk c: /i`
Enter the command	You should receive the following results.

```
The type of the file system is NTFS.
WARNING!  F parameter not specified.
Running CHKDSK in read-only mode.

WARNING!  I parameter specified.
Your drive may still be corrupt even after running CHKDSK.

CHKDSK is verifying files (stage 1 of 3)...
File verification completed.
CHKDSK is verifying indexes (stage 2 of 3)...
Index verification completed.
CHKDSK is verifying security descriptors (stage 3 of 3)...
Security descriptor verification completed.

  5116670 KB total disk space.
  1860824 KB in 10216 files.
     2568 KB in 667 indexes.
        0 KB in bad sectors.
    39258 KB in use by the system.
    27632 KB occupied by the log file.
  3214020 KB available on disk.

     4096 bytes in each allocation unit.
  1279167 total allocation units on disk.
   803505 allocation units available on disk.
```

2 Run the same command in verbose mode	Observe the results.
What is the difference in the reports?	*The Security Descriptor section—shown below in the Instructor's Edition—contains more information.*

```
CHKDSK is verifying security descriptors (stage 3 of 3)...
Cleaning up 21 unused index entries from index $SII of file 9.
Cleaning up 21 unused index entries from index $SDH of file 9.
Cleaning up 21 unused security descriptors.
Security descriptor verification completed.
```

3 What happens if you run `chkdsk` with `/f`?	*You are prompted to schedule the check so it occurs during the next system restart.*

```
C:\Documents and Settings\OSUser02>chkdsk c: /f
The type of the file system is NTFS.
Cannot lock current drive.

Chkdsk cannot run because the volume is in use by another
process.  Would you like to schedule this volume to be
checked the next time the system restarts? (Y/N) _
```

4 Schedule a check to occur during the next system restart	
Close Command Prompt	Type exit and press Enter.
5 Restart the computer	After the POST, Windows begins its startup process. Chkdsk checks the file system on C: and then restarts the computer.
6 Log on as **PAADMIN##**	

Recovering disk space

Explanation

You can recover some of the space used by temporary files and the files cached by your Internet browser. Doing so gives you more space for your applications and data files. To recover free space in Windows Vista:

1 In Computer, right-click the hard drive you want to clean up and choose Properties.
2 On the General tab, click Disk Cleanup.
3 Select the files you want to delete and the actions you want to take, and click OK.

Do it!

D-3: Using Disk Cleanup

Here's how	Here's why
1 Click **Start** and choose **Computer**	
2 Right-click **Local Disk (C:)** and choose **Properties**	To open the Properties dialog box for the disk.
3 Click **Disk Cleanup**	
Click **Files from all users on this computer** and click **Continue**	
	Disk Cleanup calculates how much space you can save on your C: drive.
4 Scroll to view the contents of the "Files to delete" list	Disk Cleanup might recommend deleting any of the following items: • Downloaded Program Files • Temporary Internet Files • Files in the Recycle Bin • Temporary files • Thumbnails It might also recommend: • Compressing old files • Cataloging files for the Content Indexer
Click **View Files**	To view the downloaded program files that Disk Cleanup is recommending that you delete.
Close the Downloaded Program Files window	
5 On the Disk Cleanup tab, clear all items that will save space except one	
Click **OK**	
Click **Delete files**	
6 Click **OK**	To close the Properties dialog box.
Close Computer	

Help students choose one set of files to delete. Students will delete the remaining items in the independent practice activity at the end of this unit.

Recovering deleted files

Explanation Deleting files in Windows involves two steps: you move the files to the Recycle Bin, and then you actually delete the files. You can recover files from the Recycle Bin by selecting them and clicking Restore. This returns them to their former locations.

When you delete a file in the Recycle Bin, the operating system doesn't truly erase the file. Instead, Windows simply marks the file as deleted in the file allocation tables. The space used by the deleted file is now available for other uses.

Using a third-party utility, you can sometimes recover these deleted files. The utility scans the file table for files that are candidates for recovery. Some utilities then scan each file's chain of clusters to determine which files are fully recoverable. Then you select the files to recover, and the utility marks the file as not deleted. The name of the file is often altered in the process; typically the first letter of the name is changed or removed.

You should install the file-recovery utility *before* you need to restore deleted files. Otherwise, as you install the utility, its files will use up the disk space containing the files you're trying to recover.

Third-party diagnostic utilities

Various vendors supply utilities you can use to diagnose disk troubles, recover data, and optimize the operations of your hard drives. Examples include Symantec's Norton SystemWorks, OnTrack Data Advisor, and Stellar Phoenix.

Troubleshooting data storage devices

As a PC technician, you should be familiar with the most common symptoms, probable causes, and suggested "first try" solutions for problems with data storage devices. The following tables list problems, probable causes, and suggested solutions for various issues with data storage devices.

Troubleshooting hard and floppy drives

Symptom	Probable cause	Suggested solution
Can't access drive at all	Cables disconnected; master/slave or SCSI ID conflict; dead drive; drive controller disabled in BIOS.	Confirm that all cables are connected fully and properly. Check the master/slave or SCSI settings. Try replacing the drive with a known good drive to see if that drive works in the system. Try the suspect drive in another system to see if it works there. These steps help you determine if the drive is good or bad. Confirm that the controller is enabled in the BIOS.
Can't boot from the hard drive	BIOS drive order prevents booting from the hard drive; hard drive isn't bootable; another drive is set to be bootable.	Confirm the boot drive order in the BIOS. Confirm that the drive is set to be bootable and is formatted as a bootable disk. Make sure you haven't set another drive to be the boot drive, or installed another boot drive into a higher-priority position on the drive chain.

Symptom	Probable cause	Suggested solution
Space on drive doesn't match advertised space	Disk unit misunderstanding; file system limitations; space being used by system recovery programs.	Sometimes the M in MB or the G in GB refers to a decimal measurement (multiples of 1000); other times, it's a binary measurement (multiples of 1024 based on powers of 2). Perhaps you have misunderstood which units are being used. The FAT32 file system is less efficient with very large drives, compared to NTFS. You can also lose space when using some sector and cluster size combinations.
Files becoming corrupted	Drive failing; bad data cable; terminator missing.	Try replacing the data cable with a new high-quality cable. Make sure all connectors are seated fully. Confirm that the SCSI chain is terminated properly. Use a disk testing utility, such as Windows Check Disk, to determine if the drive is failing.
System boots from hard drive when you do a warm restart, but doesn't do a cold boot	System booting too quickly.	Sometimes the motherboard portions of the boot process can move too quickly for a slower hard drive, which isn't ready when the CPU tries to access it. Use the BIOS setup utility to disable the Quick Boot option, and if available, enable the boot delay time option.
Drive letter incorrect	Cables connected incorrectly; master/slave set incorrectly; drive letters reassigned with Windows.	Confirm that the drive is installed in the correct location on the cable and that the master/slave settings are configured correctly. Use Disk Management (in the Computer Management console) to change drive-letter assignments.
Can't use the full space of a very large hard drive	BIOS or operating system can't support very large drives.	Install a BIOS update from your motherboard's or drive controller's manufacturer. Install the BIOS patch included with many extremely large drives. Upgrade to Windows 2000 Professional, Windows XP, or Windows Vista to use the full capacity of extremely large drives.
Drive not auto-detected during boot process	BIOS settings incorrect; bad data cable connection; failing drive.	Confirm that the BIOS settings controlling disk drive detection are set correctly. Make sure the cables are connected properly and fully seated. Try using a different data cable. Use a diagnostic utility to test the drive and confirm that it's functioning correctly.

Troubleshooting CD drives

Problem	Probable cause	Suggested solutions
No audio plays from CD	Volume turned down; speakers disconnected; CD drive not connected to sound card.	Check the volume on both the volume control (in the Windows system tray) and on the speakers. Make sure the speakers are plugged in and turned on. Make sure the CD-to-sound-card cable is connected. Check Device Manager to see if a resource conflict is preventing Windows from accessing the drive properly.
CD drive not found	Drive disabled in BIOS; driver problem; wrong drive letter.	Check BIOS settings to confirm that the drive is enabled. Make sure you're using the newest drivers. CD drives often get assigned the last drive letter, but can be assigned other letters. Make sure that the drive is truly not being found, rather than being assigned an unexpected drive letter.
Disc can't be read	Disc scratched or damaged; DVD inserted in a CD drive.	Treat all optical discs gently and store them in suitable cases or sleeves. If you must set one down without a case, lay it label side down. Make sure the disc type matches your drive type.
Buffer underrun	Buffer emptied before you finished recording.	Check the Buffer Underrun Protection checkbox in your software, if it's available.
		Record from an image on disc, rather than directly from some other source.
		Don't run anything else on the computer while recording. Disable antivirus, screensaver, or other software that might wake up and disrupt the CD burning process. Adjust virtual memory settings to prevent swapping.
Write process fails several minutes after starting; on all media you insert, the write process stops at the same point	Writing at a speed higher than the CDs or drive can support; writing faster than files can be read from the hard drive; bad CDs.	Try recording at 1X, and write from a disc image by using disc-at-once writing mode. Try another package of CDs or another brand of CDs.
Zip files are corrupted when recorded on a SCSI CD-RW drive	Bad cable connection; incorrect termination; incorrect drive ID (master/slave or SCSI ID); bad memory.	Check the SCSI cable, connection, and termination for the drive. Also check L2 cache and memory settings for potential problems.
Burned CD-RW disc can't be read on another computer	Media incompatibility; older optical drive in other computer does not support recordable CDs.	Check media compatibility. Some players and CD drives read only pressed CDs or CD-R discs, and not CD-RW discs.
		With Windows 95/98/Me, you can change the recording mode. Instead of packet-based writes, try recording with No Read Ahead enabled. (In the Control Panel, Performance, File System, CD-ROM, set Access Pattern to No Read Ahead.)

Troubleshooting DVD and Blu-ray drives

Problem	Probable cause	Suggested solutions
Disc can't be played when two displays are being used	On a laptop or other system with two displays, the overlay can't be created to play on both devices.	Use only one display when playing video through Windows Media Player. For more information, refer to `support.microsoft.com/kb/306713`.
UDF-formatted discs can't be read; you can read only some files or none; the disc might not show up in Explorer	The latest Windows service pack has not been installed.	Apply the latest Windows service pack; make sure recording software is up-to-date. For more symptoms, causes, workarounds, and other information, refer to `support.microsoft.com/kb/321640`.
Can't play movie	No playback software installed, or decoders are missing.	You must have special software for playing movies on a PC. Make sure you have such a program installed. Movies are encoded in various formats and it's possible that you won't have the correct type installed. You might find a suitable decoder at `www.free-codecs.com`.

Troubleshooting external drives and removable storage

Problem	Probable cause	Suggested solutions
Device not recognized	Device drivers not installed.	Manually install drivers for the device.
	Port inaccessible.	Verify port functionality in Device Manager; enable the device; install or update drivers as necessary.

Do it!

D-4: Troubleshooting data storage devices

Here's how

🗂 *You must set up this lab according to the "Troubleshooting Labs Setup" section of the Course Setup instructions.*

1. One or more drive-related problems have been introduced into your lab computer. Troubleshoot these problems to determine their cause(s).

2. Correct the problems you find in your PC to return it to a working state. Solving one problem might reveal the presence of another one. Troubleshoot and fix any other problems that arise.

3. Document the problem(s) you find here:

4. Document the steps you take to fix the problem(s):

Unit summary: Data storage devices

Topic A   In this topic, you learned that **file systems**, such as FAT32 and NTFS, define how operating systems access the data stored on a drive. You learned how to physically **install a hard drive** in a PC, and you learned that there are three steps to **preparing a hard drive for use** by the operating system: low-level formatting, partitioning, and high-level formatting. You also learned about various RAID levels.

Topic B   In this topic, you learned about CD, DVD, and Blu-ray drives and discs. You also learned how to **install optical drives**.

Topic C   In this topic, you examined and used a **USB flash drive**. You also learned how to install **floppy drives**, although they are slow and low-capacity compared to hard drives and optical drives, and thus sometimes aren't included in modern PCs.

Topic D   In this topic, you performed basic **disk maintenance tasks**, such as defragging and checking a disk. You learned that drives and disks can fail for various reasons, and you learned how to troubleshoot these components. You also examined common symptoms of failures and the probable causes and suggested solutions.

Review questions

1. You connect a floppy drive before the twist in the data cable. Will the operating system see this new disk as drive A or drive B?

    Unless overridden by the BIOS, the operating system should see this new drive as drive B.

2. True or false? The NTFS file system is available in 16-bit and 32-bit versions.

    False. The FAT file system is available in 16-bit and 32-bit versions.

3. What are the four steps in physically installing a hard drive in a PC?

    a. Configure drive identification options.

    b. Install the drive in the PC chassis.

    c. Connect the data and control cables to both the controller and the drive.

    d. Connect the power cable to the drive.

4. You can configure an IDE drive to be _____, _____, or _____ by using jumpers or switches on the drive.

    Master, slave, or cable-select

5. You install a floppy drive into a system. It's the only floppy drive, yet the operating system assigns it drive letter B. List two possible reasons this might happen.

    You connected the drive to the wrong connector on the floppy drive cable. The BIOS settings configure the drive to be drive B.

6 You're installing a drive and find that its data cable isn't keyed, though the motherboard connector is keyed. How can you be sure to install the drive cable in the correct orientation?

Look for pin 1 on the cable and connector. On the ribbon cable, it's typically identified by a red stripe running along the edge. On the connector, the pin is numbered or an arrow points to pin 1.

7 What's the purpose of low-level formatting a hard drive?

Low-level formatting divides the disk into tracks and divides each track into sectors. This step must be performed when a drive is brand new, usually by the manufacturer.

8 What's the purpose of partitioning a hard drive?

Partitioning divides a drive into one or more logical drives, also called volumes.

9 When you defrag your hard drive, what do you do to it?

You rearrange the clusters that make up each file so that they are contiguous and sequential on the disk.

10 You get a Sector Not Found error message when you try to use a floppy disk. What does this error indicate?

The diskette is bad.

11 List at least two reasons that you might not be able to boot from a floppy diskette.

- *The BIOS boot order doesn't include the floppy drive, or another bootable drive is listed before the floppy.*
- *You didn't put a bootable diskette into the drive.*
- *The drive or bootable diskette is faulty.*

Independent practice activity

In this activity, you'll practice installing and removing drives on a PC.

Students can remove and reinstall the floppy drive they installed during the unit.

1 Install a floppy disk drive in your system. Install it as drive A.

2 Restart your computer from the hard drive.

3 If you installed a second drive, and that drive is still installed, physically remove the additional drive from your computer.

4 Physically remove the floppy drive that you installed during this practice activity.

Unit 6
Printers and scanners

Unit time: 120 minutes

Complete this unit, and you'll know how to:

A Perform routine maintenance tasks for printers and scanners.

B Troubleshoot printer and scanner problems.

Topic A: Maintenance

This topic covers the following CompTIA A+ 220-702 exam objectives.

#	Objective
1.4	**Given a scenario, select and use the following tools** • Specialty hardware / tools • Extension magnet

1.5	**Given a scenario, detect and resolve common printer issues**
	• Issue resolution
	    – Install maintenance kit (reset page count)
	    – Clean printer

Printer maintenance

Explanation

Sometimes simple maintenance is all that's needed to keep a printer running smoothly. Check the manufacturer's documentation for each device you're supporting. The documentation will list any requirements for scheduled maintenance tasks, especially on laser printers. Also check the device's log and service history to see which maintenance tasks or repairs other technicians have performed.

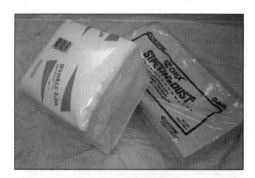

Exhibit 6-1: Cleaning cloths

Common maintenance tools to have with you when performing routine maintenance include:

- Cleaning solutions and sprays, including isopropyl alcohol and denatured alcohol
- Cleaning equipment, including soft cloths, such as those shown in Exhibit 6-1, and cotton swabs
- Lubricants
- Compressed air
- Toner vacuums and toner rags, or extension magnet brushes
- Screwdrivers (to open compartments)
- Chip puller, for removing memory chips if they need to be reseated or replaced

In the following sections, you'll learn how to perform routine maintenance on inkjet and laser printers.

When working with printers and scanners, remember to take certain safety precautions. These include following ESD safe practices, keeping dangling jewelry and neckties out of the printer, and handling components so as not to damage them. And remember the main rule for printer and scanner maintenance: Always follow the manufacturer's recommendations. When maintenance is complete, document the steps you took in the device's service log.

Inkjet printers

Inkjet printers don't need as much maintenance as laser printers. To keep an inkjet printer working properly, the main thing you need to do is change the cartridge when the ink gets low. You'll usually get a visual warning from lights on the printer, a software utility, or just poor output. Always use recommended cartridges when replacing ink supplies.

Sometimes you might have to clean the print nozzles and recalibrate the printer. You can do this by following the manufacturer's instructions, which typically have you use the printer's control panel or a software utility. Then print a test page to verify functionality. You should also clean the small well that holds the ink that's dispersed during a cleaning cycle. The well might have a sponge or absorbent pad that needs to be replaced periodically.

Keeping the inkjet printer's environment properly ventilated helps the printer last longer by preventing overheating. Another environmental concern is keeping dust out of the printer. Most inkjet printers have a very open design, which allows dust to gather inside. The accumulation of dust can result in the following:

- Stray marks on the paper if the dust gets caught on the print cartridge
- Overheating of elements if dust blocks the airflow around them

You can use a dry cloth to remove dust or paper dander, or if it's recommended by the manufacturer, use a vacuum cleaner. Clean the outside of the unit with a damp cloth or with any recommended cleaning solution.

Laser printers

Laser printers require more maintenance than inkjet printers, and the maintenance is more involved. However, regular maintenance can prevent service calls for poor print output and paper jams. Generally, there are two times when you should perform preventive maintenance on laser printers:

- **Scheduled maintenance** — Clean, lubricate, and perform adjustments based on the manufacturer's recommended schedules.
- **Unscheduled service calls** — During service calls, check the counters, such as the one shown in Exhibit 6-2. Check the manufacturer's recommendations for maintenance, and clean, lubricate, and adjust components, or replace components as needed. Before you complete the service call, examine the printer for any potential future problems, and resolve those before you leave.

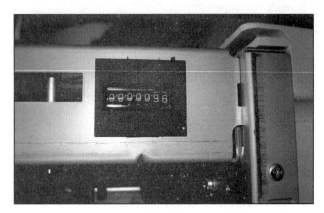

Exhibit 6-2: The counter on a laser printer

Laser printer maintenance routines might include the following tasks:

- Replace toner cartridges.
- Clean and lubricate internal components. (Be sure to follow safety procedures, as well as the manufacturer's guidelines for cleaning components.) For example, clean rollers are less likely to slip and cause paper jams.
- Replace components—such as the ozone filter, fuser assembly, or transfer roller—as recommended by the manufacturer. Often the components come in a special maintenance kit that you can get from the manufacturer. To keep a printer operating smoothly, some manufacturers recommend installing maintenance kits after a specified duration of use or a specified number of printed pages, tracked by counters. (Other printers have their counters displayed on a control panel or an on-board monitor.) After installing the maintenance kit, you might have to reset the page count. Check the documentation.
- Check the printer's firmware version and the manufacturer's Web site to see if there's a newer version available. Newer firmware can improve print quality and provide better interoperability with newer operating systems. Check the printer's documentation to find out how to access the firmware utility (usually through the printer's administrative software or by connecting to the printer through a Web browser).

Depending on your company's financial and service contracts with the manufacturer, you might receive toner and maintenance kits automatically. Some newer, large laser printers can contact the manufacturer directly to report page counts.

This contact, generally for financial purposes, can then trigger the automatic shipment of maintenance kits and replacement parts. Your company or client might have a similar arrangement; ask about it before you order any supplies.

When replacing components, take some time to clean out any accumulated toner and paper dust inside the printer. Doing so prevents this debris from hindering printer operations, and it keeps a clean printing environment. Often manufacturers' maintenance kits include cleaning materials.

When removing toner, don't use a regular vacuum cleaner or even an antistatic vacuum cleaner; use only a special toner-certified vacuum. You can also use an extension magnet brush to remove toner. If you get any toner on your hands or clothes, use cold water and soap to remove it (hot water can set the toner).

Be sure the printer is well ventilated and situated securely on a flat surface, and keep the printer trays full. Try to use only recommended supplies. Remember to follow appropriate safety precautions when working with the laser printer.

After you've completed maintenance, print a few test pages to verify functionality. You don't want to leave an inoperable printer after you've completed your service routine.

Consumables

You should always keep a sufficient supply of consumables—paper, ink cartridges, and toner cartridges—on hand. If you must order these supplies from another person who's in charge of ordering supplies for the company, ensure that your requests are submitted in a timely fashion and that you follow up on their status.

All consumables should be kept in their original packaging; in a cool, dry location, out of direct sunlight; and in a room with low humidity. If paper is too moist because of high humidity, the toner might not adhere properly. Conversely, dry paper can create static electricity, which can cause the paper to stick together, resulting in paper jams. Toner cartridges stored out of their packaging in a humid environment can cause the toner to clump.

Do it!

A-1: Performing inkjet and laser printer maintenance tasks

Here's how	Here's why
1 Turn off and unplug your inkjet printer	You're going to perform some routine maintenance tasks on an inkjet printer.
2 Obtain the appropriate manufacturer's documentation	
Find the maintenance recommendations	
3 Follow electrical and ESD safety procedures to prepare to open the printer	
4 Open the printer and remove the ink cartridges	
Remove any dust or debris in the compartment and on the outside of the printer	Use recommended cleaning solutions.
5 Follow the manufacturer's instructions to clean the print heads	
If necessary, reinstall the ink cartridges and download and install printer software	Plug in the printer, if you're using a Windows-based utility. Connect to your computer, if necessary.
6 Make sure there's enough paper	
Print a test page, and recalibrate the printer as needed	Follow the instructions to print a page and adjust settings.
7 Obtain a laser printer and its documentation	
Follow electrical and ESD safety procedures to prepare to open the printer	
8 Follow the manufacturer's cleaning and maintenance instructions	(Check the counters.) This step can include removing accumulated toner and dust and cleaning internal components. This step might also include replacing the ozone filter, which is important to prevent damage to printer components and to prevent the release of ozone into the environment around the printer.
9 Close the printer and plug it in	

Provide students with the documentation for each printer they'll be working on.

Provide students with cleaning materials and devices, according to manufacturers' instructions.

	If necessary, connect it to your computer	
10	Ensure that the printer has enough paper	
11	Print a test page	To verify that the printer is working properly.

Scanner maintenance

Explanation

Scanner maintenance generally consists of ensuring that the glass on a flatbed scanner is clean. Or if you're supporting a multifunction device, you need to ensure that the paper-feed path is clear of dust and debris, and the glass surface that documents pass over is clean and free of streaks. When cleaning printer glass, use a soft, dry cloth or a mild glass cleaner.

When you're done, make sure the glass is dry. Scan a test page or a *test chart*, which is used to provide a more objective measure of a scanner's image-reproduction ability. Then adjust the scanner's settings as necessary.

Do it!

 *Provide students with scanners and documentation.*

A-2: Performing scanner maintenance tasks

Here's how	Here's why
1 Obtain a scanner and its supporting documentation	
2 Unplug the scanner	
3 Use a soft cloth or a mild glass cleaner to clean the glass	
4 Ensure that the glass is dry Plug the scanner in	
5 Use a test chart or other document or photo to scan test pages	To determine scan quality.

Topic B: Troubleshooting

This topic covers the following CompTIA A+ 220-702 exam objectives.

#	Objective

1.5	**Given a scenario, detect and resolve common printer issues**
	• Symptoms
	  – Paper jams
	  – Blank paper
	  – Error codes
	  – Out-of-memory error
	  – Lines and smearing
	  – Garbage printout
	  – Ghosted image
	  – No connectivity
	• Issue resolution
	  – Replace fuser
	  – Replace drum
	  – Clear paper jam
	  – Power cycle
	  – Install maintenance kit (reset page count)
	  – Set IP on printer
	  – Clean printer

2.4	**Evaluate and resolve common issues**
	• Operational problems
	  – Windows-specific printing problems
	    • Print spool stalled
	    • Incorrect / incompatible driver / form printing

Printer troubleshooting

Explanation

When troubleshooting printer problems, which can include failed, distorted, and defective print jobs, you can follow some general troubleshooting steps to isolate the problem to one of the following areas:

- The application trying to print
- The printer
- The operating system and drivers
- The connection (either a printer cable or the network adapter, the network cable, and the part of the network that's between the computer and the printer)

The application

To troubleshoot the application, first restart it. If that doesn't solve the problem, try printing other files from the same application.

- If you can print other files from the same application, troubleshoot the file that wouldn't print.
- If the other files won't print either, try printing from another application, especially a simple text editor, such as Notepad.
- If you can print from another application, troubleshoot the application that's causing problems, using the manufacturer's documentation or Web site.
- If you can't print from any applications, move on to testing the printer.

The printer

To verify that the printer is online and working, check its control panel or on-board screen. Cycle the power off and on to see if that resolves the problem. Look for any service error messages, which can indicate critical operational failures. Service messages might also appear on the user's screen if the printer or print server is configured to display messages to users.

If the printer displays a service or error code, refer to the manufacturer's documentation or Web site for a description of the error and the recommended solutions. Some common error and informational messages include:

- "Add media," which indicates empty paper trays or cassettes, or if the paper supplies are full, a possible sensor problem.
- "Add supplies" or "Add toner," which can indicate a low toner supply or a sensor problem.
- "Regular maintenance," which can indicate that a part's life counter has reached a number that means it's time for regular maintenance of a specific component, such as the drum.
- "Paper jam," which indicates an obstructed paper path or a problem with a sensor.
- "Incorrect media," which can indicate a problem with the media in the trays or a problem with driver and option settings.

If there are no error codes, print an engine test page by using the printer's control panel or touch screen, or an engine-test button located somewhere on the printer (refer to the manufacturer's documentation). If the test is successful, assume that the printer is working properly. Then, on the computer, troubleshoot the operating system and drivers and the connection.

Finally, you can also print a user settings list, which details all of the settings you can modify directly on the printer (not through the operating system). You might want to check to see if these settings are correct before troubleshooting the operating system and drivers.

The operating system and drivers

If the printer is online, and you can print a test page from the printer's control panel, try to print a test page from the printer's Properties dialog box in Windows.

- If the test page prints from the Properties dialog box, you can stop troubleshooting the printer, the connection, the operating system, and the drivers. Go back and troubleshoot the application and verify that the application settings aren't conflicting with the driver settings.
- If the test page doesn't print from the Properties dialog box, try these options:
  - In the Printers window, verify that the printer status is Ready. If it's Offline, put the printer into the Ready state.
  - Use the printer's Properties dialog box to verify that the most current version of the correct driver is installed. If necessary, update the driver, or uninstall and then reinstall the drivers. This will resolve problems with incorrect drivers.
  - Verify the driver port settings, using the printer's Properties dialog box.
  - Verify that the printer driver supports any accessories and options, such as duplex printing, that are configured for the print job.
  - Check the Windows event logs for any error messages related to printing. Verify that the print spool isn't stalled.

The connection

To test a network connection, use TCP/IP utilities to verify that the computer is connected to the network and can communicate with other devices. You might need to work with a network technician.

To test a local connection, verify that the cable is securely connected at both ends, and then try printing a test page. If the test page won't print, try printing from the computer with a different cable:

- If the test page prints, the problem was probably with the cable.
- If the test page won't print, try printing from another computer, using the original cable:
  - If you can print the test page, the problem is with the original system and the drivers.
  - If you still can't print a test page, using another printer with the same connection, the problem is likely with the printer, the cable, or the drivers.

Connectivity issues might be indicated by slow printing, intermittent activity, communications errors, unexpected output, or no output at all. To detect the source of the problem, you might need to consult with a network administrator or technician, or check the manufacturer's documentation for error codes and messages, not just for printers but for any network devices, such as hubs, switches, routers, or print servers.

When troubleshooting connectivity problems, look for the following:

- Loose, broken, damaged, or improperly wired cables. You can probably check the printer cable and network cable attached to the computer and printer, but you might need assistance to check cables elsewhere in the network or to check the cable attached to a printer server locked in a server room.
- Broken or malfunctioning network devices. To verify network activity, check for blinking LEDs or link lights on network devices such as routers or hubs. This step is likely to involve a network technician.
- Incorrect protocol, network settings, or TCP/IP settings on the computer that's experiencing problems, and on network devices, such as print servers or the network printer itself.
- A bad network card on the problem computer, the network printer, or the print server. To verify network activity, check for a blinking LED light on the network card.
- Outdated firmware on network printers and other network devices, such as routers.
- Electromagnetic interference (EMI) or other interference from nearby electrical devices. Although EMI isn't usually a big problem, sometimes network cables that are too close to electrical devices can cause intermittent connectivity problems.
- Wireless connection problems, including obstacles within the line of sight of a wireless device and wireless access point. Obstacles can include walls and other structural components, and devices that can cause interference with radio waves, including other wireless devices.

Printer issues

When you've ruled out the application, the operating system, the drivers, and the connection, you've isolated the problem to the printer. Use the following sections to find a cause and solution for the specific print issue. If you aren't able to resolve the problem yourself, or you believe the solution requires a repair beyond your ability, contact a qualified printer technician.

Dark images

Cause	Solutions
Application settings; printer settings	Adjust settings to lighten the text and graphics.

Light or weak images

Cause	Solutions
Low toner	Remove the toner cartridge and shake it horizontally (or according to the manufacturer's instructions) to redistribute toner. Replace the toner cartridge as needed.
Laser failing	Test and replace the laser assembly.
Incorrect paper	Replace paper according to manufacturer's specification.

Repetitive image defects

Cause	Solutions
Drum defect	Clean the drum, if possible. Replace the drum.
Faulty registration rollers	Clean or repair rollers and gears. Replace as needed.
Debris on heated fusing roller	Unplug the printer and allow the heated roller to cool for at least 15 minutes. Clean the roller, following the manufacturer's instructions. Replace the roller or fuser assembly if necessary.

Ghosting and shadows

Cause	Solutions
Residual toner on drum	Repair or replace the cleaning blade and discharge lamps. Replace the drum if necessary.
Drum not discharging properly	Repair or replace the drum.
Primary corona not putting adequate conditioning charge on drum	Repair or replace the primary corona.

Smearing

Cause	Solutions
Dirty or worn registration rollers	Clean debris from rollers. Clean rollers. Clean and replace damaged gears.
Dirty or worn registration assembly	Clean, reinstall, or replace the registration assembly.
Dirt or debris on polygon mirror	Clean the mirror and optical components, or contact a qualified printer technician.
Damp or moist paper	Replace the paper supply with fresh paper. Store all consumables in a dry, cool location.
Incorrect paper	Replace paper with paper recommended by the manufacturer.
Fuser not at correct temperature	Inspect the thermistor and thermistor cable. Test and replace the fuser assembly. Replace worn or missing cleaning pads in the fuser assembly.

Banding

Cause	Solutions
Paper feed problem	Inspect the paper path and remove any obstructions or paper scraps.
Specially coated paper	Replace paper with paper recommended by the manufacturer.
Registration roller worn or dirty	Clean rollers. Clean and replace damaged gears.
HVPS ground loose (heavy banding)	Check that the *HPVS* (high-voltage power supply) harness isn't crimped or shorted by other assemblies.
Laser/scanner assembly failure (white horizontal lines)	Check connectors on the main logic board and mechanical control boards. Replace the boards. Replace the laser assembly.

Focus

Cause	Solutions
Not enough toner on drum	Remove the toner cartridge and shake it to redistribute the toner. Replace an empty toner cartridge.
Loose or improperly mounted laser assembly	Remount the laser assembly.
Incorrect paper	Replace paper with paper recommended by the manufacturer.
Fusing temperature or pressure too low	Replace worn or missing pads in the fuser assembly. Adjust roller pressure.
HVPS failing	Troubleshoot and replace the HVPS.

Voided areas

Cause	Solutions
Paper entering printer too early	Check the registration rollers and registration roller clutch. If the clutch is jammed in an on position, repair or replace it.
Damaged drum	Examine the drum surface; replace the drum if necessary.
Limited memory	Try printing simpler print jobs to see if they're successful. Install more memory, if possible.
Slipping gear; failing motor drive	Repair or replace gears or the motor drive assembly.

Registration, jitters, or skewing

Cause	Solutions
Problems with pickup roller or separation pad	Verify that the pickup roller is operating properly. Clean and remove any obstructions. Replace components as needed.
Faulty rollers or roller assembly	Replace worn rollers or roller assemblies.
Drive train worn or clogged	Check for proper operation of gears in the drive train; remove debris, if necessary.
Paper path obstructions	Check for and remove obstructions in the paper path.
Damaged paper tray	Verify that the paper tray isn't worn or defective. Check paper guide tabs.
Special paper	If heavy or other nonstandard paper is used, try printing with plain 20lb paper or the paper recommended by the manufacturer.
Paper in paper path at wrong angle	Check for loose or bent paper guide tabs. Check for obstructions or debris buildup in the paper path.

Misaligned color registration

Cause	Solutions
Misaligned print heads on inkjet printers	Print a color registration test page and recalibrate print heads, following manufacturer's instructions.
Misaligned or worn transfer belt	Recalibrate or replace the transfer belt.

Weak or missing color

Cause	Solutions
Low toner supply (laser printer)	Remove the toner cartridge and shake it horizontally to redistribute toner. Replace the cartridge as needed.
Low ink supply (inkjet printer)	Replace ink cartridges
Dried ink in nozzles (inkjet printer)	Follow the manufacturer's directions to clean the print head manually or by using the printer's software.
Incorrect paper	Replace paper with paper recommended by the manufacturer.

Vertical or horizontal black or white lines

Cause	Solutions
Misaligned beam detector (horizontal black lines)	Remount the beam detector. Remount the laser assembly. Replace the beam detector. Replace the laser assembly.
Dirty transfer corona (vertical white lines)	Clean the transfer corona.
Blocked laser beam or LED (vertical white lines)	Remove dust and debris from the laser aperture, LEDs, or other optical components.
Failed or failing beam sensor (horizontal white lines)	Reseat or replace cables from the beam sensor. Replace the laser assembly.
Debris in toner cartridge (vertical white lines)	Check for debris (tape, staples, etc.) in the cartridge where the magnetic roller lifts the toner out of its trough. Remove debris.

Black or blank pages

Cause	Solutions
Damaged primary corona (black pages)	Replace the primary corona.
Faulty drum (blank pages)	Replace the drum.
Defective logic board (black pages, banding)	Replace the logic board.
Defective toner cartridge	Replace the toner cartridge.

Transport/feed issues

Transport and feed issues, some of which have already been described, include the following:

- Media jamming
- Skewing
- Creasing, wrinkling, folding, and tearing
- Multiple sheets feeding in at one time (multifeeding) and misdirected media (misfeeding)
- Burning

To troubleshoot any of these issues, look for and correct the following causes:

- **Foreign objects** — Check for foreign objects, such as staples, paper clips, and tape. Clear away any jammed paper, paper scraps, or other debris.
- **Damaged media** — Verify that all media conform to the manufacturer's recommendations and aren't damaged, warped, wet, or too dry. Damaged or incorrect paper can cause burning or scorching when it reaches the fuser assembly.
- **Media-feed problems** — Check for problems with the pickup roller, separation pad, and registration assembly. Check any roller that's involved in moving the paper through the printer or multifunction device, including the rollers in any automatic document feeder. Make sure the paper is fresh and matches the manufacturer's specifications.
- **Poor media-feed timing** — Check the pickup rollers and registration assembly.
- **Separation problems** — Ensure that the transfer corona is working properly so the paper doesn't stick to the drum. Check the heated fusing roller to ensure that the paper isn't sticking to it.
- **Duplex printing problems** — Check the duplex assembly if a duplex print job is causing problems in the printer.
- **Fusing problems** — Make sure the paper is properly separating from the heated roller in the fusing assembly. Make sure the fuser is at the proper temperature. To prevent burning and scorching, check that the assembly doesn't contain any debris.
- **Media exit and delivery problems** — Make sure the exit rollers aren't blocked or jammed with any debris or foreign objects, and ensure that they're working properly. Check any finishing assemblies, such as staplers or collators, for wear or malfunction.
- **Faulty sensors** — If there are no foreign objects or debris in the paper path, and you can't find any other problems, check for malfunctioning sensors that could be giving false paper-jam errors.

You can also perform a paper path test by using the printer's control panel or on-board screen. This test pulls paper through the printer. If the printer ejects the paper, there's no paper path obstruction. If the paper jams, the printer informs you of the specific location in the paper path. You can then examine that location for paper, debris, foreign objects, or failed sensors. If the printer has multiple paper trays, you can perform the test on each tray to isolate the problem to a specific tray.

Do it!

B-1: Troubleshooting printer problems

You must set up this activity according to the Troubleshooting Labs Setup section of the Course Setup instructions.

Here's how	Here's why
1 Determine whether you can print a document from within Notepad	One or more problems were introduced into your system. You need to resolve them.
2 Determine whether you can successfully print a test page	From the printer's Properties dialog box.
If possible, print an engine test page or a user settings list	Follow the instructions in the documentation.
3 Determine whether the print quality of the page is acceptable	You might need to perform some printer maintenance to resolve print quality problems.
4 Document the problem(s) you find	**Answers will vary, based on the problems introduced into the system.**
5 Use the concepts in this topic to take the appropriate steps to resolve the problem(s) you encountered	
6 Document the steps you took to resolve the problem(s):	**Answers will vary, based on the problems introduced into the system and the steps taken to resolve them.**
7 Test the system	To verify that the problems were completely resolved.

Repeat this activity multiple times to provide students with the opportunity to troubleshoot multiple problems on more than one type of printer.

Scanner troubleshooting

Explanation

When you're troubleshooting scanner and multifunction device problems, follow the same troubleshooting steps you use to troubleshoot printers. You'll want to isolate the problem to one of the following areas:

- The application
- The operating system and drivers
- The connection:
  – Either the cable connecting the scanner directly to the computer; or the network adapter, the network cable, and the part of the network that's between the computer and the printer
  – The fax card or modem, the phone cord, and the phone line for problems with faxes on multifunction devices
- The scanner

On the computer connected to the scanner or on the multifunction device's control panel, look for any service error messages, which can indicate critical operational failures. If the scanner displays a service or error code, refer to the manufacturer's documentation or Web site for a description of the error and the suggested solutions. Some common error and informational messages for multifunction devices are:

- "Add media"
- "Add supplies" or "Low ink"
- "Media jam"

If the scanner is receiving power and is recognized by Windows but won't actually scan an image, the problem could be with an engaged carriage lock. The *carriage lock* prevents the mechanism that scans images from moving and being damaged when you transport the scanner. Typically, you find the lock underneath or in the back of the scanner.

Before you set up a scanner for a user, check to see if it has a carriage lock, and disengage it. If the user tries to scan an image when the carriage is locked, the scanner won't scan. Instead, the user will hear loud grating noises, and the scanner's internal lamp might flash, as the carriage tries to move but can't. Repeatedly attempting to scan images on a scanner with a carriage lock engaged can do serious damage to the scanner's components.

The application

First try restarting the application to reinitialize it. If that doesn't work, check the scanning application's settings to determine if they're causing the problems. Scanning settings include:

- Resolution
- Color depth
- Single-sided versus double-sided (duplex) scans
- Media size
- Exposure levels
- File format
- Reduction and enlargement
- Monochrome versus color
- ADF (automatic document feeder) versus flatbed scanner

Many scanners come with application software for scanning images by using either controls within the operating system interface or manual buttons on the front of the scanner. Typically, these buttons need software from the device manufacturer to function correctly. If a scanner is working correctly when you use the operating system interface controls but not when you use the buttons on the front of the device, verify that the software from the device manufacturer has been installed. You might want to check the manufacturer's Web site for updates as well.

Operating system and drivers

Verify that you're using the appropriate driver and driver version for the scanner or multifunction device. The scanner probably uses a TWAIN, WIA, or ISIS driver. If the scanner driver that's installed isn't compatible with the scanner or the operating system, install the correct driver and test the scanner. If the problem still isn't resolved, or if image problems persist, continue troubleshooting by using the guidelines provided next.

Connections

To test the connection, try using a different cable between the scanner and the computer. If the scanner works, suspect the cable as the problem.

If the scanner still doesn't work, test the scanner and the original cable on a different computer. If the scanner works, you can focus on the original computer by troubleshooting the operating system and drivers.

If the scanner or multifunction device is on the network, troubleshoot the network card on both the computer and the scanner, and check the network cables and devices. You might need to consult with a network technician to troubleshoot network connectivity. If you can't find any problems with the network connection, focus on the computer's operating system and drivers.

Many scanner problems are caused by improper USB connections. If the scanner doesn't work at all:

- Make sure the scanner is plugged into a built-in USB port and not a secondary USB port, such as a keyboard connection. If you have to plug the scanner into a USB hub, make sure the hub has its own power supply.
- Check the length of the cable between the scanner and the computer. USB cables should be as short as possible. A USB cable that's more than 6 feet long has trouble transferring data, especially in an environment with considerable electrical interference.
- Verify that you're using the correct USB cable and that it's plugged into the correct ports.
- If the scanner works when you first boot up Windows but then stops working, check the power management features in Windows. The operating system could be turning off (putting to sleep) the USB port due to inactivity.

Finally, some older scanners connect to the computer via a parallel cable. If the computer has a single parallel port that both a scanner and a printer must share, each time the user wants to switch between the printer and the scanner, he must restart the computer after connecting the new device.

Image quality issues

When you're troubleshooting image quality issues, refer to the table in this section, which describes some common issues and suggests possible causes and solutions.

If you can replace a part, be sure to contact the manufacturer or authorized reseller for a replacement. Sometimes you might find that it's more cost-efficient to replace the entire scanner or multifunction device than it is to replace a part. Sometimes it might not be possible to replace scanner or multifunction device components.

When testing and calibrating scanner settings, you can use a test or target chart or a calibration strip. These items provide an objective standard that can be used to measure scanner performance better than you can with user documents or photographs.

Issue	Cause	Resolution
Dark images	Scan lamp not working; glass contamination; incorrect scanner settings	Repair or replace the scan lamp; clean the glass; adjust scanner settings.
Light or weak images	Scan lamp not working; glass contamination	Replace the scan lamp. Clean the glass.
Banding; vertical or horizontal black lines or blanks	Glass contamination	Clean the glass.
Out-of-focus images	Dirty or defective mirrors, lens, or *CCD* (charge-coupled device)	Clean, repair, or replace components as needed.
Shadows	Improper alignment; defective rollers	Repair or replace rollers.
Voided areas	Limited memory; malfunctioning rollers; malfunctioning ADF; incorrect alignment; cable problems	Add more memory, if possible. Repair, clean, or replace rollers inside the multifunction device or in the ADF to correct alignment. Reseat cables, and replace as necessary.
Jitters, skewing, and registration errors	Malfunctioning rollers; malfunctioning ADF	Repair, clean, or replace rollers inside the multifunction device or in the ADF.
Misaligned color registration	Malfunctioning rollers; improper calibration; incorrect scanner software settings	Repair, clean, or replace rollers. Recalibrate the scanner or multifunction device. Verify and reconfigure scanner software settings.
Weak or missing color	Scan lamp not working; CCD problem; contaminated glass	Repair or replace the scan lamp and CCD. Clean the glass.
Vertical stripes that are brighter than surrounding image	Dirty white reference plate (also called a *calibration strip*)	If possible, clean the strip. (This might be impossible if it's sealed under the scanner glass.) Adjust driver settings.
Incomplete or distorted image	Defective storage device	Make sure the storage device has sufficient storage space for scanned files. Check with a network administrator about file size and space restrictions.

Fax issues

Typically, problems you encounter when you send faxes are similar to those you might encounter when using a scanner to create an image file. The same components that create the image for faxing also create the image file when you scan a document. Likewise, when receiving a fax, you might encounter problems similar to those you encounter when printing, because the same components are responsible for producing a printed page.

The following table describes the causes of and solutions for common fax problems you might encounter in multifunction devices.

Issue	Cause	Solution
Fax won't send	Bad fax card; non-analog line; bad cable; wrong port; no dial tone.	Replace the fax card. Connect the device to an analog phone line. Replace the phone cable. Insert the connector into the correct port. Ensure that the phone line is operable.
Can't receive faxes	Bad fax card; non-analog line; bad cable; wrong port.	Replace the fax card. Connect the device to an analog phone line. Replace the phone cable. Insert the connector into the correct port. Ensure that the phone line is operable.
Random disconnections	Noise on the line; low signal levels on the line; bad cable; call-waiting; line share devices; outdated firmware.	Contact the telephone company for line testing and service, if necessary. Replace the cable. Disable call-waiting. Remove other devices from the same phone line. Upgrade the firmware.
Slow speed	Noise on the line; low signal levels on the line; DSL interference.	Contact the telephone company for line testing and service, if necessary.
Poor quality of sent fax	Bad fax card; bad cables; low signal levels on the line; noise on the line; inappropriate document orientation.	Replace the fax card. Replace cables. Contact the telephone company for line testing and service, if necessary. Resend the document.
No dial tone	Bad fax card; bad cable; wrong port.	Replace the fax card. Replace the phone cable. Insert the connector into the correct port. Ensure that the phone line is operable.

Printers and scanners **6-23**

Do it!

B-2: Troubleshooting scanner and multifunction device problems

🎁 *You must set up this activity according to the Troubleshooting Labs Setup section of the Course Setup instructions.*

Provide students with a test chart or other material to scan.

Repeat this activity multiple times to provide students with the opportunity troubleshoot scanner and fax problems.

Here's how	Here's why
1 Determine whether you can successfully scan a test page	One or more problems were introduced into your system. You need to resolve them.
2 Determine whether the quality of the output is acceptable	
3 Document the problem(s) you find	*Answers will vary, based on the problems introduced into the system.*
4 Use the concepts in this topic to take the appropriate steps to resolve the problem(s) you encountered	
5 Document the steps you took to resolve the problem(s):	*Answers will vary, based on the problems introduced into the system and the steps taken to resolve them.*
6 Test the system	To verify that the problems were completely resolved.

Unit summary: Printers and scanners

Topic A In this topic, you learned how to maintain printers and scanners. You learned the steps you should take during **routine maintenance** of inkjet and laser printers, including replacing consumables, removing accumulated dust and toner, replacing parts based on **parts-life counters**, and ensuring a well-ventilated environment. Finally, you learned that scanners typically require little maintenance other than ensuring that the scanner glass is clean and dry.

Topic B In this topic, you learned how to **troubleshoot** printers and scanners. You learned how to isolate problems in printers and scanners and how to troubleshoot problems with image quality.

Review questions

1 True or false? You can use any vacuum cleaner to clean accumulated toner from inside a printer.

   True, but not recommended.

2 What are some of the actions you should take during routine maintenance of inkjet printers?

   Answers will include replacing ink cartridges, removing accumulated dust, and cleaning the purge unit.

3 What are some of the actions you should take during routine maintenance of laser printers?

   Answers will include replacing toner cartridges or any components based on the parts-life counters, cleaning and lubricating internal components, replacing filters, removing accumulated toner, and checking for firmware updates.

4 What should you always do when you've completed maintenance on a printer?

   Print a test page to ensure that the printer is working correctly.

5 What should you always do when you've completed maintenance on a scanner?

   Scan a test chart to ensure that the scanner is working correctly.

6 The Microsoft _____ Base is a Web site that contains problem and solution references for Microsoft applications and Windows operating systems.

   Knowledge

7 True or false? When you're troubleshooting a print job from an application, the first thing you should troubleshoot is the printer cable.

   False; check the application first.

8 When might you have to consult with a network technician or administrator when troubleshooting a network printing issue?

   When you've isolated the problem to the network or a network component.

9 Which of the following is the name given to network interference from electrical devices?

   A API

   B EPI

   C EMI

   D ECI

10 True or false? Low toner is a likely cause of repetitive image defects.

   False

11 Why might improperly stored paper cause smearing?

   The toner won't adhere to the paper properly.

12 Which of the following is the most likely cause of ghosting or shadows on printed page?

   A Accumulated toner on the transfer corona

   B Broken paper guides

   C A faulty sensor in the registration assembly

   D Residual toner on the drum

13 Which of the following are possible causes of smudged print? [Choose all that apply.]

   A Low toner

   B Damp paper

   C Debris on the laser scanning mirror

   D Limited memory

14 What problems might you see if the temperature of the fuser is too low?

   Smearing; unfocused text and graphics.

15 What's the likely culprit when printouts are skewed or misaligned?

   A problem in the paper path, including rollers and the registration assembly.

16 What problem should you suspect if you have weak or missing color on printouts?

   The color toner supply or incorrect paper.

17 List some likely problems you'd see on pages printed in a laser printer with a faulty drum.

   Repetitive image defects, blank pages, light or weak text and graphics, voided areas, and ghosts or shadows.

18 How can a paper path test help you isolate a problem in a laser printer?

   It can show you where there's a problem in the paper path, from the paper tray to the exit rollers.

19 What problems might you suspect when a scanned image is too light?

   Problems with the lamp or glass contamination.

20 What problem should you suspect when you try to send a fax, but there's no dial tone?

The fax card or cable is defective, or the cable is plugged into the wrong port on the multifunction device.

Independent practice activity

In this activity, you'll obtain maintenance information for a printer and then troubleshoot it.

1. Obtain the manufacturer and model of a laser printer in your classroom, training center, or school, or at your place of business. Go to the manufacturer's Web site and find the documentation for the printer.

2. How often does the manufacturer recommend service? Detail the maintenance steps recommended at each different page-count threshold.

   Answers will vary by manufacturer.

3. What kind of maintenance kits are available and what do they contain?

   Answers will vary by manufacturer.

4. Are there updated firmware or drivers available for download?

   Answers will vary by manufacturer.

5. Work with another student to introduce a problem into a printer.

6. Try to print a test page from the printer.

7. Examine the output, if any, to determine if it's acceptable quality.

8. Document any problems you encountered, along with the steps you took to resolve the problem.

Unit 7
Mobile computing

Unit time: 150 minutes

Complete this unit, and you'll know how to:

A Configure your mobile computer.

B Replace components in notebook computers and handheld devices.

Topic A: Configuration

Explanation

As with any Windows computer, there are many features you can configure on a notebook computer to optimize it for the way you use it every day. The Windows Mobility Center provides a central location for a variety of settings, including power and display options, that you can access with just a few clicks, instead of opening multiple windows in the Control Panel. In addition, optimizing power settings to maximize usage and battery life is an important consideration on all notebook computers.

The Windows Mobility Center

Windows Vista provides a built-in utility for mobile computers called Windows Mobility Center. This utility contains *tiles* that link to different utilities, providing a central location from which you can configure your mobile computer. You will find the Windows Mobility Center only on mobile computers (which include tablet PCs), and the tiles might vary by computer manufacturer. As you can see in Exhibit 7-1, not all computers will display all of the same tiles.

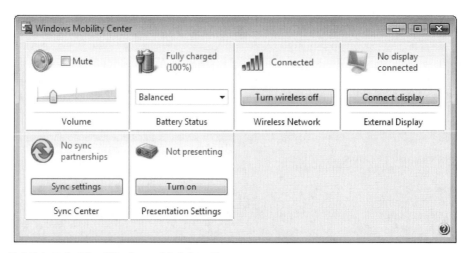

Exhibit 7-1: The Windows Mobility Center

To open the Windows Mobility Center, open the Control Panel, click Mobile PC, and then click Windows Mobility Center. You can also click the battery icon in the notification area and choose Windows Mobility Center. Typically, Windows Mobility Center will contain tiles for the following:

- Display brightness
- Volume
- Battery status
- Wireless networking status
- Screen orientation (important for tablet PCs)
- External display
- Sync Center
- Presentation settings

Mobile computing **7–3**

Do it!

A-1: Using the Windows Mobility Center

Provide students with a user name and password for an administrative user account.

You can complete this activity only on a notebook computer.

Here's how	Here's why
1 Follow your instructor's directions to log on to the notebook computer	
2 Open the Control Panel	
Click **Mobile PC** and then click **Windows Mobility Center**	
3 Adjust the brightness of the display	
4 Adjust sound volume	
5 Observe the battery status	You can see how much battery power you have remaining. You can also select a different power plan from the list.
6 Observe the Wireless Network status	You may or may not be connected to a wireless network at this point.
7 If you are using a tablet PC, observe the orientation setting	You can switch between portrait and landscape orientation.
8 Observe the External Display setting	If you don't have an external display connected, this tile will be grayed out and you'll be given the option to connect an external display.
9 Observe the Sync Center tile	You can use the Sync Center to synchronize files between your notebook and other mobile devices, such as PDAs, and between your notebook and client computers and servers on the network.
10 Observe the Presentation Settings tile	You can use this tile to quickly set up your computer for a presentation for which you'll be using a projector or other external display device.
11 Close Windows Mobility Center	Leave the Control Panel open.

Power-saving modes

Explanation

Computers use electricity as their source of power. They can use a considerable amount of power even when they sit unused and idle. Power consumption, although a bit expensive, is less of a concern with desktop computers than with portable computers that get their power from rechargeable batteries.

Modern computers include support for power-saving measures, such as shutting off unused components. Windows includes the software components required to take advantage of these power management features. A Windows computer can be in one of the following three power-saving modes:

- **Standby** — Some components are turned off or switched to a power-saving mode. For example, the monitor might switch off or your computer might run at a slower speed. Programs continue to run while your computer is in standby mode.

  Computers enter standby mode on their own after a configurable interval of no user interaction. Typically, moving the mouse or pressing a key wakes the computer from standby mode.

- **Sleep** — Most components in the computer are turned off. Power is supplied to the computer's memory chips to preserve the information held there. Most programs are stopped while the computer is in sleep mode.

  Computers typically enter sleep mode on their own after a configurable interval with no user interaction. On many desktops, you can press a special sleep key on the keyboard to put the computer to sleep. On many notebooks, closing the lid puts the computer to sleep. Typically, you must press the power button, press the sleep key, or open the laptop's cover to wake the computer from sleep mode.

- **Hibernation** — All components of the computer are turned off. The contents of memory are written to a temporary location on the hard drive. While in hibernation, the computer does not use any power. When you wake the computer, the contents of the temporary file are read into memory and programs are reactivated. Waking the computer from this state is faster than starting the computer from the off state.

  Your computer might hibernate after a configurable period of inactivity. Sometimes pressing the power button hibernates a computer, as is often the case with notebook computers. You must press the power button to wake the computer from hibernation.

The color and state of the power light indicate how power is being supplied and used:

- A solid light, typically green or blue, indicates that the computer is being powered from the outlet. With notebooks, this light indicates that the battery is fully charged.

- A solid alternate-color light, such as orange or yellow, indicates that a notebook is being powered from the outlet and its battery is being recharged.

- A blinking light indicates that the computer is in power-saving sleep mode. You can press the power button to wake it up. The color of the light varies. On some models, it's the same green or blue that indicates that the notebook is powered from the outlet. On other models, the blinking light is orange, yellow, or another color.

Power options

You can configure which components are powered down and when with standby mode. You can configure whether your computer goes to sleep and the interval after which it will do so. You can also configure whether your computer supports hibernation and how you hibernate your computer. You do all this through the Power Options window in the Control Panel.

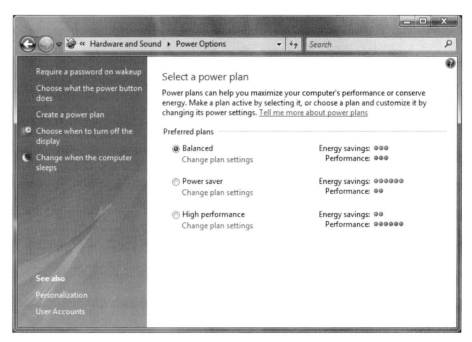

Exhibit 7-2: Selecting a power plan

Power plans

Windows Vista offers three power plans, each of which represents a set of power-saving options. You can customize the default plans, shown in Exhibit 7-2, or create your own. The standard plans are:

- **Balanced** — Balances energy savings and performance. This plan is typically used on desktop computers.
- **Power saver** — Favors energy savings over responsiveness. You might have to wait while components power up, or wake your computer more often than with another plan. This plan is typically used on notebook computers.
- **High performance** — Favors performance over energy savings. Fewer components are turned off, so the computer is more responsive. This plan is typically used with servers and computers that share their resources.

Do it!

A-2: Configuring power settings

Here's how	Here's why
1 In the address bar, click Control Panel	
Click **Hardware and Sound** and then click **Power Options**	You can also click Mobile PC and then Power Options to access the same settings.
2 Select **High performance**	⦿ High performance Change plan settings This plan favors performance over power savings.
3 Select **Power saver**	⦿ Power saver Change plan settings This plan favors power savings over performance and responsiveness.
4 Under Power saver, click **Change plan settings**	To configure power options for this plan.
5 Next to "Turn off the display," select **1 minute**	Set the option for both On battery and Plugged in.
Click **Save changes**	To set an extremely short delay before the monitor is turned off.
6 Wait one minute	The monitor will turn off.
7 Move the mouse or press ⎡SHIFT⎤	To turn the monitor back on.
8 What power-saving mode was your computer in while the monitor was off?	*Standby mode.*
9 Return the Power saver plan settings to their defaults	Click "Change plan settings," click "Restore default settings for this plan," click OK, and then click Cancel.

Sleep and hibernate modes

Explanation

The sleep and hibernate modes offer great opportunities for saving electricity when you're not using your computer. For mobile users, putting your laptop to sleep during that walk to the conference room (and the inevitable wait while the previous group takes its time leaving the room) will preserve the battery so that you can keep the computer active during your entire presentation. For longer trips—say, between clients' business locations—you will want to hibernate your computer.

Your notebook might or might not be configured to support sleep and hibernate modes the way you want. Many people find it most convenient to have their laptop go to sleep when they close the cover, and have the computer hibernate when they press the power button. You can configure these actions by following these steps in Windows Vista:

1. Open the Control Panel.
2. Click Hardware and Sound.
3. Under Power Options, click "Change what the power buttons do."
4. Using the lists, select the action you want taken when you close the lid or press the power button. You can specify different actions depending on whether the computer is running from the battery or is plugged in.
5. Click Save changes.

Do it!

A-3: Putting a notebook into hibernate and sleep modes

Here's how
1 Configure your notebook computer to go to sleep when you close the lid, and hibernate when you press the power button. Put your computer to sleep. Move the mouse or press a key to wake your computer. Hibernate your computer. Wake your computer by pressing its power button again. 2 Which is the faster power-saving mode to enter and resume from: sleep or hibernate? *Sleep mode is faster to both enter and wake from.*

Topic B: Component replacement and troubleshooting

This topic covers the following CompTIA A+ 220-702 exam objectives.

#	Objective

1.3	Given a scenario, install, configure, detect problems, troubleshoot, and repair/replace laptop components
	• Components of the LCD, including inverter, screen, and video card
	• Hard drive and memory
	• Disassembly processes for proper reassembly
	    – Document and label cable and screw locations
	    – Organize parts
	    – Refer to manufacturer documentation
	    – Use appropriate hand tools
	• Recognize internal laptop expansion slot types
	• Upgrade wireless cards and video card
	• Replace keyboard, processor, plastics, pointer devices, heat sinks, fans, system board, CMOS battery, speakers

Replacing components in notebooks

Explanation

When an internal component of a notebook computer needs replacing, most often you'll need to purchase the replacement from the manufacturer because most notebooks contain custom devices. However, PC Cards, mini PCI cards, and some other components are standardized so that you can purchase them from any manufacturer. Some third-party manufacturers make replacement components so that you have an alternative to the original equipment manufacturer.

Sometimes you can use a PC Card to replace a function that no longer works on the built-in component. If you do this, you might need to disable the built-in component to prevent a conflict between the two components.

When you need to replace an internal component, follow these general guidelines for the disassembly process to ensure proper reassembly:

- Refer to the manufacturer's documentation to locate panels or slots through which you can access internal components.
- Document and label screw locations to ensure that the correct screws are reinserted in their proper locations.
- Organize and separate new parts and any parts you remove from inside the case.
- Use hand tools appropriate for working with laptop computers.

Hot-swappable components

Hot-swappable components are those components that you can add or remove without turning the computer off. Protocols that support hot-swapping include:

- PCMCIA
- USB
- IEEE 1394 (commonly referred to as the brand name FireWire)
- Fibre Channel (used for enterprise storage)
- Serial ATA (SATA)

IDE doesn't support hot-swapping. Some computer components, such as the PC Card, require a simple hot-swap. In a simple hot-swap, you shut down the component before removing it. In the Windows operating systems, you accomplish this by clicking the Safely Remove Hardware icon in the notification area and stopping the device.

PC Cards

The expansion cards used in notebook computers are *PC Cards*. These are roughly the size of a credit card, with the thickness varying based on the type of card. There are three types of PC Cards. They all have a 68-pin female connector that plugs into a connector in the PC Card slot on the side of the computer. The Personal Computer Memory Card International Association (PCMCIA) developed and maintains the standards for PC Card adapters. For details on the PC Card standard, refer to `http://www.pcmcia.org/pccard.htm#stan`.

PC Card types

The three types of PC Card adapters are:

- **Type I** — 3.3 mm thick
- **Type II** — 5 mm thick
- **Type III** — 10.5 mm thick

Most often, you'll encounter Type II PC Card adapters. These are typically used for network adapters and modems, for adding ports such as FireWire and SCSI, and sometimes for memory. Some of the cards use a dongle to attach to a network cable or to other cables. Other cards use a pop-out port for the connector to plug into. A Type II PC Card is shown in Exhibit 7-3.

Exhibit 7-3: A Type II PC Card

Type I cards are typically used for memory, but they aren't very common because most notebook computers use SODIMMs instead. Type III cards are typically used for additional storage, such as for small hard drives. These cards aren't very common, either.

There are three types of bus connections that PC Cards might use. They're described in the following table.

Bus type	Description
CardBus	Provides 32-bit bus mastering, which allows direct communication between the card and other cards, without requiring access to the computer's CPU. Automatically uses Card and Socket Services to allocate resources required by the add-on.
Zoomed Video (ZV)	Communicates directly between the PC card and the video controller, without accessing the system bus.
eXecute In Place (XIP)	Runs commands directly from code stored on the PC Card, without using system RAM.

The conventional PCI bus is a parallel bus. Depending on the version, the PCI bus transfers either 32 or 64 bits of parallel data. A newer version of the PCI bus, called the *PCI Express bus*, uses a differential serial bus instead of a parallel bus. Compared to conventional PCI buses, the PCI Express bus has both a reduced cost and a higher bus speed. The PCI Express card is the same size as a parallel PCI card; however, the PCI Express card isn't compatible with the parallel PCI bus. Its connectors, signal voltage levels, and format are different from those of a parallel PCI bus.

Inserting and removing PC Cards

You insert the PC Card straight into the slot, and it connects to the pins in the back of the slot. Before removing a PC Card, you should stop its services by using the Safely Remove Hardware icon in the notification area. Then you press the Eject button on the case to pop the card out of the slot.

Card and Socket Services

The PC Card specification includes specifications for software support of the physical cards. This is a three-layer structure that provides plug-and-play functionality. The following table describes the software layers.

Layer	Description
Metaformat, also known as Card Information Structure (CIS)	Composed of the Basic Compatibility, Data Recording, Data Organization, and System-Specific layers. The purpose of CIS is to provide a method of data organization and data-recording-format compatibility for a variety of PC Cards.
Card Services	An API that enables sharing of device drivers and other software by PC Cards and sockets. Card Services is designed to provide support for PC Card devices to share device drivers, configuration utilities, and applications. It's also designed to provide a single resource for functions shared by the software.
Socket Services	BIOS-level software that manages PC Cards and detects their insertion and removal. This layer provides the upper layers with information about the sockets, including the number of sockets, the number of windows, and the power needed for the PC Card.

Installing PC Cards

To install a PC Card, you simply slide it into the PC Card slot on the side of the notebook. Be sure to install it with the correct side up so that you don't bend any of the pins. There's often an arrow or other indicator showing which way the card should be inserted. Install any device drivers or software if you're prompted to do so.

In Windows 2000 Professional, Windows XP, and Windows Vista, after you've installed a removable device, such as a PC Card, an icon appears in the notification area. You can use the Safely Remove Hardware icon to open the Safely Remove Hardware dialog box, which lists the removable hardware devices that are installed. You can view the properties of a device or stop a device from this dialog box. Exhibit 7-4 shows the icon and dialog box.

Exhibit 7-4: The Safely Remove Hardware icon and dialog box

Before removing a device, you should always stop the service first. This ensures that the device isn't being accessed by any programs or services. If it's a storage device, stopping it ensures that it isn't in the middle of writing information. Data can become corrupted if you remove the storage device while it's being written to.

After stopping the device, you can press the eject button on the computer to release the PC Card from the slot. The button is usually located next to the slot.

Do it!

B-1: Adding and removing hot-swappable components

Here's how	Here's why
1 If necessary, log on to the notebook computer, using the administrative credentials provided by your instructor	
2 Attach the USB device provided by your instructor	Windows detects the device and places an icon in the notification area.
If necessary, turn on power to the device	
If prompted, install any drivers for the device	Windows Vista doesn't ship with drivers for all devices. Although it detects the device, you might need to install manufacturer-provided drivers for it to function correctly.
3 Test the device	To verify that it is installed correctly and functioning as expected.
4 In the notification area, right-click the device icon and choose **Safely Remove Hardware**	To open the Safely Remove Hardware dialog box so you can stop the component services.
Select your device and click **Stop**	To open the "Stop a Hardware device" dialog box.
Click **OK**	To confirm the device to be stopped.
Click **OK**	(If necessary.) To accept the message that the device has stopped.
Click **Close**	You can now detach the device safely.
5 Detach the USB device	

You need a USB device for each student.

Non-hot-swappable components

Explanation

A component that isn't hot-swappable requires that you shut down the computer before you add or remove the component. You might hear this process referred to as *coldplug*. In notebook computers, internal components, such as the hard disk and memory, are often coldplug devices.

If you're adding or removing a coldplug component in a notebook computer, you should remove the battery in addition to unplugging the AC power. The battery continues to supply power to the notebook even when the notebook is off. Replacing components while the battery is still in the notebook might permanently damage the unit.

Mini PCI cards

Another expansion card you might find in notebooks and other portable computer equipment is the *mini PCI card*. This type of card has the same functionality as a standard PCI card used in desktop computers, but in a smaller format. It's typically used for communications that are integrated into the notebook, including modems, wired and wireless network cards, and video cards. These cards are installed inside the notebook case, rather than being installed externally like PCI Cards. Exhibit 7-5 shows a built-in modem and network adapter provided by a mini PCI card.

Exhibit 7-5: Built-in modem and network provided by mini PCI cards

Memory

The location of notebook memory modules varies greatly. In some notebooks, you install memory by unscrewing a cover from a compartment on the underside of the case. In others, you need to remove the keyboard from the case to access the memory area.

Memory has become more standardized for notebook computers than it was in the past. Previously, each notebook used its own version of memory. Now, it's easier to find a notebook that uses a standard SODIMM or something similar.

When you're determining the amount of memory to put in a notebook computer, you should be aware of a standard process called *shared video memory*. In this process, the graphics card uses a portion of the computer's RAM in addition to any on-board memory of its own. Most often this happens when the graphics card is set to one of the higher display modes. Shared video memory can leave you with less memory than you expected for your applications.

For example, if you buy a notebook with 1 GB of memory and 128 MB of shared video memory, and you set your display to a high pixel depth with a 32-bit color palette or you use graphics-intensive applications, you might find that you have only 896 MB of available memory (1024-128=896).

Refer to the notebook's documentation for instructions on installing memory. As with all internal components, you shouldn't install memory until you shut down the computer, unplug the power cord, and remove the battery. You don't want to turn on the computer accidentally while you're installing or replacing the memory.

Drives

Notebook computers are equipped with a hard drive and a DVD or CD drive. It's unusual to find a modern notebook with a floppy drive. The DVD or CD drive might or might not be an RW drive. Hard drives in notebooks typically have a smaller capacity than hard drives in desktop computers.

The notebook hard drive has a small form factor; it's usually a 2.5" drive. The hard drive is designed to use less power than typical desktop drives. It's often slower than the desktop hard drive as well.

The hard drive can be accessed from the bottom of the notebook computer. By unscrewing one or more screws, you can remove an access cover and then slide out the hard drive. Removing it might be necessary if the drive fails or if you want to replace it with a higher-capacity drive. Exhibit 7-6 shows a notebook hard drive.

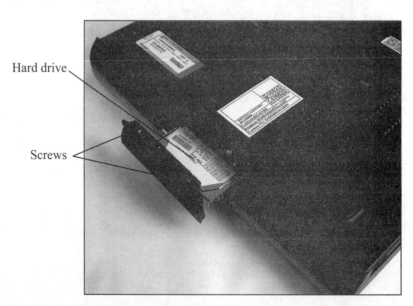

Exhibit 7-6: Removing the hard drive from a notebook computer

Some notebook computers enable the user to exchange the CD or DVD drive with a floppy or other drive. If the computer is equipped in this manner, you press a release lever or button to eject the drive, and then insert the other drive in its space. If you need to use both drives simultaneously, there might be an adapter you can use to connect the floppy drive externally. If your notebook doesn't include such a feature, and you really need a floppy drive, you can purchase a floppy drive that connects via the USB port of any computer.

Network adapters and modems

Network adapters, both wired and wireless, are standard equipment on notebook computers now. These adapters used to be PC Cards that you added to a notebook, but now they're typically built in. Ethernet 10/100 network cards are the most common network adapters used in notebooks. You can upgrade or replace these as needed to correct problems or improve performance. Modems are typically built-in adapters as well.

Other components

Other components you might need to replace on a notebook computer include:

- The processor
- Heat sinks
- Fans
- The system board
- The CMOS battery
- Speakers
- Plastic components, such as internal brackets, wire harnesses, memory covers, and support assemblies

Refer to the notebook's documentation to determine which parts can be replaced and how to access them.

Do it!

B-2: Replacing an internal component in a notebook

Here's how	Here's why
1 Shut down the notebook computer	
Unplug the computer	From the electrical outlet.
Remove the battery	From the battery compartment.
2 Using the appropriate tools, access the internal component you'll replace	Refer to your notebook's documentation for instructions to access the given component.
3 Remove the old component from the computer	Follow the directions in the documentation.
4 Install the new component	Again, refer to the documentation for your notebook.
5 Using the appropriate tools, close the compartment containing the internal component you replaced	
6 Start the computer and log on as **PAADMIN##**	To verify that the computer successfully boots and finds the new component.

If you don't have additional internal components for the computers, students can remove and then replace a current component.

Repeat this activity with additional components to give students experience replacing multiple components.

Peripherals

Explanation

Most notebook computers include one or more USB ports. Other notebooks might include parallel ports and a VGA port. Many people like to connect their notebooks to external peripherals while they aren't mobile. The notebook might or might not include a PS/2 port. If it does, you can connect an external keyboard to it. If not, you'll need a USB keyboard if you want to use an external keyboard. An S-Video port might also be included.

If your notebook features a single PS/2 port, you can purchase a Y-adapter so that you can plug in both an external mouse and a keyboard. The keyboard and mouse ports on the adapter are labeled. Take care to connect the keyboard and mouse to the proper ports, or they won't work.

Do it!

B-3: Adding peripherals

Provide students with a variety of peripheral devices to connect to their notebook computers.

Here's how	Here's why
1 Identify the peripheral ports on your notebook	Check your answers against the notebook's documentation. There are typically USB, VGA, and parallel ports, but there might be others.
2 Determine which port should be used to connect the given peripheral device	
3 Connect the device	
If necessary, connect power to the device	
If necessary, turn the device on	
4 Verify that the device works	

Problems with portable computers

Explanation

As you service notebook computers, you'll find that they have some problems that are similar to those you see in desktop computers and some that are unique to portable devices.

Added components not recognized

When you insert a PC Card or a memory module, it should be recognized by the system. PC Cards might require that you install device drivers, but other than that, you shouldn't need to do anything. Memory modules should be automatically recognized as well. If either of these components isn't found, or if the system doesn't boot after they're installed, chances are that they aren't fully installed. Try removing the component and reinstalling it.

PC Cards are hot-swappable and can be inserted while the notebook is running. Memory modules, however, should be installed only while the system is turned off. In fact, on some systems, the memory is installed under the keyboard, so you have to turn the computer off to install the memory.

Sometimes it's helpful to remove any unnecessary peripheral devices. If removing another peripheral device solves the problem, there's probably a system resource conflict between the two devices. Most of the time, the operating system automatically assigns appropriate system resources to devices. However, some older devices might require specific I/O addresses that conflict with other devices on the system. In this situation, you will need to either manually assign the resources to avoid the conflict or upgrade the component.

The display

The monitor is an integrated component of a notebook computer, just as the keyboard is. The monitor forms the hinged cover for the laptop. The monitor is a very thin LCD device. Modern notebook monitors are *active-matrix* monitors that use *TFT (thin-film transistor)* technology to provide the highest resolution available. The TFT layer of the active-matrix monitor stores the electrical state of each pixel as all of the pixels are updated. This technology provides an exceptionally clear display.

The video adapter in the computer converts data into the signals required to produce the image you see on your screen. Today's video adapters create the signals needed to display full-color images and video.

In LCD monitors, manufacturers use backlights to illuminate the LCD from the side or back and to increase visibility in low-light situations. Backlight sources can be an incandescent light bulb, one or more *light-emitting diodes* (LEDs), an *electroluminescent panel* (ELP), or a *cold cathode fluorescent lamp* (CCFL).

- Incandescent backlighting might be used in notebook computers for which high screen brightness is needed. However, incandescent bulbs have a limited life. They also generate a large amount of heat, which requires the bulbs to be mounted a certain distance from the screen.
- LED backlighting is used in small, inexpensive LCD notebook monitors.
- ELP backlighting is used in larger notebook displays. An inverter provides the ELP with the relatively high-voltage AC it needs to function.
- CCFL backlighting is also used in large displays. CCFLs use an inverter and a diffuser.

Many laptop display problems are caused by the Fn key's being set to the wrong monitor setting—for example, it's set to use an external monitor when one isn't connected. If you're experiencing display problems, you should:

1. Toggle the monitor Fn key to switch between the settings.
2. Connect a known working external monitor if one isn't connected, or disconnect it if it is.
3. Adjust the backlight or brightness setting of the display.
4. Reboot the computer in Safe mode, which loads standard VGA drivers. If the display loads in Safe mode, you need to reset the display settings for a normal boot.

Additional monitor problems can be caused by the user's choosing incorrect resolution settings. A monitor's resolution is the number of pixels across and down that a video adapter can create. Sometimes users select settings that are incompatible with their monitor. You'll need to correct the settings, and you might need to boot into Safe mode to do this. More complex monitor problems can be caused by a faulty LCD backlight bulb, LCD inverter cable, LCD inverter, or motherboard.

A laptop usually has a button that, when pressed, turns off the monitor; this button turns off the laptop when the lid is closed. Sometimes this LCD cutoff switch gets stuck, preventing the laptop's screen from working. Work it loose and see if that fixes the problem.

If the display goes black or is dim, the problem is often the inverter, which provides power for the backlight. The inverter can be replaced; be sure to get one that's compatible with your system. The connectors vary between inverters, depending on the system you're working on. Follow the manufacturer's instructions to replace the inverter.

Another problem you might encounter is *pixelation*, a condition in which the individual pixels that make up an image are visible to the naked eye. This occurs when the image being displayed requires more colors or better resolution than the monitor can produce. Using an external monitor with higher capabilities is the best solution to this problem.

The layers of the LCD screen are held together with a thin frame and sometimes tape. This frame is then held to the laptop case by a plastic bezel. The bezel is held by several screws, usually located under rubber pads on the front of the display. Sometimes there are additional screws on the back or on the fixed portion of the hinge. The sides and top of the case might also have locking tabs that you need to release to get into the monitor.

Keyboards

The keyboard on a notebook computer is smaller than a standard desktop keyboard. Typically, notebook keyboards include the alphanumeric keys, function keys, and the most important "system" keys, such as Enter, Backspace, and so forth. Unlike desktop keyboards, notebooks rarely contain dedicated numeric keypads, and some keys serve dual purposes.

To access the alternate purpose of a dual-purpose key, you press the key while holding down the Fn key. For example, to increase the brightness of your laptop's screen, you might press the F2 function key while holding down the Fn key. The alternate actions of these dual-purpose keys are usually written in small, light type on the edge of the keys.

Sometimes the function keys work as a toggle. If a user is typing and getting unexpected results, such as trying to type a "j" and getting the number "1" instead, perhaps a function key was activated.

To replace a keyboard, follow the manufacturer's instructions for removing the keyboard and disconnecting its cables.

Pointing devices

Notebook computers have integrated pointing devices built into the middle of the keyboard or placed below the keys. Some notebook keyboards have a small pointer, much like a joystick, that can be pushed up, down, left, and right to move the mouse. Separate buttons below the Spacebar are used as the left and right mouse buttons.

The cases of some notebook computers aren't very substantial, and resting your hands on the surface next to the touchpad can result in the sensors perceiving that you've moved the mouse pointer. This can be bothersome, so you'll want to advise users to rest their hands lightly on the surface to avoid this problem.

To replace a pointing device, follow the manufacturer's instructions for accessing and then removing the device. Often a repair is as simple as replacing a worn finger joystick device with a newer one; however, you might need to access a finger pad from inside the system case.

The stylus

On a PDA, you access applications through the touch screen. Using the stylus, you tap the application you want to use. You can then interact with the handheld device through menus, handwriting recognition software, an external or on-screen keyboard, or icons within the application.

To tell the PDA where the boundaries of its screen are, you need to calibrate it when you set it up for the first time (or if it's been unpowered long enough that it's completely lost the settings). You're prompted to tap the screen at the center and the four corners. This process gives the operating system the boundaries of the screen, and the OS can then calculate where you're pointing when you tap the screen with the stylus.

If a user is having problems entering or selecting information with the stylus, you might need to recalibrate the device through the operating system. If that doesn't work, try resetting the device first and then recalibrating. There's usually a spot on the back of the case where you insert a pointed tool to reach and press the Reset button. If recalibration and resetting don't fix the problem, the screen might need to be replaced.

Do it!

You must set up this lab according to the Troubleshooting Labs Setup section of the Course Setup instructions.

B-4: Troubleshooting portable-computer problems

Here's how	Here's why
1 Determine whether you can use the built-in keyboard, monitor, and pointing device	One or more problems were introduced into your system. You need to resolve them.
Determine whether you can use the external keyboard, monitor, and pointing device	These can be connected directly to ports on the notebook or to a port replicator or docking station.
Determine whether the notebook can be used from battery power	
2 Document the problem(s) you find:	*Answers will vary based on the problems introduced into the system.*
3 Take the appropriate steps to resolve the problem(s) you encountered	
4 Document the steps you take to resolve the problem(s):	*Answers will vary based on the problems introduced into the system and the steps taken to resolve them.*
5 Test the system	To verify that the problems were completely resolved.

Troubleshooting power problems

Explanation

There are three power-related measurements you should know for the laptop you are working on:

- **Voltage** — The rate at which power is drawn by the laptop's power adapter
- **Amperage rating** — The strength of the current
- **Polarity** — Positive or negative

This information is often stamped on the transformer case of the laptop's power cord. It's also documented in the laptop's operating manual.

Remember this formula: `volts × amps = watts`. You'll find that many laptops run on fewer than 100 watts of power.

The power connector in your laptop has two possible positions: the positive lead is on either the inside pin or the outside connector. You need to match it up correctly with the adapter; otherwise, you can burn out the laptop's circuits. If a laptop arrives for service and doesn't have its original power cord, you can substitute one—just make sure you use one that has the correct power settings.

You can purchase a 12-volt power adapter that connects to the auxiliary power socket in a vehicle or airplane. These adapters are usually available from the notebook's manufacturer or from a third party that sells adapters to fit your notebook model. The 12-volt power adapters also work in the cigarette lighter of older-model cars. Again, you'll need to make sure you get an adapter with the correct power measurements for your laptop.

Replacing the battery

You can remove the battery from the battery compartment to insert a new one. Replacement is necessary if you're mobile for long periods of time and must replace a discharged battery with a fully charged one to continue working. Also, if the battery has reached the end of its useful life, you'll need to replace it.

The battery compartment is typically located on the bottom of the notebook. The compartment has a slider or button that you press to eject the battery. Because manufacturers expect this component to be changed by users, it isn't held in place with screws or other holders that require tools.

Examine the power options on the classroom notebooks to see what can be configured. Point out that options vary among systems, some options might not be included on computers students encounter in the field, and additional options might be available.

Power issues with notebook computers

To determine how power is being supplied and used on a notebook computer, you examine the color and state of the power light. Check the documentation for your notebook to determine the colors and steadiness modes it uses to indicate power use.

Even rechargeable notebook batteries eventually wear out. Most batteries can be recharged about 500 times and still hold a charge. This duration usually works out to about two or three years of life expectancy for battery power. When the battery no longer takes or holds a charge, you need to replace the battery. Most often, you need to obtain one from the notebook's manufacturer, although there are some third-party manufacturers of replacement batteries. Be careful if you replace the battery with one that isn't specifically designed for your laptop or isn't from a reputable manufacturer. Batteries have been known to overheat, becoming a fire hazard.

The notification area usually contains an icon that indicates how much battery power remains. If you point to this icon, it displays the percentage of battery power remaining and the estimated time it will last. Usually, if you right-click or double-click the icon, you can configure settings to extend battery life by turning off components after a period of inactivity. There might also be predefined settings for specific needs, such as watching DVDs under battery power, or getting the most performance even if it means using up battery power faster.

Some notebook computers don't work at all, even from AC power, if the battery is depleted. If you remove the battery completely from these systems, you can power on the system. Other systems require that you have the battery installed, even if it won't hold a charge, because it's used to complete the electrical circuit in the notebook.

When troubleshooting power problems in a laptop, you want to verify power. To do so:

- Look at the notebook's power lights for an indication of its power source.
- Use a multimeter to test whether the power cord is delivering power from the wall outlet.
- Try swapping the AC adapter with another that's known to work.
- Try replacing the battery with another one.

Power issues with handheld computers

Because handheld devices are battery-operated, the batteries need to be replaced or recharged to keep the devices functioning properly. Most handheld devices have a flat, round battery that helps prevent data loss if the main batteries are fully discharged. However, if the handheld device is left uncharged long enough, even this battery can't maintain your data forever.

Data can be lost if the device isn't recharged or the battery isn't replaced in a timely manner. Therefore, backing up your PDA's data to your desktop computer is a good practice. Typically, you'll have a backup from when you synchronized the data between the PDA and the computer. If you lose power, you might also lose device settings. If this happens, you'll need to reset all of the calibrations and any other customized settings.

Mobile computing **7-23**

Do it!

B-5: Identifying power problems

🗔 *You must set up this lab according to the "Troubleshooting Labs Setup" section of the Course Setup instructions.*

Here's how	Here's why
1 Try to power on your notebook, using just battery power	
What do the power indicator lights show?	*The notebook doesn't power up from the battery. There are no power indicator lights on.*
2 Identify the polarity of your notebook's power cord	
3 Connect the power cord to the notebook	
Connect the power cord to the wall outlet	
4 Try to power on your notebook, using power from the wall outlet	
What do the power indicator lights show?	*If the notebook powers up, the power lights indicate power to the system coming from the AC adapter. If it doesn't power up, the lights are off.*
5 If the notebook doesn't power up, test the power from the power cord by using a multimeter	
6 If your test shows that power coming through the power cord is good, what could the power problem be?	*The battery is depleted and the notebook requires a charged battery to make the electrical connections to power up from the AC power adapter.*
How might you solve that problem?	*You can replace the battery with a charged one, or you might be able to remove the battery from the system and power up by using the AC adapter.*
7 Test your solution	

Unit summary: Mobile computing

Topic A In this topic, you configured a mobile computer. You examined the **Windows Mobility Center**, and you learned how to configure **power settings**.

Topic B In this topic, you learned how to replace the internal components of a notebook computer. Internal components are categorized into **hot-swappable** and **coldplug** devices. You also learned how to connect **peripheral devices** to a notebook computer to add functionality, and you learned how to troubleshoot components of a portable computer.

Review questions

1 What category of components can you replace in a computer without turning off the power?

   Hot-swappable

2 For what category of components should you turn off the power to the computer before attempting to replace them?

   Coldplug

3 In Windows XP and Vista, what category of components can you remove by using the Safely Eject Hardware icon in the notification area?

   Hot-swappable

4 When you're upgrading memory, why should you care about shared video memory?

   Shared video memory can use some of the RAM installed, leaving less RAM available for other operations.

5 If a notebook doesn't have a PS/2 port, how can you connect an external keyboard?

   You can use the USB port. You can either purchase a USB keyboard or purchase an adapter to change the PS/2 connection to USB.

6 You've installed a new peripheral device. When it doesn't work, you remove unnecessary peripheral devices during troubleshooting. The new device now works. What's most likely the problem, and how do you solve it?

   There's a resource assignment conflict between the new device and an existing device. You need to manually assign non-conflicting resources, such as an I/O address, to one of the devices.

7 Which power-saving mode uses the least amount of power: Standby, Sleep, or Hibernation?

   Hibernation

8 Which power-saving mode takes the least amount of time to wake from: Standby, Sleep, or Hibernation?

   Standby

9 What is a power plan?

   A power plan is a group of power-saving settings.

10 How do you switch between internal and external monitors on most notebook computers?

Press the Fn key with another key to indicate that you want to use the external or internal monitor.

11 What's one of the most common user-caused problems with laptop displays?

Users cause many laptop display problems by inadvertently switching the Fn key to the wrong monitor setting—for example, setting it to use an external monitor when one isn't connected.

12 A user calls to tell you that his computer "just turned off" on him, and now a light is blinking. What's the problem, and how can you resolve it?

A blinking light indicates that the notebook is in power-saving sleep mode. Tell the user to press the power button to wake up the notebook.

13 Why is it important to know the voltage and amperage of a laptop's power cord?

If you connect a power cord that doesn't supply the correct voltage and regulate the amperage to the unit, you can damage internal components.

14 On Windows Vista notebook systems, which utilities can you use to view battery usage and configure power settings?

You can double-click the battery icon in the notification area to open the utility for your particular notebook. With this utility, you can view battery usage information and configure power-saving settings when the notebook runs on battery power.

You can also use the Windows Mobility Center to see the battery status and configure power settings.

15 If the power supply in a PDA has been discharged for long periods of time, what can happen?

You can lose data and might need to recalibrate the device.

Independent practice activity

In this activity, you'll practice working with notebook components.

1 Unplug the notebook computer from the AC power source.
2 Double-click the battery icon in the notification area.
3 View the battery's current charge status.
4 Modify the power settings to conserve battery power.
5 Shut down the system.
6 Use the appropriate tools to replace an internal component with one supplied by your instructor.
7 Reboot the system to verify that the new internal device is recognized.
8 Add a hot-swappable device to your system.
9 Verify that the hot-swappable device is functional.
10 Properly remove the hot-swappable device from your system.

Unit 8
Windows management

Unit time: 210 minutes

Complete this unit, and you'll know how to:

A Manage directories and files.

B Manage the operating system.

C Participate in a Remote Assistance session, and connect to another computer using Remote Desktop.

Topic A: Directory and file management

This topic covers the following CompTIA A+ 220-702 exam objectives.

#	Objective
2.1	Select the appropriate commands and options to troubleshoot and resolve problems <ul><li>DIR</li><li>EDIT</li><li>COPY (/a /v /y)</li><li>XCOPY</li><li>MD / CD / RD</li><li>[command name] /?</li></ul>
2.2	Differentiate between Windows operating system directory structures (Windows 2000, XP, and Vista) <ul><li>User file locations</li><li>System file locations</li><li>Fonts</li><li>Temporary files</li><li>Program files</li><li>Offline files and folders</li></ul>
2.3	Given a scenario, select and use system utilities / tools and evaluate the results <ul><li>Disk Manager<ul><li>– Mount points</li><li>– Mounting a drive</li></ul></li></ul>

The command-line utility

Explanation

Windows 2000 Professional, Windows XP, and Windows Vista include a utility that enables the user to interact with the operating system in a non-graphical user interface. Using this utility, you enter character-based commands to run applications and other utilities. To access the MS-DOS command-line interpreter, Command.com, do any of the following:

- Click Start and choose All Programs, Accessories, Command Prompt.
- In Windows XP Professional, Windows XP Home Edition, and Windows 2000 Professional, click Start and choose Run. In the Open box, enter `command` or `cmd`, and then click OK.
- In Windows Vista, click Start, type `cmd` in the Search box, and press Enter.

The command-line utility is a helpful tool to use when you're performing management tasks. You can combine multiple commands into one batch or script file, which will run all of the commands in the file. You can run the commands locally or remotely.

Windows management   8-3

Directory structures

You divide hard disks into usable storage spaces through *partitions*. Depending on the operating system you're using and the maximum hard disk size it supports, you can configure a hard disk as a single large partition or as multiple smaller partitions. In Microsoft operating systems, each partition is assigned a drive letter and is considered the *root* of the directory structure for that partition.

Underneath the root directory, you organize information by creating *directories* (also called *folders*). You use directories to group your files into logical categories, making information easier to find.

When you install Windows, it creates a default directly structure that includes locations for user files, system files, and other files used by applications and the operating system. The following table lists the default file locations for three versions of Windows. A typical installation will put these folders on the computer's C:\ drive.

File type	Windows 2000	Windows XP	Windows Vista
User files	Documents and Settings	Documents and Settings	Users
System files	Winnt	Windows	Windows
Fonts	Winnt\Fonts	Windows\Fonts	Windows\Fonts
Temporary files	Winnt\Temp	Windows\Temp	Windows\Temp
Program files	Program Files	Program Files	Program Files
Offline files and folders	Winnt\CSC	Windows\CSC	Windows\CSC

The CSC folder is hidden by default, and it doesn't contain any editable or readable files. To see the files in the offline-files cache, open the cache by using Offline Files and Sync Center in the Control Panel.

Navigation

To navigate the directory structure on a hard disk, you can use MS-DOS commands from the command line or use Windows Explorer in any version of Windows.

MS-DOS navigation commands include:

- `command` or `cmd` — Starts an instance of the MS-DOS command interpreter, Command.com.
- `dir` — Displays a list of the current or specified directory's files and subdirectories.
- `chdir` or `cd` — Changes the current directory to the specified directory.

Command (cmd)

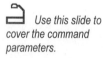

Use this slide to cover the command parameters.

If students aren't familiar with command syntax conventions, briefly explain them.

To use this command, you can enter it in either of two ways:

```
command
cmd
```

Optional parameters and switches include those shown below and described in the following table.

```
command drive:path device /e:nnnn /p /c string /msg
```

In syntax statements such as this, information that you must supply for a parameter (such as *path*) is indicated by italics. Switches, which provide options for controlling the execution of a command, are preceded by the "/" symbol (as in `/p`).

Parameter/Switch	Description
`drive:path`	Specifies where the command.com file is stored on the hard disk. If you don't specify a path, the command searches the current directory and any directories listed in the system's PATH statement.
`device`	Specifies an alternative device you want to use to enter MS-DOS commands. Valid values for the `device` parameter are `prn`, `lpt1`, `lpt2`, `lpt3`, `con`, `aux`, `com1`, `com2`, `com3`, and `com4`.
`/e:nnnn`	Specifies the environment size, where `nnnn` is the number of bytes. Valid values for `nnnn` are from 160 to 32768. If you don't specify the `/e:nnnn` value, the default value of 256 is used.
`/p`	Is used only with the `shell` command in the config.sys file. This switch makes a new copy of the command interpreter permanent.
`/c string`	Specifies that the command interpreter should run the command stated in the string value and then stop.
`/msg`	Specifies that all error messages be stored in memory. You must use this switch with the `/p` switch.

Dir

Use this slide to cover the command parameters.

The syntax of `dir` is:

```
dir
```

Optional parameters and switches include those shown below and described in the following table:

```
dir drive:path filename /p /w /a:attributes /o:sortorder /s ▶
/b /l
```

Parameter/ Switch	Description
`drive:path`	Specifies the drive and directory for which you want to see a listing. If you don't specify a `drive:path`, the command lists the contents of the current directory.
`filename`	Specifies a particular file or group of files for which you want to see a listing. For example: `dir *.exe` shows all executable files.
`/p`	Displays the listing one screen at a time. To advance to the next screen of listings, you can press any key.
`/w`	Displays the listing in wide format instead of as a single-column list.
`/a:attributes`	Specifies which directories and files you want displayed, according to their attributes. Valid attribute values include: h Hidden files -h Non-hidden files s System files -s Non-system files d Directories -d Files only (not directories) a Files ready for archiving -a Files that haven't changed since the last archive r Read-only files -r Non-read-only files
`/o:sortorder`	Controls the order in which the `dir` command displays the results. Valid *sortorder* values include: n Alphabetical order by name -n Reverse alphabetical order by name e Alphabetical order by file extension -e Reverse alphabetical order by extension d Chronological by date and time, oldest to newest -d Chronological by date and time, newest to oldest s By size, smallest to largest -s By size, largest to smallest g Grouped directories, then files -g Grouped files, then directories
`/s`	Lists every occurrence of a specified file in the specified directory and its subdirectories.
`/b`	Lists each directory name or file name, with one per line. No heading information or summary is displayed with this switch. The `/b` switch overrides the `/w` switch.
`/l`	Displays unsorted directory names and file names in lowercase.

You can use the wildcard characters ? and * to display a subset of directories and files. For example, `dir *.txt` displays all files with the .txt extension; `dir 200?.txt` displays all files whose names contain "200" with any final character and the .txt extension, such as 2000.txt, 2001.txt, 2002.txt, and so on.

Chdir (cd)

To use this command, you can enter it in either of two ways:

```
chdir
cd
```

Each command displays the name of the current drive and directory. Optional parameters are listed in the following table.

Parameter	Description
`chdir drive:path` (or `cd drive:path`)	Changes the current drive and directory to the one specified.
`chdir..` (or `cd..`)	Changes the current directory to its parent directory.
`chdir \` (or `cd \`)	Changes the current directory to the root directory of the current drive.

Windows Explorer

If necessary, remind students that directories are called folders in Windows Explorer.

To navigate the directory structure by using Windows Explorer:

1. Click Start and choose All Programs, Accessories, Windows Explorer.
   The left pane in Windows Explorer is the navigation pane; the right pane is the details pane.
2. In the navigation pane, click the plus sign (+) next to a drive or folder to expand the tree and display the subfolders in that drive or folder.
3. Select a drive or subfolder in the navigation pane to view its contents (subfolders and files) in the details pane.

Help

You can get general information about command-line commands by entering the following at the command line:

```
help
```

You can get command-specific help by entering the following at the command line:

```
command /?
```

Substitute the word `command` with the name of the command for which you want to get help.

Windows management **8–7**

Do it!

A-1: Using the command prompt

Here's how	Here's why
1 If necessary, log on to Windows as **PAADMIN##**	The password is !pass1234.
2 Click **Start**, type **cmd**, and press ← ENTER	To open a Command Prompt window. You could also choose Command Prompt from the Start menu, but for this activity, you'll run the MS-DOS cmd command.
3 Type **help** and press ← ENTER	The operating system returns a list of available commands and a brief description of each.
4 Type **dir /?** and press ← ENTER	Use the help information displayed to determine the answer to the following question.
5 What would be the result of the following command? `dir c:\windows\system32\*.exe /p /o:-n`	*A list of all .exe files in c:\windows\system32, one screen at a time, in reverse alphabetical order.*
Type the preceding command and press ← ENTER	
6 Press SPACEBAR	To display the next screen of files.
Continue to press SPACEBAR	Until you reach the end of the directory listing.

Point out that only the first screen of files is displayed, and the file names are in reverse alphabetical order.

Do it!

A-2: Navigating a directory tree

Here's how	Here's why

1 What command would you use to change from the current directory to the root of drive C:?
 	
Enter the command
	Use either of the following:
	`chdir \`
	`cd \`

2 What command would you use to change from the root of C: to C:\Windows\Temp?
 	
Enter the command
	Use either of the following:
	`chdir c:\windows\temp`
	`cd c:\windows\temp`

3 What command would you use to navigate to the parent directory?
 	
Enter the command
	Use either of the following:
	`chdir ..`
	`cd ..`

4 Change the directory to **C:\Users\PAADMIN##**	

A Command Prompt window is open.

These activities assume that users have logged in with the user name PAADMIN##. Tell students the proper path if they are using a different account.

Windows management **8-9**

Creating directories

Explanation

As with navigating the directory structure, you can create directories at the command prompt or through Windows Explorer.

To create a directory at the command prompt, you use the `mkdir` (or `md`) command. The syntax is:

```
mkdir drive:path
md drive:path
```

Parameter	Description
drive	Specifies the drive on which you want to create the directory.
path	Specifies the name and location of the new directory. The maximum length of any single path from the root directory is 63 characters, including backslashes (\).

To create a directory in Windows Explorer:
1 In the navigation pane, select the drive or folder where you want to create the folder.
2 Choose File, New, Folder, or in Windows Vista, click Organize and choose New Folder.
3 Type the name of the new folder.
4 Press Enter.

When you create a directory in Windows Explorer, the maximum depth of the folder structure is limited by the maximum number of allowable characters in a file path, which is 255. This total number of characters includes the characters representing the drive, plus any file extensions.

Spaces in MS-DOS commands

The Windows operating systems use two different command interpreters to process commands at a command prompt. When you're entering MS-DOS commands that include space characters, they're processed differently, depending on the version of Windows you're using:

- In Windows 95 and Windows 98, command.com doesn't allow spaces.
- In Windows NT Workstation and later versions of Windows, cmd.exe treats the spaces as delimiters and processes the command by treating each word after the command as a separate parameter.

To force the command interpreter to recognize the spaces, you should enclose in quotation marks any file or folder names that include spaces.

For example, the command:

```
md c:\my business files
```

is invalid in Windows 95 and 98. In Windows NT Workstation, Windows 2000 Professional, and all versions of Windows XP and Windows Vista, that command would create three directories: c:\my, c:\business, and c:\files.

To create a single directory called "my business files," you need to enter:

```
md "c:\my business files"
```

Do it!

A-3: Creating directories

Here's how	Here's why
1 What command would you use to create a directory called **marketing** at the root of the C: drive? Enter the command	`md c:\marketing`
2 What command would you use to view only directories at the root of the C: drive? Enter the command	`dir c:\ /a:d`

```
 Directory of c:\

02/04/2009  02:16 PM    <DIR>          $Recycle.Bin
02/04/2009  03:48 PM    <DIR>          Boot
11/02/2006  08:00 AM    <JUNCTION>     Documents and Settings [C:\Users]
07/18/2009  02:20 PM    <DIR>          marketing
05/30/2009  10:55 AM    <DIR>          Program Files
04/11/2009  01:19 AM    <DIR>          ProgramData
07/18/2009  12:00 AM    <DIR>          System Volume Information
02/04/2009  02:16 PM    <DIR>          Users
02/16/2009  04:35 PM    <DIR>          Windows
               0 File(s)              0 bytes
               9 Dir(s)  26,514,616,320 bytes free
```

To verify that the marketing directory was created successfully. Your screen should look similar to the one shown here. Your directories might vary from those listed in the graphic.

Copying directories

Explanation

You can use the MS-DOS `copy` and `xcopy` commands and Windows Explorer to copy directories and their contents. The `copy` command copies one or more files to another location. The `xcopy` command copies files (not including hidden and system files), directories, and subdirectories.

Copy

The syntax for the `copy` command is:

```
copy source destination
```

Parameter	Description
source	Specifies the location and name of the file you want to copy. The source can consist of a drive letter and colon, a directory name, a file name, or any combination of these items.
destination	Specifies the location and name of the file you want to copy to. The destination can consist of a drive letter and colon, a directory name, a file name, or any combination of these items.

Optional parameters and switches for the `copy` command include those shown below and described in the following table:

```
copy /a/b source /a/b + source /a/b + ... destination /a/b /v
```

Switch	Description
/a	Indicates that the file is an ASCII text file.
	When the /a switch precedes a list of file names, the switch applies to all file names that follow it, until /b is encountered. When the /a switch follows a file name, the switch applies to the file preceding it and to all files that follow it, until /b is encountered.
/b	Indicates a binary file. The /b switch works the same as the /a switch.
+	Allows you to list multiple files to copy.
/v	Verifies that the new files are written successfully.
/-y and /y	Suppresses (/-y) or displays (/y) the prompt to confirm that you want to overwrite files.

Xcopy

The syntax for the `xcopy` command is:

```
xcopy source destination
```

Parameter	Description
source	Specifies the location and names of the files you want to copy. The source must include either a drive or a path.
destination	Specifies the destination of the files you want to copy. The destination can consist of a drive letter and colon, a directory name, a file name, or any combination of these items.

Optional parameters and switches for the `xcopy` command include those shown below and described in the following table:

```
xcopy source destination /a/m /d:date /p /s /e /v /w
```

Switch	Description
/a	Copies only source files that have the archive file attribute set.
/m	Copies source files that have the archive file attribute set. The /m switch turns off the archive file attribute.
/d:date	Copies only source files modified on or after the date you specify.
/p	Prompts you to confirm the creation of each destination file.
/s	Copies directories and subdirectories unless they're empty. Without the /s switch, `xcopy` works within a single directory.
/e	Copies subdirectories, even if they're empty.
/v	Verifies each file as it's written to make sure it's identical to the source file.
/w	Displays the message, "Press any key to begin copying file(s)." You must respond before the copy process begins.

Windows Explorer

To copy a directory and its contents in Windows Explorer:

1. In the navigation pane, select the directory you want to copy. To select multiple directories, hold down the Ctrl key and select each directory.
2. Choose Edit, Copy, or in Windows Vista, click Organize and choose Copy.
3. In the navigation pane, select the location that you want the directory and its contents to be copied to.
4. Choose Edit, Paste, or Organize, Paste.

Windows management **8-13**

Do it!

A-4: Copying a directory and its contents

Here's how	Here's why
1 Change the directory to **C:\Windows\System32\Drivers**	(Enter cd \Windows\System32\Drivers.) This directory contains a folder named etc.
What command would you use to copy the etc folder and its contents to the root of C: and verify that the files were copied correctly? Enter the command	`xcopy etc c:\etc\ /v`
2 Verify that the etc directory and its files were copied to C:\	Use the `dir` command.

3 If the folder C:\Windows\System32\Drivers\etc contained subfolders that you wanted to copy with the files, even if the subfolders were empty, what command would you use?	*First, change directories:*
	`cd \windows\system32\drivers`
	
	Then enter the xcopy command:
	`xcopy etc c:\etc\ /e /v`

Dir c:\ /a:d
Dir c:\etc

Removing directories

Explanation

You can remove a directory by using the MS-DOS `rmdir` (`rd`) command, the `deltree` command, or Windows Explorer.

Rmdir (rd)

Before you can delete a directory by using `rmdir` (`rd`) in MS-DOS, you must delete any files and subdirectories in that directory. The directory must be empty except for the "." and ".." symbols and must not contain any hidden or system files. If the directory contains hidden or system files, you must first use the `attrib` command to remove the hidden and system attributes from the files.

The syntax for the `rmdir` (`rd`) command is:

    rmdir drive:path
    rd drive:path

The *drive:path* parameter specifies the location and name of the directory you want to delete.

You can't use `rmdir` (`rd`) to delete the current directory. You must change to another directory.

Deltree

The `deltree` command, which was introduced with Windows NT, is an external command available in MS-DOS versions 6.0 and later. Using `deltree`, you can delete a directory and all of its subdirectories and files, including hidden and system files. Unlike with `rmdir` (`rd`), the directory doesn't need to be empty.

The syntax of the `deltree` command is:

    deltree drive:path

The *drive:path* parameter specifies the location and name of the directory you want to delete.

Optional parameters and switches for the `deltree` command include:

    deltree /y drive:path drive:path

Parameter/ Switch	Description
/y	Deletes the directory and its contents without prompting you for confirmation.
drive:path	Enables you to specify multiple directories to delete.

Windows Explorer

To remove a directory and its contents by using Windows Explorer:

1. Select the folder you want to remove. (You can use either pane.)
2. Choose File, Delete, or in Windows Vista, click Organize and choose Delete.
3. Click Yes to confirm that the folder and its contents should be moved to the Recycle Bin.

Windows management **8–15**

Do it!

A-5: Removing directories

Here's how	Here's why
1 Delete the **C:\etc** folder	
2 Were you successful? Why or why not?	*The operation was unsuccessful because the etc folder contains files. A directory must be empty before you can delete it with the `rd` command.*
3 Delete the contents of the etc folder	Change to the C:\etc folder and enter `del *.*`. Confirm that you want to delete the files.
4 Change to the C drive, and delete the **etc** folder	
5 Verify that the etc folder has been deleted but the Marketing folder is still there	

Explain to students why they can't use the external MS-DOS command deltree.

Text files

Explanation

You can create a text file by using the MS-DOS `edit` command or a Windows GUI text-editing application such as Notepad.

To create a text file in the edit utility:

1. At the MS-DOS prompt, type `edit` and press Enter.
2. Enter the desired text.
3. If your mouse driver is loaded and functional, you can use the mouse to choose File, Save As. Otherwise, press Alt, F, A.
4. To change the current directory, press Alt+D. Use the arrow keys and Enter to navigate to the desired directory.
5. To move the insertion point to the File Name box, press Alt+N.
6. In the File Name box, type a file name, including the extension.
7. Press Tab several times to highlight the OK button, and then press Enter.
8. Press Alt, F, X to exit the edit utility.

To create a text file by using the Windows GUI text editor, Notepad:

1. Click Start and choose All Programs, Accessories, Notepad.
2. Enter the desired text.
3. Choose File, Save As.
4. From the Save in list, select the desired directory.
5. In the File name box, type a name for your file.
6. Verify that Text Documents (*.txt) is selected in the Save as type box.
7. Click Save.
8. Choose File, Exit.

Windows management **8–17**

Do it!

A Command Prompt window is open.

A-6: Creating a text file

Here's how	Here's why
1 Enter **edit**	To start the MS-DOS text editor. Because you ran the `edit` command from within a Command Prompt window, your mouse driver is loaded and available. However, you'll use keyboard shortcuts to choose menu items in this activity.
2 Type **This is my first text file created with the MS-DOS text editor.**	
3 Press `ALT`	The menu bar is highlighted. The commands are shown with their keyboard shortcuts in white.
Press `F`	To display the File menu. The keyboard shortcuts for File menu items are also displayed in white.
Press `A`	To open the Save As dialog box.
4 Press `ALT` + `D`	(While holding down Alt, press D.) To move the insertion point to the Directories box.
Press `↓` several times to highlight C	C: is added to the File Name box.
Press `ALT` + `N`	To move the insertion point back to the File Name box.
Press `END`	To move to the end of the File Name box, leaving C: entered in the box.
5 Type **\Users\PAADMIN##\My Text File.txt**	
Observe the buttons at the bottom of the Save As box	OK is highlighted.
Press `↵ ENTER`	To activate the OK button and save the file as My Text File on the C drive.
6 Press `ALT`, `F`, `X`	(In sequence, not simultaneously.) To close the text editor window.

Editing text files

Explanation

You can edit a text file by using the MS-DOS `edit` command or a Windows GUI text editing application, such as Notepad.

To edit a text file with the `edit` command:

1 At the MS-DOS prompt, type `edit` *drive*:*path**filename* and press Enter.
2 Modify the text as needed.
3 If your mouse driver is loaded and functional, you can use the mouse to choose File, Save. Otherwise, press Alt, F, S.
4 Press Alt, F, X to exit the edit program.

To edit a text file in Notepad:

1 Click Start and choose All Programs, Accessories, Notepad.
2 Choose File, Open.
3 In the Look in list, navigate to the folder containing the text file.
4 In the file list, select the desired file.
5 Click Open.
6 Modify the text.
7 Save the file and then exit the program.

Do it!

A-7: Editing a text file

A Command Prompt window is open.

Students can press Up Arrow to scroll through previous commands. They can then edit a command instead of retyping it.

Here's how	Here's why
1 Enter the following command: `edit "C:\Users\PAADMIN##\My Text File.txt"`	The text file opens in the MS-DOS text editor.
2 Press `END`	To move the insertion point to the end of the sentence.
3 Press `SPACEBAR` Type **I have edited this file by using edit.**	The text continues on one line. The MS-DOS text editor doesn't have the word-wrap feature that's included in GUI text editors, such as Notepad.
4 Press `ALT`, `F`, `S`	To save the changes in your file.
5 Press `ALT`, `F`, `X`	To exit the text editor.
6 Close the Command Prompt window	

Windows management **8–19**

Mounting a volume to a local folder

Explanation

Instead of assigning a drive letter to a volume, you can mount it to a local folder on an NTFS partition. Disk Management will assign a drive path instead of a drive letter. Windows creates what's called a *mount point* between the volume and the file system; the mount point provides invisible access to the mounted drive.

To mount a volume, in Disk Management, right-click the partition or volume you want to mount and click Change Drive Letter and Paths. Click Add, and click "Mount in the following empty NTFS folder." Type the path to the folder, or click Browse to find it.

Do it!

A-8: Mounting a volume

Here's how	Here's why
1 Click **Start**, right-click **Computer**, and choose **Manage**	To open Computer Management.
Click **Continue**	
2 Under Storage, select **Disk Management**	
3 Right-click the unallocated space on your primary disk and choose **New Simple Volume**	
Click **Next**	
4 In the size box, enter **5000**, and click **Next**	To create a 5 MB volume.
5 Select **Mount in the following empty NTFS folder**, and in the box, type **C:\Marketing**	To mount the new volume to the empty C:\Marketing folder.
Click **Next**	
6 Edit the Volume label box to read **My mount**	
Check **Perform a quick format** and click **Next**	
Click **Finish**	

There is a C:\Marketing folder and it is empty.

7	Open **Computer** and display the C:\ drive	
	Observe the new icon for the Marketing folder	Name 📄 marketing 📁 Program Files 📁 Users 📁 Windows It has changed to reflect the mounted volume.
8	Right-click the **Marketing** folder and choose **Properties**	
	Observe the General tab	marketing Type: Mounted Volume Location: C:\ Target: My mount You can see the mounted-drive icon and the Mounted Volume type in the description.
	Click **Cancel**	
9	In Disk Management, right-click **My mount** and choose **Change Drive Letter and Paths**	
	Click **Remove**	To remove the mount point.
	Click **Yes**	
10	In Computer, observe the Marketing folder	The icon has changed. The mount point has been removed.
11	Close all open windows	

Topic B: Resource management

This topic covers the following CompTIA A+ 220-702 exam objectives.

#	Objective
2.1	**Select the appropriate commands and options to troubleshoot and resolve problems** • NET
2.3	**Given a scenario, select and use system utilities / tools and evaluate the results** • Administrative Tools • Services • Regional and language settings

2.4	**Evaluate and resolve common issues**
	• Error messages and conditions
	  – System performance and optimization
	    • Aero settings
	    • Indexing settings
	    • Sidebar settings
	    • Background processes
	    • Startup file maintenance

Services

Explanation

When it comes to optimizing and securing a computer, one of the first things you can do is disable any unnecessary components, such as services. When a service is unnecessarily installed or is no longer used, you should disable it. Running unnecessary services consumes resources, such as memory and the CPU, and adds overhead to the system. If you're having a problem with a component on a computer, see if the service is running.

The Services console

You use the Services console (part of the Microsoft Management Console, or MMC) is shown in Exhibit 8-1. You can use it to configure a variety of settings related to how services function and respond to potential problems.

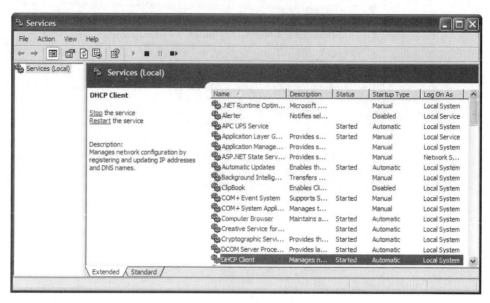

Exhibit 8-1: The Services console in Windows XP

The properties of a service are set on four dialog-box tabs, as follows:

- **General** — Displays the service's name and description, the path to the executable file, the startup parameters, and buttons you can click to start, stop, pause, and resume a service.
- **Log On** — Allows you to specify the user name that a service runs as, along with the hardware profiles for which the service is enabled.
- **Recovery** — Allows you to configure the computer's response when a service fails, including various actions depending on the number of failures. You can specify a program that the operating system should run when a service failure occurs.
- **Dependencies** — Specifies the services that a service depends on to function correctly, as well as the services that depend on this service in order to function.

Before you stop or disable a service, check to see if you're running any necessary services that depend on the service you want to disable. To do this, you use the Dependencies tab in the service's Properties dialog box. Exhibit 8-2 shows the Dependencies tab for the DHCP Client service.

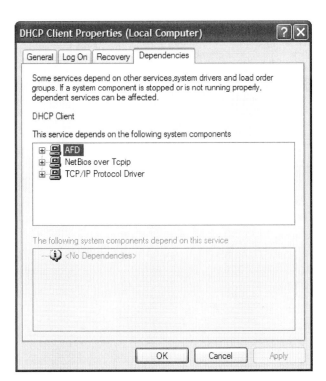

Exhibit 8-2: Dependencies for the DHCP Client service

Do it! **B-1: Configuring Windows services**

Here's how	Here's why
1 Click **Start** and choose **Control Panel**	
2 Click **System and Maintenance**	
3 Click **Administrative Tools**	
Double-click **Services** and click **Continue**	To open the Services console.
4 Right-click **Performance Logs and Alerts** and choose **Properties**	This service enables Performance Logs and Alerts. It's stopped and won't start unless you manually start it.
5 From the Startup type list, select **Automatic**	This sets the service to start automatically the next time the computer restarts.
6 Click **Apply**	
Click **Start**	To manually start the service.
7 Activate the Log On tab	To display the properties of the account under which the service runs.
8 Activate the Recovery tab	
9 From the First failure list, select **Restart the Service**	If necessary.
From the Second failure list, select **Run a Program**	
In the Program box, enter **cmd.exe**	This causes the Command Prompt program to start if the service fails for a second time.

10	Activate the Dependencies tab	
	Observe the list of services that the service depends on	The service depends on the Remote Procedure Call (RPC) service. A problem with RPC could cause problems with this service. There are no services that depend on the Performance Logs and Alerts service.
11	Click **OK**	To close the dialog box. The service is now listed as started.
12	Right-click **Performance Logs and Alerts** and choose **Stop**	To manually stop the service. Remember that the startup type is set to automatic, so the service will start again automatically the next time the computer restarts.
13	Close all open windows	

The net command

Explanation

Windows 2000, Windows XP, and Windows Vista include a command-line utility that you can use to manage and monitor the operating system. The `net` command provides a quick way to access specific information and perform several functions at the command line. The following table describes some of the parameters that are available for this command.

Parameter	Description
continue	Restarts a paused service.
pause	Pauses a service.
print	Displays print jobs and queues.
session	Lists or disconnects sessions between the computer and other computers.
share	Lists shares on the local computer, and shares local resources.
start	Lists running services, and starts a service.
stop	Stops services.
use	Connects and disconnects the computer from a network share.
view	Displays a list of computers on the network, and lists shared resources on a specific computer when used with a computer name.

Administrative command prompt

Some `net` command operations, such as starting and stopping services, require you to use an administrative command prompt. To open an administrative command prompt, click Start, right-click Command Prompt, and choose "Run as administrator."

Do it!

B-2: Using the net command

Here's how	Here's why
1 Click **Start** and choose **All Programs**, **Accessories**	
Right-click **Command Prompt**	
Choose **Run as administrator** and click **Continue**	To open the Command Prompt window with administrative privileges.
2 Enter **net view**	To see a list of computers on the network.
3 Enter **net share**	To see a list of shared folders on your computer.
Do you have any shared folders?	*Answers will vary.*

	4 Enter **net share Marketing=C:\Marketing**	To share the Marketing folder.
	5 Enter **net share**	To confirm that you've shared the folder and the share name is Marketing.
Assign students to work in pairs, or have students connect to your computer.	6 Enter **net use \\\\computername\Marketing**	To connect to the shared Users folder on another computer in the classroom.
Have students share user names and passwords.	Enter a user name when prompted	
	Enter a password when prompted	
	7 Enter **net use**	To confirm that you've connected to the shared folder.
	8 Enter **net use \\\\computername\Marketing /delete**	To remove the connection.
	9 Enter **net use**	To confirm that you've removed the connection to the shared Marketing folder on the other computer.
	10 Enter **net share marketing /delete**	To stop sharing the Marketing folder.
	11 Enter **net share**	To verify that the folder is no longer shared.
	12 Enter **net start**	To display the list of services running on your computer.
	13 Enter **net stop spooler**	To stop the Print Spooler service.
	Enter **net start spooler**	To start the service again.
	14 Enter **exit**	To close the Command Prompt window.

The Startup program group

Explanation

Many types of applications, such as work productivity, network connectivity, entertainment, and operating system support, can be installed on your Windows 2000 Professional, Windows XP, or Windows Vista computer. When they're installed, some applications are programmed to start up automatically, or to start up some of their components automatically, when you log into Windows. You find these applications or application components in your Startup program group, as shown in Exhibit 8-3.

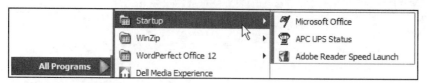

Exhibit 8-3: The Startup program group

Users can add applications to the Startup group manually by dragging items to it or by using Windows Explorer to copy and paste. Sometimes the addition is intentional, but sometimes it's inadvertent, and the addition can cause problems with startup. To edit the Startup program group, you can drag items onto or off of the Start menu. You can also right-click Start and choose Open All Users. Use Windows Explorer to copy and remove items.

Do it!

B-3: Observing the Startup program group

Here's how	Here's why
1 Click **Start** and choose **All Programs**, **Startup**	To display the list of applications that run automatically at startup. You can drag items onto and off of this menu.
2 Close the Start menu	
3 Right-click **Start** and choose **Explore All Users**	
In the navigation pane, expand **Programs**	
Select **Startup**	This shows the Startup program group items that apply to all users who log on to this computer. You can add or delete items from this window just as in any other file management window.
4 Close all open windows	

Regional and language settings

Explanation

Although regional and language settings are typically configured during Windows installation and then never touched again, you can reconfigure the settings at any time in the Control Panel. To access the settings in Windows Vista, open the Control Panel, click Clock, Language, and Region, and then click Regional and Language Options. (In Windows XP, open the Control Panel and double-click Regional and Language Options.)

The following table describes the settings you can configure on each tab of the Regional and Language Options dialog box.

Tab	Settings
Formats	The display of numbers, currency, dates, and times. All formats have default groups of settings, but all are customizable.
Location	Your computer's location, which can affect some applications that provide location-specific content.
Keyboards and Languages	Keyboard input configuration based on language and region, and language settings.
Administrative	The language for non-Unicode applications, and user settings.

Do it! **B-4: Exploring regional and language settings**

Here's how	Here's why
1 Open the Control Panel and click **Clock, Language, and Region**	
Click **Regional and Language Options**	To open the Regional and Language Options dialog box.
2 Observe the Formats tab	You can use these settings to control the display of currency, numbers, and dates and times. The current format was set during the Windows installation.
3 Click **Customize this format** and observe the settings on the various tabs	In the Customize Regional Options dialog box, you can configure very specific display settings, including decimal displays, currency formats, hour and minute displays, and long and short dates.
Click **Cancel**	To close the Customize Regional Options dialog box.
4 Activate and observe the Location tab	Again, the location was set during installation.
Display the **Current location** list	You can select any country in this list to specify your current location.
Press (ESC)	To close the list.
5 Activate and observe the Keyboards and Languages tab	You can change your keyboard input settings and the language Windows uses. You can install additional language packs to customize menus and dialog boxes.
6 Activate and observe the Administrative tab	You can configure the language for non-Unicode programs, and you can copy regional settings to new user accounts and specific system accounts.
7 Click **Cancel**	To close the Regional and Language Options dialog box.
Return to the main Control Panel window	Click the Back button.

Indexing

Explanation

Because it's faster to search through an index than it is to search through every file on a computer, Windows builds an index of files from specific folders in the directory structure. In Windows Vista, by default the index is built from the Offline Files, the Start Menu folder, and the Users folder. Because most users will store their files in their Documents or Pictures folders, the Users folder is a prime location for indexing. If users complain that their files aren't showing up when they search or that the search is slow, check to see if the correct folders are being indexed. If necessary, reconfigure the index by adding new folders, and then rebuild it.

To reconfigure or troubleshoot indexing in Windows Vista, open the Control Panel, click System and Maintenance, and then click Indexing Options. You can add or remove folders in the index list, and you can control index settings such as the index location and whether encrypted files are indexed. You can also rebuild the index or restore index settings to their defaults.

Do it!

B-5: Modifying indexing settings

Here's how	Here's why
1 In the Control Panel, click **System and Maintenance** and then click **Indexing Options**	To open the Indexing Options dialog box.
Observe the locations	You can see a list of folders from which Windows builds the index.
2 Click **Modify**	To open the Indexed Locations dialog box.
Click **Show all locations** and click **Continue**	
3 In the "Change selected locations" box, expand the C: drive	Don't check the C: drive.
Under the C: drive, check **Marketing**	So that Windows will index this folder.
Observe the "Summary of selected locations" box	Summary of selected locations Included Locations Internet Explorer History (P… marketing Offline Files (PAVISTA01\PA… Start Menu Users
	The Marketing folder has been added to the list.
4 Click **OK**	To close the Indexed Locations dialog box. The Marketing folder has been added to the list of indexed locations in the Indexing Options dialog box.
5 Click **Advanced** and then click **Continue**	To open the Advanced Options dialog box.
Observe the settings on the Index Settings tab	You can choose how Windows indexes encrypted files, you can rebuild the index, and you can change the location of the index.
6 Activate the File Types tab	
Scroll through the list	You can choose which file types are indexed.
7 Click **Cancel**	To close the Advanced Options dialog box.
Click **Close**	To close the Indexing Options dialog box.
Close the Control Panel	

Windows Aero

Explanation

Windows Aero is the name of the new user interface (UI) that Microsoft introduced with Windows Vista. The Windows UI had remained much the same from the introduction of Windows 95 up through Windows XP in 2001. This new UI includes the following features:

- Translucent windows, taskbar, and Start menu
- Taskbar thumbnails, which provide a preview of the windows they represent
- Three-dimensional Windows Flip, shown in Exhibit 8-4, which allows you to flip between open windows while seeing what's in each window

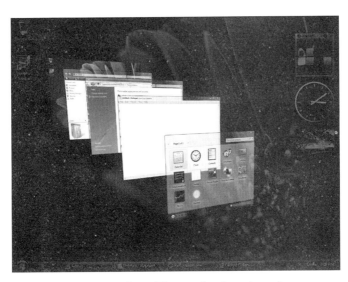

Exhibit 8-4: 3D Windows Flip in the Aero interface

Technical requirements

Windows Aero is available in Windows Vista Home Premium, Business, Windows, and Ultimate. The Windows Aero UI has several technical requirements:

- 1 GHz 32-bit (x86) or 64-bit (x64) processor
- 1 GB of system memory
- 128 MB graphics card
- DirectX 9–compatible graphics processor that supports a Windows Display Driver Model (WDDM) driver, Pixel Shader 2.0 in hardware, and 32 bits per pixel

Although you can install and use Windows Vista on a computer with a slower processor, less memory, and a non-compatible graphics card and processor, you won't be able to use the Windows Aero interface.

Personalizing the appearance of Windows

You can customize the appearance of Windows to suit your preferences by using the Personalization settings in the Control Panel. To access these settings, right-click the desktop and choose Personalize.

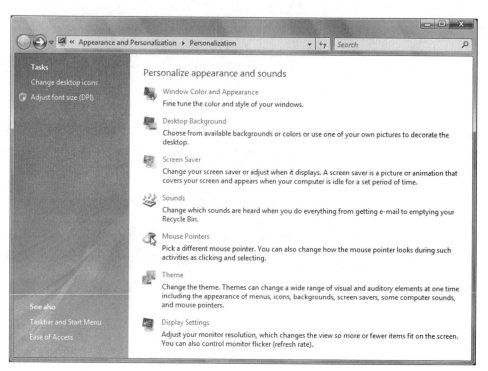

Exhibit 8-5: Personalization settings

The following table describes some of what you can do with the various settings.

Category	Use settings to...
Window Color and Appearance	Enable window transparency, and change the colors used for various window components.
Desktop Background	Add wallpaper, a background pattern, or a color to the desktop.
Screen Saver	Activate and control screen savers.
Sounds	Choose sound effects you hear when working with Windows.
Theme	Change the overall design of your system by using predefined combinations of backgrounds, sounds, colors, and icons.

Changing the desktop background

You can modify the desktop background, setting it to a color, pattern, or wallpaper of your choice. *Wallpaper* is a picture that appears on the desktop background. To change the desktop background:

1 Click Start and choose Control Panel.
2 Click Appearance and Personalization. You can also right-click an empty area of the desktop and choose Personalize to get to this step.
3 Click Desktop Background.
4 Select a picture category from the list, and then select the picture you want. You can also browse to a picture file you have saved elsewhere.

Exhibit 8-6: Choosing a background

Do it!

B-6: Personalizing the appearance of Windows

Here's how	Here's why
1 Click **Start** and choose **Documents**	To open the Documents folder.
Click **Start**	To display the Start menu.
2 Observe the Start menu, the edges of the Documents folder window, and the taskbar	The right side of the Start menu, the edges of the window, and most of the taskbar are translucent, showing features and objects beneath them. This is the Windows Aero interface.
3 Close Documents	
4 Right-click the desktop and choose **Personalize**	To open the Personalization window.
5 Click **Window Color and Appearance**	
Observe the settings	You can change the colors of the window and configure window transparency.
6 Select a new color and observe the window	You can see what the color would look like.
Experiment with the Color intensity slider bar	To lighten or darken the color you selected.
7 Clear **Enable transparency**	To see what the effect would be if window transparency were disabled.
Click **OK**	To save your settings.
8 Click **Desktop Background**	To choose a new desktop background.
From the Picture Location list, select **Sample Pictures**	You can choose wallpaper images from your Pictures folder, sample wallpapers included with Windows, images from the Public Pictures folder, or images from elsewhere.
9 From the Picture Location list, select **Windows Wallpapers**	
Select a new background	The desktop changes right away, so you can see how it will look.
After you find a background you like, click **OK**	To accept the new background and return to the Appearance and Personalization settings.
10 Close all open windows	

Troubleshooting Windows Aero

Explanation

Typically, you don't need to enable Windows Aero. If you install the correct version of Windows Vista on a computer that meets the technical requirements, Windows Aero is the default UI. If Windows Aero isn't displayed, or if you're not seeing all of its effects, you can troubleshoot the problem by using the suggestions in the following table.

Possible cause	Solution
Edition of Windows Vista doesn't support Windows Aero	Install Windows Vista Home Premium, Business, Enterprise, or Ultimate. You can upgrade from Windows Vista Home Premium and Windows Vista Business to Windows Vista Ultimate.
Hardware doesn't support Windows Aero	Check the computer's hardware against the published requirements, and install new hardware as necessary.
Video card driver out of date	Install a new driver for the video card.
Incorrect display settings	Verify that the color setting is 32-bit and the refresh rate is set to at least 10 Hz.
Incorrect desktop theme	Set the desktop theme to Windows Vista, and the color scheme to Windows Aero. Verify that window transparency is enabled.
Window transparency not enabled; power settings on a mobile computer disable window transparency	Enable window transparency. On a mobile computer, select a power plan other than the power saver plan, and verify that window transparency is enabled.
Application doesn't support Windows Aero	Upgrade to a new version of the application, if possible.

Do it!

B-7: Troubleshooting Windows Aero settings

Here's how	Here's why
1 True or false? All applications support Windows Aero	*False. Some applications don't. You can check for upgrades for any applications that don't currently support Windows Aero.*
2 If a computer doesn't display the Windows Aero UI, what's the first thing you should check?	*Check whether the currently installed version of Windows Vista supports Windows Aero.*
What's the second?	*Check that the computer meets the hardware requirements.*

Windows Sidebar

Explanation

The *Windows Sidebar*, shown in Exhibit 8-7, holds small programs that Microsoft calls gadgets. Essentially, *gadgets* perform small, simple functions that you might commonly need but that don't need your full attention. Examples include a clock, a calculator, sticky notes, news feeds, and small games and slide shows. To open the Windows Sidebar when it's closed, click Start and choose All Programs, Accessories, Windows Sidebar.

Exhibit 8-7: Gadgets in the Windows Sidebar

Gadgets can be added to, moved in, and removed from the Windows Sidebar as you wish. A few gadgets are present by default, but you can change these easily. You can even drag gadgets onto the desktop and leave them there.

To move a gadget, click its handle and drag it to where you want it. Gadgets in the Windows Sidebar will automatically rearrange themselves when you move one of them. When you drag a gadget, you need to grab its handle, because with some gadgets, clicking directly on them means that you want to do something like write a new reminder note or open a news article.

You add new gadgets from the Gadget Gallery, shown in Exhibit 8-8. To open it, click the plus button at the top of the Sidebar, or right-click the Sidebar and choose Add Gadgets. You can then right-click the gadget you want and choose Add, or just double-click the gadget to add it. The gallery also has a link for getting gadgets online.

Exhibit 8-8: The Gadget Gallery in Windows Vista

Configuring gadget settings

Many gadgets have properties you can set. For instance, you can choose different faces for the clock or different colors for the sticky notes. When you hold the mouse pointer over a gadget, its control buttons appear to the right. Click the button that looks like a wrench to open the gadget's settings; Exhibit 8-9 shows an example. You can also right-click the gadget and choose Options.

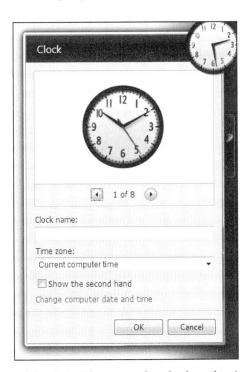

Exhibit 8-9: Changing the clock gadget's settings

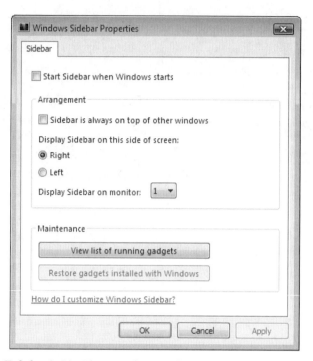

Exhibit 8-10: The Windows Sidebar Properties dialog box

Setting the Windows Sidebar properties

To open the Windows Sidebar Properties dialog box, shown in Exhibit 8-10, right-click a blank area of the Windows Sidebar and choose Properties. Here you can adjust whether the Windows Sidebar is always on top, when it starts, and what side of the screen it starts on. For instance, to prevent the Sidebar from opening when Windows starts, do this:

1. Right-click a blank area of the Sidebar and choose Properties.
2. Clear the "Start Sidebar when Windows starts" checkbox.
3. Click OK.

Removing gadgets

To remove a gadget, click the Close button (the X button) to the right of it. You can also right-click the gadget and choose Close Gadget.

Hiding and exiting the Windows Sidebar

To hide the Windows Sidebar, right-click it and choose Close Sidebar to minimize it to an icon in the notification area. When you hide Windows Sidebar, the gadgets continue to run even though they are not visible. To display the Windows Sidebar again, click its icon in the notification area.

To exit the Windows Sidebar, right-click the Sidebar's icon in the notification area and choose Exit. When you exit Windows Sidebar, the gadgets are closed, too.

Windows management **8–41**

B-8: Configuring the Windows Sidebar

Do it!

Here's how	Here's why
1 Click **Start** and choose **All Programs**, **Accessories**, **Windows Sidebar** *(Skip this step if Windows Sidebar is already running.)*	To open the Windows Sidebar.
2 Observe the Sidebar	A default selection of gadgets is loaded, including a clock and a slideshow. A faded background partially obscures the desktop background.
3 Point to a blank area under the gadgets	Windows displays a border around the Windows Sidebar area.
4 Drag the clock to the bottom of the Windows Sidebar *(Drag it to the top if it's already at the bottom.)*	You can click and hold anywhere on the clock face. Notice how the other gadgets move when you drop the clock at its new location.
5 Point to the clock and then, to its right, click as shown	The button that looks like a wrench will open the clock's settings, shown in Exhibit 8-9.
6 Change the clock face to one of your choosing	Use the arrow buttons under the face in the settings dialog box.
7 Click **OK**	To close the settings and change the clock.
8 Right-click a blank area of the Sidebar and choose **Add Gadgets...**	To open the Gadget Gallery.
9 Double-click **Notes**	To add it to the Windows Sidebar.
10 Close the Gadget Gallery	
11 Right-click a blank area of the Windows Sidebar and choose **Properties**	To open the Properties dialog box. You can use it to configure the Windows Sidebar.
12 Check **Sidebar is always on top of other windows**	So that the Windows Sidebar will always appear on top of open windows. This way, it will always be displayed and not hidden behind a window.
13 Click **View list of running gadgets**	To display a list of gadgets that are installed. You can use this dialog box to remove gadgets from the Windows Sidebar.
14 Click **Close** and then click **OK**	To close the dialog boxes.

15	Point to the Notes gadget Click where indicated	To close the gadget.
	Click **Close Gadget**	To confirm that you want to close Notes.
16	Right-click a blank part of the Sidebar and choose **Close Sidebar**	The Sidebar and its gadgets disappear, but the Sidebar is still running.
17	In the notification area, click	(Probably the leftmost button in that area.) To show the Windows Sidebar again.
18	Right-click and choose **Exit**	In the notification area.
	If necessary, click **Exit Sidebar**	To exit the Windows Sidebar.

Windows management 8–43

Topic C: Remote management

This topic covers the following CompTIA A+ 220-702 exam objectives.

#	Objective
2.3	**Given a scenario, select and use system utilities / tools and evaluate the results** • Remote Desktop Protocol (Remote Desktop / Remote Assistance)

Remote Assistance

Explanation

Remote Assistance provides a way for a user to ask someone at another computer for help with a computer problem. Remote Assistance allows the helping user to see the other user's desktop and, when permitted, to take control of that system temporarily to resolve problems. Some organizations might have a network configuration that prevents a second user from taking control of the first computer's keyboard and mouse; this will depend on your specific network setup. Theoretically, depending on network configuration, you can ask for and receive help on just about any Windows Vista computer in the world.

The Remote Assistance session works like this:

1 You invite someone to help you by creating and making available an invitation. You can send an e-mail message to the person you're asking for help, or you can create an invitation file that you can put in a shared location, attach to an e-mail message, or send through an instant messaging program. You must also give the helper the password associated with the invitation.

2 The helper accepts your invitation and enters the password.

3 You show the helper the problems you're experiencing. He or she can then answer your question or take control of your computer (if permitted) to fix the problem.

4 Either you or the helper then ends the session.

In Windows Vista, Remote Assistance is enabled by default. To configure Remote Assistance settings, click Start, right-click Computer, and choose Properties. Under Tasks, click Remote settings, and enter a password if prompted. On the Remote tab, you can enable or disable Remote Assistance. Click Advanced to enable or disable remote control of your computer and to set time limits for invitations.

To create an invitation, open Windows Help and Support, click Ask, and then click the Windows Remote Assistance link. Click "Invite someone you trust to help you"; choose to use e-mail to invite the friend or create an invitation; and then complete the wizard.

Do it!

C-1: Requesting Remote Assistance

Here's how	Here's why
1 Click **Start**, right-click **Computer**, and choose **Properties**	You're going to configure Remote Assistance and then request assistance from the instructor.
Under Tasks, click **Remote settings**	
Click **Continue**	
2 Observe the Remote Assistance section	Remote Assistance is currently enabled. You can clear the checkbox to disable Remote Assistance.
3 Click **Advanced**	
Observe the Remote control section	You can disable remote control by clearing this checkbox. Currently it's enabled, but your friend will still need to request permission before taking control.
Observe the Invitations section	You can set a time limit on invitations you create.
4 In the number list, select **1**	Set the maximum amount of time invitations can remain open: 1 Hours
	To set the time limit to 1 hour. After that time, invitations will expire.
5 Click **OK** twice, and close the System window	
6 Open Windows Help and Support	You're going to request help from your instructor.
Under Ask someone, click **Windows Remote Assistance**	
7 Click **Invite someone you trust to help you**	You can then send an e-mail message or save the invitation as a file.
8 Click **Save this invitation as a file**	If you had an open invitation that you'd already created, you could use that one by clicking it.
Click **Browse** and locate and select the **Public Documents** folder	This is an easy location to put an invitation in.

If students are asked whether to get the latest online Help content, have them click Yes.

Public Folder sharing has been enabled.

Windows management

9	In the File name box, type ***firstname*'s Invitation** Click **Save**	Where *firstname* is your first name.
10	Enter and confirm a password of **!pass1234** Click **Finish**	You will need to give this password to your helper so he or she can accept the invitation.
11	Observe the Windows Remote Assistance window	Remote Assistance indicates that it's waiting for an incoming connection. At this point, you'd notify your helper that you've created an invitation and put it in the Public Documents folder on your computer. You'd also tell your helper what the password is.

Do it!

C-2: Participating in a Remote Assistance session

Here's how

You can participate with all of the students one by one, or select a student and have other students watch the session.

1 Wait for your instructor to accept your invitation. Click **Yes** when asked whether to accept the connection.

2 Click **Chat** and explain to your instructor what the problem is. Open your personal folder and Windows Calendar.

3 Allow your instructor to take control of your session. Watch as your instructor opens and closes folder windows and programs.

4 End the session.

5 Access the remote settings and disable Remote Assistance.

Remote Desktop

Explanation

You can use Remote Desktop and the Remote Desktop Protocol (RDP) to connect to remote Windows Vista computers—"remote" meaning a computer that is on another desk, in another building, across a campus, on a different floor in the same building, or almost anywhere in the world. Using Remote Desktop, you can access any program or folder, the Control Panel, network configuration tools, and just about any other feature on the remote computer.

Exhibit 8-11: A remote connection

To enable Remote Desktop in Windows Vista, click Start, right-click Computer, and choose Properties. Click Remote settings, and enter an administrative password or click Continue. Then select one of the "Allow connections…" options. Remote Desktop is enabled by default, but you need to verify that it's enabled on the computer you want to connect to.

Not every user can connect remotely with Remote Desktop. By default, computer administrators already have permission, but you can select other users and allow them to make remote connections.

To allow users to connect, open the System Properties dialog box, activate the Remote tab, and click Select Users. Click Add, type the name of the user account, and click OK.

Windows management **8-47**

Do it!

C-3: Enabling Remote Desktop

Here's how	Here's why
1 Click **Start**, right-click **Computer**, and choose **Properties**	
2 Click **Remote settings** and click **Continue**	You will enable Remote Desktop.
3 In the Remote Desktop section, verify that "Allow connections from computer running any version of Remote Desktop (less secure)" is selected	Only users with administrative privileges can enable this feature.
4 Click **Select Users** and observe the Remote Desktop Users dialog box	Except for your PAADMIN## account, no users are permitted to access the computer through Remote Desktop. You can add any users to this list.
5 Click **Cancel**	To close the Remote Desktop Users dialog box.
6 Click **OK**	To close the System Properties dialog box.
Close any open windows	

If students see a window about sleep settings, have them click OK.

Connecting remotely

Explanation

You can connect to a Windows Vista or Windows XP computer with Remote Desktop enabled from any Windows computer with Remote Desktop Connection, unless the remote computer is in sleep mode or in hibernation. When you connect to the remote computer, its console is locked, preventing anyone from working on it while the remote connection is established. Although the Remote Desktop feature redirects output to the remote computer, all programs and utilities run locally on the remote computer.

To access Remote Desktop Connection in Windows Vista, click Start and choose All Programs, Accessories, Remote Desktop Connection.

Windows management **8–49**

Do it!

Pair two students together for this activity. One partner should connect while the other observes.

C-4: Making a Remote Desktop connection

Here's how	Here's why
1 At one partner's computer, click **Start** and choose **All Programs**, **Accessories**, **Remote Desktop Connection**	
2 In the Computer box, enter the name of your partner's computer	Get this information from your partner.
Click **Options**	To display more of the dialog box.
Observe the tabs	You can use the settings on these tabs to configure the remote connection. You will be prompted for a user name and password when you connect.
3 Click **Connect**	
In the User name box, type your partner's PAADMIN## user name	
In the Password box, type **!pass1234**	Or whatever your partner's password is.
4 Click **OK**	To connect to your partner's remote computer.
Click **Yes**	To log your partner off of the other computer.
5 On the remote computer, click **OK**	(If necessary.) To allow the connection.
6 Experiment with opening programs and folders on the remote computer	
7 Observe the title bar	You can see the name of the computer you're connected to, and there are Minimize, Restore Down, and Close buttons.
8 Experiment with the Control menu buttons	To see what it's like to minimize, maximize, and restore the Remote Desktop Connection window.
9 Click **Start** and log off	To close the remote connection to your partner's computer.
On the remote computer, log back on	
10 Switch roles with your partner and repeat the activity	

Unit summary: Windows management

Topic A In this topic, you learned how to manage directories and files by using the **command-line utility** and the Windows Explorer GUI. You learned how to navigate the **directory structure** and how to create, copy, and delete files and directories.

Topic B In this topic, you learned how to manage Windows **services** by using the Services console and the **net command**. You also learned how to identify startup items and how to manage those items by using the **Startup program group**. You then learned how to configure regional and language settings, and you configured indexing, Windows Aero, and the Windows Sidebar.

Topic C In this topic, you learned how to manage and troubleshoot problems remotely by using the **Remote Desktop** and **Remote Assistance** features.

Review questions

1 Hard disks are divided into usable storage spaces through:

   A Files

   B Folders

   C Directories

   D Partitions

2 To organize information under the root of a hard disk partition, you can use which of the following? [Choose all that apply.]

   A Files

   B Folders

   C Directories

   D Partitions

3 Which command-line command is used to change the current directory?

   A `dir`

   B `cd`

   C `md`

   D `rd`

4 Which utility enables you to connect to a remote computer and work as if you were sitting at that computer?

   Remote Desktop

5 What `dir` command would you use to view all hidden files in C:\Windows\System32 in alphabetical order, by extension, across multiple columns?

   dir c:\windows\system32 /w /a:h /o:e

Windows management **8–51**

6 True or false? Remote Assistance is enabled by default.

True

7 True or false? By default, any user can offer assistance to another user by using the Remote Assistance utility.

False

8 When you're creating a directory in Windows Explorer, what's the maximum depth of the folder structure?

A 63 characters

B 254 characters

C 255 characters

D Unlimited

9 What's the difference between the command-line commands `copy` and `xcopy`?

The copy command copies one or more files to another location. The xcopy command copies files (not including hidden and system files), directories, and subdirectories.

10 True or false? By default, any user can make a Remote Desktop connection.

False

Independent practice activity

In this activity, you'll practice managing your Windows computer.

1. Using a Command Prompt window, create two folders on your C: drive. Give them any names you choose.
2. Using the edit utility, create two text files in one of the folders.
3. Use the Command Prompt window to copy the two files to the other folder.
4. Configure Windows to index both folders.
5. Use the `net` command to share both folders. Display a list of shared folders on your computer to verify that they've been shared. (*Hint:* You will need to run Command Prompt in Administrator mode.)
6. Stop sharing both folders.
7. Use the Command Prompt window to delete both folders and their contents.
8. Add an application such as Notepad to your Startup group.
9. Log off and log back on to verify that your chosen application runs on startup.
10. Remove the application from the Startup group.
11. Log off and log back on to verify that your chosen application no longer runs on startup.
12. Configure Windows Aero with a new, personalized look.
13. Work with another student in a Remote Assistance session. Choose who will be the helper and who will ask for help. Create a scenario that your student partner can help you answer.

Unit 9
Windows maintenance

Unit time: 240 minutes

Complete this unit, and you'll know how to:

A Monitor the operating system.

B Perform operating system maintenance tasks.

C Configure Task Scheduler.

D Troubleshoot operating system problems.

Topic A: Monitoring

This topic covers the following CompTIA A+ 220-702 exam objectives.

#	Objective
2.3	**Given a scenario, select and use system utilities / tools and evaluate the results** • System Monitor • Administrative Tools 　– Event Viewer 　– Performance Monitor • Task Manager 　– Process list 　– Resource usage 　– Process priority 　– Termination
2.4	**Evaluate and resolve common issues** • Error Messages and Conditions 　– Event Viewer (errors in the event log)

Resource Overview

Explanation

Reliability and Performance Monitor contains an important tool called *Resource Overview*, which you can use to assess and maintain the health of your system. As shown in Exhibit 9-1, Resource Overview is the first tool you see when you open Reliability and Performance Monitor. It provides real-time graphs and detailed information about four key components:

- **CPU** — Displays CPU utilization.
- **Hard disk** — Displays the disk input/output statistics.
- **Network** — Details network traffic.
- **Memory (RAM)** — Displays memory statistics, including the percent of memory used and the number of hard page faults.

Under the graphs are corresponding sections that you can expand to see more detailed information. Just click the associated graph to see more detailed information about that component's current performance.

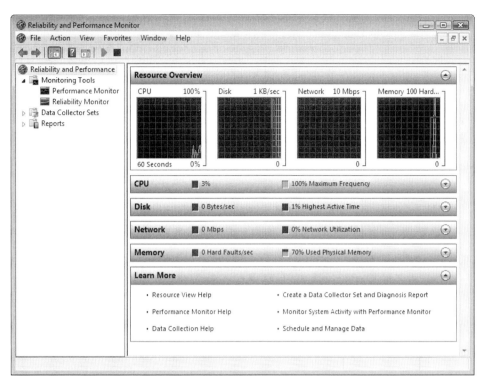

Exhibit 9-1: Resource Overview

To open Reliability and Performance Monitor and display Resource Overview:

1. In the Control Panel, click System and Maintenance. Then click Performance Information and Tools.
2. In the left pane, click Advanced tools.
3. Click "Open Reliability and Performance Monitor." Click Continue.

You can also view Reliability and Performance information in the Computer Management console.

Do it!

A-1: Viewing real-time performance data in Resource Overview

Here's how	Here's why
1 Open Computer Management	
2 Under System Tools, select **Reliability and Performance**	To display the Resource Overview.
3 Observe the four graphs	Each graph is scrolling to the left, showing you the level of activity for each component.
4 Click the CPU graph	To display the details. You can see which applications and processes are accessing the CPU.
5 Click the CPU graph again	To close its details section.

Performance Monitor

Explanation

You use Performance Monitor, shown in Exhibit 9-2, to monitor computer performance in real time (in one-second intervals), or in the form of saved reports of real-time data. (Performance Monitor was known as System Monitor in Windows 2000.) Hundreds of computer performance variables called *counters* are available for you to measure and assess a computer's performance. For example, you can:

- Create a baseline to compare system performance over time.
- Monitor system resource usage.
- Identify performance problems.
- Identify performance bottlenecks.

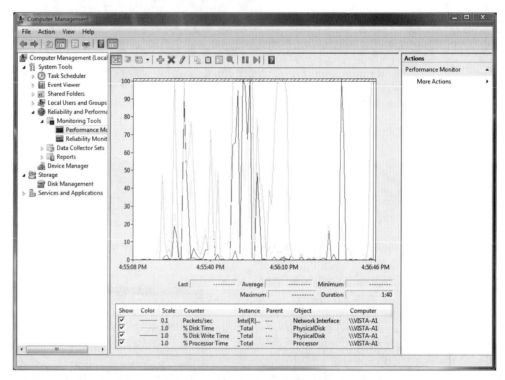

Exhibit 9-2: Performance Monitor real-time graph in Windows Vista

The counters are categorized by *performance object*, which is any resource that you can measure. Here are some of the more commonly used performance objects:

- Cache
- Memory
- Objects
- Paging File
- PhysicalDisk
- Process
- Processor
- System
- Thread

Bottlenecks

A bottleneck occurs when a shortage of a particular system resource causes a performance problem. You can identify some common system-resource shortages by using the following counters:

Counter	Description
Processor: % Processor Time	Monitors how hard your processor is working. A number consistently exceeding 75% indicates that your processor is being overworked. If purchasing a new system with a more powerful processor is not an option, you can try to take some of the burden off the processor by: • Adding more RAM to the system • Reducing the number of programs that run simultaneously • Verifying that an individual program is not taking control of the processor and then failing to release it
Process: Thread Count	Displays the numbers of threads active in a process. *Threads* are pieces of software code that are loaded into memory. When an application opens, it can take control of multiple memory threads to accomplish its tasks. When the application closes, it should release the threads, thereby freeing them up for other applications. When an application opens threads in memory but fails to close them, this situation is called a *memory leak*. (It's typically caused by poor application programming.) Monitoring the Thread Count can help you identify memory leaks in applications.
Memory: Pages/sec	Monitors the rate at which pages are read from or written to disk. This counter can point to page faults that cause system delays. You might need to add RAM.
PhysicalDisk: Disk Transfers/sec	Records the rate of read and write operations on your disk. If the value recorded exceeds 25 disk I/Os per second, you have poor disk-response time. This can cause a bottleneck that affects response time for applications running on your system. It might be time to upgrade your hardware to use faster disks or scale out your application to better handle the load. (Scaling out an application means adding one or more servers to your distributed software application.)

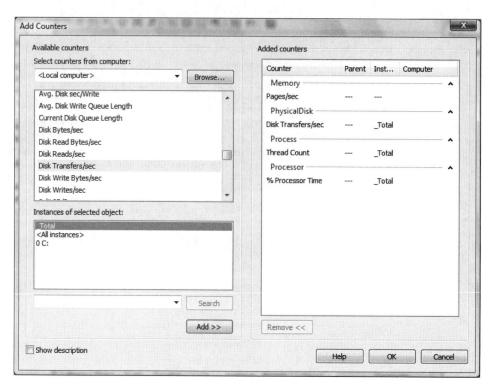

Exhibit 9-3: Adding counters

Real-time monitoring

To monitor resources in real time, you add counters to the Performance Monitor graph. Right-click the graph and choose Add Counters to open the dialog box shown in Exhibit 9-3. Then, in the Add Counters dialog box:

1. Specify whether you want to monitor resources on the local computer or a remote computer.
2. In the list of performance objects, expand the performance object that contains the counter you want to add.
3. Select the desired counter.
4. Select an instance of the counter. *Instances* are unique copies of a performance object (for example, a network card or hard disk).
5. Click Add.
6. When you've added all the counters you want, click OK.

Do it!

A-2: Monitoring performance

Here's how	Here's why
1 In the console tree, expand **Reliability and Performance**	
Under Monitoring Tools, select **Performance Monitor**	To open Performance Monitor.
2 Observe the empty graph	After you add counters, this is where the real-time data will be displayed. Under the graph is a list of the counters it displays (it's empty now).
3 Right-click the empty graph and choose **Add Counters...**	
4 Click the down-arrow next to Processor	To expand that performance object and display its associated counters.
5 Select **%Processor Time** and observe the "Instances of selected object" box	Depending on the number of processors (or if you have a dual-core processor), you might see more than one instance.
Select **_Total** and click **Add**	To add the total %Processor Time to the list of added counters.
6 Scroll up, collapse **Processor**, and expand **Process**	It's easier to scroll when you don't have performance objects expanded.
Select **Thread Count** and observe the list of instances	All of the process threads are listed. If you needed to monitor a specific thread, you could select it from the list.
Verify that **_Total** is selected, and click **Add**	
7 Add **Memory: Pages/sec** and **PhysicalDisk: Disk Transfers/sec** to the Added counters list	Repeat the procedure of expanding the performance object, selecting the counter, and clicking Add.
8 After you've added all four counters, click **OK**	

9	Observe the graph	The real-time monitoring has begun. In a moment, you'll generate some activity to see how the graph spikes when you use the computer.
	Observe the list of counters	You can see the four counters you added, and each has been assigned a different color. You can uncheck one of the checkboxes to remove the counter's display from the graph. The counter will be temporarily hidden, but not deleted.
10	Open Internet Explorer, and then open the Control Panel and the Documents folder	To generate activity on the computer.
	Switch to Computer Management and observe the graph	The activity has generated some data, so you might see counters you didn't see just a few minutes ago.
11	Browse to a couple of Web pages	To generate more activity and some network traffic.
	Observe the graph	You can use this data to help determine where there might be some performance bottlenecks on your computer. Depending on what information you're trying to find, you can add or remove dozens of counters to measure a computer's performance.
12	Close all open windows except for Computer Management	

If students are asked to customize their Internet Explorer settings, tell them to leave Suggested Sites off and use express settings.

Performance Monitor configuration

Explanation

As with other Windows utilities, you can customize Performance Monitor to suit your needs. The following table describes some of the more useful buttons on the toolbar above the graph.

Button	Use to...
	Open saved log files and display them in Performance Monitor.
	Change the Performance Monitor display from a line graph to a histogram or a text-based report.
	Add and delete counters.
	Highlight counters so you can see their lines on the graph more easily.
	Open the Performance Monitor Properties dialog box.
	Pause and restart the real-time display.
	Update data, one click at a time.

You can also use the Performance Monitor Properties dialog box to configure Performance Monitor and the display of data. The following table describes the tabs and the settings you can configure on them.

Tab	Use to configure...
General	The display of components, such as the legend and the toolbar; how much data is displayed in the histogram and report views; whether Performance Monitor should collect samples automatically; how often samples should be collected; and how long the samples should be displayed.
Source	Whether the data source to be displayed is real-time data or comes from a saved log file.
Data	How data is displayed, including which counters should be displayed, and the color, scale, width, and style of the line displayed for each counter.
Graph	Graph elements, such as the view, scroll style, title and vertical axis labels, and scale.
Appearance	General appearance values, including colors and font.

Do it!

A-3: Configuring Performance Monitor

Here's how	Here's why
1 On the Performance Monitor toolbar, click	To open the Properties dialog box.
2 Activate the General tab and observe the settings	You can configure some display options and the performance sample interval.
3 Change Sample every to **2**, and the Duration to **30**	Graph elements — Sample every: 2 seconds; Duration: 30 seconds. The data will now be updated every two seconds, and the graph will display 30 seconds' worth of data.
Click **OK** and observe the changes in the line graph	It updates more slowly and doesn't contain as much data as it did before.
4 Open the Properties dialog box	
Change the Sample every and Duration settings back to **1** and **100**, respectively	
5 Activate the Data tab	
Select the **Disk Transfer/sec** counter and change the line width to the thickest setting	
Select the **%Processor Time** counter and change it to a dark color (if necessary)	
Change the counter's line style to the dash style, as shown	Style: — — —
6 Activate the Graph tab	
Change the scroll style to **Scroll**	
Change the vertical scale maximum to **50**	
7 Click **OK** and observe the changes	More of the data is displayed, some of the lines are different, and the data is scrolling right to left.

Have students open and close programs again to generate activity.

8	On the Performance Monitor toolbar, click [icon]	To change the line graph to a histogram, which provides another way to display the data graphically.
	Click [icon] again	To change the histogram to a text-based report. The data is still presented in real time, but it's text-based rather than graphical.
	Return the display to a line graph	
9	In the list of counters, select the **Disk Transfers/sec** counter, and then click [icon]	To highlight the counter.
	Click the button again	To turn off highlighting.
10	Click [icon]	To freeze the display.
	Click [icon] a few times	To update the data manually.
	Click [icon]	To unfreeze the display.
11	In the list of counters, select the **Thread Count** counter and click [icon]	To delete the counter.

Reliability Monitor

Explanation

In addition to knowing how well your system components are operating, you'll also want to know the overall reliability of your system, including the hardware components, applications, and the Windows Vista operating system itself. Reliability Monitor is one tool you can use to assess the stability of a system over a period of time and pinpoint any components that might be causing system problems.

Reliability Monitor tracks the following events that affect system stability:

- Software installs and uninstalls
- Application failures
- Hardware failures
- Windows failures
- Miscellaneous failures

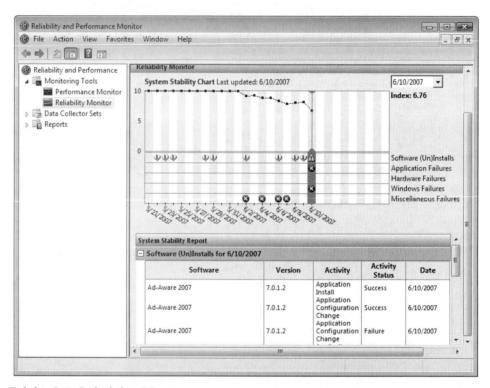

Exhibit 9-4: Reliability Monitor

Reliability Monitor, shown in Exhibit 9-4, provides two features you can use to track and troubleshoot system health:

- **System Stability Chart** — A calendar-based chart that tracks reliability and the events that affect it over a 28-day period. Each day Reliability Monitor assigns a number, called the *Stability Index*, to system stability. The Index ranges from 1.0 (least stable) to 10.0 (most stable). You can track the rise and fall of the index and match that number to the logged events to help determine what exactly is affecting system stability.

    You can display specific date ranges and see a current average index. In Exhibit 9-4, you can see that several events began to affect the index and brought it down from 10.0 to 6.76. Resolving the problems that caused those events will increase system stability.

- **System Stability Report** — A report that provides details for the day you select in the System Stability Chart. You can use the report to see details about the events that affected the Stability Index that day.

To open Reliability Monitor, open the Control Panel, click System and Maintenance, and click Performance Information and Tools. In the left pane, click Advanced tools, and then click Open Reliability and Performance Monitor. In the tree pane, select Reliability Monitor. You can also open Reliability Monitor in Computer Management.

Do it!

A-4: Determining a system's Stability Index

Here's how	Here's why
1 In Reliability and Performance Monitor, under Monitoring Tools, select **Reliability Monitor**	
2 Observe the System Stability Chart	The Stability Index is represented by a black line, with a dot on each day to indicate that day's number. If there have been any events, they're logged as icons to indicate an informational event, a warning, or an error.
3 If possible, select a day with an icon and observe the System Stability Report	To see the event details for that day. Only event categories that logged events will open in the report. You can use this information to track problems and increase system stability.
4 Select any other days with icons	To view the events on those days.
5 What's your current Stability Index? Is it trending up or down? Why?	*Answers will vary.*
6 How might you increase the Stability Index?	*Answers might include: uninstall problem applications; and replace hardware components.*
7 Close all open windows	

Encourage students to share their details.

Task Manager

Explanation

Ctrl+Shift+Esc also opens Task Manager.

As you know, Task Manager is a Windows GUI utility that provides information about the applications, processes, and services that are running on a computer. A version of Task Manager is available in all Windows operating systems.

To open Task Manager, press Ctrl+Alt+Delete and then click Task Manager. You can also right-click an empty part of the taskbar and choose Task Manager.

Depending on the version of Windows installed, Task Manager will contain some or all of the tabs described in the following table.

Tab	Description
Application	Displays the status of applications running on the computer. You can end an application, switch to a running application, or start an application.
Processes	Displays information about the processes that are running on the computer. Each process entry displays the name of the executable file, the name of the account running the application (it might be a system service account), the process's percentage of CPU usage, and the amount of memory the process is using.
	You can end processes from this tab, and you can configure process priority so that a process runs as Low, Below Normal, Normal, Above Normal, High, or Realtime priority. The operating system kernel responds to processes with a higher priority before responding to those with a lower priority. Be careful if you set the priority for a process too high; other programs might slow down because they are getting less I/O time.
Services	Displays a list of running and stopped services. You can open the Services console from this tab.
Performance	Displays a dynamic representation of the most common performance indicators for your computer. You'll see graphs for CPU and page file usage; summary totals for the number of handles, threads, and processes running; and totals for physical, kernel, and commit-charge memory.
Networking	Displays a dynamic graphical representation of your current network utilization. For each network adapter installed, Task Manager lists the percentage of network utilization, the link speed of the connection, and the state of the connection.
Users	Displays the names and status of any users currently logged on. You can log users off or disconnect them by using this tab. The Users tab is available on Windows XP and Windows Vista computers that aren't members of a domain and that have Fast User Switching enabled. (Several features can affect Fast User Switching, such as domain membership and Offline Files.)

The Performance tab was covered in Unit 3, "Memory systems."

Exhibit 9-5 shows all of the Windows Task Manager tabs in Windows Vista.

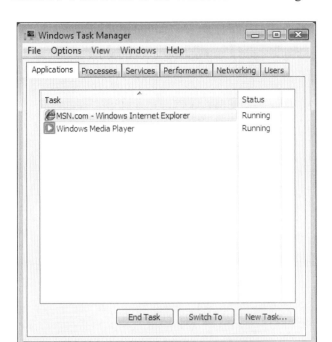

Exhibit 9-5: Task Manager in Windows Vista

The Applications tab

You can use the Applications tab in Task Manager to end a running application. This is helpful when a general protection fault (GPF) occurs and an application isn't responding to keyboard or mouse input. To end a running application:

1. On the Applications tab, select the application you want to end.
2. Click End Task.
3. If the application still isn't responding, Windows will display a dialog box telling you that the application isn't responding. Click End Task.

You can also use the Applications tab to switch to another application. For example, if an application is running, but is running in the background or doesn't have a taskbar button displayed, you can use Task Manager to switch to the application.

1. On the Applications tab, select the application you want to switch to.
2. Click Switch To. This minimizes Task Manager and places the selected application on top of the desktop.

You can start a new instance of an application from within Task Manager. This is helpful if the explorer.exe process has stopped and you have lost your Start menu, taskbar, and desktop items. Creating a new task to start explorer.exe will fix the problem. To do so:

1. On the Applications tab, click New Task.
2. In the Open box, type the name of the executable file (or browse to navigate to it).
3. Click OK.

Do it!

A-5: Monitoring applications

Here's how	Here's why
1 Open Documents and a Command Prompt window Minimize both windows	
2 Right-click an empty section of the taskbar and choose **Task Manager**	
3 Activate the Applications tab	
4 Select **Documents** and click **Switch To**	Task Manager minimizes to the taskbar, and the Documents folder is now active.
5 On the taskbar, click **Windows Task Manager**	
6 Select **Command Prompt**	If this application had experienced a GPF, its status would be "Not responding."
7 Click **End Task**	To end the Command Prompt application.
8 Click **New Task**	
In the Open box, type **notepad** and then click **OK**	An instance of Notepad runs, and it's listed on the Applications tab.

The Processes tab

Explanation

The Processes tab is helpful when you need to determine if a running process is overwhelming the processor and slowing the system down. Here's how you do that:

1. Activate the Processes tab.
2. As you complete tasks on the computer, observe the CPU column. You should see the number spike as each process takes processor time, and then the number should return to normal.

    If a process has a high percentage of CPU usage that doesn't return to normal, you might have to end the process.
3. Select the name of the executable file for the process that's overwhelming the CPU.
4. Click End Process.
5. A warning box states that terminating the process can cause undesirable results. To end the process, click End Process (in Windows Vista) or Yes (in Windows 2000 and XP).

Do it!

A-6: Ending a process

Here's how	Here's why
1 Activate the Processes tab and click **Show processes from all users** Click **Continue**	
2 Click **Memory**	(The column heading.) To sort the list of processes by memory consumption.
3 Click **Image Name**	(The column heading.) To sort the list of processes by name.
4 Select **notepad.exe** Click **End Process**	
Click **End Process**	The selected instance of Notepad closes, and its executable file is removed from the list of processes.
5 Right-click a process and choose **Set Priority**	
Observe the priority settings	You can assign a process a priority to give it more processing time. Be careful when adjusting these settings because they could cause some programs to slow down or stop responding.
6 Click a blank area of the desktop	To close the shortcut menu.

Memory is a column heading.

The Networking tab

Explanation

You can use the data displayed on the Networking tab in Task Manager to quickly see how much of your computer's network bandwidth you're using.

If multiple network adapters are installed in the computer, the chart displays a combination of the network traffic for all adapters. The bottom of the tab displays information about multiple adapters individually, allowing you to compare the traffic on each one.

You can change the columns displayed in the summary area for each adapter by choosing View, Select Columns. Exhibit 9-6 shows the options. Information on each option is available on Microsoft's Web site at:
`http://www.microsoft.com/resources/documentation/windows/`▶
`xp/all/proddocs/en-us/taskman_whats_there_w.mspx`.

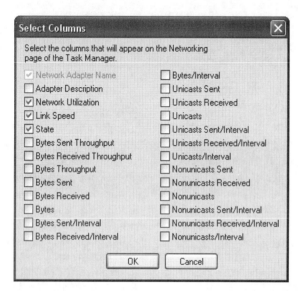

Exhibit 9-6: Data types that can be displayed under the Networking graph.

The Users tab

You can use the Users tab in Task Manager to monitor the users logged on to the computer and to disconnect them, log them off, or send them a message. The columns on the Users tab include the items in the following table.

Item	Description
User	Lists the user names of people logged on to this computer.
ID	Shows a numeric ID assigned to identify the user session on the computer.
Status	Indicates the current status of the user session: Active or Disconnected.
Client Name	If applicable, indicates the name of the computer using the session.
Session	Displays the session type. (You'll need to scroll to the right to see this column.)

Do it!

A-7: Monitoring network utilization and users

Here's how	Here's why
1 Activate the Networking tab	In Task Manager.
2 Move Task Manager to the lower-right corner of your screen	You will view the network utilization data as you work with Internet Explorer.
3 Open Internet Explorer	Task Manager remains on top.
4 In Task Manager, observe the Local Area Connection graph	There were small spikes in network traffic as you accessed the Internet through the local network.
5 Observe the box below the graph	It shows details about your network adapter.
6 Activate and observe the Users tab	You can view the status of logged-on users, and you can log them off and disconnect them from this tab. You can even send them a message.
7 Close Task Manager and any open windows	

Event monitoring

Explanation

Event Viewer, shown in Exhibit 9-7, is a Windows utility that enables you to monitor events that occur on your system. The events that are recorded can help you determine the cause of problems you're having with a particular application, a component of the operating system, or a suspected security breach.

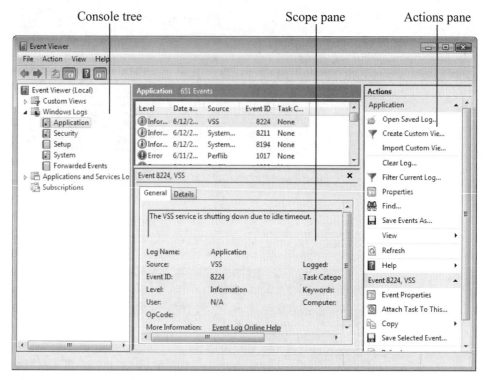

Exhibit 9-7: Event Viewer in Windows Vista

In Windows Vista, events are kept in the *logs*, which are described in the following table.

Log	Contains
Application	Events logged by individual applications. The types of events an application logs in Event Viewer are determined by the application's developers and might vary considerably among applications and vendors.
Security	Events relating to the security of the computer.
Setup	Events related to the installation of applications.
System	Events reported by Windows system components. The operating system determines which components report errors to the Event Viewer log.
Forwarded Events	Events forwarded from remote computers as a result of an event subscription.

Each of the logs displays the following information for each recorded event.

Item	Description
Source	The program, system component, or individual component of a large program that recorded the event.
Event ID (Vista); Event (2000/XP)	An ID that identifies the type of event. Event IDs are coded into the operating system and individual applications and can be used by product support personnel to troubleshoot problems.
Level (Vista); Type (2000/XP)	The type of event that is recorded: Error, Warning, Information, Success Audit (Security Log only), or Failure Audit (Security Log only).
User	The name of the user who was logged on when the event was recorded. Many components run under a system account, so you might see SYSTEM in this column, even if a user was logged on when the event occurred.
OpCode	The point at which the event was recorded.
Logged	The date and time the event was logged.
Task Category (Vista); Category (2000/XP)	Additional information about the component that logged the event.
Keywords	Words that you can use to search for more information about the event.
Computer	The name of the computer where the event occurred.

Event types

There are five types of events, which are listed in the following table.

Event type	Description
Error	A significant problem; for example, a service fails to start.
Warning	An event that is not a significant or immediate problem, but could become a significant problem in the future. For example, disk space is running low.
Information	The successful operation of a task; for example, a network driver loads successfully.
Success Audit (Security Log only)	A successful security event; for example, a user logs on successfully.
Failure Audit (Security Log only)	An unsuccessful security event; for example, a user attempts to log on, but fails to submit proper credentials.

Double-clicking an individual event opens an Event Properties dialog box, as shown in Exhibit 9-8, with a description of the event. You can use the arrow buttons to view information about the previous (up arrow) or next (down arrow) event.

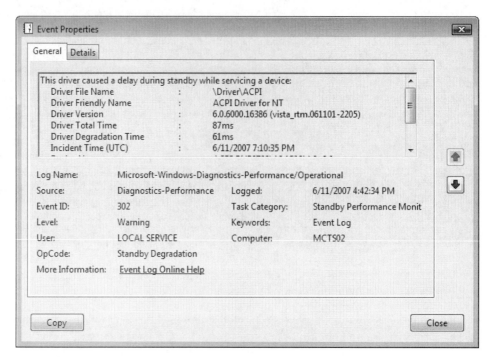

Exhibit 9-8: An Event Properties dialog box in Windows Vista

To open Event Viewer, open the Control Panel and click System and Maintenance. Click Administrative Tools, and then double-click Event Viewer.

Do it!

A-8: Viewing the event logs

Here's how	Here's why
1 Click **Start** and choose **Control Panel** Click **System and Maintenance**	
2 Click **Administrative Tools** and double-click **Event Viewer** Click **Continue**	
3 In the console tree, double-click **Windows Logs**	To display the event logs.
4 Select **Application**	You can maximize the window to see the information in the details pane.
Observe the column headers	The most important identifying information is displayed. Not all of the details are shown in the list of events.
5 Observe the events	The events are listed from the most recent to the oldest, by default.
Double-click the first event	To open the Event Properties dialog box, which displays a more detailed description of the event. You can use detailed event information to determine why an application, service, hardware device, or Windows Vista component failed.
6 Click ⬇	To move to the next event in the Application log.
Click **Close**	To close the Event Properties dialog box and return to Event Viewer and the Application log.
7 In the console tree, select **Security** and scroll through the list of events	To view security-related events, which relate to logons and logoffs.
Select **System** and scroll through the list of events	To view the events recorded by the operating system and its components.
8 Select the Application log	

Changing the event display

Explanation

Using the View menu, you can sort and filter the display of events in each event log, and you can search for events that meet particular criteria. These features are helpful in quickly narrowing down a full event log to only certain events.

Sorting events

By default, events are listed from the newest to the oldest, by date and time, but you can easily change the sort order by clicking any column heading. A single click on the column heading sorts the events in ascending order (an up-arrow appears in the column heading, as shown in Exhibit 9-9). A second click sorts events in descending order (a down-arrow appears in the column heading). You can also use the View, Sort By command to sort by column heading. To return the view to the default, choose View, Remove Sorting.

Up arrow shows that the log is sorted in ascending order by Level

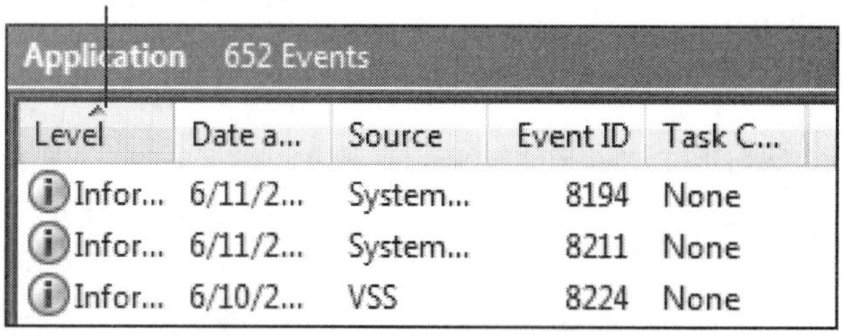

Exhibit 9-9: An Application log sorted by Level

Grouping events

In Windows Vista, you can group events in a log by column heading. Choose View, Group By, and choose a column heading by which to group the events. You can then choose View, Collapse All Groups to see just the groups, and then expand each group as necessary. Exhibit 9-10 shows the Application log grouped by Level. To remove the grouping, choose View, Remove grouping of events.

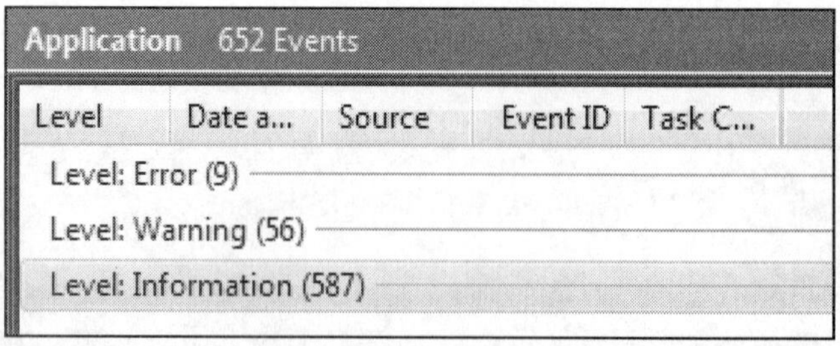

Exhibit 9-10: Grouped events

Filtering events

To display only certain events in Windows Vista, you can apply a filter to the view. Here's how:

1. In the console tree, select the log where you want to filter events.
2. In the Actions pane, click Filter Current Log. (To show or hide the Actions pane, click the Show/Hide Action Pane button on the toolbar.)
3. Check and clear event types as needed.
4. Select filter criteria as needed from each of the following areas:
   - Logged
   - Level
   - Source
   - Event ID
   - Task category
   - Keywords
   - User
   - Computer
5. Click OK.

To remove the filter, click Clear Filter in the Actions pane.

If you filter events instead of sorting them, you can use the Event Properties dialog box to navigate between the details of only the events that meet your filtering criteria.

Point out the filter's components and the results.

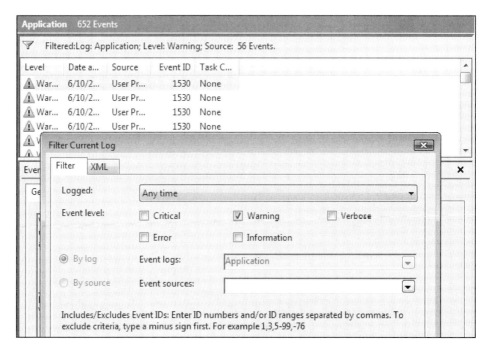

Exhibit 9-11: An Application log with a filter applied

Do it!

A-9: Controlling the display of an event log

Here's how	Here's why
1 Click **Level**	*[Screenshot: Application 652 Events, with columns Level, Date a..., Source]* To sort the list of events in the Application log alphabetically by level. The arrow in the column heading is pointing up.
Click **Level** again	To reverse the sort order. The arrow is pointing down.
2 Sort by the **Source** column heading	
3 Choose **View**, **Remove sorting**	To return the log to the default view.
4 In the Actions pane, click **Filter Current Log…**	To open the Filter Current Log dialog box, with the Filter tab active.
Under Event level, check **Error** and **Warning**	To display only warning and error messages. *[Screenshot: Event level: Critical ☐, Warning ☑, Verbose ☐, Error ☑, Information ☐]*
5 Open the Event sources list	You can choose to display events from just one source.
Select **Application**	
Click in a blank area of the dialog box	To close the list.
6 Open the Task category list	With an event source selected, you can further refine your filter to show events from specific categories.
Close the Category list	
Observe the Event ID, Keywords, User, and Computer(s) boxes	You can enter values in these boxes to further refine your filter.
At the top of the dialog box, open and observe the Logged list	You can show only events that occur within a specified date range.
7 Click **OK**	To apply the filter.

The Application log should be selected.

8	Do any events match the filter criteria?	*Answers will vary.*
9	Observe the top of the event list	The filter criteria are displayed.

> ▽ Filtered:Log: Application; Levels: Error, Warning; Source: Application 0 Events.

10	In the Actions pane, click **Clear Filter**	To remove the filter.
11	Close all open windows	

Topic B: Maintenance

This topic covers the following CompTIA A+ 220-702 exam objective.

#	Objective
2.3	**Given a scenario, select and use system utilities / tools and evaluate the results** • Disk management tools – NTBACKUP • System Restore

Backups

Explanation

Microsoft operating systems include a backup utility you can use to create copies of your files so you can recover your data if a system failure occurs. On a bootable computer, you should back up any critical data before you attempt to troubleshoot any problems.

Windows Backup

The Backup utility is installed with Windows 2000 Professional, Windows XP Professional, and Windows Vista Business and Ultimate. You can use Windows Backup to:

- Archive selected files and folders on your hard disk in another location, including on removable storage devices.
- Restore the archived files and folders to your hard disk.
- Make a copy of your computer's system state, which includes:
  - Registry
  - Boot files
  - COM+ class registration database
  - IIS metadirectory
  - Windows File Protection system files
- Copy your computer's system partition, the boot partition, and the files needed to start up the system.

The most common use of the Backup utility is to back up critical data and operating system files to ensure that recovery is possible if files are accidentally deleted or a disaster occurs.

You access the Windows Backup utility through System Tools. The utility can be used in two modes: Wizard mode and Advanced mode. Wizard mode walks you step-by-step through the process of creating a backup or restoring files. Advanced mode gives you complete control over the file and folder selection process.

Once you have decided how often, when, and with what methods backups should be made, you can use the Backup utility to schedule them. You can schedule backups to occur daily, weekly, monthly, and on specified days or at specified times.

Windows XP backup types

The Windows Backup utility supports five types of backups, described in the following table.

Type	Backs up...
Copy	Selected files. Does not clear the archive attribute, which shows that the file has been backed up.
Daily	All selected files that were modified the day of the daily backup. Does not clear the archive attribute.
Differential	Selected files that have been created or modified since the last normal or incremental backup. Does not clear the archive attribute. Differential backups require that you have the most recent normal backup in addition to the differential backup if you want to restore files.
Incremental	Selected files that have been created or modified since the last normal or incremental backup. Clears the archive attribute. Incremental backups require that you have the most recent normal backup in addition to the incremental backup if you want to restore files.
Normal	All selected files. Clears the archive attribute. With a normal backup, you need only the most recent copy of the backup file to restore from backup.

Copy backups can be used between normal and incremental backups without affecting their settings.

Windows Backup in Windows Vista

Backups can be saved on any removable media, on a directory on your hard disk, in a shared folder on the network, or on another computer on the network. Because Windows Vista has CD and DVD writing built in, you can even back up your files directly to one of those discs.

With Windows Backup, you can:

- Create automatic backups of your personal files.
- Restore files that you previously backed up.
- Create a Complete PC Backup.

To perform any backup actions, you must be logged on as an administrator. You cannot provide administrative credentials on demand to back up files with Windows Backup. You can restore files as a standard user, but only to your personal folder or the Public Documents folder.

Automatic backups

You can schedule automatic backups of your files by using Windows Backup. This option is designed to make copies of your photos, documents, video files, and music files. It does not back up system settings or installed programs.

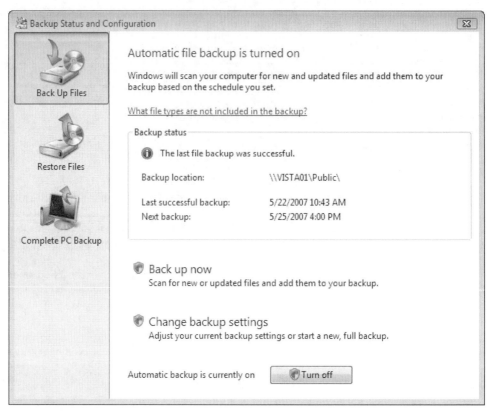

Exhibit 9-12: Backup Status and Configuration in Windows Vista

To configure and enable automatic backups:

1 Log on as an administrative user.
2 Choose Start and choose All Programs, Accessories, System Tools, Backup Status and Configuration.
3 Click "Set up automatic file backup." Click Continue to acknowledge that you're performing a system modification.
4 As needed, check or clear the options for each type of file you want the utility to back up. Click Next.
5 Select a location for your backed-up files. Click Next.
6 Using the How Often, When, and What time lists, specify when you want automatic backups to be run. Click Finish.
7 Click OK to save your backup schedule and to begin backing up your files now. If you selected an optical disc drive for your backup files, Windows will prompt you to insert a disc when it is ready to write your files.

Do it!

B-1: Scheduling a backup

If student computers do not have CD or DVD writers and sufficient blank discs, you can have students back up to a network server.

Here's how	Here's why
1 Create a folder named **Files** in the Documents folder, and create two text documents in the Files folder	You'll use these for the backup and restore activities.
Close any open windows	
2 Click **Start** and choose **All Programs**, **Accessories**, **System Tools**, **Backup Status and Configuration**	To open the Backup Status and Configuration window.
3 Click **Set up automatic file backup**	
Click **Continue**	Windows searches for a suitable backup device.
4 Follow your instructor's directions to select your computer's optical drive or a network location	
Click **Next**	You are prompted to choose which disks to back up.
5 Clear checkboxes for all disks except C:	
Click **Next**	You are prompted to choose which types of files to back up.
6 Clear checkboxes for all types except Pictures and Documents	
Click **Next**	You are prompted to set the schedule for future backups.
7 Configure the backup schedule as shown	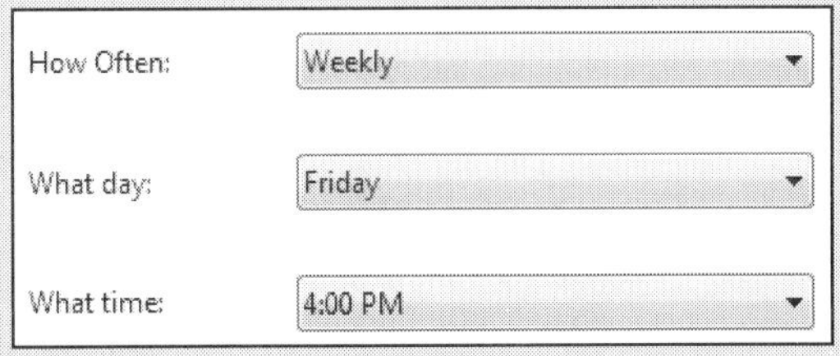 How Often: Weekly What day: Friday What time: 4:00 PM
8 Click **Save settings and start backup**	

9	If you're backing up to a CD or DVD, click the balloon message stating that File Backup needs your attention	
	Insert a blank CD or DVD into your computer	You will be prompted to format the CD.
	Click **OK**, and when prompted to format the disc, click **Format**	The backup begins. You could click Close now and continue using your PC. The backup would continue running.
	If prompted, insert additional discs and observe as the backup progresses	
10	If you're backing up to a network location, observe the Backup status box as the backup begins	
11	Observe as the files are backed up	Once you have enabled automatic backups, you can perform subsequent backups by clicking "Run backup now." Or you can wait, and Windows Backup will run automatically on the schedule you specified. 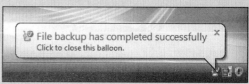 A system message informs you that the backup is done.
	Click **Close**	(If necessary.) To close the notification window.
12	Leave Windows Backup open	

Restoring files

Explanation

Restoring files is as easy as backing them up:

1 Open Backup Status and Configuration.
2 Click Restore Files.
3 Select either "Files from the latest backup" or "Files from an older backup." Click Next.
4 Browse to locate the files you want to restore, or specify to restore all of the files. Click Next.
5 Click Start Restore.
6 Click Finish.

Windows maintenance **9–33**

Do it!

B-2: Restoring files from backup

If the previous activity could not be completed, show and explain the restore options.

Here's how	Here's why
1 Delete the Files folder from your Documents folder	
2 Minimize the Documents window	
3 In the Backup Status and Configuration window, click **Restore Files**	
4 Click **Restore files**	You are prompted to choose what to restore.
5 If necessary, select **Files from the latest backup**	
Click **Next**	
6 Click **Add files**	
7 Double-click **Files**	To open it.
SHIFT +click to select all of the files	You're going to restore these files.
Click **Add**	
8 Click **Next**	You are prompted to choose whether to restore the files to their original location or to a new location.
Click **Start restore**	To restore the files to their original location. The restore will take a few seconds.
Click **Finish**	To close the Restore Files Wizard.
9 Switch to the Documents window and observe the folder's contents	The folder you deleted is back, along with the files inside the folder.
10 Close Backup Status and Configuration	

System Restore

Explanation

The System Restore utility in Windows Vista and Windows XP creates snapshots of your computer's configuration. There are three types of snapshots:

- **System checkpoints** — Created automatically when Windows Vista or XP detects the beginning of a request to make a system configuration change.
- **Manual restore points** — Manually created by a user, using the System Restore utility.
- **Installation restore points** — Created automatically when certain programs are installed.

Using the System Restore utility, you can restore your computer to a previous configuration with the settings recorded in a system checkpoint, a manual restore point, or an installation restore point. This is helpful in recovering a system that's not functioning properly due to newly installed hardware or software or updated configuration settings. The restore process might also help you recover from a virus or worm that has infected your computer. Before you begin troubleshooting, you can create a system restore point, so you can return the computer to its original state if your troubleshooting solutions cause larger or additional problems.

Windows Vista automatically creates restore points every day and just before you make certain system changes, such as installing new software. You can also manually create a restore point at any time.

To manually create a restore point in Windows Vista:

1. Open the Control Panel.
2. Click System and Maintenance, and then click System.
3. On the left, click System Protection.
4. Click Continue, or enter the administrator's password.
5. Click Create.
6. Type a brief description of the restore point in the text box.
7. Click Create.

In Windows XP, click Start and choose All Programs, Accessories, System Tools, System Restore. Select "Create a restore point" and click Next. Enter a descriptive name for the restore point, and click Create.

Windows maintenance **9–35**

Do it! **B-3: Creating a restore point**

Here's how	Here's why
1 Open the Control Panel	
2 Click **System and Maintenance**	
3 Click **System**	To open the System window.
4 On the left, click **System Protection**	
Click **Continue**	
5 Click **Create**	
6 In the "Create a restore point" box, enter **My Restore Point**	System Restore tags restore points with the date and time, so you need to type only a brief description.
7 Click **Create**	The restore point is created.
8 Click **OK**	To close the dialog box stating that the restore point was successfully created.
9 Observe the date and time of the most recent restore point	It's the restore point you just created.
10 Click **OK**	To close the System Properties dialog box.
Close the Control Panel	

This button will be disabled while Windows searches for available disks.

Student restore point dates won't match the screenshot.

Restoring the system

Explanation

Before you use System Restore to undo a change, if the change involved a hardware device, first try using Driver Rollback. It reverses fewer system changes. If Driver Rollback doesn't solve the problem, then revert the system to a restore point.

Using Driver Rollback, you can replace a newly installed driver that isn't working with a previously installed one that was working. To do so:

1 Open Device Manager.
2 Open the Properties dialog box for the device that's no longer working correctly.
3 Activate the Driver tab.
4 Click Rollback Driver (or Roll Back Driver in Windows Vista).
5 Click Yes to confirm.

Driver Rollback is available in Windows 2000 Professional and all versions of Windows XP and Windows Vista.

To use System Restore to restore data in Windows Vista:

1 Click Start and choose All Programs, Accessories, System Tools, System Restore.
2 When prompted, enter the administrator's password and click Submit.
3 Choose the appropriate restore point to which to restore your system. Click Next.
4 Click Finish. The computer will restore the previous settings and restart.
5 Log back in and confirm the restoration.

Windows reboots and restores the system state to the settings saved in the restore point. Changes in user data aren't affected, but any installation or configuration changes made after the restore point are lost.

System Restore doesn't replace the process of uninstalling a program. To completely remove the files installed by a program, Microsoft recommends that you remove the program by using the Add or Remove Programs utility or the program's own uninstall utility.

Booting to a system restore point

If the Windows GUI won't load during normal startup, use the Advanced startup options to boot into Safe mode. You'll be prompted to go directly to System Restore or boot into Safe mode. Choose to boot directly to System Restore.

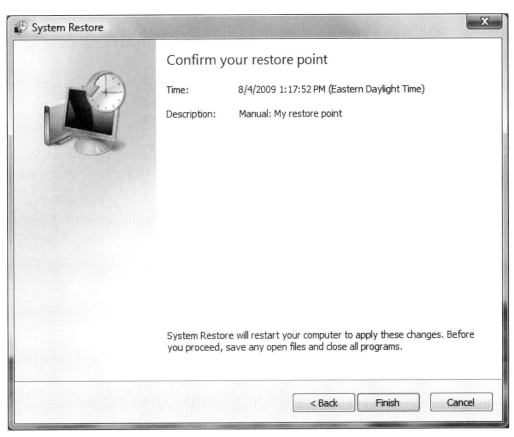

Exhibit 9-13: Restoring to a specific point in time with System Restore

Do it!

B-4: Restoring a computer to a previous state

Here's how	Here's why
1 Click **Start** and choose **All Programs**	
2 Choose **Accessories**, **System Tools**, **System Restore**	To open System Restore.
Click **Continue**	
3 Select **Choose a different restore point**	
Click **Next**	
4 In the list, select **Manual: My Restore Point**	(If necessary.) You'll restore to this point.
Click **Next**	
5 Click **Finish**	To begin the system restore. This process will take a few minutes.
Click **Yes**	To confirm your intent to restore to the restore point. System Restore begins restoring your computer; it will restart your computer during the process.
6 Log on to Windows	
7 Click **Close**	To close the System Restore message box that tells you your system has been restored.

Topic C: Task Scheduler

This topic covers the following CompTIA A+ 220-702 exam objective.

#	Objective
2.3	Given a scenario, select and use system utilities / tools and evaluate the results • Task Scheduler

Using Task Scheduler

Explanation

Task Scheduler, shown in Exhibit 9-14, is a utility you can use to schedule routine maintenance tasks or to act on the occurrence of a specific event. Task Scheduler can run behind the scenes with no user intervention, or it can accept input from the logged-on user.

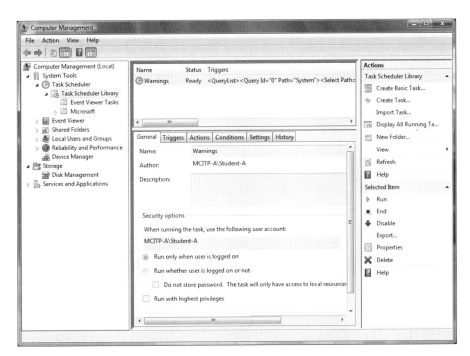

Exhibit 9-14: Task Scheduler

To create a task manually:

1. Open Computer Management, and expand Task Scheduler in the tree pane.
2. Right-click Task Scheduler Library and choose Create Task.
3. Using the five tabs in the dialog box, configure general properties, triggers, actions, conditions, and settings. (We'll cover each of these tabs in the following sections.)

If you want help with creating a task, you can have a wizard walk you through these five tabs, but you won't have the same range of options. To start the wizard, right-click Task Scheduler Library and choose Create Basic Task.

General properties

On this tab, you assign a name to the task, and you can enter an optional description. You can also configure security options, including which user credentials the task uses to run. By default, the task will run as the currently logged-on user. You can choose to have the task run only when the user is logged on or run whether the user is logged on or not. You can also choose to run the task with the highest privileges assigned to that user account.

Triggers

The *trigger* is the event that prompts the task to run. Triggers include a scheduled start time, a logon, startup, idle time, an event, and workstation locking and unlocking. To configure a trigger:

1 On the Triggers tab, click New.
2 In the New Trigger dialog box, select a trigger type from the "Begin the task list."
3 Configure the settings for the trigger type, whether it's a date and time or an event from an event log.
4 Configure advanced settings, including delay and repeat intervals, timeouts, and expiration dates.

Actions

The *action* is the task that's performed in response to the trigger. You can configure one of three actions: start a program, send an e-mail message, or display a message. To create an action:

1 On the Actions tab, click New.
2 From the Action list, select one of the three actions:
   - If the action is "Start a program," select the program and add any additional configuration parameters.
   - If the action is "Send an e-mail," enter the sender and recipient e-mail addresses, a subject line, the message text, any attachments, and an address for a Simple Mail Transfer Protocol (SMTP) server for the outgoing e-mail message.
   - If the action is "Display a message," type the title and body of the message.

Conditions

You can choose the conditions under which the task will run, in addition to any trigger settings. The options are:

- **Idle** — You can choose to start or stop the task depending on whether the computer is idle and how long the computer is idle.
- **Power** — You can configure the task to run only if the computer is connected to an AC power source, and to stop if the computer switches to battery power. You can also specify that the computer should wake up to run the task.
- **Network** — You can choose to run the task only if a specified network connection is available or if any connection at all is available.

Settings

You can configure additional settings that will control the task's behavior. These settings include whether the task can be run on demand, when and how often to restart the task if it fails, when to stop the task, and when to delete the task if it's not run.

Do it!

C-1: Creating a basic task

Here's how	Here's why
1 Open Computer Management	You're going to create two tasks. In this activity, you'll create a weekly reminder. In the next activity, you'll create a task to run Windows Defender when you lock your computer.
2 Expand Task Scheduler and select **Task Scheduler Library** In the Actions panel, click **Create Basic Task**	
3 Name the task **Weekly Invoice Reminder** and click **Next**	
4 Select **Weekly** and click **Next** On the Weekly page, select **Friday**, and change the time to **9:00:00 AM** Click **Next**	
5 On the Action page, select **Display a message** and click **Next** In the Title box, type **REMINDER** In the Message box, type **REMEMBER THE WEEKLY INVOICES** Click **Next**	
6 On the Summary page, observe the "Open the Properties dialog for this task when I click Finish" checkbox	You can access all of the options on the General, Triggers, Alerts, Conditions, and Settings tabs in the Properties dialog box.
7 Click **Finish** Observe the new task in the library list, and the five tabs from its Properties dialog box displayed below	You can select a task in the list and view its settings on the five tabs. But to edit the task's settings, you need to open its Properties dialog box.

If the task does not appear, have students right-click the list and choose Refresh.

8	Observe the History tab	The task was successfully registered.
9	Right-click the task in the list and choose **Run**	To test the task.
	If necessary, select the **REMINDER** taskbar button	To display the message box.
10	Click **OK**	To close the message box.
11	Right-click the task in the list and choose **Properties**	
	Select each tab and observe its contents	You can reconfigure the task by changing just about any setting.
12	On the Triggers tab, select the trigger and click **Edit**	
	Clear **Friday** and check **Monday** instead	To reconfigure the task to run every Monday morning.
	Click **OK**	
13	On the Actions tab, select the action and click **Edit**	
	Edit the message to read **REMEMBER THIS WEEK'S INVOICES**	
	Click **OK**	
14	On the Conditions tab, select **Wake the computer to run this task**	
15	On the Settings tab, select **Run task as soon as possible after a scheduled start is missed**	
	Click **OK**	To close the dialog box and apply the new settings.

Windows maintenance 9-43

Do it!

C-2: Creating a task manually

Here's how	Here's why
1 Right-click **Task Scheduler Library** and choose **Create Task...**	
2 On the General tab, name the task **Windows Defender on Lock**	
3 On the Triggers tab, click **New**	
From the "Begin the task" list, select **On workstation lock**	
Under Advanced settings, check **Delay task for**, and change the time to **30 seconds**	
Click **OK**	
4 On the Actions tab, click **New**	
In the Action list, verify that **Start a program** is selected	
Click **Browse** and browse to C:\Program Files\Windows Defender	
Select **MpCmdRun** and click **Open**	This is the command-line version of Windows Defender.
5 In the Add arguments box, type **scan -1**	`scan -1`
	To perform a quick scan.
Click **OK**	
6 In the Create Task dialog box, click **OK**	To create the task.
7 Lock your computer and wait at least one minute	To trigger the action. You might see or hear the hard disk as the Windows Defender scan is started.
8 Log back on and observe the task list	The Windows Defender on Lock task ran when you locked your computer.

⚠ *Be sure students type the hyphen before the number 1.*

Students might have to press F5 to refresh the view.

Topic D: Troubleshooting

This topic covers the following CompTIA A+ 220-702 exam objectives.

#	Objective

2.4	**Evaluate and resolve common issues**
	• Operational Problems
	   – Auto-restart errors
	   – Bluescreen error
	   – System lockup
	   – Device drivers failure (input / output devices)
	   – Application install, start or load failure
	   – Service fails to start
	• Error Messages and Conditions
	   – Boot
	      • Invalid boot disk
	      • Inaccessible boot drive
	      • Missing NTLDR
	   – Startup
	      • Device / service failed to start
	      • Device / program in registry not found
	• System Performance and Optimization
	   – Startup file maintenance
	   – Background processes

Computer startup problems

Explanation

There are operating-system problems you'll need to troubleshoot that manifest themselves as symptoms during computer startup. These errors can be grouped into three categories:

- **Boot errors** — The computer system doesn't boot successfully.
- **Operating system startup errors** — The computer system boots successfully, but reports an error message when loading the operating system.
- **Operating system load errors** — The computer successfully boots, but the operating system interface doesn't load properly.

Boot errors

To resolve boot errors, you need to have access to your computer's system BIOS or CMOS, a boot disk, and disk-based utilities.

To identify and resolve boot errors, use the troubleshooting techniques described in the following table.

Boot error	Cause	Resolution
Invalid boot or non-system disk error	A floppy or CD-ROM that isn't bootable is in a bootable drive.	Check that there isn't a disk in the floppy or CD-ROM drive.
	The system BIOS or CMOS isn't configured properly to boot to the hard disk.	Verify that system BIOS or CMOS boot-order settings are correct.
	The hard disk drive doesn't have the Windows boot files on it.	Depending on the OS, boot from your emergency repair disk, your Windows installation CD-ROM, or your restore CD.
	The hard disk drive isn't connected properly.	If the computer was moved recently or if the hard drive was just installed, check that the hard disk is properly connected to the computer.
	The hard disk is bad.	If the previous solutions fail to resolve the problem, the hard disk might be bad and might need to be replaced.
Inaccessible boot device	The system BIOS or CMOS isn't configured properly to boot to the hard disk.	Verify that system BIOS or CMOS boot-order settings are correct.
	The hard disk drive isn't connected properly.	If the computer was moved recently or if the hard drive was just installed, check that the hard disk is properly connected to the computer.
	The motherboard was recently changed, or you moved the Windows system disk to another computer with a different motherboard.	Reinstall Windows to fix the Registry entries and drivers for the mass storage controller hardware. You might be able to use a Microsoft generic driver until you can find the proper driver.
	The hard disk is bad.	If the previous solutions fail to resolve the problem, the hard disk might be bad and might need to be replaced.

Boot error	Cause	Resolution
NTLDR is missing, or Couldn't find NTLDR	A floppy or CD-ROM that isn't bootable is in a bootable drive.	Check that there isn't a disk in the floppy or CD-ROM drive.
	The system BIOS or CMOS isn't configured properly to boot to the hard disk.	Verify that system BIOS or CMOS boot-order settings are correct.
	The boot.ini file is configured incorrectly.	View the contents of boot.ini. Edit if necessary.
	The Ntldr file is missing or corrupt.	Copy the Ntldr file from the Windows installation CD-ROM, a Windows boot disk, or another computer. If other Windows files are missing or corrupt, you might have to reinstall the operating system to resolve the problem.
	The hard disk drive isn't connected properly.	If the computer was moved recently or if the hard drive was just installed, check that the hard disk is properly connected to the computer.
	There's a corrupt boot sector or MBR.	There might be a virus. Use your virus removal software.
	You're trying to upgrade from FAT32 to a Windows version that doesn't support FAT32.	Boot into the previous version of the operating system, back up data, and complete a fresh installation of the new operating system.
	The hard disk is bad.	If the previous solutions fail to resolve the problem, the hard disk might be bad and might need to be replaced.
Bad or missing Command interpreter	A floppy or CD-ROM that isn't bootable is in a bootable drive.	Check that there isn't a disk in the floppy or CD-ROM drive.
	The system BIOS or CMOS isn't configured properly to boot to the hard disk.	Verify that system BIOS or CMOS boot-order settings are correct.
	The command.com, msdos.sys, io.sys, or drvspace file was deleted, was renamed, or has become corrupt.	Boot the computer by using a boot disk. Replace the missing or corrupt file.
	The hard disk is bad.	If the previous solutions fail to resolve the problem, the hard disk might be bad and might need to be replaced.

Startup errors

To identify and resolve startup errors, you can use troubleshooting techniques described in the following table.

Startup message	Cause	Resolution
Error in CONFIG.SYS line ##	There's a problem with the specified line in the config.sys file.	View the specified line in config.sys. Look for typing errors or calls to files that don't exist. Edit as necessary to resolve the problem.
Himem.sys not loaded	The himem.sys file is missing or corrupt.	Copy a new version of himem.sys to the hard disk. Verify that the reference to himem.sys is correct in config.sys.
	There's a problem with physical memory.	If the previous solution fails to solve the problem, the physical memory might be bad and might need to be replaced. Himem.sys runs a check on RAM and can't do so if a RAM chip is bad.
Missing or corrupt Himem.sys	The himem.sys file is missing or corrupt.	Copy a new version of himem.sys to the hard disk. Verify that the reference to himem.sys is correct in config.sys.
	There's a problem with physical memory.	If the previous solution fails to solve the problem, the physical memory might be bad and might need to be replaced. Himem.sys runs a check on RAM and can't do so if a RAM chip is bad.
Device/service has failed to start; Device/program in Registry not found	Windows is trying to load a device or service that won't load properly.	Check the Event Viewer logs to determine which device or service failed to load. Check the installation or configuration of the device (by using Device Manager) or service (by using the Services console). Reinstall the device or service if necessary.

Operating system load errors

Common operating system load errors and troubleshooting techniques are listed in the following table.

Error	Cause	Resolution
Failure to start GUI	Explorer.exe is missing or corrupt.	Copy Explorer.exe from the Windows installation CD-ROM, a Windows boot disk, or another computer. If other Windows files are missing or corrupt, you might have to reinstall the operating system to resolve the problem.
Windows Protection Error—illegal operation	An application asks the operating system to process an operation that the OS doesn't recognize.	Illegal-operation messages typically have an error code or something else you can use to research the exact cause and resolution of the specific error.
	Outdated device drivers need to be updated.	If the device driver is being loaded by the operating system at Startup, try to boot into Safe mode and roll back or update the driver.
		If the illegal operation causes a GPF (or Blue-screen error), you might need to reboot the computer.
		An incorrect or corrupt device driver can cause an auto-restart error (the computer reboots automatically when it tries to load the driver). After you identify the driver causing the problem, you need to replace it.
User-modified settings cause improper operation at startup	The user has changed a system setting that causes the computer to hang at startup.	If available, boot using one of the Startup modes to reverse the changes. On Windows XP and Windows Vista computers, roll back to a system restore point.
Application install, start, or load failure	Someone tries to install or start an application that isn't compatible with the operating system.	Research the application to see if a patch is available that allows it to run on your operating system. You might need to upgrade the application to one whose coding functions according to the application rules of your OS.

Remind students that a GPF (general protection fault) is also called the Blue Screen of Death (BSOD).

Windows maintenance 9–49

Do it!

D-1: Troubleshooting Windows startup errors

Questions and answers

1 You recently installed a new hard disk in a user's computer. You installed Windows XP Professional and the needed applications, and then copied the user's data to the new drive. The computer was functioning just fine in your office. You delivered it to the user's office, and when you started it up, you received the message "NTLDR is missing." What is the likely cause?

When you connected the new hard disk, the connections weren't made tightly. When you transported the computer from one place to the other, the connections loosened just enough to prevent the hard disk from functioning.

2 If your first solution doesn't resolve the problem, what is another likely cause of the "Missing NTLDR" message?

When installing applications or moving over the user's data, you left a floppy or CD-ROM that isn't bootable in a bootable drive.

3 You are installing Windows XP on a computer for a user. When you start Windows XP, it loads the desktop, but then you receive a "Windows Protection Error—illegal operation" message. Each time you restart the computer, the same thing happens. What do you think the problem is, and how can you resolve it?

The computer might be using an outdated device driver for a device that loads during startup. The computer contains a device that isn't compatible with Windows XP.

- *Boot into Safe mode:*
  - *Check the Event Logs to see if an error was recorded about a device or service not starting.*
  - *Check Device Manager to see if there is a warning or error icon next to a device.*
  - *Run the Windows XP compatibility wizard to determine if there is a device that is installed but isn't supported.*
- *Use Device Manager's Update Driver Wizard to fix a device driver problem.*

Advanced startup options

Explanation

If you're having a problem with Windows Vista, and you can't get it to start, you can use the advanced startup options to diagnose and fix startup problems. To access the menu for the startup modes, boot the computer and press F8 after you hear your computer's startup beep. You should press F8 during the first few moments of the boot process—before the Windows logo/splash screen is displayed.

The following table describes the advanced startup options that are available when you boot Windows Vista.

Option	Description
Safe mode	Boots the computer with a minimum configuration, such as mouse, keyboard, and standard monitor device drivers. Can be used to solve problems with a new hardware installation or problems caused by user settings.
Safe mode with networking	Boots the computer with a minimum configuration, plus networking devices and drivers. Use this mode when files you need to resolve problems are stored on the network.
Safe mode with command prompt	If Safe mode does not load the operating system, you can try this startup mode to get a command prompt. You can then use your MS-DOS-based utilities to troubleshoot and resolve startup problems. You do not have network access.
Enable boot logging	The operating system loads normally. All files used during the boot process are recorded in a file called ntbtlog.txt. If you're having a problem with a device, check ntbtlog.txt to see which devices loaded successfully and which did not. The file is stored in the C:\Windows folder in Windows Vista.
Enable VGA mode	Boots the operating system with a generic VGA display driver. Use this mode to correct improper video or display settings or to fix a non-functioning video driver.
Last Known Good Configuration	Uses the boot settings stored in the Registry from the last successful boot. If the system was configured incorrectly, you can use this option to reverse all system setting changes made after the last successful boot.
Debugging mode	Allows you to move system boot logs via a serial port from a failing computer to another computer for evaluation. This option sends the boot information to the serial port.
Start Windows normally	Boots the computer as if you hadn't entered the Advanced boot options menu.

Although Safe mode is a good tool to help you figure out if the computer can start at all, most of the other advanced startup options are available for experienced computer administrators. Be careful when you're using advanced startup options to troubleshoot operating system errors. Sometimes you should call for additional help from experienced personnel.

Do it!

D-2: Booting the computer using advanced startup options

Here's how	Here's why
1 Click **Start**, click the arrow next to the lock, and choose **Restart**	You will boot the computer into Safe mode for troubleshooting a problem. Make sure you watch the computer screen carefully so you know when to press F8 in the next step.
2 After the Windows shutdown screen disappears, when the black startup screen is displayed, press [F8]	You might need to press it more than once to get the correct timing to display the operating system start menu.
If necessary, press [F8] again	To display the advanced boot options.
Observe the menu choices	Safe mode is selected by default.
Press [← ENTER]	To start Windows Vista in Safe mode. You can see the list of files and drivers loaded during Safe-mode startup.
3 Log on as **PAADMIN##**	
Observe the desktop	It appears with a plain black background with white Safe-mode text in all four corners. Windows Help and Support is open to explain Safe mode.
4 Open your personal folder	You have access to all of your files, just as you normally would.
Close the window	
5 Open the Computer folder	You have access to local disks and optical drives.
Close the window	
6 Open Internet Explorer	You don't have network capabilities, so you can't access the Internet. In Safe mode, you can uninstall a program you installed or undo a setting you changed in Windows Vista. You can also uninstall a hardware device or run a virus-protection scan—anything that you think might help resolve the problem that's preventing the computer from starting.
7 Restart the computer	

Point out the different look for the Start menu.

8 At the startup screen, press `F8` Press `↓` to scroll down and select **Safe Mode with Networking** Press `↵ ENTER`	To start up in Safe mode with networking capabilities.
9 Log on to the computer	
10 Open Internet Explorer	To access the Web; you now have Internet and network capabilities. You can use this startup option if you need to access a file on the network that can help you resolve the startup problem. You can also use this mode to put important files on another computer for safekeeping while you try to figure out the problem on this computer.
11 Restart the computer and boot normally Log on to Windows again	

The System Configuration utility

Explanation

Using the System Configuration utility, also called *Msconfig*, you can view, disable, and enable services and software that run at startup. Msconfig.exe is included with Windows XP and Windows Vista. In this utility, you check and clear checkboxes to enable or disable startup configuration options, as opposed to using a text editor to manually edit startup files. Using the checkboxes, you can quickly make configuration changes to test solutions to a startup problem.

To start the System Configuration utility, click Start, choose Run, type msconfig, and click OK.

Startup modes for troubleshooting

The General tab in the System Configuration utility allows you to start the computer in any of three modes when troubleshooting:

- **Normal Startup** — Loads all device drivers and services.
- **Diagnostic Startup** — Loads only basic devices and services.
- **Selective Startup** — Loads only the selected files and services. In Windows XP, the choices are:
    - System.ini
    - Win.ini
    - System services
    - Startup items
    - Choice of boot.ini file

Windows Vista has slightly different choices that mirror the last three choices in the previous list: Load system services; Load startup items; and Use original boot configuration.

To prevent individual lines or items in a specific configuration file from loading, activate the tab for the desired configuration file and clear the checkbox next to the line or item that you don't want to load.

When you're done troubleshooting, you need to verify that all of the configuration files and all of the items that are listed in those files are loaded. Then activate the General tab and select Normal Startup.

D-3: Using the System Configuration utility

Do it!

Here's how	Here's why
1 Click **Start** Enter **msconfig** Click **Continue**	You will see how you can use the System Configuration utility to troubleshoot startup problems with Windows Vista.

2 Observe the General tab	Startup selection
	● Normal startup
	  Load all device drivers and services
	○ Diagnostic startup
	  Load basic devices and services only
	○ Selective startup
	  ☑ Load system services
	  ☑ Load startup items
	  ☑ Use original boot configuration
	
	You can use this tab to boot into a diagnostic mode without pressing F8 during startup.

Select **Diagnostic Startup**	To load just basic devices and services.
Click **OK**	
3 Click **Restart**	The computer boots into a diagnostic mode without your having to press F8 at startup.
Log on as **PAADMIN##**	You can now troubleshoot any problems you're having with the operating system. A minimal UI has been loaded.
4 Open System Configuration	You must switch back to Normal Startup after you are done troubleshooting.
5 Select **Normal Startup** Click **OK**	To load all device drivers and services.
When prompted, restart the computer and log on as **PAADMIN##**	The desktop is normal.
6 Run msconfig	
7 Activate the Boot tab	You can configure boot options, including which operating system to boot to and whether to perform a safe boot.

If a new Allow/Cancel UAC dialog appears, tell students to click Allow.

8 Activate the Services tab

Service	Manufacturer	Status
Application Experience	Microsoft Corporation	Running
Application Layer Gateway Service	Microsoft Corporation	Stopped
Application Management	Microsoft Corporation	Stopped
Windows Audio Endpoint Builder	Microsoft Corporation	Running
Windows Audio	Microsoft Corporation	Running
Base Filtering Engine	Microsoft Corporation	Running
Background Intelligent Transfer ...	Microsoft Corporation	Stopped
Computer Browser	Microsoft Corporation	Running
Certificate Propagation	Microsoft Corporation	Running
Microsoft .NET Framework NGEN...	Microsoft Corporation	Stopped
COM+ System Application	Microsoft Corporation	Stopped
Cryptographic Services	Microsoft Corporation	Running

Here you can enable and disable individual services. The status of each service is listed, so you can see which services are running or stopped, as shown here.

9 Activate the Startup tab

You can enable or disable programs in your Startup group.

10 Activate the Tools tab

This tab provides a list of utilities you can use in your troubleshooting efforts. Just select a utility and click Launch.

Leave System Configuration open.

Windows Diagnostics

Explanation

As an IT Technician, in order to manage or maintain the operating system, you must be able to determine exactly what you have on the system. Windows includes a utility that collects and reports information about the configuration of the specified computer. You can use this tool from within Windows or from a command line, with switches.

The System Information window

To open Windows Diagnostics from within Windows, click Start and choose All Programs, Accessories, System Tools, System Information. The System Information window, shown in Exhibit 9-6, opens. You can also run msinfo32 at a command prompt.

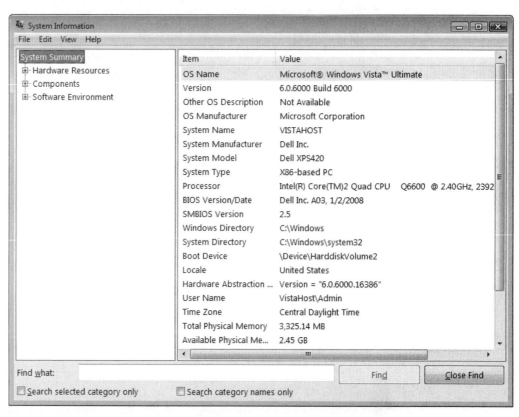

Exhibit 9-15: The System Information window in Windows Vista

The System Information window displays system summary information plus detailed information in the following categories:

- Hardware Resources
- Components
- Software Environment
- Internet Settings (in some Windows versions)

System information for remote computers

To display the statistics of a remote computer, choose View, Remote Computer and enter the name of the computer. For you to run msinfo32 to report on a remote computer, the remote computer must have Windows Management Instrumentation (WMI) installed. This is a Windows component that's installed by default. You must also have appropriate privileges to view system information on a remote computer.

The ver command

The `ver` command is a command-line utility that displays the version of MS-DOS or Windows running on the computer. It's available in all client versions of Windows.

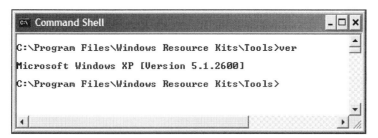

Exhibit 9-16: The ver command in Windows XP

D-4: Running Windows Diagnostics

Do it!

System Configuration is open and the Tools tab is active.

Here's how	Here's why
1 Select **System Information** and click **Launch**	
Maximize the System Information window	
Observe the Summary information	The details pane shows general information about the configuration of your computer.

2 If necessary, expand Hardware Resources	⊟ Hardware Resources
	   Conflicts/Sharing
	   DMA
	   Forced Hardware
	   I/O
	   IRQs
	   Memory
	
	To display the categories listed.

Describe to students what they are seeing in each subcategory. Select each subcategory and observe the information it reports	

3 Expand Components	⊟ Components
	  ⊞ Multimedia
	    CD-ROM
	    Sound Device
	    Display
	    Infrared
	  ⊞ Input
	    Modem
	  ⊞ Network
	  ⊞ Ports
	  ⊞ Storage
	    Printing
	    Problem Devices
	    USB
	
	To display the categories listed.

Describe to students what they are seeing in each subcategory. Select each subcategory and observe the information it reports	If necessary, expand any subcategories that contain additional categories.

4 Expand Software Environment, and select each subcategory and observe the information it reports	Software Environment — System Drivers — Signed Drivers — Environment Variables — Print Jobs — Network Connections — Running Tasks — Loaded Modules — Services — Program Groups — Startup Programs — OLE Registration — Windows Error Reporting
	To display the categories listed.
5 Close the System Information window, and then close System Configuration	
6 Open a Command Prompt window	
Type **ver** and press ⏎ ENTER	`Microsoft Windows [Version 6.0.6000]`
	The version of Windows you are using is reported at the command line.
Close all open windows	

System File Checker

Explanation

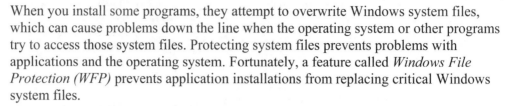

When you install some programs, they attempt to overwrite Windows system files, which can cause problems down the line when the operating system or other programs try to access those system files. Protecting system files prevents problems with applications and the operating system. Fortunately, a feature called *Windows File Protection (WFP)* prevents application installations from replacing critical Windows system files.

To verify that you have the original protected system files, you can use the command-line tool called *System File Checker* to scan all protected files. If System File Checker discovers that a protected file has been overwritten, it retrieves the correct version of the file from the cache folder (the folder that holds needed system files) or the Windows CD-ROM and replaces the incorrect file.

To use the System File Checker to scan all protected system files, open a Command Prompt window and enter `sfc /scannow`. If prompted, insert the Windows CD-ROM and complete the scan. In Windows XP, you can also use the `/scanonce` switch to scan once at the next reboot, and use the `/scanboot` switch to scan at every boot. For help with the System File Checker syntax, enter `sfc /?` at the command prompt.

Do it!

D-5: Using System File Checker

Here's how	Here's why
1 Open an administrative Command Prompt window	Click Start, choose Accessories, right-click Command Prompt, and choose Run as administrator.
2 Enter **sfc /scannow**	To verify that the protected operating system files are the originals.
	You might be prompted for the Windows installation files if the service pack and hotfixes you've installed have replaced some of the original operating system files.
Click **Cancel**	
Click **Yes**	To skip the file.
Click **Cancel**	To stop the scan.

Unit summary: Windows maintenance

Topic A   In this topic, you learned how to monitor the operating system. You used **Task Manager** to monitor applications, users, performance, and network utilization and to end a process. You used **Event Viewer** to monitor events on the computer. You worked with the three logs—Application, Security, and System—on both local and remote computers. You learned how to sort, filter, and search through events in the log. In addition, you learned how to manage the **Event log files** and change their options.

Topic B   In this topic, you learned how to perform operating system **maintenance** tasks that can help prevent problems from occurring with Windows computers. These tasks include **backing up** and **restoring** data, creating a system restore point, and restoring to a restore point.

Topic C   In this topic, you used **Task Scheduler** to create and configure scheduled tasks. You created a basic task by using a wizard, and then you created a task manually.

Topic D   In this topic, you learned how to use various Windows troubleshooting tools to identify and resolve **operating system problems**. You identified the symptoms, causes, and resolutions of common startup errors. You also learned how to use startup modes and the **System Configuration utility** to troubleshoot.

Review questions

1. What's the GUI utility that provides information on processes that are running on a computer?

    A Event Viewer

    B Task Manager

    C System Monitor

    D Windows Diagnostic

2. Which tab in Task Manager can you use to end an application that has experienced a general protection fault and isn't responding to keyboard or mouse input?

    A Applications

    B Networking

    C Performance

    D Processes

    E Users

3. Which tab in Task Manager can you use to determine if an application is overloading the CPU?

    A Applications

    B Networking

    C Performance

    D Processes

4. Which Event Viewer log would you monitor if you believed that an unauthorized person might be accessing a computer after hours?

    Security

5 Which event types are used only in the Security log? [Choose all that apply.]

   A Error
   B Warning
   C Information
   D Success Audit
   E Failure Audit

6 Which of the following display types can you use to display data in Performance Monitor? [Choose all that apply.]

   A Line graph
   B Pie chart
   C Histogram
   D Pictogram

7 In Event Viewer, what is the difference between sorting a view and filtering a view?

   When you sort a view, it groups all events displayed in ascending or descending order by the column heading you clicked on. When you filter a view, it displays only those events that meet your criteria.

8 In Task Scheduler, a(n) _____ causes an action to be performed.

   trigger

9 True or false? You can configure a pop-up message, a text message, and an e-mail message as actions in Task Scheduler.

   False. You can't configure a text message.

10 When you use Windows Backup to back up the system state, which files are backed up?

   - *Registry*
   - *Boot files*
   - *COM+ class registration database*
   - *IIS metadirectory*
   - *Windows File Protection system files*

11 What are the two modes you can run Windows Backup in?

   Wizard mode and Advanced mode.

12 Which backup type requires that you have the most recent normal backup in addition to this backup if you want to restore files? [Choose all that apply.]

   A Copy
   B Daily
   C Differential
   D Incremental
   E Normal

13 For what intervals can you schedule backups?

- Daily
- Weekly
- Monthly
- At predefined times
- On predefined days

14 When Windows detects the beginning of a request to make a system configuration change, what type of restore point is created?

A System checkpoint

B Manual restore point

C Installation restore point

D Automatic checkpoint

15 Which type of error presents as the computer system booting successfully, but reports an error message when loading the operating system?

A Boot error

B Operating system startup error

C Operating system load error

D Hardware error

16 A floppy or CD-ROM that isn't bootable in a bootable drive can cause which boot errors? [Choose all that apply.]

A Invalid boot or non-system disk error

B Inaccessible boot device

C NTLDR is missing, or Couldn't find NTLDR

D Bad or missing Command interpreter

17 A problem with physical memory can cause which operating system startup errors? [Choose all that apply.]

A Error in CONFIG.SYS line ##

B Himem.sys not loaded

C Missing or corrupt Himem.sys

D Device/service has failed to start

18 An outdated device driver that needs to be updated can cause which operating system load error?

A Failure to start GUI

B Windows Protection Error—illegal operation

C User-modified settings cause improper operation at startup

D Application install, start, or load failure

19 If you're having problems with a device, which startup mode can you use to record all files used during the boot process in a file called ntbtlog.txt?

Enable boot logging

20 In the System Configuration utility, which mode can you use to load only basic devices and services while troubleshooting a problem?

  A Normal

  B Diagnostic

  C Selective

  D Debug

21 Can you use System Restore to uninstall a program?

No. System Restore doesn't replace the process of uninstalling a program. To completely remove the files installed by a program, Microsoft recommends that you remove the program by using the Add or Remove Programs utility or the program's own uninstall utility.

Independent practice activity

In this activity, you'll practice maintaining your Windows computer.

1 View events recorded on your computer by the operating system.

2 Sort the events by type.

3 Create a filter to display just Warning and Error system events.

4 Return the display to all system events.

5 Run Notepad and Internet Explorer.

6 Open Task Manager.

7 Use the Applications tab to end Notepad.

8 Find the process for Internet Explorer and end it.

9 End the explorer.exe process.

10 Use the Applications tab to start a new task for explorer.exe.

11 Close Task Manager.

12 Create a task to start Windows Calendar every weekday morning at 9:00 so you can check your appointments for the day.

13 Run the new task to ensure that it works correctly.

14 Restart the computer and use the advanced startup options to enable boot logging. Log on and open the log file. Verify that there were no errors.

Unit 10
SOHO networking

Unit time: 150 minutes

Complete this unit, and you'll know how to:

A Discuss networking components.

B Install and configure a small-office/home-office network.

Topic A: Networking basics

This topic covers the following CompTIA A+ 220-702 exam objective.

#	Objective

3.2	**Install and configure a small office / home office (SOHO) network**
	• Connection types
	  – Dial-up
	  – Broadband
	    • DSL
	    • Cable
	    • Satellite
	    • ISDN
	  – Wireless
	    • All 802.11
	    • WEP
	    • WPA
	    • SSID
	    • MAC filtering
	  – Routers / Access Points
	    • Disable SSID broadcast
	    • MAC filtering
	    • Firewall
	  – LAN (10/100/1000BaseT, Speeds)
	  – Bluetooth (1.0 vs. 2.0)
	  – Cellular
	  – Basic VoIP (consumer applications)
	• Basics of hardware and software firewall configuration
	  – Port assignment / setting up rules (exceptions)
	  – Port forwarding / port triggering
	• Physical installation
	  – Wireless router placement
	  – Cable length

Network connection types

Explanation

In this day and age, you can assume that all small-office/home-office (SOHO) networks are going to connect to the Internet in one way or another. The connection might be used to browse the Web, communicate with customers through e-mail, or connect to a private network at an office or school to check e-mail or transfer files. This section describe ways that a SOHO can connect to the Internet through an Internet service provider (ISP) and private networks.

POTS/PSTN

The slowest but least expensive Internet connection to an ISP is known as *plain old telephone service* (POTS). Also referred to as the *public switched telephone network* (PSTN), it's the network of the world's public circuit-switched telephone networks. Until recently, this was the most common method of home connection. You'd have to use a dial-up connection each time you wanted to connect to the ISP over the telephone line, as illustrated in Exhibit 10-1.

The connection isn't continuous, and when the line isn't connected to an ISP, it can be used for regular telephone service or any other telecommunications function. Data speed on a regular telephone line is a maximum of 56 Kbps.

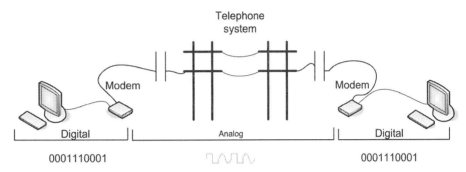

Exhibit 10-1: Communication via POTS/PSTN

ISDN

Integrated Services Digital Network (ISDN) technology also uses a telephone line to transmit data, but unlike POTS, the data isn't converted to analog form. The modem used must be digital. An ISDN line is digital and consists of two phone circuits, both carried on one pair of wires, along with a slower, third circuit, used for control signals.

Each data circuit can transmit data at up to 64 Kbps, and the two circuits can be combined to move data at a speed of 128 Kbps. This configuration of an ISDN line is known as the *basic rate interface (BRI)* and is intended for home and small-business users. Another, higher-cost ISDN level of service is called *primary service interface (PRI)* and is intended for larger organizations. It has 23 data channels and a control channel.

DSL

A *Digital Subscriber Line (DSL)* is a high-speed data and voice transmission line that uses telephone wires for data transmission but carries the digital data at frequencies well above those used for voice transmission. Voice and digital data can be transmitted on the same line at the same time. The regular voice telephone line must be dialed for each use, but the DSL part of the line is always connected to the computer.

A DSL can transmit data at speeds up to 1.5 Mbps in both directions, or it can be set up as an *asymmetric* line (ADSL), which can transmit up to 640 Kbps upstream (to the ISP) and 7.1 Mbps downstream (from the ISP). Higher bandwidth can be achieved by bonding multiple DSL lines.

Cable

A *cable modem* connects to the cable television line that's already installed or available in many homes. These devices are actually *transceivers* (transmitter/receivers), rather than modems, but they are commonly known as cable modems. With a cable modem, digital data is converted to analog signals and placed on the cable at the same time as the incoming television signal. The modem converts incoming analog data signals into digital data for the computer.

The data frequencies differ from the television signal frequencies, and the two signals don't interfere with one another on the cable. Depending on the individual configuration, a cable modem can transmit data at speeds from 500 Kbps up to 30 Mbps, and downstream data transfers are typically faster than upstream transfers. A cable connection is illustrated in Exhibit 10-2.

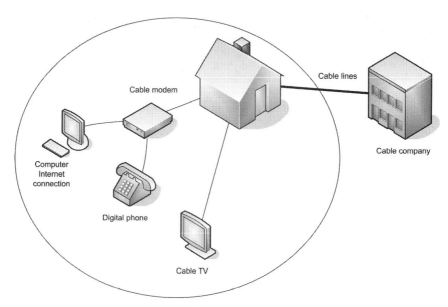

Exhibit 10-2: Cable connections

Many cable companies now offer *Voice over IP (VoIP)* service, also known as digital phone service, to their users. With VoIP, you can make telephone calls over a data network such as the Internet. VoIP converts the analog signals from digital back to voice at the other end so you can speak to anyone with a regular phone number.

To use VoIP, you need a high-speed Internet connection. You make calls by using one of the following sets of equipment:

- A regular telephone with an analog telephone adapter (ATA).
- An IP phone that has an RJ-45 connector instead of an RJ-11 connector; the RJ-45 connector plugs directly into your router.
- Software from your VoIP provider, a microphone, speakers, and a sound card for computer-to-computer communication.

The benefits of using VoIP include the following: a lower cost due to using established data networks; and the ability to take your VoIP phone to any location that has a data network, plug into that network, and receive calls as if you were on your home network. VoIP data transmission speeds and reliability are the same as for a data network.

Satellite

A satellite-link Internet connection to an ISP is now available nationwide. It's especially attractive in rural areas where telephone-based services might be limited and cable sometimes isn't available. A satellite communication link uses a dish similar to a satellite television dish, mounted on the building, to communicate with a stationary satellite in orbit. The server is connected to the dish antenna. Incoming Internet data travels from the ISP to the satellite in orbit, and then down to the dish and into the LAN server.

The speed of the connection varies according to the ISP but can go up to 1.5 Mbps. The uplink connection from the LAN to the ISP is usually a telephone-line/modem connection and isn't as fast as the satellite downlink.

A digital radio signal from the LAN up to the satellite—which in turn sends the signal to the ISP—is also available. However, it costs much more than the telephone connection, which is usually adequate for sent data. Exhibit 10-3 illustrates how a satellite ISP sends data at high speed to LANs via a stationary satellite and receives data from the LAN over a slower telephone/modem line.

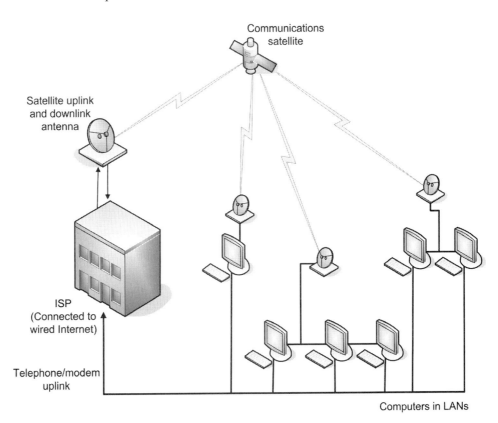

Exhibit 10-3: Satellite ISP configuration

Wireless

The term "wireless" refers to several technologies and systems that don't use cables for communication, including public radio, cellular telephones, one-way paging, satellites, infrared light, and private, proprietary radio. Because of the expense and the concern that increasing the use of wireless technology might affect our health, airplane control systems, pacemakers, and other similar items, wireless isn't as popular as wired data transmission. However, wireless is an important technology for mobile devices and for Internet access in remote locations where other methods aren't an option.

For Internet access, two popular applications of wireless are:
- Fixed-point wireless, sometimes called *Wireless Local Loop (WLL)*
- Mobile wireless

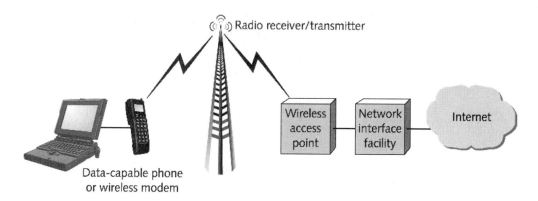

Exhibit 10-4: A wireless WAN

Cellular

All of the major cellular phone companies now provide Internet connection service for their customers. Wherever you have cell phone reception, you can connect to the Internet through your Internet-capable phone or laptop by using a cellular network PC card. Cell phone companies typically charge an additional monthly fee for this service.

The connection speed for cellular Internet service is faster than dial-up, but slower than DSL or cable. There are currently three connection technologies in use: Enhanced Data rates for GSM Evolution (EDGE), Evolution-Data Optimized (EV-DO), and High-Speed Downlink Packet Access (HSDPA).

At the time this course was written, many cellular providers were promoting their *3G* and *4G* networks. The 3G networks are wide-area cell-phone networks that evolved to incorporate high-speed Internet access and video telephony. The 3G standard is based on the ITU's IMT-2000 standard and doesn't specify a standard data rate. It typically provides a minimum speed of 2 Mbps and a maximum of 14.4 Mbps for stationary users, and 348 Kbps in a moving vehicle. The 3G networks use EV-DO technology. The 4G networks are capable of speeds of 100 Mbps while moving and 1 Gbps while stationary.

The 4G standard is still in development. Access to 4G networks will be provided by such schemes as the following: Code Division Multiple Access (CDMA); Multi-carrier code division multiple access (MC-CDMA); and Frequency Division Multiple Access (FDMA) schemes, such as Orthogonal FDMA (OFDMA), Single Carrier FDMA (SC-FDMA), and Interleaved FDMA.

Bluetooth

Bluetooth is a short-distance—up to 10 meters—radio communications technology developed by the Bluetooth Special Interest Group, which includes more than a thousand companies. Bluetooth is designed to enable devices—such as cell phones, PDAs, personal audio players, PC peripherals, and PCs—to discover the presence of other Bluetooth devices within range. Once detected, these devices self-configure and begin communicating with each other. With Bluetooth devices, you shouldn't have to configure any communications parameters, such as network addresses.

Bluetooth 1.0 was more difficult to configure and has since been replaced with Bluetooth 2.0 and Bluetooth 3.0. Bluetooth 3.0, adopted as a new standard in 2009, is the fastest Bluetooth yet, using the wireless standard 802.11 for communication.

Network address translation

Network address translation (NAT) devices correlate internal and external addresses. A SOHO network might have just a single IP address on the Internet, but dozens of private (internal) IP addresses. All Internet communications will appear to come from that single public IP address. The NAT router makes sure that inbound and outbound packets arrive at the correct destination. Unless an internal system has initiated a communication session, external devices cannot find or communicate with internal devices due to the translated network addressing scheme.

There are a couple of good reasons to use NAT:

- **Availability of addresses** — The American Registry for Internet Numbers (ARIN) regulates and assigns IP addresses that can be used directly on the Internet. Companies must apply and pay for the use of address ranges, and typically must justify the addresses they request. Rather than going through the trouble for every new block of network devices they add, companies use a private range of addresses within their network.
- **Security** — By using private addresses within the company, network administrators make it more difficult for hackers and automated malware on the Internet to discover and compromise internal systems.

In the SOHO environment, the typical cable or DSL modem provides NAT functionality to map internal addresses to one or more IP addresses assigned by the Internet service provider. In a corporate environment, routers, firewalls, or other devices provide large-scale address translation services.

Firewalls and proxy servers

A *firewall* is a device that controls traffic between networks, typically between a public network and a private internal network. Firewalls examine the contents of network traffic and permit or block transmission based on rules.

At their core, all firewalls protect networks by using some combination of the following techniques:

- NAT (network address translation)
- Basic packet filtering
- Stateful packet inspection (SPI)

Basic firewalls use only one technique, usually NAT, but firewalls that are more comprehensive use all of the techniques combined. Of course, as you add features, complexity and cost increase.

Stateless packet filters examine IP addresses and ports to determine whether a packet should be passed on or forwarded. Stateful packet filters monitor outbound and inbound traffic by watching addresses, ports, and connection data. Stateful packet filters can determine whether a packet is part of an existing communication stream or a new stream.

Some more advanced firewalls "understand" the data contained in packets and thus can enforce more complex rules. For example, an Application-layer firewall might determine that an inbound packet is carrying an HTTP (Web) request and is going to a permitted address and port. Such a packet would be transmitted. Packets carrying other protocols or going to other addresses might be blocked.

Proxy servers

A *proxy server* is a type of firewall that services requests on behalf of clients. With a proxy server, a client's request is not actually sent to the remote host. Instead, it goes to the proxy server, which then sends the request to the remote node on behalf of the client. Before sending the packet, the proxy server replaces the original sender's address and other identifying information with its own. When the response arrives, the proxy server looks up the original sending computer's information, updates the incoming packet, and forwards it to the client.

By these actions, a proxy server masks internal IP addresses, as a NAT device does. It also blocks unwanted inbound traffic—there will be no corresponding outbound connection data in its tables, so the packets will be dropped. Many proxy servers also provide caching functions. The contents of popular Web pages, for example, could be saved on the proxy server and served from there, rather than by sending requests out across a WAN link.

Do it!

Discuss with students why they believe their answer is the best choice in each scenario.

A-1: Selecting a connection technology

Exercises

1 For each user, select the appropriate connection technology.

Susan is a salesperson who travels extensively. She needs to send and receive communication with the home office and clients while in transit. What's Susan's best choice for connection technology?

Wireless. Many locations such as coffee houses, airport terminals, and other public buildings, have wireless access points that Susan could use to connect to her company's LAN through the Internet.

Another option is cellular: Susan could use a cellular network card in her laptop to communicate with the company's LAN from anywhere she has cell phone service. Depending on how often Susan connects and how time-critical her data is, this option might be best even with its cost.

James is an architect who works out of his home in a mountainous region. James must send and receive large CAD drawings to and from clients and builders. What is James's best choice for connection technology?

With James's remote location, he's probably too far away to connect via cable or DSL lines. Dial-up service using PSTN would likely be terribly slow for uploading and downloading the CAD drawings. Although it might be more expensive, the best bet would be satellite service with transfer speeds that are the same for uploading and downloading.

Grace lives next to James in the Adirondack mountains. She is retired and uses e-mail to communicate with her children and grandchildren all over the country. Sometimes they send her digital pictures attached to the messages so she can see the grandchildren. She occasionally uses her Web browser to look up information. What is Grace's best choice for connection technology?

Grace's livelihood doesn't rely on her Internet connection; she doesn't send large files; and she receives picture files occasionally. An inexpensive dial-up service, using the phone lines already connected to Grace's house, would serve her needs just fine.

Outlander Spices currently spends thousands of dollars a month for local and long distance telephone service. Like most companies, they have high-speed Internet connections to most locations. What connection technology could they use to support their telephone needs and save money?

Voice over IP (VoIP).

2 Describe the ways that the cellular telephone system can be used to make Internet connections.

Cellular PC cards enable you to connect your laptop computer to your cell phone or directly to the cellular network. However, the most common method is to use the Internet features built into your cell phone or handheld computer. Such devices enable you to browse the Web, manage your e-mail, and receive alerts (such as from stock market or sports monitoring sites).

Ethernet

Explanation

Ethernet is the most popular form of LAN in use today. It's popular because it strikes a good balance between ease of setup and use, speed, and cost. Four types of Ethernet architecture are available now. Each type is distinguished primarily by the speed at which it operates.

- **10 Gigabit Ethernet** (also called **10GbE**) — Is the fastest of the Ethernet standards. With a data rate of 10 Gbps (gigabits per second), it is 10 times faster than Gigabit Ethernet.
- **1000-Mbps Ethernet** (or **Gigabit Ethernet**) — Operates at a speed of 1000 Mbps (1000 megabits per second = 1 gigabit per second). It's used for large, high-speed LANs and heavy-traffic server connections. Few, if any, home networks require Gigabit Ethernet.
- **100-Mbps Ethernet** (or **Fast Ethernet**) — Operates at a speed of 100 Mbps. It can also handle data at 10 Mbps, and this feature allows devices running at the slower speed to operate on the same network as devices operating at 100 Mbps.
- **10-Mbps Ethernet** (or **Twisted-Pair Ethernet**) — Operates at a speed of 10 Mbps. The first Ethernet version was developed by the Xerox Corporation in the 1970s and later became known as Ethernet IEEE 802.3.

Each Ethernet version can be set up with various types of wire or cable. However, the different speeds of the versions and the conditions in which they operate usually dictate what type of connecting wires you need to use. Designations for the different Ethernet standards are based on the medium each standard uses:

- **BASE-X** and **BASE-R** standards — Run over fiber optic cable.
- **BASE-W** standards — Run over fiber optic cables; referred to as *Wide Area Network Physical Layer (WAN PHY)*. BASE-W standards use the same types of fiber and support the same distances as 10GBASE-R standards; however, with BASE-W, Ethernet frames are encapsulated in SONET frames.
- **BASE-T** standards — Run over twisted-pair cable, either shielded or unshielded.
- **BASE-CX** standards — Run over shielded copper twisted-pair cable.

Most current Ethernet installations use shielded twisted-pair (STP) cable, unshielded twisted-pair (UTP) cable, or fiber optic cable. Older Ethernet installations used either 50-ohm RG58/U coaxial cable (also known as thin Ethernet or 10Base2) or 50-ohm RG8/U coaxial (known as thick Ethernet or 10Base5). However, these are both obsolete now.

10 Gigabit Ethernet standards

The following table lists the 10 Gigabit Ethernet standards and their specifications.

Standard	Medium	Distance
10GBASE-T	Copper twisted-pair, shielded or unshielded	100 meters with CAT6a; up to 55 meters with CAT6
10GBASE-SR, 10GBASE-SW	Multi-mode fiber	26 meter or 82 meters, depending on cable type 300 meters over 50 µm (microns) at 2000 MHz per km with OM3 multi-mode fiber
10GBASE-LR, 10GBASE-LW	Single-mode fiber	10 km
10GBASE-ER, 10GBASE-EW	Single-mode fiber	40 km
10GBASE-ZR, 10GBASE-ZW	Single-mode fiber	80 km

Gigabit Ethernet standards

The following table lists the gigabit Ethernet standards and their specifications.

Standard	Medium	Distance
1000BASE-T	Unshielded twisted-pair: CAT5, CAT5e, or CAT6	100 meters per network segment
1000BASE-CX	Balanced copper shielded twisted-pair	25 meters
1000BASE-LX	Single-mode optic fiber	5 km
1000BASE-LX10	Single-mode optic fiber	10 km
1000BASE-BX10	Single-mode fiber, over single-strand fiber	10 km
1000BASE-LH	Single-mode optic fiber	10km
1000BASE-ZX	Single-mode optic fiber	70 km
1000BASE-SX	Multi-mode optic fiber	500 meters

Fast Ethernet standards

The following table lists the Fast Ethernet standards and their specifications.

Standard	Medium	Distance	Notes
100BASE-TX	Twisted-pair copper: CAT5 or above	100 meters per network segment	Runs over two pairs: one pair of twisted wires in each direction. The most common Fast Ethernet.
100BASE-T4	Twisted-pair copper: CAT3		Requires four pairs: one pair for transmitting; one for receiving; and remaining pairs switch direction as negotiated. An early implementation of Fast Ethernet
100BASE-T2	Twisted-pair copper		Runs over two pairs.
100BASE-FX	Single- or multi-mode fiber	400 meters for half-duplex; 2 km for full-duplex over MMF	Uses two strands: one for receiving and one for transmitting. Not compatible with 10BASE-FL.
100BASE-SX	Multi-mode fiber	300 meters	Uses two strands of MMF: one for receiving and one for transmitting. Backward-compatible with 10BASE-FL.
100BASE-BX	Single-mode fiber	20 km	Uses a single strand of SMF.

Do it!

A-2: Describing Ethernet standards

Questions	Answers
1 Which is the fastest Ethernet standard?	10 Gigabit Ethernet (10GbE). With a data rate of 10 gigabits per second, it is 10 times faster than Gigabit Ethernet.
2 Which Ethernet standards run over fiber optic cables?	BASE-X, BASE-R, and BASE-W
3 What type of cabling do most current Ethernet networks use?	Shielded twisted-pair (STP), unshielded twisted-pair (UTP), or fiber optic cable.
4 Which 10 Gigabit Ethernet standard can run the longest distance?	10GBASE-ZR and 10GBASE-ZW, at distances up to 80 km.
5 What type of cabling would you use for a 1000BASE-T Ethernet network?	Unshielded twisted-pair: CAT5, CAT5e, or CAT6.
6 What's the difference between 100BASE-TX and 1000BASE-T cabling?	1000BASE-T uses all four wire pairs. 100BASE-TX runs over two pairs—one pair of twisted wires in each direction.

Wireless LAN connection components

Explanation

To establish a wireless LAN, you need wireless network cards in the computers and a wireless router or a *wireless access point (WAP)* device on the network. The router or WAP broadcasts radio signals, and the wireless network cards pick up the broadcasts.

Wireless NICs

Wired-network adapters of all current types (PCI, PC Card, and USB, shown in Exhibit 10-5) come in wireless versions. Wireless capability is built into many newer laptops as standard equipment and can easily be added to laptops by using wireless PC Card or USB NICs. Desktops are also easily outfitted with wireless capabilities by adding PCI Card or USB wireless NICs. If wireless access is available, these cards can communicate with a wireless access point—examples are shown in Exhibit 10-6—allowing you to access the network without using cables. This is especially useful in places like libraries, where wandering around with a laptop while maintaining network access can be very convenient.

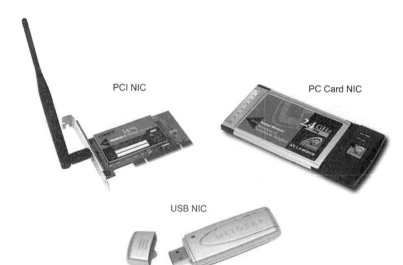

Exhibit 10-5: Wireless NICs

Wireless access points

The access point (AP) contains the following: at least one interface for connecting to the wired network (this interface is typically called the "WAN port"); and transmitting equipment for connecting with the wireless clients.

APs often integrate other networking functions. Many include Ethernet networking ports for connecting wired devices and thus function as switches. Many APs include routing capabilities, and such devices most often also include firewall functions. The popular Linksys Wireless-G family of wireless routers is one such example of multifunction APs. Two brands of wireless access points are shown in Exhibit 10-6.

Exhibit 10-6: Wireless access points

Manufacturers of wireless LAN equipment will often promote access ranges of 550 meters. As shown in the following table, as you move farther away from an access point, the data transfer speed drops. Remember that interference from your building's structure and environmental noise can also affect data throughput.

IEEE speed	Data speed	Distance from AP
High	4.3 Mbps	40 to 125 meters
Medium	2.6 Mbps	55 to 200 meters
Standard	1.4 Mbps	90 to 400 meters
Standard low	0.8 Mbps	115 to 550 meters

TIPS *You can use the analogy of a light bulb and light to describe AP radio signals. The farther you move away from the light source, the less light you get from it. Eventually, you'll be in darkness. If the light passes through an object such as a curtain, the light will be dimmed, if not totally blocked.*

You should place your wireless LAN access points within 60 to 90 meters of the wireless clients. When determining the number and placement of WAPs, you need to account for obstructions in the floor plan. For example, in a large room with no walls, you could centrally place one WAP to service up to 200 devices.

There are two methods for determining correct WAP placement: an informal site survey and a formal site survey.

- In an *informal site survey*, you temporarily set up the WAPs at the locations you're considering for permanent placement. Then you use a wireless client to test the signal strength of connections within the range that WAP will service, preferably testing from actual client desk locations. If the connection signals are strong where you need them to be, you go back and permanently mount and install the WAPs. If not, you move the WAPs and retest.

- In a *formal site survey*, you use field-strength measuring equipment. You install a test antenna in each estimated WAP location and then use the field-strength measuring equipment to determine the exact strength of a test signal at various points within the WAP's range. You move the test antenna to obtain the best possible signal for the wireless coverage area. Once you've determined the exact locations for the WAPs, you can permanently mount and install them.

Do it!

A-3: Examining wireless devices

Here's how	Here's why
1 In wireless communications, what replaces the wire?	**Radio waves or infrared light.**
2 Does your classroom have a wireless access point visible?	**Answers will vary.**
3 If so, where is it placed in relation to client computers?	**Answers will vary.**
4 Walk around the classroom with a wireless client (such as a notebook computer) and observe the signal strength reported by Windows Vista	(If the equipment is available.) An icon in the system tray reports the signal strength for the wireless connection.

Wireless standards

Explanation

The *IEEE 802.11 standard* specifies a technology that operates in the 2.4–2.5 GHz band. Wireless networks operate according to the specifications of the IEEE 802.11 standards. The 802.11 standard defines an access point as a device that functions as a transparent bridge between the wireless clients and either a private wired network in the home or office or the Internet. The access point contains at least one interface for connecting to the wired network, and it contains transmitting equipment for connecting with the wireless clients.

The current and future wireless network standards under 802.11 are listed in the following table.

Standard	Description
802.11a	Ratified in 1999, 802.11a uses Orthogonal Frequency Division Multiplexing (OFDM) signaling to transmit data. OFDM offers significant performance benefits compared with the more traditional spread-spectrum systems. OFDM is a modulation technique for transmitting large amounts of digital data over radio waves. Capacity per channel is 54 Mbps with real throughput at about 31 Mbps. It operates at a frequency of 5 GHz, which supports eight overlapping channels.
802.11b	Ratified in 1999, 802.11b is one of the most commonly used 802.1x technologies. Uses Direct Sequence Spread Spectrum (DSSS). Capacity per channel is 11 Mbps with real throughput at about 6 Mbps. It operates at a frequency of 2.4 GHz, which supports three non-overlapping channels.
802.11c	Pertains to the operation of bridge connections. Was moved to the 802.1 standards set.
802.11d	Ratified in 2001, 802.11d aims to produce versions of 802.11b that are compatible with other frequencies so it can be used in countries where the 2.4 GHz band isn't available.
802.11e	Not yet ratified, 802.11e adds Quality of Service (QoS) capabilities to 802.11 networks. It uses a Time Division Multiple Access (TDMA) data signaling scheme and adds extra error correction.
802.11F	Ratified in 2003, 802.11F improves the handover mechanism in 802.11 so users can maintain a connection while roaming. It's designed to give network users the same roaming freedom that cell phone users have.
802.11g	Ratified in 2003, 802.11g is a combination of 802.11a and 802.11b. It can use either DSSS or OFDM to transmit data. Capacity per channel is 54 Mbps with real throughput at about 12 Mbps. It operates at a frequency of 2.4 GHz. It's a commonly used 802.11 technology.
802.11h	Ratified in 2003, 802.11h attempts to improve on 802.11a by adding better control over radio channel selection and transmission power.
802.11i	Ratified in 2004, 802.11i deals with security. This is an entirely new standard based on the Advanced Encryption Standard (AES). This standard has a feature called Robust Security Network (RSN), which defines two security methodologies. The first is for legacy-based hardware using RC4, and the second one is for new hardware based on AES.
802.11j	Ratified in 2004, 802.11j allows 802.11a and HiperLAN2 networks to coexist in the same airwaves. The 802.11j standard changed the 5GHz signaling capabilities to support Japanese regulatory requirements.
802.11k	A wireless network management system, currently in progress.
802.11l	This letter was skipped by the IEEE governing board to avoid confusion with 802.11i.
802.11m	This standard maintains the documentation for the 802.11 family.
802.11n	Currently in progress, 802.11n is a 200+ Mbps standard.

Although devices that support the 802.11a standard are generally incompatible with those that support 802.11b, some devices are equipped to support either 802.11a or 802.11b. The newest approved standard, 802.11g, allows 802.11b and 802.11g devices to operate together on the same network. This standard was created specifically for backward compatibility with the 802.11b standard. Many modern APs support multiple standards. For example, one AP might offer concurrent support for 802.11a, b, g, and n clients, in addition to 100 Mbps wired network clients.

Network protocols

Network *protocols* are the languages that computers, servers, and network devices use to communicate with each other. Protocols send data across the network in units called *packets*. The following table describes some common protocols you can use in Windows networks.

Protocol	Description
TCP/IP	(Transmission Control Protocol/Internet Protocol) A routable, non-proprietary protocol that's the predominant Windows network protocol. It's supported by all versions of Windows and most other non-Microsoft operating systems. TCP/IP is also the protocol of the Internet.
IPX/SPX	(Internetwork Packet Exchange/Sequenced Packet Exchange) A routable, proprietary protocol that was the native protocol in early versions of Novell NetWare. Later versions of NetWare supported TCP/IP as the native protocol. Windows computers can connect to IPX/SPX networks and NetWare servers by using Microsoft's version of IPX/SPX, called NWLink. To share files and printers on a NetWare server, you must install the Microsoft Client for NetWare.
AppleTalk	A routable network protocol supported by Apple Macintosh computers. Windows NT and Windows 2000 support AppleTalk. Mac OS X (10.2 and later) supports TCP/IP and can connect to Windows networks without requiring AppleTalk support. AppleTalk computers are called *nodes* and can be configured as parts of *zones* for sharing resources. As with other networks, each node on an AppleTalk network must be configured with a unique network address.
NetBEUI	(NetBIOS Extended User Interface) A non-routable, proprietary Microsoft protocol that's supported in Windows 9x/Me, Windows NT, and Windows 2000. NetBEUI uses NetBIOS (Network Basic Input/Output System) services to communicate with other computers on a network. (NetBIOS helps with computer names and some basic communication services.) Although it isn't technically supported in Windows XP, you can install it by manually copying files from the installation CD-ROM. What's nice about NetBEUI is that it has no settings to configure. You install the protocol, connect the computer to the network, and it just works. The drawback is that it isn't routable, so it can't pass data from one network segment to another. This means that it can't be used for remote access or any communication outside a single segment.

Wireless networks send and receive information by using one of these major wireless protocols:

- **Wi-Fi** (Wireless Fidelity) — The most widely used wireless technology at present. Wi-Fi began as the 802.11b IEEE standard, but most implementations have been upgraded to use the newer 802.11g standard. The 802.11b and 802.11g standards have an indoor transmission range of up to 35 meters.
- **IEEE 802.11a** — An improved version of the original Wi-Fi technology and based on the same IEEE 802 standard. Devices supporting the 802.11a standard have an indoor transmission range of up to 35 meters and are not compatible with 802.11b.
- **WiMAX** (IEEE 802.16 Air Interface Standard) — A point-to-multipoint broadband wireless access standard. It's an emerging wireless connection standard for long distances.
- **Bluetooth** — A standard for short-range wireless communication and data synchronization between devices. As discussed earlier, the latest version of Bluetooth uses the 802.11 standard for communication between devices.

Do it!

A-4: Comparing network protocols

Questions and answers

1. Which protocol was used in early versions of Novell NetWare?

    A   TCP/IP

    B   NetBEUI

    C   IPX/SPX

    D   AppleTalk

2. What is the predominant protocol in Windows networks?

    A   TCP/IP

    B   NetBEUI

    C   IPX/SPX

    D   AppleTalk

3. Which protocol requires no configuration?

    A   TCP/IP

    B   NetBEUI

    C   IPX/SPX

    D   AppleTalk

4. List the major wireless protocols.

    Wi-Fi (802.11b and 802.11g), Bluetooth, 802.11a, and WiMAX.

5. Are 802.11b products compatible with 802.11a products?

    No. However, 802.11g products are usually backward-compatible with 802.11b.

WLAN security risks

Explanation

Wireless devices present a whole new set of threats that network administrators might be unaware of. The most obvious risks concerning wireless networks are theft and rogue devices. Most cell phones, text pagers, PDAs, and wireless NICs are small enough that they can easily be lost or stolen. Because they are easy to conceal and contain valuable information about a company, they have become favorite targets of intruders. Wireless LANs can be subject to session hijacking and man-in-the-middle attacks. Additional risks remain because anyone can purchase an access point and set it up.

Wireless access points, when set up right out of the box, have no security configured. They broadcast their presence—in essence saying, "Hey, my name is xxx, here I am!" The free availability of 802.11 network audit tools, such as AirSnort and NetStumbler, and even some PDAs, means that breaking into wireless networks configured with weak security is quite easy. These tools can be used to check wireless security by identifying unauthorized clients or access points and verifying encryption usage.

There are other tools, however, in the form of management software. To eliminate 802.11 shortcomings and to help improve the image of wireless technology on the market, the Institute of Electronic and Electric Engineers (IEEE) and the Wireless Ethernet Compatibility Alliance (WECA) proposed standards for significantly improved user authentication and media access control mechanisms.

Additional risks associated with wireless networks include the following:

- The 802.1x transmissions generate detectable radio-frequency traffic in all directions. Persons wanting to intercept the data transmitted over the network might use many solutions to increase the distance over which detection is possible, including the use of metal tubes such as a Pringles can or a large tomato juice can.

- Without the use of an encryption standard of some type, data is passed in clear text form. Even though technologies such as Wired Equivalent Privacy (WEP) encrypt the data, they still lack good security. A determined listener can easily obtain enough traffic data to calculate the encryption key in use.

- The authentication mechanism is one-way, so it's easy for an intruder to wait until authentication is completed and then generate a signal to the client to trick it into thinking it has been disconnected from the access point. Meanwhile, the intruder, pretending to be the original client, begins to send data traffic to the server.

- The client connection request is a one-way open broadcast. This gives an intruder the opportunity to act as an access point to the client, and act as a client to the real network access point. An intruder can watch all data transactions between the client and access point, and then modify, insert, or delete packets at will.

- A popular pastime is *war driving*, which involves driving around with a laptop system configured to listen for open wireless access points. Several Web sites provide detailed information locating unsecured networks. These sites provide locations, sometimes on city maps, for the convenience of others looking for open access links to the Internet. This is an attractive method not only to capture data from networks, but also to connect to someone else's network, use their bandwidth, and pay nothing for it.

- *War chalking* is the process of marking buildings, curbs, and other landmarks to indicate the presence of an available access point and its connection details by utilizing a set of symbols and shorthand.

WLAN security components

There are four components to security on a wireless network:
- Access control
- Encryption
- Authentication
- Isolation

Access control

You can use various techniques to control which clients can access your AP. The simplest, and least effective, is to simply turn off SSID broadcasts. This "hides" the presence of your AP. However, the SSID (service set identifier) is also included in routine client-to-AP traffic. Thus, it's easy for appropriately configured devices to detect SSIDs that aren't explicitly broadcast.

A stronger method is to enable a MAC filter on your AP. The MAC address is the hardware-level address of a client's network adapter. On most APs, you can enter a list of permitted MACs, or blocked MACs, to limit connections. This method prevents access to resources on your network, but it's awkward to implement because each WAP must be configured with the MAC address of each wireless network card. This method is also not satisfactory because your data is still vulnerable to being read with a packet sniffer. Someone with a packet sniffer could view your MAC address and then configure his or her computer to use the same MAC address after you turn off your computer, effectively impersonating you on the network.

As with the SSID, valid MAC addresses are transmitted across the wireless network. Thus, a malicious user could detect a valid MAC address, configure his computer to impersonate that MAC address, and gain access to the AP.

Encryption

You can encrypt communications between your AP and clients. Various techniques exist, with some more secure than others. To make a connection, clients must use the same encryption scheme and possess the appropriate encryption key. Once connected, a static or dynamically changing key provides ongoing encryption.

In theory, encryption blocks unapproved connections to your AP. Additionally, as long as the encryption scheme is sufficiently strong, your data streams are kept private from eavesdroppers. As you will see, not all wireless encryption systems are sufficiently robust to actually provide these protections.

Authentication

Through RADIUS (Remote Authentication Dial-In User Service) or other systems, you can enable client authentication over your wireless network. Using a system similar to the user authentication mechanism you use to log onto a computer, an AP can authenticate the identity of a wireless client.

Authentication provides much stronger access control protection than does SSID hiding or MAC filtering. You should still use encryption with authentication. Without it, eavesdroppers could access the data that legitimate clients transmit when those clients have connected to the AP. Authentication typically requires the use of additional software or hardware devices, such as a RADIUS server.

Isolation

Isolation is a means of segregating network traffic. There are two types: wireless client isolation and network isolation.

With *wireless client isolation*, also called *AP isolation*, wireless clients are put onto individual VLANs (virtual LANs) so that they cannot access each other. This method is commonly used in public wireless networks to prevent one user from accessing another user's computer. Imagine the risk you face in a library or coffee shop, where another user might try to access your shared folders or even mount brute-force attacks on your PC over the Wi-Fi hotspot network.

You might also want to provide *network isolation*. For example, you might want to permit wireless clients to access the Internet and your corporate mail server, which is on your wired network. However, you might also want to prevent wireless clients from accessing other wired nodes, such as your file servers.

Some APs offer network isolation through custom routing configurations. You can also enable such isolation through your general network design and firewall configuration.

Transmission encryption

You should enable transmission encryption on your wireless routers unless you have a very good reason not to. Transmission encryption limits which clients can connect to your AP and protects data from eavesdropping during transmissions.

Products certified by the Wi-Fi Alliance as Wi-Fi compatible must support at least the WPA Personal level of encryption. As of this writing, products don't have to support the 802.11i standard, but the requirement will soon take effect.

Encryption method	Description
WEP	Wired Equivalent Privacy (WEP) was built into the 802.11 standards for wireless connectivity that govern how data can be encrypted while in transit on the wireless network. It uses a 64-bit or 128-bit symmetric encryption cipher. For WEP to work, a key is configured on both the WAP and the client. This key is used to encrypt the data transmitted between the WAP and the client. There are no standards for how the WEP key is to be placed on the clients and the WAP. Most implementations require you to type in the key manually on each client and the WAP.

Although WEP is an easy way to prevent casual hackers from viewing the traffic transmitted on your wireless LAN, it is the least secure encryption technique. WEP has known design flaws that make it relatively easy to crack. However, it is the only viable option for 802.11b and other older wireless clients. |
| WPA Personal | Wi-Fi Protected Access (WPA) was developed to overcome the weaknesses in WEP. It uses the RC4 symmetric cipher with a 128-bit key. WPA Personal uses a "pre-shared key" (PSK), which simply means that you must enter a passphrase on both the AP and the clients.

The actual encryption key is built from this passphrase and various other data, such as the sending node's MAC address. With the Temporal Key Integrity Protocol (TKIP) option, the full encryption key changes for each packet.

WPA authorizes and identifies users based on a secret key that changes automatically at a regular interval. WPA uses TKIP to change the temporal key every 10,000 packets. This ensures much greater security than the standard WEP. |
WPA2	WPA2 builds on WPA by adding more features from the 802.11i standard. Notably, WPA2 uses the Advanced Encryption System (AES) cipher for stronger encryption.
WPA Enterprise	This method works in conjunction with an 802.1X authentication server, which distributes unique keys to each individual. Communications between the client and AP are encrypted using the individual's key.
RADIUS	Remote Access Dial-in User Service (RADIUS) uses a specialized server for authentication and uses WEP for data encryption, as illustrated in Exhibit 10-7. The authentication server can include keys as part of the accept message that's sent back to the WAP. In addition, clients can usually request a key change. This ability ensures that keys are changed regularly to limit the ability of hackers to view information on the wireless network.
802.11i	This standard defines security mechanisms for wireless networks. As of this writing, 802.11i-compatible devices are relatively rare. However, the popularity of this new technology will grow as more people use wireless as their primary means of connecting to a network.

WPA Personal and PSK are roughly synonymous.

WPA with AES is roughly synonymous with WPA2.

You can configure a Windows server to act as a RADIUS server.

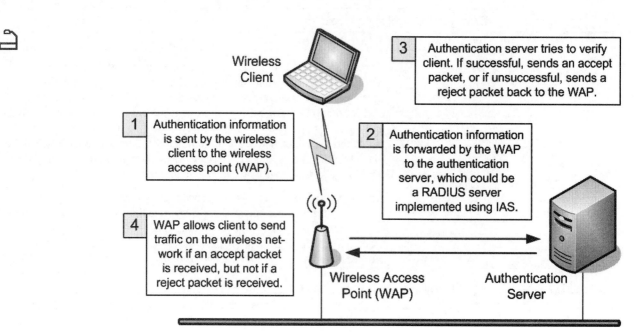

Exhibit 10-7: The 802.1x standard protocol authentication process

Do it! **A-5: Identifying the technology used to implement WLANs**

Questions and answers

1 What are the two technologies you can use to secure your wireless networks?

Wired Equivalent Privacy (WEP) and Wi-Fi Protected Access (WPA)

2 You've recently been hired as a consultant to evaluate Outlander Spices' wireless network security. What items should you check in evaluating their security practices?

Answers might include:

- *Is WEP enabled on their wireless devices? If not, enable WEP.*

- *Have they changed the default administrator passwords on their wireless access points? If not, change the default administrative password on the devices, and use a complex password.*

- *Are the default service set identifiers (SSIDs) still being used on their WAPs? If so, change the SSIDs. (Don't use meaningful names such as division or department names.)*

- *Are they still broadcasting SSIDs? If so, disable the Broadcast SSID setting so the client SSID and the WAP SSID match.*

- *Are they using RADIUS to add authentication to their WAP? If not, consider setting up a RADIUS server to authenticate the wireless connections with the WAP.*

- *Is the wireless network in a DMZ? If not, consider setting up an Internet-only zone and placing the wireless network in it to add a layer of encryption and authentication that makes the wireless network secure enough for sensitive data.*

- *Are wireless clients getting their IP addresses assigned statically or dynamically from a DHCP server? If the wireless clients are using DHCP, change to static IP addresses for wireless clients.*

- *Are MAC filters in place? If not, enable MAC address filtering on access points to prevent unauthorized wireless NICs from accessing the network.*

Topic B: Installing a wireless network

This topic covers the following CompTIA A+ 220-702 exam objective.

#	Objective

3.2	**Install and configure a small office / home office (SOHO) network**
	• Connection types
	   – Wireless
	      • DHCP settings
	   – Routers / Access Points
	      • Disable DHCP
	      • Use static IP
	      • Change SSID from default
	      • Disable SSID broadcast
	      • Change default username and password
	      • Update firmware
	• Basics of hardware and software firewall configuration
	   – Port assignment / setting up rules (exceptions)
	   – Port forwarding / port triggering
	• Physical installation
	   – Wireless router placement

Configuring a wireless access point

Explanation

After you have connected your wireless access point to your wired network, you need to configure it. When setting up your AP, you assign a service set identifier (SSID), which is essentially a name for your wireless network. It is possible, and sometimes likely, that multiple wireless networks will be accessible from a given location. In such cases, clients use the SSID to distinguish between WLANs and connect to a particular network.

An AP typically broadcasts the SSID. In this way, clients can discover the presence of a nearby AP. Such broadcasts identify the security mechanisms in place to enable clients to auto-configure connections.

Securing your AP

Out of the box, your wireless access point isn't secure. To make your AP more secure, you should complete the following configuration tasks:

- **Set the most secure transmission encryption method compatible with your clients** — Options might include WEP, WPA Personal, WPA2, WPA Enterprise, RADIUS, and 802.11i.
- **Update the access point's firmware version**.
- **Change default administrator accounts and passwords for the access point** — Many devices don't have a default password set on the Administrator account. Programs like AirSnort identify the manufacturer based on the MAC address, so if you only change the SSID, an informed hacker can still easily gain access. Also, changing the name of the widely available administrator accounts presents an added barrier to anyone trying to connect to the AP.
- **Change the default SSIDs** — When you change the SSID, don't use anything that reflects your company's main names, divisions, products, or address. Doing so would make your organization an easy target. If an SSID name is enticing enough, it might attract hackers.
- **Disable SSID broadcasts** — SSID broadcasting is enabled by default. When you disable this feature, an SSID must be configured in the client to match the SSID of the access point.
- **Separate the wireless network from the wired network** — Consider using an additional level of authentication, such as RADIUS, before you permit an association with your access points. RADIUS is an authentication, authorization, and accounting protocol for network access. The wireless clients can be separated so the connections not only use RADIUS authentication, but are also logged.
- **Put the wireless network in an Internet-access-only zone or a demilitarized zone (DMZ)** — Place your wireless access points in a DMZ, and have your wireless users tunnel into your network through a VPN (virtual private network). Setting up a VLAN for your DMZ requires extra effort on your part, but this solution adds a layer of encryption and authentication that makes your wireless network secure enough for sensitive data.
- **Disable DHCP within the WLAN to keep a tighter control over users** — Assign static IP addresses to your wireless clients. Doing this creates more administrative overhead to manage, but makes it harder to access your network.
- **Enable MAC address filtering on access points to limit unauthorized wireless NICs** — Many access points allow you to control access based on the MAC address of the NIC attempting to associate with it. If the MAC address of the wireless client's NIC isn't in the access point's table, access is denied. Although there are ways of spoofing a MAC address, it takes an additional level of sophistication.
- **Enable 802.1x** — This is the recommended method of authentication and encryption for enhanced security on computers running versions of Windows later than Windows XP. The use of 802.1x offers an effective solution for authenticating and controlling user traffic to a protected network, as well as dynamically varying encryption keys. The 802.1x standard ties EAP to both the wired and wireless LAN media and supports multiple authentication methods, such as token cards, Kerberos, one-time passwords, certificates, and public key authentication. You configure 802.1x encryption from the IEEE 802.1x tab of the policy setting's Properties dialog box.

A network administrator should periodically survey the site, by using a tool such as NetStumbler or AirSnort, to see if any rogue access points are installed on the network. In addition, the administrator can take a notebook equipped with a wireless sniffer and an external antenna outside the office building to see what information inside the building can be accessed by someone parked in the parking lot or across the street.

Do it!

B-1: Configuring a wireless access point (instructor demo)

You need a wireless access point installed on your classroom network for this activity. The steps were written for a D-Link WAP. If your WAP is different, alter the steps accordingly.

You also need your computer's MAC address.

Here's how	Here's why
1 Open Internet Explorer and enter the IP address of your WAP	You are prompted for administrator credentials on the WAP.
2 Enter the appropriate user name and password for your WAP and click **OK**	
3 Activate the Wireless Settings tab	
Edit the SSID box to read **123ABC567**	Remember, one of the security guidelines for creating a more secure SSID is that it not reflect your company's main names, divisions, products, or address.
For SSID broadcast, select **Disabled**	
For Security, select **WEP** and record the WEP key	WEP key: _____
Check **Apply**	The device restarts itself.
4 Activate the Tools tab	
In the New password and Confirm password boxes, enter **!pass4321**	
Check **Apply**	

5 Activate the Advanced tab

  Select **MAC filters**

  Choose **Only allow computers with MAC address listed below to access the network**

  In the Name box, enter your computer's name

  In the MAC address box, enter your computer's MAC address

  Check **Apply**

6 Close Internet Explorer

Tell students they would continue to add MAC addresses for all computers they wanted to give access to the WAP.

Configuring wireless clients

Explanation

When you implement an authenticating server, such as RADIUS, the wireless client must submit its credentials with the authenticating server before wireless network access is established. When the client computer is in range of the wireless AP, it tries to connect to the WLAN that is active on that AP.

If the wireless AP is configured to allow only secured or 802.1x-authenticated connections, it issues a challenge to the client. The wireless AP then sets up a restricted channel that allows the client to communicate with only the RADIUS server. The RADIUS server accepts a connection only from a trusted wireless AP, or one that has been configured as a RADIUS client on the Microsoft Internet Authentication Service (IAS) server and provides the shared secret key for that RADIUS client. The RADIUS server validates the client credentials against the directory.

If the client is successfully authenticated, the RADIUS server decides whether to authorize the client to use the WLAN. If the client is granted access, the RADIUS server transmits the client's master key to the wireless AP. The client and wireless AP now share common key information they can use to encrypt and decrypt the WLAN traffic passing between them. How you configure Windows clients to participate in this process depends on the operating system.

Windows Vista and Windows XP wireless clients

Wireless Auto Configuration dynamically selects the wireless network to which a connection attempt is made, based on configured preferences or default settings. Computers running Windows Vista and Windows XP support *Wireless Zero Configuration*, which enables computers to automatically connect to available wireless networks. By default, Windows Vista and Windows XP client computers can choose from available wireless networks and connect automatically without user action. Wireless Zero Configuration automatically configures such items as TCP/IP settings, DNS server addresses, and IAS server addresses. Wireless Zero Configuration includes support for 802.1x authentication and encryption.

The default settings for Wireless Zero Configuration using IEEE 802.1x authentication include:

- "Infrastructure before ad hoc mode, and computer authentication before user authentication."
- "WEP authentication attempts to perform an IEEE 802.11 shared key authentication if the network adapter has been preconfigured with a WEP shared key; otherwise, the network adapter reverts to the open system authentication."

Although the IEEE 802.1x security enhancements are available in Windows Vista and Windows XP, the network adapters and access points must also be compatible with this standard for deployment.

You can change the default settings to allow guest access, which isn't enabled by default. You shouldn't turn on guest access on a laptop using Wireless Zero Configuration. An unauthorized user could establish an ad hoc connection to the laptop and gain access to confidential information on it.

Windows 2000 Professional wireless clients

Computers running Windows 2000 Professional don't support Wireless Zero Configuration. You can configure a wireless network card for connection by using EAP-TLS or PEAP authentication, just as you can when configuring Windows Vista and Windows XP computers.

Only Windows Vista and Windows XP computers natively support IEEE 802.1x authentication. Microsoft provides an 802.1x Authentication Client download, which allows Windows 2000 computers to use the 802.1x standard. This download can be found at `http://support.microsoft.com/kb/313664`.

Windows CE wireless clients

Palmtop computers running Windows CE .NET include Wireless Zero Configuration and manual configuration options similar to those in Windows Vista and Windows XP. They support 802.11a and Native Wireless Fidelity (Wi-Fi). You can configure older Windows CE palmtop computers for wireless networking. The settings are similar to those for Windows 2000 Professional.

Do it! **B-2: Configuring a wireless client (instructor demo)**

Here's how	Here's why
1 On the computer with a wireless NIC, click **Start** and choose **Control Panel**, **Network and Internet** Click **Network and Sharing Center** Under Tasks, click **Manage wireless networks**	You'll configure the client to connect by using the settings on the wireless access point.
2 Click **Add** Click **Manually create a network profile**	Because you disabled the broadcast of the SSID, you must manually configure the connection.
3 In the Network name box, enter **123ABC567** In the Security type box, select **WEP** Select **Manually assign a network key**	
4 In the Security Key/Passphrase box, enter the WEP key you recorded in the previous activity	
5 Check **Connect even if the network is not broadcasting** Click **Next**	
6 Click **Connect to...** Select **123ABC567** Click **Connect**	This item must match the SSID of the WAP you want to connect to.
7 Close all open windows	

Your WAP is set to allow your computer access, as directed in the previous activity.

To complete this activity, you need a computer with a wireless NIC.

Unit summary: SOHO networking

Topic A In this topic, you looked at the technologies used to create wired and wireless connections between devices in a **SOHO network**. You identified the hardware components, protocols, and communication standards needed to create a SOHO network.

Topic B In this topic, you learned how to create a wireless network connection between a client and an access point. You also learned how to secure the communication by using the four components critical to security on a wireless network: **access control**, **encryption**, **authentication**, and **isolation**.

Review questions

1 Which wireless technology is used to create a direct connection between two devices?

  A Bluetooth

  C Radio

  D Wi-Fi

  E WiMAX

2 You should place your WLAN access points within how many meters of the wireless clients?

  A 40 to 125

  B 55 to 200

  C 60 to 90

  D 90 to 400

  E 115 to 550

3 To obtain the IEEE speed designated as high, clients must be within how many meters of the AP?

  A 40 to 125

  B 55 to 200

  C 60 to 90

  D 90 to 400

  E 115 to 550

4 In a(n) _____ site survey, you temporarily set up your WAPs at the locations you're considering for permanent placement.

  informal

5 Which of the following is the most widely used wireless technology at present?

  A 802.11a

  B Bluetooth

  C Wi-Fi

  D WiMAX

6 True or false? The 802.11b, 802.11a, and 802.11g standards are all considered Wi-Fi.

   True

7 Ratified in 2003, which standard is a combination of 802.11a and 802.11b?

   A 802.11c

   B 802.11g

   C 802.11h

   D 802.11n

8 Of the four components to security on a wireless network, to which one does a RADIUS server belong?

   A Access control

   B Authentication

   C Encryption

   D Isolation

9 War _____ is the process of using a set of symbols and shorthand to mark buildings, curbs, and other landmarks to indicate the presence of an available access point and its connection details.

   Chalking

10 Which encryption method uses the Advanced Encryption System (AES) cipher for stronger encryption?

   A 802.11i

   B WEP

   C WPA Personal

   D WPA2

11 An AP typically broadcasts its _____ so clients can discover its presence.

   SSID

12 True or false? Wireless Zero Configuration enables Windows Vista and Windows XP computers to automatically connect to available wireless networks.

   True

13 True or false? Windows 2000 Professional clients have no way of supporting IEEE 802.1x authentication.

   False. Microsoft provides an 802.1x Authentication Client download, which allows Windows 2000 computers to use the 802.1x standard.

Independent practice activity

In this activity, you'll practice adding a wireless access point and client to your network. You might need to work with one or more other students, depending on the number of wireless routers available.

1. Remove the network cable from your NIC.
2. Connect the network cable to your wireless router.
3. Connect a second network cable from the wireless router to your NIC.
4. Connect the power to the wireless router.
5. Check the router documentation for instructions for accessing the configuration utility.
6. Verify that you have Internet connectivity. If you don't, check the router documentation for instructions on configuring Internet access.
7. Change the SSID name to your lab number followed by your first name (for example, 06Jane). Most often, you use an Internet browser to connect to an IP address such as 192.168.1.1.
8. Following the directions in the wireless router's documentation, configure WPA or WEP.
9. Remove the network cable from your NIC.
10. Install a wireless NIC on your computer. If you don't have an empty PCI slot, you can remove your secondary wired NIC and install the wireless card.
11. Create a connection to your WAP. (There is a DHCP server in the classroom that you should be able to use to assign an IP address to the wireless NIC.) Configure WPA or WEP on the connection to match what you just set in the wireless router.
12. Verify that you have Internet connectivity.
13. Uninstall the wireless NIC from your computer. If necessary, reinstall your wired NIC.
14. Unplug the network cable from the wireless router. Plug the network cable back into your wired NIC.

Unit 11
Network troubleshooting

Unit time: 120 minutes

Complete this unit, and you'll know how to:

A Prepare toolkits for troubleshooting.

B Troubleshoot client-side connectivity issues.

Topic A: Troubleshooting basics

This topic covers the following CompTIA A+ 220-702 exam objective.

#	Objective
1.4	Given a scenario, select and use the following tools • Specialty hardware / tools • Cable testers

The troubleshooting toolkit

Explanation

Support technicians need tools that perform a wide variety of functions. Repair toolkits are available for amateurs and for professionals. These specialty hardware toolkits contain versions of the tools appropriate for working with networking components. You can also assemble your own toolkit with the following items:

- **A variety of screwdrivers** — You should have large and small versions of flat-blade, Phillips, and Torx screwdrivers.
- **Small and large needle-nose pliers** — These are useful for grasping objects.
- **Tweezers** — Also used for grasping objects.
- **Three-pronged "grabber"** — For picking up screws or other objects in areas too small to get your fingers into.
- **A small flashlight** — A small penlight or a light that can be clamped to the computer case can prove quite useful.
- **Antistatic bags** — To protect components that are sensitive to static electricity.

   ⚠ Never lay a component on the outside of an antistatic bag. The bag is designed to collect static charges on the outside of it, so if you place a component on the bag, the collected static charges might discharge onto the component.

- **Small containers** — For holding screws and small components that are easily lost.
- **Grounding wrist straps and ESD antistatic mats** — To protect the equipment from any static you might be carrying on your body.

   ⚠ A grounding wrist strap should never be worn when you're working on the interior of a monitor, but in all other cases, this is a highly recommended ESD protection tool.

- **Antistatic sprays** — Useful if your clothes are likely to generate static.

The following additional items are important for every toolkit.

Tool	Used to...
Multimeter	Test equipment with readings of ohms, amps, and volts. Comparing the readings with the appropriate values for a component helps you determine if there's a problem with the component.
Nut driver	Remove hex-head nuts.
Cable stripper	Remove the outer insulation from network cables and expose the wires inside them. Usually, this item also includes wire cutters to cut the cable or wire.
Snips	Cut or trim cables.
Punchdown tool	Connect wires to a punchdown block.
Crimper	Crimp a connector onto a network cable. It comes in varieties for RJ-11, RJ-45, and coaxial cable.
Butt set	Test and verify telephone lines.
Time-domain reflectometer (TDR)	Locate problems in metallic wires, such as coaxial cable and twisted-pair network cables.
Optical time-domain reflectometer (OTDR)	Locate faults in optical fiber.
Certifier	Test and verify network cable speeds by sending data packets across the network. You can use certifiers to verify that network segments are operating at optimal levels.
Temperature monitor	Monitor temperature in various environments, especially in rooms containing networking devices. High temperatures can damage some network devices, including servers. Monitors can be configured to warn you when the temperature has exceeded a specific limit, so you can take corrective action.
Voltage event recorder	Measure electrical properties to determine whether there's an adequate power supply and what the quality of that power supply is.

The software toolkit

Most people think of hardware tools when you speak of assembling a toolkit for a network technician. However, there are several software tools you'll need for a complete troubleshooting toolkit, especially when you're troubleshooting clients and servers and their network connections.

Tool	Description
Disk containing common drivers	If your company has standardized a specific set of equipment with common drivers, having a disk with you can make it easy to install the drivers quickly if you have to remove them to fix a problem or if they become corrupted. Many companies place the files on a central server location, but if you can't access the server due to the problem you're trying to fix, having the drivers on the server won't do you any good.
Antivirus software	You should include a boot disk from which you can boot a system that has been infected with a boot virus. Norton and McAfee are examples of companies that make antivirus software you can use to create such a disk. Follow the manufacturer's directions to clean the virus from the system. Sometimes you need to boot from the antivirus software CD when you need to clean a system, so configure CMOS to be able to boot from CD.
Boot disk	A bootable floppy disk or boot CD-ROM is useful if you can no longer boot from the hard drive. On this CD or floppy disk, you should have basic commands that enable you to perform simple tasks.
Operating system CD or DVD	Having a copy of the operating system CD enables you to get to the CAB files that you might need when installing or repairing some piece of hardware. It's also useful if you need to boot from the CD or if files or drivers have been corrupted and need to be replaced.
Documentation about common problems	If you encounter a set of common problems and need documentation on how to fix them, a CD or flash drive with that information can prove valuable. If the documentation is in a searchable format, then you can easily find the information you need to fix a problem you've encountered in the past.

Web sites for the manufacturers of the equipment you support should be included somewhere in your toolkit. A bookmark list, a paper list, or a document containing the URLs is useful. Being able to access the support sites directly is beneficial when you need to obtain updated drivers or look for solutions to problems. Another useful site is drivers.com. You can download drivers for many components, including some from companies no longer in operation.

A CD binder is useful for carrying these tools with you. CD binders come in a variety of sizes. You can also copy the files to a USB flash drive instead of to a CD if you prefer.

Do it!

A-1: Identifying common toolkit components

Here's how	Here's why
1 Open a Web browser and go to a search site	You'll examine the components of a hardware technician's toolkit.
2 Search for **computer maintenance toolkit**	
3 Compare your results with those of other students	Options range from small kits with a few tools for a modest price, to comprehensive kits for a facility specializing just in hardware repairs.
4 Which tools would you include in your toolkit for your job?	*Answers will vary but should include, at a minimum, a variety of screwdrivers, needle-nose pliers, tweezers, snips, cable strippers, a punchdown tool, and a flashlight.*
5 When would you use a crimper?	*You'd use a crimper if you needed to join a cable and a connector.*
When would you use a punchdown tool?	*You'd use a punchdown tool if you needed to connect a wire to a punchdown block.*
6 What software tools would you include in your troubleshooting kit?	*Answers will vary, but should include a boot disk, common drivers, and an operating system CD.*
7 When would you use a certifier?	*You'd use a certifier to verify that the cabling in a network segment was operating according to its published standard.*
When would you use a temperature monitor?	*A temperature monitor will tell you when the temperature in a server room has exceed the optimal level.*
8 Search for diagnostic software. What are some examples you find?	*Answers might include software from SmithMicro and from Ultra-X, among others.*
9 In addition to the software mentioned in the text, are there any other tools you would include?	*Answers will vary.*

Topic B: Troubleshooting the network

This topic covers the following CompTIA A+ 220-702 exam objectives.

#	Objective
1.4	Given a scenario, select and use the following tools • Specialty hardware / tools • Cable testers
2.1	Select the appropriate commands and options to troubleshoot and resolve problems • IPCONFIG (/all /release /renew) • PING (-t –l) • TRACERT • NSLOOKUP

3.1	Troubleshoot client-side connectivity issues, using appropriate tools
	• TCP/IP settings
	  – Gateway
	  – Subnet mask
	  – DNS
	  – DHCP (dynamic vs. static)
	  – NAT (private and public)
	• Characteristics of TCP/IP
	  – Loopback addresses
	  – Automatic IP addressing
	• Mail protocol settings
	  – SMTP
	  – IMAP
	  – POP
	• FTP settings
	  – Ports
	  – IP addresses
	  – Exceptions
	  – Programs
	• Proxy settings
	  – Ports
	  – IP addresses
	  – Exceptions
	  – Programs

#	Objective

	Troubleshoot client-side connectivity issues, using appropriate tools (continued)
	• Tools (use and interpret results)
	   – Ping
	   – Tracert
	   – Nslookup
	   – Netstat
	   – Ipconfig
	   – telnet
	   – SSH
	• Secure connection protocols
	   – SSH
	   – HTTPS
	• Firewall settings
	   – Open and closed ports
	   – Program filters

Troubleshooting wired connections

Explanation

Problems with wired connections can have many sources. Some are physically based, such as a bad network cable; and some are software based, such as an invalid TCP/IP address.

Electrical interference

Electrical interference is a common problem that occurs on networks and degrades data signals. *Network noise* is any electrical signal on the network cable that isn't part of the sender's original signal. Noise is generated both internally and externally.

Internally, twisted-pair cables produce relatively little electrical interference—the twists cancel each other out. Any variation in the thickness of the wire, the cable insulation, or the capacitance of wires or insulation causes a mismatch and creates noise between the pairs. Good cables minimize the internally produced noise, but don't remove it altogether.

Electrical interference can also come from many external sources. You should always install cables in separate conduits, away from items such as electric motors (like those found in elevators), fluorescent lights, and air conditioners. In areas where there's an abundance of electrical noise, you can use shielded cables or other technologies, such as fiber optic cables, to avoid interference.

When a data signal travels down a conductor, it creates an electrical field, which interferes with any wires close by. This kind of interference is called *crosstalk*. Crosstalk increases at higher frequencies and with parallel wires. The twists in twisted-pair cables cancel this effect; however, it's important that the twists are symmetrical and that adjacent pairs have different twists.

Other physical issues

In addition to crosstalk and interference, you should be aware of the additional issues described in the following table.

Issue	Description
Attenuation	Attenuation is the decrease in signal strength along the length of a network wire. The longer the wire, the greater the degree of signal attenuation. You can solve this problem by shortening the cable or by inserting a device such as a repeater. Attenuation is expressed in negative decibels (dB).
Collisions	On Ethernet networks, collisions are the result of multiple network hosts transmitting data simultaneously. Some collisions are expected in any network, but too many collisions can cause a bottleneck and prevent the transmission of data.
Open impedance mismatch (echo)	Line echo is typically the result of impedance mismatch, which is caused by the termination or wiring conversion from four-wire telephone circuits to two wires.

Cable testing devices

You can use a cable testing device, like the one shown in Exhibit 11-1, to test the physical cables and network functions. For example, you can determine how a network handles varying loads of data, and whether the network throughput matches the cable and device ratings. You can purchase cable testing devices for your particular LAN or purchase one that's compatible with multiple network types. For example, testing devices are available for 10 and 100 Base-T networks.

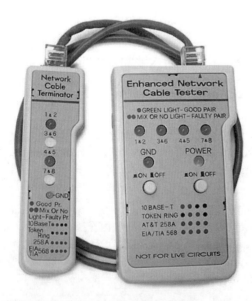

Exhibit 11-1: A cable testing device

Your cable testing device might be able to perform the following physical cable tests:

- Locating incorrectly wired cables, open cables, and shorts
- Locating missing cables
- Locating cables that don't support your network type (for example, 100 Base-T)
- Testing hub connections
- Testing PC connections
- Testing installed cables
- Testing patch cables
- Locating and tracing inactive cables

Network analyzers

One example of a network analyzer is Network Associates' NetXRay.

A *network analyzer*, sometimes called a *protocol analyzer*, is a portable device that can be hand-carried to a network location and set up to monitor and diagnose problems with a network. A network analyzer, shown in Exhibit 11-2, can help you troubleshoot difficulties that can occur because of problems with the hardware or software. A network analyzer can identify problems with:

- Cabling
- Jacks
- Network cards
- Hubs
- Other hardware that works at the lower levels of the OSI model

A network analyzer can also diagnose problems with TCP/IP, including TCP/IP packet errors. It can analyze where a packet is coming from or going to, and whether the protocols within the packet are used correctly. The packets can be captured and analyzed at any point on the network, such as when the cabling is connected to a wall jack. The analyzer can be attached between the cable and the jack, and can read and analyze packets as they pass.

Exhibit 11-2: A portable network analyzer

One problem you might encounter when using a network analyzer is that it can capture too much data, making it difficult to find the data that applies to the problem at hand. Fortunately, you can specify filters that weed out data that isn't involved in the problem.

A network analyzer can be a laptop computer with a proprietary operating system and other software specifically designed to capture and analyze packets on a network.

Network optimization

Fixing network problems can be as easy as replacing a worn cable, but sometimes network problems require bigger fixes. For example, some network communication problems require a reconfiguration of the entire network, either for all network communication or for specific types.

- Many networks have servers that contain highly sensitive data that must be available around the clock. To increase the amount of uptime for these servers and provide a high level of availability, a network administrator must build in a level of fault tolerance so that there is a way to quickly recover from a server or network problem.

  For example, a server farm provides a high level of fault tolerance by spreading sensitive data and applications across a number of servers. If one server were to fail, the remaining servers would still provide services to network users. In addition, RAID provides data redundancy, which can allow a server administrator to recover data from a failed hard disk in a server.

- To decrease response times for Internet users and to reduce the load on gateway servers, you can deploy proxy servers that use a caching engine to store frequently requested Web addresses. These servers can store Web content that users access frequently, and return that content to the users faster than they could retrieve the content directly from the Web.
- Many applications, such as Voice over IP (VoIP) and video applications, are particularly prone to *latency sensitivity*, which is caused when the network breaks the data into different-size packets that might be transmitted out of sequence. The latency sensitivity can cause jitters in the video or voice transmissions, severely reducing their quality and potentially rendering them useless.

  Quality of Service (QoS) mechanisms and policies on the network can be used to prioritize video and VoIP transmission to ensure that the packets receive priority over other types of network traffic. The QoS mechanisms can help reduce and eliminate jitters and other types of interference.

When troubleshooting network problems, you should be aware of these issues and escalate them if necessary.

Do it!

B-1: Testing the physical network

Students need a basic cable tester and a throughput/load tester or network analyzer.

Students will test the section of cable between their PC and the classroom hub.

Explain to students what problems their tester can find.

Students will test the speed and load capacity of the network.

Configure filters as necessary to ensure that the analyzer produces the necessary results.

Here's how	Here's why
1 Follow your instructor's directions to attach your cable tester to your computer's network cable	You're going to test the section of cable between your computer and the classroom hub.
2 Follow your instructor's directions to attach your cable tester to the network cable ending at the classroom hub	
3 Follow your instructor's directions to test the section of cable and read the tester's display	
4 Follow your instructor's directions to remove the cable tester and reattach the cables	
5 Follow your instructor's directions to connect the network analyzer to the network	You're going to conduct load and throughput testing.
6 Follow your instructor's directions to conduct load testing and throughput testing	
7 Follow your instructor's directions to remove the network analyzer	

Troubleshooting wireless network connections

Explanation

As with other types of troubleshooting, troubleshooting wireless network connections begins with identifying the components that make up the wireless communication process. These components include:

- The Windows operating system and the network adapter's driver
- The wireless network adapter
- The wireless radio frequency signal
- The wireless access point

Isolating problems

Your task is to isolate the problem by asking various questions. Questions you should ask include:

- Is the wireless network adapter listed in Device Manager? If so, does Device Manager report that the adapter is working properly?

  If it doesn't, you should suspect a problem with the network adapter driver or even the card itself. You should also verify whether the wireless network adapter's radio has been turned off.

  If Device Manager reports that the network adapter is working properly, you should suspect a problem with its configuration or the wireless access point.

- Is the computer's wireless network connection configured to use the appropriate encryption method for the wireless access point?

  If it isn't, change the configuration of the wireless network connection to use the correct security settings.

- Is the computer detecting the wireless access point? If so, what is the strength of the wireless signal? (You can determine the strength of the wireless signal by using the "Connect to a wireless network" wizard.)

  If the wireless signal is weak, this is an indication that the computer might be too far from the wireless access point. The WAP might also be experiencing interference from the environment (such as metal file cabinets). You might also try installing equipment designed to boost the signal strength of the WAP.

- Is the wireless access point configured correctly? Specifically, is it configured to use the appropriate encryption algorithm for the network cards used in your environment?

  For WAPs configured to use WPA or WPA2 with a pre-shared key, has anyone changed this key on the wireless access point? If so, you must enter the new key in your profile for connecting to the network.

The following table describes some common problems you might encounter with wireless connections.

Symptom	Probable cause	Suggested solution
Unable to connect to infrared wireless device	Out of range; obstructions blocking ports; infrared serial port disabled in BIOS or operating system.	Move closer to the device. Remove obstructions and gently clean the infrared port windows. Use the BIOS setup utility and Device Manager to confirm that the infrared port is enabled.
Unable to connect to radio wireless device	Out of range; interference from electrical motors or equipment; drivers not installed; wireless router turned off; security settings prevent connections.	Move closer to the device, and move away from sources of interference. Use Device Manager to confirm that the wireless device is installed and that there are no conflicts. Confirm that your router is turned on. Confirm that you have sufficient permissions to connect to the wireless device.
Unable to connect to Bluetooth wireless device	Out of range; interference from electrical motors or equipment; drivers not installed; security settings prevent connections.	Move closer to the device, and move away from sources of interference. Use Device Manager to confirm that the wireless device is installed and that there are no conflicts. Confirm that you have sufficient permissions to connect to the wireless device.

Do it!

B-2: Troubleshooting wireless networking

Questions and answers

1. A user reports that she doesn't see any wireless networks when she runs the "Connect to a wireless network" wizard. What are some things you should check on her computer?

   You should check the status of the computer's wireless network adapter in Device Manager. You should also check whether the network adapter's radio is turned on or off. Finally, check whether the network adapter is configured to use the appropriate security settings for your network's WAPs.

2. Several users report this morning that they cannot connect to the network. These users connect wirelessly via a wireless access point. What are two things you should check to troubleshoot this problem?

   You should first verify that the WAP is turned on and functioning properly. Next, check to see if anyone changed the pre-shared key on the WAP.

3. Users report that they are intermittently losing their connections to the wireless network. What should you check?

   You should check to see if any metal components, such as file cabinets, might be interfering with the signal. You should also verify that users aren't trying to connect to a wireless access point from too far away.

Troubleshooting TCP/IP

Explanation

One of the most common complaints you'll hear from users is that they can't get to something on the network, or "the Internet is down." When you hear a complaint about network connectivity, your first step should be to check the user's network connection and TCP/IP settings.

If you find a problem on the client computer, it's your job to fix it, usually by correcting TCP/IP properties. If you suspect a problem with the network as a whole or with a particular server on the network, you'll need to contact the appropriate individual, typically the network administrator, to escalate the problem.

TCP/IP utilities

TCP/IP includes a group of utilities that can be used to troubleshoot problems with TCP/IP. The following table lists the utilities and their purposes.

Utility	Purpose
IPCONFIG	Displays the host's IP address and other configuration information. Some parameters are: `ipconfig /all` — Displays all information about the connection. `ipconfig /release` — Releases the current IP address. `ipconfig /renew` — Requests a new IP address. `ipconfig /?` — Displays information about `ipconfig`.
FTP (File Transfer Protocol)	Transfers files over a network.
Nbtstat	Displays NetBIOS over TCP/IP statistics, NetBIOS name tables, and the NetBIOS name cache. You can use this utility with switches to remove or correct NetBIOS name cache entries.
Netstat	Displays a list of a computer's active incoming and outgoing connections.
NSLookup	Reports the IP address of an entered host name, or the host name of an entered IP address.
Ping (Packet Internet Groper)	Verifies a connection to a network between two hosts, using Internet Control Message Protocol echo requests.
Route	Allows you to manually control network routing tables.
Telnet	Allows you to communicate with another computer on the network remotely, entering commands on the local computer that control the remote computer.
Trace Route	Traces and displays the route taken from the host to a remote destination; `tracert` is one example of a trace-routing utility.

Most of these commands are entered from a command prompt. To open a Command Prompt window in any version of Windows, run the `cmd` command. From the Command Prompt, you can enter a Windows or DOS command, including any of those in the previous table.

Do it!

B-3: Identifying TCP/IP utilities used for troubleshooting

Questions and answers

1. A user opens a browser window and tries to contact your intranet server at www.domain.class. The user receives a message that the site can't be found. What's the first TCP/IP utility you should try?

   Ping the server at www.domain.class from a command prompt. If that fails, ping the server's IP address. If that's successful, you know the problem lies with DNS.

2. Users in one location have complained that load time for the company's intranet site is slow. No one in any other location is reporting a problem. What TCP/IP utility can you use to diagnose the problem?

   You can use tracert from a computer at multiple locations and compare the hop count. You will probably find that the hop count is higher in the location reporting slow intranet performance.

Network troubleshooting **11–17**

IPCONFIG

Explanation

When a user complains of network problems, you should first check the TCP/IP settings on the user's computer. In any version of Windows, use IPCONFIG, as shown in Exhibit 11-3, to display and modify the current TCP/IP configuration, including the IP address, subnet mask, default gateway, and DNS server address.

Several switches can be added to the `ipconfig` command to display the current IP information (`ipconfig /all`), release the IP address (`ipconfig /release`), and renew the IP address (`ipconfig /renew`) for all connections. The following table describes some common switches.

Switch	Use to...
`/release [adapter name]` `/release6 [adapter name]`	Release a leased IPv4 or IPv6 address (respectively) so that it returns to the pool of available addresses on the DHCP server. You can specify the name of the network connection for which you want to release the leased address. If you don't specify a connection name, Windows Vista releases the leased IP addresses for all network connections. You might use this option when a computer cannot obtain an address from a DHCP server (typically when the server is unavailable) or if you want to force the computer to obtain a new lease (because the DHCP server's IP addressing parameters have changed).
`/renew [adapter name]` `/renew6 [adapter name]`	Renew a leased IPv4 or IPv6 address. As with the `/release` parameter, you can specify the name of the network connection for which you want to renew the IP address lease. If you don't specify a network connection name, Windows Vista attempts to renew all leased IP addresses for all network connections configured to use DHCP. Use this option to try to renew a computer's IP address lease. If the computer can't communicate with the DHCP server from which it obtained its IP address, or you have disabled the scope (pool) of IP addresses from which the computer obtained its IP address, the DHCP server will deny the computer's lease renewal request. At this point, the computer will start over with the IP address leasing process by broadcasting a DHCP request packet.
`/flushdns`	Delete all name resolution information (host names and their IP addresses) from the client's DNS Resolver cache. For example, you might use this parameter to troubleshoot name resolution problems that occur after you change a server's IP address. If computers still have the server's name and old IP address in the DNS Resolver cache, they won't be able to communicate with the server until this cache is deleted.
`/displaydns`	Display the contents of the DNS Resolver cache.
`/registerdns`	Renew all IP address leases from DHCP servers, and re-register the computer's host name and IP address on your network's DNS servers.

Check to see if the IP address and subnet mask are correct, and verify the default gateway and DNS server addresses. When you do this, you might find that the computer has no IP address configured or has configured itself with an automatic private address. If so, this gives you a couple of options:

- If IP addressing information is assigned by a DHCP server, suspect a problem with a DHCP server itself or with the network between the user's computer and the DHCP server. First, verify that the network card is working correctly and is attached to the network cable, which is in turn plugged into the appropriate network port on the wall or floor. Try to release and then renew the IP address from the DHCP server. If you can verify these things, and you can't get an IP address from the DHCP server, then escalate the call to the appropriate network administrator.
- If IP addressing is assigned manually, then assign the correct information, such as IP address, default gateway, subnet mask, or DNS server address, and test to see if connectivity is restored.

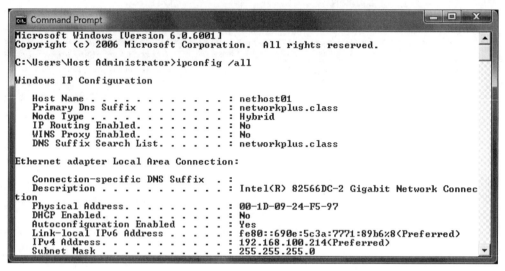

Exhibit 11-3: IPCONFIG

Network troubleshooting **11-19**

Do it!

B-4: Using IPCONFIG to display TCP/IP settings

Here's how	Here's why
1 Click **Start** and enter **cmd**	To open a Command Prompt window. You're going to use IPCONFIG to view your IP address settings.
2 At the command prompt, enter **ipconfig**	To display your current IP address, subnet mask, and default gateway, as shown here.

```
C:\Users\hostadmin01>ipconfig

Windows IP Configuration

Ethernet adapter Local Area Connection:

   Connection-specific DNS Suffix  . : networkplus.class
   Link-local IPv6 Address . . . . . : fe80::3585:ffb7:fa18:8e72%11
   IPv4 Address. . . . . . . . . . . : 192.168.157.17
   Subnet Mask . . . . . . . . . . . : 255.255.255.0
   Default Gateway . . . . . . . . . : 192.168.157.1
```

This is a quick way to find a computer's basic IP address information.

3 At the command prompt, enter **ipconfig /all**	To display extended IP addressing information, as shown here.

```
C:\Users\hostadmin01>ipconfig /all

Windows IP Configuration

   Host Name . . . . . . . . . . . . : nethost01
   Primary Dns Suffix  . . . . . . . : networkplus.class
   Node Type . . . . . . . . . . . . : Hybrid
   IP Routing Enabled. . . . . . . . : No
   WINS Proxy Enabled. . . . . . . . : No
   DNS Suffix Search List. . . . . . : networkplus.class

Ethernet adapter Local Area Connection:

   Connection-specific DNS Suffix  . : networkplus.class
   Description . . . . . . . . . . . : Broadcom NetXtreme Gigabit Ethernet
   Physical Address. . . . . . . . . : 00-1E-C9-47-59-31
   DHCP Enabled. . . . . . . . . . . : Yes
   Autoconfiguration Enabled . . . . : Yes
   Link-local IPv6 Address . . . . . : fe80::3585:ffb7:fa18:8e72%11(Preferred)
   IPv4 Address. . . . . . . . . . . : 192.168.157.17(Preferred)
   Subnet Mask . . . . . . . . . . . : 255.255.255.0
   Lease Obtained. . . . . . . . . . : Monday, December 08, 2008 1:43:26 PM
   Lease Expires . . . . . . . . . . : Sunday, December 14, 2008 1:43:25 PM
   Default Gateway . . . . . . . . . : 192.168.157.1
   DHCP Server . . . . . . . . . . . : 192.168.157.5
   DNS Servers . . . . . . . . . . . : 192.168.157.5
   NetBIOS over Tcpip. . . . . . . . : Enabled
```

It can be easier to view this information at the Command Prompt than to click through a few dialog boxes to find the same information in the Windows GUI.

Explanation

Ping and basic TCP/IP connectivity

While you're in the MS-DOS Prompt or Command Prompt window, you can use another tool to verify basic TCP/IP connectivity. *Ping (Packet Internet Groper)* is a simple program that allows one computer to send a test packet to another computer and then receive a reply. You use ping to determine whether another computer is available for communication on a TCP/IP network.

After you have verified that the computer has a valid IP address, you can use the `ping` command to see if you can communicate with another computer on the network. You'll need to know the NetBIOS name, DNS name, or IP address of the other computer—perhaps a router or server that you know is operational. At the MS-DOS or command prompt, enter

```
ping computer
```

where `computer` is the other computer's name or IP address. A successful result looks similar to Exhibit 11-4.

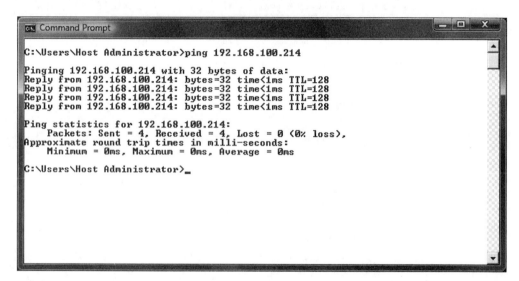

Exhibit 11-4: Successful ping results

When you issue the `ping` command from the command prompt, followed by an IP address or a domain name, `ping` communicates over a TCP/IP network to another node on the network. It sends an Internet Control Message Packet (ICMP) Echo Request and expects to receive an ICMP Echo Reply in return. Packets are exchanged and then reported on screen to verify connectivity on the network.

If you can't use ping successfully, try the following:

- If you used ping with a domain name, use the IP address of the remote host instead. If that works, the problem is with name resolution.
- Try to ping a different computer. Can you communicate with any other computer on the network? Ping the loopback address, 127.0.0.1, to see if you have any connectivity on the network.
- If you can't communicate with any other computer on the network, use IPCONFIG to verify that the computer has been assigned an IP address.
- Verify all network configuration settings, including IP address, subnet mask, and default gateway.
- Reboot the computer to verify that TCP/IP has been loaded.
- Try removing TCP/IP and reinstalling it. Perhaps the initial installation was corrupted.
- Check the physical connections. Is the network cable plugged in or is there a telephone connection? Do you get a dial tone?

If all of these methods fail to produce results, you might need to escalate the issue.

Do it!

B-5: Testing TCP/IP connectivity

Here's how	Here's why
1 In the Command Prompt window, type **ping 127.0.0.1** and press ⏎ ENTER	(The window should still be open from the previous activity.) This is the *loopback address*, which verifies that TCP/IP is working on this computer. Pinging the loopback address tests a computer's own basic network setup. You should receive four successful responses.
2 Type **ipconfig /all** and press ⏎ ENTER	Record your IP address and your default gateway address. IP address: _____ Default gateway address: _____
3 Ping your IP address	To verify that TCP/IP communication can be sent out on the network cable from your NIC card and back in again. You should receive four successful responses.
4 Ping the instructor's computer	To verify that you have connectivity to other computers on your local subnet. You should receive four successful responses.
5 Ping the IP address of your classroom's gateway	To verify that you can reach the gateway that connects you to other subnets. You should receive four successful responses.

Explain to students that with a TCP/IP connectivity problem, they can use ping to test connectivity from their computer outward, verifying successful communication closest to them first.

Give students your IP address.

6 How does being able to successfully ping the IP address of your default gateway help you when troubleshooting?

If you can ping your default gateway, you know that the computer you're working on has a functioning network adapter, the network cabling is intact between this computer and the router, and TCP/IP is configured correctly on the computer.

7 Users are complaining that they are unable to access one of your organization's file and print servers (even though they had just been using this server). You discover that another person in Desktop Support moved the server to a new subnet. What might be the cause of users not being able to access this server? How can you resolve the problem?

If someone moved the server to another subnet, the server's IP address had to change. It's possible that the users have the server's name and old IP address stored in the DNS cache on their computers. When they try to connect to the server, their computers are using the old IP address instead of the new one. To resolve the problem, open a Command Prompt window and enter `ipconfig /flushdns`.

NSLookup

Explanation

When two computers communicate with each other by using TCP/IP across the network, the Domain Name System (DNS) server is responsible for resolving the names you specify to their associated IP addresses. Active Directory domains also use DNS to provide users and computers with access to the network's resources.

To verify that your computer can communicate with its DNS server(s), enter `nslookup [host or FQDN]`. Your computer succeeds in communicating with the DNS server if the server responds with the IP address of one or more computers. You'll sometimes see multiple IP addresses for a given *fully qualified domain name* (FQDN), such as `www.cnn.com`. In this example, the Web site administrators have configured multiple Web servers to host its content. DNS servers then use a technique referred to as "round robin" to balance the workload across those servers.

Tracert

If a user is telling you that he or she can't access resources on the network, you should verify that the user's client software is configured properly. You should also verify that File and Printer Sharing is installed and enabled on the computer the user is trying to access.

You can perform an additional test on the network by using the `tracert` command to check the network path between two computers. At an MS-DOS or command prompt, enter `tracert computer` where `computer` is the name or IP address of a destination.

Do it!

B-6: Using NSLookup and Tracert

Here's how

1	At the command prompt, enter **nslookup**	To test your DNS configuration. In class, the classroom DNS server's IP address will be returned.
		In other environments, depending on the configuration, you might see a DNS server name and IP address returned, or you might see just an IP address and an error message telling you that NSLookup can't find the server name. This is a DNS server configuration issue.
2	Enter **nslookup** followed by a Web address	Try www.yahoo.com. You should see DNS addressing information for that domain.
3	Enter **exit**	To exit NSLookup.
4	Enter **tracert [IP_address of a classroom server]**	To trace the path to a server in your network. This is a short path, so the results are returned promptly.
5	Enter **tracert www.yahoo.com**	To trace the route to Yahoo's Web server. This takes a while longer.
6	Close the Command Prompt window	

Be prepared to offer another DNS server's IP address if you didn't use this IP address during setup.

Ports

Explanation

TCP/IP components are responsible for getting data ready to move across the network. The most common task performed by one component is breaking down an entire message into smaller pieces, called *packets*, that can move more easily across the network. The two component protocols in the TCP/IP protocol suite are *Transmission Control Protocol (TCP)* and *User Datagram Protocol (UDP)*.

One of the defining characteristics of these TCP/IP components is the use of port numbers. Each service running on a server listens at a port number. Port numbers 0 to 1024 are reserved for privileged services (well-known ports). Each protocol knows which service it should deliver the packets to. The combination of an IP address and a port number is referred to as a *socket*.

Applications that are using incorrect port numbers, and firewalls that don't have necessary port exceptions, can prevent network communications. In addition, incorrect port forwarding configuration on firewalls can block communication with internal resources when a user attempts to access them from outside the firewall. By contrast, port forwarding through a firewall directs traffic to the computer on the internal network that sent outgoing traffic from a specific port. Incorrectly configuring port forwarding can also disrupt network communications.

The following table shows well-known services and the ports they use.

Service	Port
FTP	TCP 21, 20
	20 is used for FTP data; 21 is used for FTP control
SSH	TCP 22, UDP 22
Telnet	TCP 23
SMTP	TCP 25
DNS	TCP 53, UDP 53
BOOTP and DHCP	UDP 67, 68
Trivial FTP (TFTP)	UDP 69
HTTP	TCP 80
POP3	TCP 110
NNTP	TCP 119
NTP	UDP 123
IMAP	TCP 143, UDP 143
SNMP	TCP 161, UDP 161
Secure HTTP	TCP 443

Do it!

B-7: Using port numbers

Here's how	Here's why
1 Open Internet Explorer and go to **www.microsoft.com**	In the United States, the page at http://www.microsoft.com/en/us/default.aspx is displayed. The Web browser automatically connects you to port 80 on this server.
2 In the address bar, type **http://www.microsoft.com:21**	
Press ← ENTER	The Web browser can't connect because port 21 isn't used for HTTP.
3 In the address bar, type **http://www.microsoft.com:80**	
Press ← ENTER	The Web browser connects and gives you the same Web page as in step 1.
4 In the address bar, type **ftp://ftp.microsoft.com**	
Press ← ENTER	The Web browser automatically connects you to port 21 when you use FTP.
5 In the address bar, type **ftp://ftp.microsoft.com:80**	
Press ← ENTER	The Web browser can't connect because port 80 isn't used for FTP.
6 In the address bar, type **ftp://ftp.microsoft.com:21**	
Press ← ENTER	The Web browser connects and gives you the same information as in step 4.
7 Click **Start**	
In the Start Search box, type **cmd**	
Press ← ENTER	To open a Command Prompt window.

Network troubleshooting **11–27**

8 At the command prompt, type
netstat –an |find /i "listening"

Press ⏎ ENTER

```
C:\Users\VistaHost>netstat -an |find /i "listening"
  TCP    0.0.0.0:135            0.0.0.0:0              LISTENING
  TCP    0.0.0.0:445            0.0.0.0:0              LISTENING
  TCP    0.0.0.0:5357           0.0.0.0:0              LISTENING
  TCP    0.0.0.0:49152          0.0.0.0:0              LISTENING
  TCP    0.0.0.0:49153          0.0.0.0:0              LISTENING
  TCP    0.0.0.0:49154          0.0.0.0:0              LISTENING
  TCP    0.0.0.0:49155          0.0.0.0:0              LISTENING
  TCP    0.0.0.0:49156          0.0.0.0:0              LISTENING
  TCP    127.0.0.1:12025        0.0.0.0:0              LISTENING
  TCP    127.0.0.1:12080        0.0.0.0:0              LISTENING
  TCP    127.0.0.1:12110        0.0.0.0:0              LISTENING
  TCP    127.0.0.1:12119        0.0.0.0:0              LISTENING
  TCP    127.0.0.1:12143        0.0.0.0:0              LISTENING
  TCP    192.168.157.4:139      0.0.0.0:0              LISTENING
  TCP    [::]:135               [::]:0                 LISTENING
  TCP    [::]:445               [::]:0                 LISTENING
  TCP    [::]:5357              [::]:0                 LISTENING
  TCP    [::]:49152             [::]:0                 LISTENING
  TCP    [::]:49153             [::]:0                 LISTENING
  TCP    [::]:49154             [::]:0                 LISTENING
  TCP    [::]:49155             [::]:0                 LISTENING
  TCP    [::]:49156             [::]:0                 LISTENING
```

The first column shows the service, and the second column shows the port the service is listening on.

9 At the command prompt, enter
exit

To close the Command Prompt window.

Troubleshooting other client connection issues

Explanation

Beyond the basic networking functionality of TCP/IP, there are other networking settings you will likely have to troubleshoot. Before checking specific connection issues such as those that follow, always verify basic network connectivity.

Secure connection protocols

HTTP (Hypertext Transfer Protocol) is the most common protocol used on the Internet today. This is the protocol used by Web browsers and Web servers. HTTP defines the commands that Web browsers can send and the way Web servers can respond.

Secure Web servers use *SSL (Secure Sockets Layer)* to enable an encrypted communication channel between themselves and users' Web browsers. SSL is a public-key/private-key encryption protocol used to transmit data securely over the Internet, using TCP/IP. The URLs of Web sites that require SSL begin with `https://` instead of `http://`. When you connect using SSL, the connection itself is secure, and so is any data transferred across it.

Secure Shell (SSH) exchanges data between two network nodes over a secure channel. It operates at the OSI Network layer. SSH was designed as a replacement for Telnet and other insecure remote shells, which sent data (including passwords) in plain text. This left the data open for interception. SSH encryption provides data confidentiality and integrity over an insecure network, such as the Internet. Its primary use is to access shell accounts on Linux and UNIX systems.

When you're troubleshooting these connection protocols, verify that server addresses are correct, and that the client computers support the version of the protocol that the server requires.

FTP

File Transfer Protocol (FTP) is a simple file-sharing protocol. It includes commands for uploading and downloading files, as well as for requesting directory listings from remote servers. This protocol has been around the Internet for a long time and was originally implemented in UNIX during the 1980s. The first industry-distributed document, or *Request for Comment* (RFC), describing FTP was created in 1985.

Web servers (using HTTP) and e-mail software (using SMTP) must encode data so it appears as text when it travels over the Internet. FTP, however, offers an alternative. FTP can transfer binary files over the Internet without the encoding-and-decoding overhead, making it a popular protocol for moving files over the Internet.

Note: Although there are still FTP servers running on the Internet, there are fewer than in previous years. FTP is slowly becoming obsolete because of its inherent lack of security and because HTTP can upload and download files.

FTP is implemented in standalone FTP clients as well as in Web browsers. It is safe to say that most FTP users today are using Web browsers.

When troubleshooting FTP connections, verify that the IP address of the FTP server is correct and that the FTP client is trying to access the correct port. Also verify that firewalls on both the client and server sides have port exceptions for FTP traffic. In addition, the client software should have an exception in any software firewall on the client computer.

E-mail settings

Simple Mail Transfer Protocol (SMTP) is used to send and receive e-mail messages between e-mail servers. It is also used by e-mail client software, such as Outlook, to send messages to the server. SMTP is never used by a client computer to retrieve e-mail from a server. Other protocols control the retrieval of e-mail messages.

Post Office Protocol version 3 (POP3) is the most common protocol used for retrieving e-mail messages. This protocol has commands to download and delete messages from the mail server. POP3 does not support sending messages. By default, most e-mail client software using POP3 copies all messages onto the local hard drive and then erases them from the server. However, you can change the configuration so that messages can be left on the server. POP3 supports only a single inbox and does not support multiple folders for storage on the server.

Internet Message Access Protocol version 4 (IMAP4) is another common protocol used to retrieve e-mail messages. The capabilities of IMAP4 are beyond those of POP3. For example, IMAP can download message headers, which you can use to choose which messages you want to download. In addition, IMAP4 allows the use of multiple folders to store messages on the server side.

When you're troubleshooting SMTP, POP3, and IMAP in any e-mail client, be sure you have the correct e-mail server addresses and the correct ports and security authentication protocols and passwords. If there's a mismatch in any of this information, e-mail transmission will fail.

NAT and proxy servers

Most NAT devices consistently work well and don't require much maintenance or troubleshooting. Typically, you will need to ensure that the device is powered on and the TCP/IP settings are correct. Verify that it has Internet and local network connectivity. Sometimes powering down the device will cause it to reset its connections. Also verify that network clients using NAT have the correct TCP/IP configuration, including the default gateway.

You can troubleshoot proxy servers in the same way as NAT devices. In addition, verify that any software (including Web browsers) on the client computer has the correct proxy server address and port number, and any authentication settings are correct. Also verify that the necessary firewall exceptions are in place to allow communication with the proxy server.

Do it!

B-8: Troubleshooting client-side connectivity issues

Here's how	Here's why

1 A user reports that she's not able to send or receive e-mail. What steps should you take?

You should first verify client network connectivity. Then check her e-mail settings to ensure that she has the correct e-mail server addresses, user name and password, ports, and authentication settings.

2 If the user still reports problems after you've checked the settings on her computer, what's a likely next step?

If she's still having problems, verify that the e-mail server is functional.

3 What are some reasons a user could have problems accessing an FTP server?

Answers will include: incorrect IP addressing information on the client or on the server; a network problem between the client and the FTP server; and incorrectly configured firewall port exceptions and/or program filters on both the client and network firewalls.

4 A user reports that he's having trouble accessing the Web. You've verified that he has local network connectivity. What other issues might be causing this problem?

Answers will include firewall port exception and program filter settings, and the proxy server address and port number.

Windows Network Diagnostics

Explanation

One of the tools built into Windows Vista for troubleshooting network problems is Windows Network Diagnostics. This utility automates many of the steps for troubleshooting TCP/IP and network connectivity. You can access Windows Network Diagnostics by using a number of methods. For example, Exhibit 11-5 shows the Network and Sharing Center of a computer that can't connect to the Internet. You could launch Windows Network Diagnostics on this computer by clicking the "Diagnose and repair" link in the Tasks pane or clicking the red "X" displayed on the Internet connection.

Other methods for launching Windows Network Diagnostics include the following:

- Right-click the Network icon in the system tray and choose "Diagnose and repair."
- In the Network Connections window, right-click the appropriate network connection and choose Diagnose.

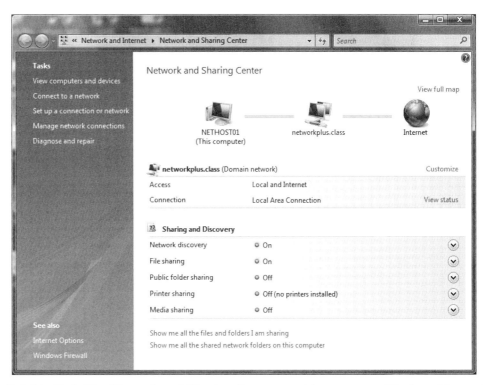

Exhibit 11-5: The Network and Sharing Center provides access to Windows Network Diagnostics

Windows Network Diagnostics tasks

When you run Windows Network Diagnostics, it attempts to diagnose many of the common problems encountered on TCP/IP networks. For example, it can typically identify problems such as an incorrect subnet mask or default gateway address, a DNS server that is down, a disabled network adapter, or a network adapter that you need to reset, as shown in Exhibit 11-6. Click one of the options displayed to see if it solves the problem.

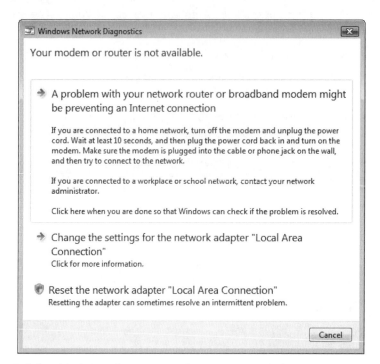

Exhibit 11-6: Windows Network Diagnostics helps you resolve many common TCP/IP problems

Wireless networks

Windows Network Diagnostics can help you resolve problems with wireless networks, too. The utility will attempt to identify the cause of the problem you're experiencing, and then walk you through the steps to correct the problem. In addition, information about the problems the utility detects is recorded in the System log, with the Event ID of 6100. You can review these events to help identify the cause of the problem with the wireless network.

Network troubleshooting **11-33**

Do it!

B-9: Troubleshooting with Windows Network Diagnostics

Here's how	Here's why
1 Click **Start** and right-click **Network** Choose **Properties**	To open the Network and Sharing Center.
2 In the Tasks pane, click **Manage network connections**	
3 In the Network Connections window, right-click **Local Area Connection** and choose **Properties**	To open the Properties dialog box for the local area connection.
Click **Continue**	
4 On the Networking tab, select **Internet Protocol Version 4 (TCP/IPv4)** Click **Properties**	To open the Properties dialog box for the TCP/IP protocol.
5 Enter a non-working IP address and invalid gateway and DNS server addresses	To deliberately misconfigure your computer so that it cannot connect to the Internet. You will troubleshoot the "problem" in upcoming steps.
Click **OK**	To save your changes.
Click **Yes**	You'll see that Windows Vista already recognizes a problem.
Click **Close** Close the Network Connections window	
6 In the Network and Sharing Center, click **Diagnose and repair**	To open Windows Network Diagnostics so that you can diagnose why your computer can't access the Internet.
7 Read the message box	Windows cannot communicate with the Primary DNS Server. It can't repair the problem automatically.
Click **Cancel**	
8 Click **Manage network connections**	

Guide students in selecting IP addresses that won't enable them to access the Internet.

9	Right-click **Local Area Connection** and choose **Properties**	
	Click **Continue**	
	On the Networking tab, select **Internet Protocol Version 4 (TCP/IPv4)**	
	Click **Properties**	To open the Properties dialog box for the TCP/IP protocol.
10	Configure your computer to use DHCP to obtain both an IP address and a DNS server address	So that your computer can connect to the Internet.
	Click **OK** and **Close**	To save your changes.
11	Close Network Connections	
12	Verify that you can connect to the Internet	Use Internet Explorer or observe the connection information reported in the Network and Sharing Center.
13	Close all open windows	
14	You have just run Windows Network Diagnostics to identify a problem with a computer's wireless connection. You want to view the information reported by the utility in the computer's event logs. Which event log should you check?	
	You should check the System log for any events with an event ID of 6100.	

Unit summary: Network troubleshooting

Topic A In this topic, you learned how to build hardware and software **toolkits** to help in your troubleshooting practice.

Topic B In this topic, you learned to troubleshoot the network. You learned to troubleshoot the **physical network** by troubleshooting cables and wireless devices. Then you learned how to troubleshoot the **logical network** by troubleshooting TCP/IP and client connectivity issues.

Review questions

1 At a minimum, which IPv4 address components must you configure in order to communicate on your local subnet? [Choose all that apply.]

   A IP address

   B Subnet mask

   C Default gateway

   D DNS server address

2 Which utility enables you to reset a computer's network adapter?

   A Network Map

   B Windows Network Diagnostics

   C IPCONFIG

   D Local Area Connection

3 What steps can you take to minimize electrical interference on a wired LAN?

   Install cables in separate conduits, away from items such as electric motors, fluorescent lights, and air conditioners. In areas where there's an abundance of electrical noise, use shielded cables or other technologies such as fiber optic cables to avoid interference.

4 What might be the cause if you cannot connect to a radio wireless device?

   Answers include:

   - *Out of range*
   - *Interference from electrical motors or equipment*
   - *Drivers not installed*
   - *Wireless router turned off*
   - *Security settings preventing connections*

5 Which command displays the IP address of the host and other configuration information?

   A `getmac`

   B `ipconfig`

   C `nslookup`

   D `ping`

6 List four physical cable tests you can perform with a cable testing device.

   Answers include:
   - *Locating miswired cables*
   - *Locating missing cables*
   - *Locating cables that don't support your network type (for example, 100 Base-T)*
   - *Testing hub connections*
   - *Testing PC connections*
   - *Testing installed cables*
   - *Testing patch cables*
   - *Locating and tracing inactive cables*

7 A network analyzer can detect problems with what four pieces of hardware?
   - Cabling
   - Jacks
   - Network cards
   - Hubs

8 What information does the `ipconfig` command report?
   - *Connection-specific DNS suffix*
   - *IP address*
   - *Subnet mask*
   - *Default gateway*

9 What command should you enter to view the Host Name and DNS Server address?

   ipconfig /all

10 Which command would you use to verify name resolution (DNS) settings?

   A `ipconfig`

   B `ping`

   C `nslookup`

   D `tracert`

11 What is the difference between SMTP and POP3?

   SMTP is used primarily for sending e-mail, and POP3 is used for retrieving e-mail.

12 _____ is the decrease in signal strength along the length of a network wire.

   Attenuation

13 True or false? QoS can be used to prioritize video and VoIP transmission to reduce jitters.

   True

14 Which `ipconfig` switch is used to delete all name resolution information from the client's DNS Resolver cache?

   `/flushdns`

Independent practice activity

In this activity, you will discuss and apply various troubleshooting techniques.

Note: Form teams and discuss the following questions. There are no definite answers for these questions.

1 A user is unable to access the network from his or her workstation. Role-play troubleshooting this user's problem.

2 On an IP network that's connected to the Internet through a router providing network address translation, Jim reports that he can't browse the Internet. List the steps to resolve the problem.

   a   *Launch your Web browser and verify that you can browse.*

   b   *Ping Jim's computer.*

   c   *If you receive a response that indicates that his host adapter is active, verify that the appropriate name servers are defined.*

   d   *If they are, verify that the default gateway is specified to be the router's LAN IP address.*

   e   *If it isn't set, set the gateway address. Then reboot.*

   f   *If you can browse the Web, inform Jim about the nature of the problem.*

   g   *Document the problem, the symptoms, and the resolution.*

Unit 12
Security

Unit time: 180 minutes

Complete this unit, and you'll know how to:

A Recognize and mitigate common security threats.

B Implement and troubleshoot security measures.

Topic A: Common security threats

This topic covers the following CompTIA A+ 220-702 exam objectives.

#	Objective

4.1	Given a scenario, prevent, troubleshoot, and remove viruses and malware
	• Use antivirus software
	• Identify malware symptoms
	• Quarantine infected systems
	• Research malware types, symptoms, and solutions (virus encyclopedias)
	• Remediate infected systems
	• Update antivirus software
	   – Signature and engine updates
	   – Automatic vs. manual
	• Schedule scans
	• Repair boot blocks
	• Scan and removal techniques
	   – Safe mode
	   – Boot environment
	• Educate end user

Overview of security threats

Explanation

The goals of security are integrity, confidentiality, and availability. Threats to even the most secure systems' data challenge administrators and users every day. The cost of lost assets must be balanced against the cost of securing the network; your company must decide how much risk it is willing to take.

When data integrity is compromised, an organization must typically spend a lot of time and money to correct the consequences of the attack. If data confidentiality is compromised, the consequences aren't always immediate, but they are usually costly. Application availability can be compromised by network outages, causing organizations to lose millions of dollars in just a few hours.

There are four primary causes of compromised security:

- Technology weaknesses
- Configuration weaknesses
- Policy weaknesses
- Human error or malice

Technology weaknesses

Computer and network technologies have intrinsic security weaknesses in the following areas:

- **TCP/IP** — This protocol suite was designed as an open standard to facilitate communications. Due to its wide usage, there are plenty of experts and expert tools that can compromise this open technology. It cannot guard a network against message-modification attacks or protect connections against unauthorized-access attacks.
- **Operating systems** — UNIX, Linux, and Microsoft Windows, for example, need the latest patches, updates, and upgrades applied to protect users.
- **Network equipment** — Routers, firewalls, and switches must be protected through the use of passwords, authentication, routing protocols, and firewalls.

Configuration weaknesses

Poor configuration of even the most secure technology is often caused by one of the following weaknesses:

- **Unsecured accounts** — User account information transmitted unsecurely across the network exposes user names and passwords to programs used to monitor network activity. These programs, such as packet sniffers, can capture and analyze the data within IP packets on an Ethernet network or dial-up connection.
- **System accounts with weak passwords** — If no strong password policies are defined on the network, users can create passwords that can be easily guessed or cracked.
- **Poorly configured Internet services** — If Java and JavaScript are enabled in Web browsers, attacks can be made using hostile Java applets. High-security data should not be stored on a Web server; you should store data such as Social Security numbers and credit card numbers behind a firewall that can be accessed only through user authentication and authorization.
- **Unsecured default settings** — Many products have default settings that contain security holes.
- **Poorly configured network equipment** — Incorrect configuration of network devices can cause significant security problems. For example, incorrectly configured access control lists, routing protocols, or Simple Network Management Protocol (SNMP) community strings can open up large security holes.
- **Trojan horses** — These programs contain destructive code but appear to be harmless; they are enemies in disguise. They can delete data, mail copies of themselves to e-mail address lists, and open up other computers for attack.
- **Viruses** — Viruses have become possibly the single largest threat to network security. They replicate themselves and infect computers when triggered by a specific event. The effect can be minimal and only an inconvenience, or a virus can be more destructive and cause major problems, such as deleting or corrupting files or slowing down entire systems.

Human error and malice

Human error and malice constitute a significant percentage of breaches in network security. Even well-trained and conscientious users can cause great harm to security systems, often without knowing it.

Users can unwittingly contribute to security breaches in several ways:

- **Accident** — The mistaken destruction, modification, disclosure, or incorrect classification of information.
- **Ignorance** — Inadequate security awareness, lack of security guidelines, lack of proper documentation, lack of knowledge. Users might inadvertently give information on security weaknesses to attackers.
- **Workload** — Too many or too few system administrators.

Conversely, ill-willed employees or professional hackers and criminals can access valuable assets through:

- **Dishonesty** — Dishonesty encompasses fraud, theft, embezzlement, and the selling of confidential corporate information.
- **Impersonation** — Attackers might impersonate employees over the phone in an attempt to persuade users or administrators to give out user names, passwords, modem numbers, and so on.
- **Disgruntled employees** — Employees who were fired, laid off, or given a reprimand might infect the network with a virus or delete files. These people know the network and the value of the information on it and thus are often a huge security threat.
- **Snoops** — Individuals take part in corporate espionage by gaining unauthorized access to confidential data and providing this information to competitors.
- **Denial-of-service (DoS) attacks** — These attacks swamp network equipment such as Web servers or routers with useless service requests, causing the systems to become sluggish in responding to valid requests or even to crash.
- **Identity theft** — An attacker gains access to someone's personal information and uses it to commit fraud. Identity theft often takes the form of financial abuse, but it can also be used to obtain accounts that are then used to attack networks.

Security **12–5**

Do it! **A-1: Identifying common security threats**

Questions and answers

1 Which of the following computer and network technologies have intrinsic security weaknesses?

   A TCP/IP
   B Operating systems
   C Network equipment
   D All of the above

2 What is a crime called in which one person masquerades under the identity of another?

   A Identity theft
   B Confidentiality
   C Integrity
   D All of the above

3 Which of the following is not a primary cause of network security threats?

   A Encryption algorithm
   B Technology weaknesses
   C Policy weaknesses
   D Configuration weaknesses
   E Human error

4 True or false? Trojan horses are destructive programs that masquerade as benign applications.

   True

5 Which of the following is not considered a configuration weakness?

   A Unsecured accounts
   B Poorly configured Internet services
   C Viruses
   D Human ignorance

Social engineering

Explanation

Social engineering is the equivalent of hacking vulnerabilities in computer systems to gain access—except that it occurs in the world of people. Social engineering exploits trust between people to gain information that attackers can then use to gain access to computer systems. These trust exploits usually, though not always, involve a verbal trick, a hoax, or a believable lie. The goals of social engineering techniques include fraud, network intrusion, industrial espionage, identity theft, and a desire to disrupt a system or network.

Targets for social engineering techniques tend to be large organizations, where it is common for employees who have never actually met to communicate with each other. Other targets include employees who have information desired by attackers: industrial/military secrets, personal information about specific individuals, or resources such as long-distance or network access.

Social engineering techniques are often used when the attacker cannot find a way to penetrate the victim's systems with other methods. For example, when strong perimeter security and encryption foil an attacker's efforts to penetrate the network, social engineering might be the only avenue left. A slip of words is all the attacker needs to gain access to your well-defended systems.

Shoulder surfing

Shoulder surfing is a social engineering attack in which someone attempts to observe secret information by looking over your shoulder (or using other methods, described next). Imagine someone standing behind you as you log onto your workstation. By watching your fingers, the person can determine your password, and then later log on as you.

Shoulder surfing has forms that don't directly involve PCs. Consider the old long-distance calling-card attack—before cheap long distance and cell phones, people often subscribed to calling-card plans. By entering a long code number before dialing a phone number, you could get cheaper rates or bill the call to a third party. Spies would reportedly watch public telephones from afar through a telescope to watch as you entered the number, hoping to record your calling-card number. They'd then use that number to place long-distance calls.

A modern version of the calling-card attack involves learning your credit or debit card number and your PIN (personal identification number). With these numbers, an attacker could bill catalog or online purchases to your card. Cases have been reported of thieves using digital cameras to snap photos of the front and back of cards as people pay for merchandise in a store.

Dumpster diving

Digging useful information out of an organization's trash bin is another form of attack, one that exploits the implicit trust people have that once something is in the trash, it's gone forever. Experience shows that this is a very bad assumption, because dumpster diving is an incredible source of information for those who need to penetrate an organization in order to learn its secrets. The following table lists the useful types of information that can be obtained from trash or recycling bins:

Item	Description
Internal phone directories	Provide names and numbers of people to target and impersonate. Many user names are based on legal names.
Organizational charts	Provide information about people who are in positions of authority within the organization.
Policy manuals	Indicate how secure (or insecure) the company really is.
Calendars	Identify which employees are out of town at a particular time.
Outdated hardware	Provides all sorts of useful information; for example, hard drives might be restored, with data still accessible.
System manuals, network diagrams, and other sources of technical information	Include the exact information that attackers might seek, including the IP addresses of key assets, network topologies, locations of firewalls and intrusion detection systems, operating systems, applications in use, and more.

Online attacks

Online attacks use instant-messaging chat and e-mail venues to exploit trust relationships. Attackers might try to induce their victims to execute a piece of code by convincing them that they need it ("We have detected a virus, and you have to run this program to remove it—if you don't run it, you won't be able to use our service") or because it is something interesting, such as a game. While users are online, they tend to be more aware of hackers, and are careful about revealing personal information in chat sessions and e-mail. If a user installs the attacking program from a link, the attacker's code tricks the user into entering a user name and password in a pop-up window.

Social engineering countermeasures

There are a number of steps that organizations can take to protect themselves against social engineering attacks. At the heart of all of these countermeasures is a solid organizational policy that dictates expected behaviors and communicates security needs to every person in the company.

1 Take proper care of trash and other discarded items.
   - For all types of sensitive information on paper, use a paper shredder or locked recycle box instead of a trash can.
   - Ensure that all magnetic media are bulk-erased before they are discarded.
   - Keep trash dumpsters in secured areas so that no one has access to their contents.

2 User education and awareness training are critical. Ensure that all system users have periodic training about network security.
   - Make employees aware of social engineering scams and how they work.
   - Inform users about your organization's password policy (for example, never give your password out to anybody at all, by any means at all).
   - Give recognition to people who have avoided making mistakes or who have caught real mistakes in a situation that might have been a social engineering attack.
   - Ensure that people know what to do if they spot a social engineering attack.

Do it!

A-2: Discussing social engineering

Questions and answers

1. Which of the following are the best ways to protect your organization against revealing sensitive information to dumpster divers?

    A Use a paper shredder or locked recycle box.

    B Teach employees to construct strong passwords.

    C Add a firewall.

    D Keep trash dumpsters in secured areas.

2. How can you help system users avoid social engineering attacks?

    Answers might include:

    - *Make employees aware of social engineering scams and how they work.*
    - *Inform users about your organization's password policy.*
    - *Give recognition to people who have avoided making mistakes or who have caught real mistakes in a situation that might have been a social engineering attack.*
    - *Ensure that people know what to do if they spot a social engineering attack.*

3. Give examples of shoulder surfing in the context of both corporate and individual security.

    Corporations: An attacker looks over someone's shoulder to learn a password. Later, he logs on as that individual to access data or further attack network resources.

    Individuals: A thief takes a photo of your credit card as you pay for goods and then uses your credit card number to make an online purchase.

Viruses, worms, and Trojan horses

Explanation

Viruses constitute one of the biggest threats to network security. Network administrators need to keep a constant lookout for them and prevent their spread. They are designed to replicate themselves and infect computers when triggered by a specific event. The effect of some viruses is minimal and only an inconvenience, but others are more destructive and cause major problems, such as deleting files or slowing down entire systems.

Worms

Worms are programs that replicate themselves over the network. The replication is done without a user's intervention. A worm attaches itself to a file or a packet on the network and travels of its own accord. It can copy itself to multiple computers, bringing the entire network down. One method worms use to spread themselves is to send themselves to everyone in a user's e-mail address book. The intent of a worm infiltration is to cause a malicious attack. Such an attack often uses up computer resources to the point that the system, or even the entire network, can no longer function or is shut down.

Trojan horses

Trojan horses are delivery vehicles for destructive code. These appear to be harmless programs but are enemies in disguise. They can delete data, mail copies of themselves to e-mail address lists, and open up other computers for attack. Trojan horses are often distributed via spam—a great reason to block spam—or through compromised Web sites.

A *logic bomb* is code that is hidden within a program and designed to run when some condition is met. For example, the code might run on a particular date. Or perhaps the bomb's author sets some sort of condition that would be met after he or she is fired, at which time the code would run. Because a logic bomb is contained within another, presumably useful, program, you could consider it a type of Trojan horse.

Antivirus software

To stop viruses and worms, you should install antivirus software on individual computers, servers, and other network devices, such as firewalls. Most antivirus software runs a real-time antivirus scanner. A real-time antivirus scanner is software that's designed to scan every file accessed on a computer and thereby catch viruses and worms before they can infect the computer. This software runs each time a computer is turned on.

The real-time scanner helps antivirus software stop infections from different sources, including Web browsers, e-mail attachments, storage media, or local area networks. You can also boot into Safe mode to gain access to files that might normally be locked during normal Windows operation.

Most antivirus software works by using a *checksum*, a value that is calculated by applying a mathematical formula to data. When the data is transmitted, the checksum is recalculated. If the checksums don't match, the data has been altered, possibly by a virus or worm. The process of calculating and recording checksums to protect against viruses and worms is called *inoculation*.

Definition files

Antivirus software must be updated to keep up with new viruses and worms. The software can find only those threats that it knows to look for; therefore, the manufacturer constantly provides software updates, called *virus definitions*, as new viruses and worms are discovered. It's important to use antivirus software that automatically checks and updates its virus definitions, as well as the software engine itself, from the manufacturer's Web site. Having outdated virus definitions is the number-one cause of virus or worm infection.

Antivirus products

The following table lists several antivirus software products and their manufacturers' Web sites. Most of these sites offer detailed information about common viruses and worms. The sites even offer removal tools you can download for free and use to remove worms and viruses from infected computers. One of the best ways to protect your computers against viruses and worms is to stay informed. Web sites like www.datafellows.com and www.symantec.com provide descriptions of the latest threats.

Software	Web address
Norton AntiVirus by Symantec, Inc.	www.symantec.com
ESET Smart Security	www.eset.com
McAfee VirusScan by McAfee Associates, Inc.	www.mcafee.com
ESafe by Aladdin Knowledge Systems, Ltd	www.esafe.com
F-Prot by FRISK Software International	www.f-prot.com
PC-cillin by Trend Micro (for home use); NeaTSuite by Trend Micro (for networks)	www.trendmicro.com
avast! by ALWIL Software	www.avast.com

E-mail servers should also have antivirus software installed to protect computers on your local area network. Microsoft Forefront is an example of network antivirus software that scans all inbound and outbound e-mail, filters e-mail based on attachment type, and blocks spam.

Do it!

Antivirus programs are frequently changed and updated, so before class, test this activity with the current version of the program.

A-3: Installing antivirus software

Here's how	Here's why
1 Use Internet Explorer to download the Professional version of avast! from the avast.com Web site	
If prompted, select **Ask me later** and click **OK**	(In the Phishing Filter dialog box.) To delay setting the Phishing filter.
2 Install the avast! antivirus software	Follow the prompts to complete a default installation of the software.
3 When prompted to perform a boot-time scan of your computer, click **Yes**	
4 Restart your computer	Your computer scans when you reboot. Note the name and location of the report file: _____ When the scan is complete, avast! briefly displays a summary report of files scanned and infections found.
5 Log on to Windows	
6 Open the avast! report file	
Observe its contents	If no infections were found, it displays the same summary report shown at the end of the boot scan. If problems were found, more details are provided in this file.
Close the file and any open windows	
7 Click the avast! On-Access Scanner icon in the system tray	It's the blue icon with an "a" on it. The status should be Active.
Scroll through the list of information being protected	
Click **OK**	To close the avast! window.
8 Compare and contrast Trojan horses and logic bombs	*Both Trojan horses and logic bombs are programs containing unpublished, and typically damaging, hidden capabilities. Unlike Trojan horses, logic bombs are not necessarily built for transmission to other systems.*

TIPS *The boot scan can take 15 to 20 minutes to complete.*

Security   **12–13**

Spyware

Explanation

Spyware is software that gets installed on your system without your knowledge. It can cause a lot of problems for the user, including gathering personal or other sensitive information. Spyware can also change the computer's configuration. For example, it might change the home page in your browser. In addition, it often displays advertisements, earning this type of spyware the name *adware*. All of this can slow down your computer's performance, and the pop-ups can be so frequent that you can't really do any work.

Spyware is often installed when you are installing another application, especially free applications that you download from the Internet. For this reason, you need to be sure that you know exactly what you are installing. Sometimes the license agreement and privacy statement state that the spyware will be installed, but most people tend not to read those documents very closely. Spyware is often found on peer-to-peer and file-sharing networks. Spyware can also integrate itself into Internet Explorer, causing frequent browser crashes.

One way to reduce the amount of spyware on your system is to use a good pop-up blocker. Windows Vista includes pop-up blocker and anti-spyware software called Windows Defender. This real-time protection software makes recommendations to the user when it detects spyware. You can also schedule the software to perform scans.

When Windows Defender detects spyware on a computer, it displays information about the threat, including the location on the computer, a rating of the risk it poses to you and your information, and its recommendation as to what action you should take. The alert levels are described in the following table.

Alert level	Description
Severe	Especially malicious programs that will affect the privacy and security of your computer and can damage your system. Windows Defender recommends that you remove such software immediately.
High	Spyware programs that might affect the privacy and security of your computer and could damage your system. The changes the program makes on your computer are usually done without your consent. Windows Defender recommends that you remove such software immediately.
Medium	Spyware programs that could potentially gather personal information or make system changes and have a negative impact on your computer's performance. The software will not be automatically deleted. You will need to evaluate the way the software operates and determine whether it poses a threat to your system. If the publisher of the software is unfamiliar to you or is an untrusted publisher, you should block or remove the software.
Low	This software was typically installed with your knowledge and according to the licensing terms you agreed to, but it still might collect information or change the configuration of the computer. If the software was installed without your knowledge, review the alert details and determine whether you want to remove it.
Not yet classified	These programs typically do no harm unless they were installed without your knowledge. If a program is something you recognize and trust, go ahead and allow it to be run. If you don't recognize the publisher or the software, evaluate the alert details to determine your course of action.

If clients are running Windows XP with SP2, you can download Windows Defender from Microsoft and install it on those systems to protect them. Windows Defender is integrated into Windows Vista.

Another free product that is available for spyware removal is Spybot Search & Destroy. It is available from `www.safer-networking.org`. Each time you want to scan and remove spyware from your system with Spybot, you need to update the spyware definitions first. You might want to consider running both Spybot and Windows Defender; what one program might miss, the other might catch. It is often difficult for a single product to find all of the spyware on a system.

Do it!

A-4: Scanning your system for spyware

Here's how	Here's why
1 Open the Windows Security Center	In the Control Panel.
2 Click **Windows Defender**	
3 Click **Tools**	
Click **Options**	
4 Verify that "Automatically scan my computer (recommended)" is checked	
Verify that "Check for updated definitions before scanning" is checked	
Verify that "Apply default actions to items detected during a scan" is checked	
5 Display the **High alert items** list	The default setting is to perform the action based on the definition for the items detected.
Close the list	
6 Click **Save**	(If necessary.) To save your changes and close the Options window.
Click **Continue**	
7 Click **Scan**	To perform a quick scan. If you want to do a full scan, you'll need to go into Options, set the Type to "Full system scan," and schedule a scan.
If prompted, check for updates	To download updated definition files.

If students did not need to change any settings, have them click Cancel.

8	After the scan is complete, click	The Help button.
	If prompted, click **Yes**	To allow Windows Help and Support to search online for updated content.
	Under Getting Started, click **Understanding Windows Defender alert levels**	
9	Review the alert levels	The chart indicates the actions that are taken when items for each alert level are detected.
10	Close Windows Help and Support, and leave Windows Defender open	

Explanation

Operating and configuring Windows Defender

With any spyware protection software, you must regularly update *signatures*, which identify spyware programs. Windows Defender is integrated with Windows, which means that new signatures will be downloaded and installed automatically by Windows Update (assuming you have Windows Update enabled).

Windows Defender configuration

The default configuration of Windows Defender is sufficient for most users. Depending on how you use your computer, you might want to increase or decrease the frequency at which Windows Defender scans it for spyware.

You should scan your computer for spyware regularly. Just how often you scan depends on your Internet usage: heavily used computers are much more likely to gather spyware than are infrequently used PCs. You should probably scan at least once a week.

History

The History list displays actions that Windows Defender has taken in the past. This information can include the dates and times of system scans, the spyware programs detected, and the actions taken with those programs.

Quarantined programs

Windows Defender disables or removes spyware programs from your computers. Disabled programs are said to be "quarantined." Like an infectious person who is kept apart from other people, quarantined programs are rendered inactive so they cannot infect or further harm your computer. The Quarantined programs list in Windows Defender displays the names of any programs that have been quarantined.

Blocking, disabling, and removing malware

Windows Defender will automatically stop some forms of malware from running when your PC starts. For example, a virus might install itself onto your computer and try to run when you turn on your PC. Windows Defender will block programs like that, particularly those that attempt some action that would typically require you to enter the administrator's password.

After your computer has started up, Windows Defender will display a list of blocked programs—you will see an icon in the notification area of the taskbar. Right-click the Windows Defender icon and choose "Blocked startup programs" to see the list.

Running a blocked program

If Windows Defender has blocked a program that you think should have run, you can run it from the blocked-programs list. Point to "Run blocked program" and click the program you want to run. You might need to enter the administrator's password to proceed.

Disabling a blocked program

You can disable a program so that it cannot run at startup. You might do this if you think a program is a virus but it has not been removed by your antivirus software. To disable a program:

1. Open Windows Defender.
2. On the toolbar, click Tools.
3. Click Software Explorer.
4. From the Category list, select Startup Programs (if necessary).
5. Locate and select the program you want to disable.
6. Click Disable.

Removing a blocked program

You can remove a program entirely. This is the surest way to prevent a program from running on your computer at startup. To remove a program:

1. On the Windows Defender toolbar, click Tools.
2. Click Software Explorer.
3. From the Category list, select Startup Programs (if necessary).
4. Locate and select the program you want to remove.
5. Click Remove.

A-5: Disabling a program

Do it!

Windows Defender is open and has finished scanning the computer.

Here's how	Here's why
1 Observe the status section of the Windows Defender window	It displays the date and time of the last scan and last update, and indicates whether real-time protection is enabled.
2 Click **History**	To display the list of spyware programs detected on your computer and the actions taken with them.
3 Click **Quarantined items**	To display the list of programs that Windows Defender has disabled on your PC.
4 Click **Tools**	To open the Tools and Settings page. You can access the list of quarantined programs from this page or configure program options.
5 Click **Software Explorer** 	Windows Defender displays a list of startup programs that ran or are running on your computer.
6 Select **Microsoft Windows Explorer** 	The right pane displays details about the program. This program is the core Windows program that displays windows, dialog boxes, and so forth.

⚠ *Make sure students don't disable or remove any drivers or programs.*

7 Observe the program control buttons	[Remove] [Disable] [Enable]
	Because explorer.exe is a core part of Windows, you cannot remove or disable it. If you had selected an add-on program, whether malware or simply another startup program, you could disable or remove the program with these buttons. You could also enable a blocked program from here.
8 From the Category list, select **Currently Running Programs**	
Observe the list	You can see some Windows components, Windows Defender, and the avast! software. You can use the buttons under the descriptions to disable the program or to open Task Manager, which you can use to stop running programs.
9 Close all open windows	

BIOS updates

Explanation

The BIOS that comes in your computer doesn't usually need to be updated. Sometimes, however, you might need to upgrade the BIOS. The computer manufacturer will know whether device problems are caused by BIOS problems. Also, if new technology becomes available that isn't supported by the current BIOS, the computer manufacturer might release a new version of the BIOS that includes support for it.

BIOS manufacturers don't supply consumers with updates. They are released to the computer manufacturers, who built the BIOS into the computers.

Determining the BIOS version

You can find the version of BIOS installed in your system by using the System Information tool. With System Summary selected in the System Information window, record the value listed in the BIOS Version/Date field. This field lists BIOS version data, which you can use to determine if a newer version is available on your PC maker's Web site. If there's a SMBIOS Version field, record the value listed in it. The SMBIOS is used by PC inventorying programs to collect data about the computer. SMBIOS updates are usually included with BIOS updates. Not all PCs include a SMBIOS, however; older computers probably won't.

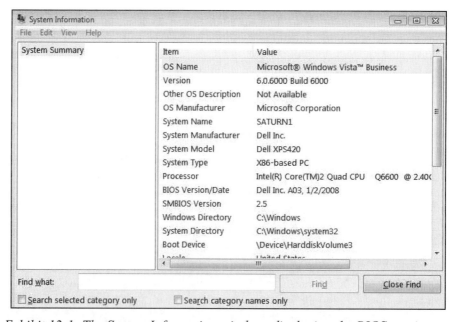

Exhibit 12-1: The System Information window, displaying the BIOS version

Security   **12-21**

Flashing the BIOS

To update the BIOS in your system:

1. Use the System Information tool to determine your current BIOS version.
2. Visit your PC manufacturer's Web site and navigate to the support pages to locate the BIOS update files. Compare the version number and release date with the information reported by the System Information tool to determine if a new BIOS version is available.
3. Download the installation file for the new BIOS version. Make sure you choose the version that matches your PC model.
4. If it's not part of the BIOS installation file, download the appropriate BIOS flashing utility from your PC manufacturer's Web site. Make sure you choose the version that matches your PC model and operating system.
5. Close all open applications.
6. Open the flashing utility and follow the instructions it provides to update the BIOS.
7. Restart your PC when prompted.

Do it!

A-6: Determining whether you need to update your computer's BIOS

TIPS
If you've completed this activity on classroom computers during a previous class, there probably won't be a newer BIOS for students to install.

Here's how	Here's why
1 Run **msinfo32**	
2 Record your BIOS and SMBIOS information	Manufacturer: Version: Date: SMBIOS Version:
3 Close System Information	
4 Visit your PC manufacturer's Web site and determine if a newer version of the BIOS is available	

Topic B: Implementing and troubleshooting security

This topic covers the following CompTIA A+ 220-702 exam objectives.

#	Objective

2.4	**Evaluate and resolve common issues**
	• Error Messages and Conditions
	   – System Performance and Optimization
	      • UAC

4.2	**Implement security and troubleshoot common issues**
	• Operating systems
	   – Local users and groups: Administrator, Power Users, Guest, Users
	   – Vista User Access Control (UAC)
	   – NTFS vs. Share permissions
	      • Allow vs. deny
	      • Difference between moving and copying folders and files
	      • File attributes
	   – Shared files and folders
	      • Administrative shares vs. local shares
	      • Permission propagation
	      • Inheritance
	   – System files and folders
	   – Encryption (BitLocker, EFS)
	   – User authentication
	• System
	   – BIOS security
	      • TPM

Windows Vista user accounts

Explanation

Like its predecessors, Windows Vista includes features that support shared use of a single PC. More than one person can use a single PC while maintaining separate sets of preferences (desktop wallpaper, recent documents, favorites) and privileges (resources, such as files and folders, to which access is permitted). Windows Vista stores these settings in a user account.

User accounts

A user account is a collection of settings and privileges associated with a person (or persons, if multiple people choose to share the same account). When you log on to Windows Vista (even if it logs you on automatically without prompting you for a user name and password), the operating system loads the settings and privileges defined in your user account. Your experience with the PC is tailored to you, thanks to the user account.

User account types

Although this is a prerequisite, be sure that students understand the difference between local and domain user accounts.

Windows Vista supports two general types of user accounts: computer administrator and standard user. Administrators have full control of the computer, while standard user accounts can use programs but cannot make system changes that affect other user accounts. The following table summarizes some of the privileges allowed for each account type.

Administrator	User	Privilege
✓	✓	Use programs.
✓	✓	Change account picture, and add, change, and delete account password.
✓		Change account name or account type.
✓	✓	Add, delete, and change files in personal Documents and Public Documents folders.
✓		Add and delete files other than those in personal Documents and Public Documents.
✓		Add and delete user accounts and change other users' passwords.
✓		Add programs.
✓		Add hardware (other than printers).
✓	✓	Add a local printer.
✓	✓	Add a network printer.
✓		Change system settings.

A Guest account is built in but is not active by default. The Guest account can use installed programs, but has limited privileges and cannot even change the account picture or password.

You can designate user accounts as Power Users by adding them to the local Power Users group. Despite the name, Power Users don't really have any more administrative control over the computer than standard users. However, they might have sufficient permissions to run some applications that standard users can't.

Windows XP and Windows 2000 also have Guest, Administrator, and Power User accounts.

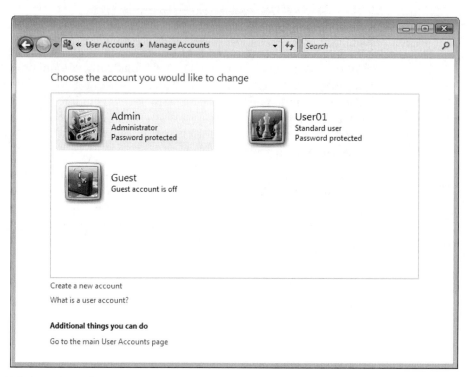

Exhibit 12-2: The Manage Accounts window in Windows Vista

Creating user accounts

Only an administrator account (or a standard user providing administrator credentials) can create a user account. User accounts are managed through the Control Panel.

1. In the Control Panel, click User Accounts and Family Safety.
2. Click "Add or remove user accounts."
3. When prompted, enter administrative-level credentials (password, or user name and password), or click Continue.
4. Click "Create a new account."
5. Enter a name for the new user. The name can contain spaces, but not any of the following characters: /\ [ ] " ; : < > + - , ? *
6. Select the account type: Standard user or Administrator.
7. Click Create Account.

Security **12-25**

Do it!

B-1: Creating local user accounts

Here's how	Here's why
1 Click **Start** and choose **Control Panel**	
2 Under User Accounts and Family Safety, click **Add or remove user accounts**	(In Vista Business, under User Accounts.)
3 When prompted, click **Continue**	
4 Click **Create a new account**	
5 Enter **Anne** for the user name	Name the account This name will appear or Anne A user name can contain spaces, but cannot contain any of the following characters: / \ [ ] " ; : < > + - , ? *
6 Observe the types of user account	You can create a standard user or administrator account from this window. The default is standard user.
7 Click **Create Account**	To create a standard user account named Anne.
Observe the Manage Accounts window	The new account is listed with the other accounts on your computer.
8 Create a standard user account named **Robert**	Use the same settings you did for the user account Anne.

User account pictures might not show up unless students are logged in as an administrator.

Passwords

Explanation

You can easily improve security by requiring logon passwords. Windows provides tools you can use to enable passwords, as well as set, change, and delete passwords.

Passwords require a user to enter a secret word—actually, any string of letters, numbers, and characters—before he or she can log on or switch to another account. Standard users can set and change their own passwords, and an administrator can set and change passwords for any user on the system. You can add a password hint to remind yourself of your password, but if a password is forgotten, an administrator must change the password for you. Passwords are set in the User Accounts window.

Password rules

When using passwords, you must adhere to these Windows rules:

- A password can contain letters, numbers, and characters, but it cannot start or end with a space.
- Passwords are case sensitive.
- Passwords must be between 1 and 127 characters long.
- In a business environment, the system or network administrator might have implemented more restrictive rules. Check with him or her to determine the complete set of rules that apply to you.

Password recommendations

Although the preceding rules explain the limits, you should follow these general guidelines when setting your passwords:

- Match the strength of your password to your needs for security. For example, home computer users can often use very simple passwords (or no password) because there is little risk or potential for loss from unauthorized access to the PC. (However, if that PC is connected to the Internet, it's essential that you use a strong password to help protect the computer from attack.) User accounts in a business environment should be password-protected, but are likely to need less secure passwords for standard users than for administrative users.
- Set a password that is easy to remember, but hard to guess. It is not secure to use your spouse's name, kids' names, pets' names, and so forth as your password.
- Longer passwords are more secure than shorter passwords, with those more than 15 characters being the most secure. Try using a phrase, such as DigitalPhotographyFan, to create an easily remembered long password.
- Use a mix of upper- and lowercase letters, numbers, and characters in your password. Avoid common substitution schemes, such as replacing Os with zeros, Es with threes, and so forth.
- Don't write down your passwords. Some security experts suggest that writing down passwords is okay if you can store the written copy in a secure place, such as a locked cabinet. Check with your corporate security officer for the policy set by your company in this matter.

You might ask students to suggest some passwords and then discuss why they are or aren't secure.

Creating a user password

To create a user password for an account that doesn't have one:

1. In the Manage Accounts window, click the user account for which you want to set a password. If prompted, enter the administrator's password.
2. Click "Create a password" to open the dialog box shown in Exhibit 12-3.
3. Type the password twice.
4. (Optional) Enter a password hint. The hint is visible to all users, so it should be something to remind the user of his or her password without giving it away to others.
5. Click Create password.

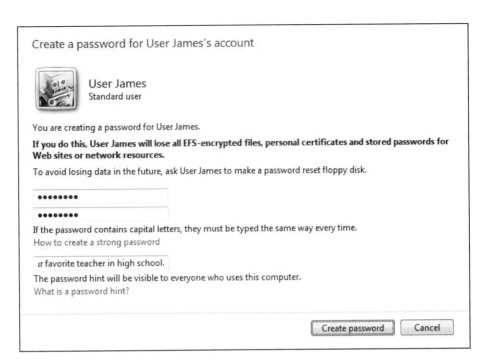

Exhibit 12-3: Creating a password

Do it!

B-2: Creating a password

Here's how	Here's why
1 Click **Anne**	In the Manage Accounts window. You'll add a password to this account.
2 Click **Create a password**	
3 In the New password box, enter **p@ssword**	Passwords are case sensitive and should include non-alphabetic characters.
4 In the Confirm new password box, enter **p@ssword**	To confirm the password and guard against typos.
5 In the "Type a word or phrase to use as a password hint" box, enter **This is too easy!**	Remember that hints are visible to anyone. It should jog your memory, but not be useful to anyone else.
6 Click **Create password** Click ⬅	To return to the Manage Accounts window.
Observe the Anne user account	It shows that the account is password-protected.
7 Close the Manage Accounts window	
8 Log off your account and log on as **Anne**	To test the account. Use the password you just created.
9 Log off Anne and log back on as **PAADMIN##**	
10 Create a password of **p@ssword** for the user account Robert	
11 Test the new password for Robert by logging on with that account	
12 Log back on as **PAADMIN##**	

Requiring a new password

Explanation

When you create a user account for someone who will use your computer, you know the user's password. He might not like the password you have chosen. Additionally, he might not want you to know his password and have access to his files.

You can configure an account to require the user to change the password the first time the user logs on. Additionally, you can set passwords to expire and require periodic changing.

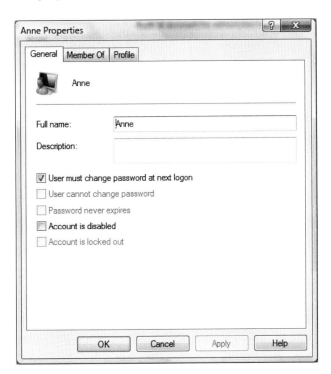

Exhibit 12-4: Requiring a user to supply a new password

Do it!

B-3: Requiring a new password

Here's how	Here's why
1 Click **Start**	
Right-click **Computer** and choose **Manage**	To open Computer Management.
2 Click **Continue**	You must be logged on as an administrator or provide administrator credentials to use the Computer Management console.
3 In the tree pane, click where indicated	▷ 📁 Shared Folders 　 👥 Local Users and Groups 　 ⚙️ Reliability and Performa To expand Local Users and Groups.
Select the **Users** folder	A list of user accounts on your computer is displayed in the details pane.
4 Right-click **Anne** and choose **Properties**	To open the Properties dialog box for this user account.
5 Clear **Password never expires**	To make available the option to require a new password. It's currently grayed out.
6 Check **User must change password at next logon**	
7 Click **OK**	
8 Close Computer Management	
Log off your account and log on as **Anne**	
Change the password to **Pa$$321**	To fulfill the requirement you just implemented.
9 Log off Anne and log back on as **PAADMIN##**	

Disabling user accounts

Explanation

If you aren't using an account but don't want to delete it, you can disable it to prevent anyone else from logging on with that account. Windows preserves all of the settings, files, and permissions associated with a disabled account. Later, you can enable the account, and its settings will be intact. You disable and enable accounts by using the Computer Management console.

Exhibit 12-5: Disabling an account

Deleting accounts

When you no longer need a user account, you can delete it. You must be logged in as an administrator. You can delete administrator and standard user accounts, except for the account you used to log on.

When you delete an account, Windows will prompt you to delete all files associated with the account. Doing so is optional. You can keep the files associated with the account. Administrators will have access to those files, but standard users won't.

Do it!

B-4: Disabling local user accounts

Here's how	Here's why
1 Open Computer Management	
Expand Local Users and Groups, and then select the **Users** folder	
2 Right-click **Anne** and choose **Properties**	
3 Check **Account is disabled**	
4 Click **OK**	The down-pointing arrow on the account's icon indicates that it's disabled.
5 Close Computer Management	

User Account Control

Explanation

Microsoft has recommended for years that administrative users log on and work with a standard user-level account unless they actually need special administrative privileges for certain tasks. This security scheme protects a computer in a number of ways, including the following:

- Administrators can't inadvertently change system settings, delete important files, or do other system harm as they could if they logged on regularly as an administrative user.
- Unauthorized users can't walk up to an unattended administrator computer and make system changes on it or on other computers on the network.

However, previous Windows versions have not made such a work style convenient. System administrators had to frequently log off as the standard user and log back on as an administrator to perform many duties. This meant closing applications, saving work in progress, and interrupting their workflow.

User Account Control (UAC) in Windows Vista is designed to make it convenient to follow Microsoft's security recommendation. You are permitted to make more system changes than you could before when logged on as a standard user. More important, whenever you attempt an action that requires administrative privileges, you are prompted for credentials; this step helps protect against malware being installed or making changes without your permission. If you supply appropriate administrative credentials, you are permitted to perform the action. You don't need to log out and log back in as an administrator.

Advise students that they should take advantage of UAC. They should always log on as a standard user rather than as an administrator.

Elevation prompts

Windows Vista displays different elevation prompts based on the privileges of the user account that is logged on when an application needs administrative privileges. When you are logged on to Windows Vista as a local administrator, it displays a consent prompt, as shown in Exhibit 12-6, whenever a program needs elevated privileges to accomplish a task. You can identify the Windows Vista commands or programs that need administrative privileges by looking for the shield icon. For example, in Exhibit 12-6, you can see that Windows Vista requires administrative privileges when you want to open one or more ports in Windows Firewall to enable an application to communicate through the firewall.

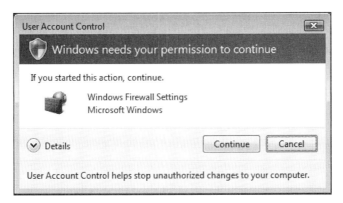

Exhibit 12-6: The User Account Control consent prompt

If you're logged on as a standard user and attempt to perform a task that requires administrative privileges, you'll see a credential prompt, as shown in Exhibit 12-7. This prompt requires you to enter the user name and password for a local or domain administrator account before Windows Vista will grant the necessary privileges for the application to run.

Exhibit 12-7: The User Account Control credential prompt

When elevated permissions are required, UAC will present one of the alerts in the following table. You'll need to provide the appropriate administrative credentials or speak to a computer administrator to continue.

Alert	You'll see this alert when...
Windows needs your permission to continue	The operating system wants to perform a function that will modify the computer or operating system settings.
A program needs your permission to continue	A program with a valid digital signature wants to start.
An unidentified program wants access to your computer	A program without a valid digital signature wants to start. A program without a valid digital signature is not necessarily a malicious program.
This program has been blocked	The computer administrator has blocked you from starting the program you're trying to start.

Tasks that require administrative privileges in Windows Vista include:
- Installing and removing applications
- Installing a device driver, Windows updates, or an ActiveX control
- Configuring Windows Firewall
- Creating, modifying, and deleting local user accounts
- Configuring Parental Controls
- Scheduling tasks
- Restoring backups
- Modifying the configuration of User Account Control (by editing the local group policy)

Administrator accounts

Even though UAC is helpful, you or your system administrator might still assign administrator accounts to you and others who use your PC. Having separate accounts for each administrator helps track system changes. Also, when an administrator-level user no longer needs access to the PC, you can simply delete his or her user and administrator accounts. You won't have to change and distribute passwords to all of the other administrative-level users of the PC.

UAC configuration

You can configure the behavior of UAC by using the Local Security Policy console (part of the Microsoft Management Console, or MMC). This console, like Computer Management, is a tool that administrators use to configure a Windows Vista computer. This console is used to modify the *local security policy*, which is a collection of settings that cover all aspects of a computer's security.

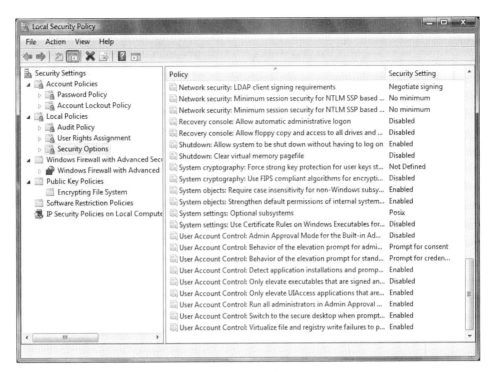

Exhibit 12-8: The Local Security Policy console

You must be very careful when making changes in the Local Security Policy console because you could negatively affect the security of the computer. You must also consult with the network administrator to determine which network-wide security policies are in effect. Although you can configure UAC through the Local Security Policy console, chances are, in many organizations you won't need to make any changes, and you might even be prohibited from changing the local security policy.

You can configure the following UAC settings in the Local Security Policy console. To open it, click Start and type secpol.msc.

Configuring local security policy is beyond the scope of this course. Just briefly present these settings to students so they know what the settings are and how to access them.

UAC policy setting	Description	Default setting
Admin Approval Mode for the Built-in Administrator account	Determines how Admin Approval mode operates for the built-in Administrator user account.	Disabled
Behavior of the elevation prompt for administrators in Admin Approval Mode	Determines how the elevation prompt behaves for computer administrators.	Prompt for consent
Behavior of the elevation prompt for standard users	Determines how the elevation prompt behaves for standard user accounts.	Prompt for credentials
Detect application installations and prompt for elevation	Dictates how approval works for program installations.	Enabled
Only elevate executables that are signed and validated	Requires a security key check on certain applications.	Disabled
Only elevate UIAccess applications that are installed in secure locations	Requires installation of certain programs in specific secure locations.	Disabled
Run all administrators in Admin Approval Mode	Determines system-wide UAC security policy behavior.	Enabled
Switch to the secure desktop when prompting for elevation	Determines which type of desktop a user will see during an elevation request.	Enabled
Virtualize file and registry write failures to per-user locations	Configures security on older applications.	Enabled

Disabling UAC

You can disable UAC altogether, but doing so would leave your computer exposed to a variety of security threats. To disable UAC, in User Accounts, click "Turn User Account Control on or off." Provide the necessary administrative credentials or click Continue. Clear the "Use User Account Control (UAC) to help protect your computer" checkbox, and click OK.

Security **12-37**

Do it!

B-5: Configuring UAC

Here's how	Here's why
1 Click **Start** and enter **secpol.msc**	To open the Local Security Policy console. You're going to examine the UAC settings in the local security policy.
Click **Continue**	
If necessary, maximize the window	
2 Double-click **Local Policies**	To expand it.
Select **Security Options**	To display the settings in the details pane.
3 Scroll to the bottom of the list	
Observe the User Account Control settings	The settings described previously are listed in order.
4 Double-click **Admin Approval Mode for the Built-in Administrator account**	
5 Observe the settings	○ Enabled ◉ Disabled
	You can choose between Enabled or Disabled to turn this security setting on or off.
6 Activate the Explain tab	To display an explanation of this policy setting and the effects of the Enabled and the Disabled settings. Sometimes configuring policies can be confusing, so it helps to have the effects of each setting explained explicitly.
7 Click **Cancel**	To close the dialog box without making any changes.
8 Double-click **Behavior of the elevation prompt for standard users**	
Click the drop-down arrow and observe the settings	They are different from the Enabled and Disabled settings you saw in the last dialog box.
Prompt for credentials ▼ Automatically deny elevation requests Prompt for credentials	

Tell students they can also open the Local Security Policy through the Administrative Tools section of the Control Panel.

Tell students to expand the Policy column if necessary.

9	Activate the Explain tab	To read the explanation for each setting.
10	Click **Cancel**	To close the dialog box without making changes. Always check with your network administrator or other administrator before configuring local security policy settings.
11	Close the Local Security Policy console	

File system security

Explanation

You can use the *access control list (ACL)* for a folder to allow or deny various permissions for users. All of the permissions granted to the user either directly or through groups are combined for the *effective permissions* the user has for the file or folder. Permissions flow down through the file structure, with the user inheriting the permissions from the folders above. Implicit denial causes privileges to be denied unless there are explicit permissions granted.

For files and folders in Windows Vista, you can specify the permissions described in the following table.

Point out that when the permission is set to Deny, users won't be able to do the things listed in the second column of this table.

Permission	When set to Allow
Full control	Users can view folder and file contents, modify files and folders, create files and folders, and run programs. This permission applies to the current folder and all folders below it unless another permission is set to prohibit inheritance of the permission into subfolders.
Modify	Users can modify files and folders, but cannot create them.
Read & execute	Users can view the contents of files and folders. They can also run programs located in the folder.
Read	Users can view folder contents, and open files and folders.
Write	Users can create and modify files and folders.
Special permissions	Users can perform management tasks, such as managing documents.

You should always grant a user the least privileges necessary. In other words, if someone needs only to read a file, grant the Read permission, not Write, Modify, and so forth. This approach ensures that users won't make inadvertent or forbidden changes in your data

"Access Denied" errors

One of the problems you can expect to troubleshoot as a desktop support technician occurs when a user is denied access to a resource. Troubleshooting this problem involves asking a typical series of questions, such as:

- Is everyone denied access to the resource, or is only that user denied access? Use this question to determine if the problem lies with the shared resource or the configuration of a single user account.
- If only one user is denied access, can this user access any shared resources on the network? Use this question to determine if there's a problem with the user's networking components (network adapter, cabling, or configuration).

If your isolating questions lead you to determine that the problem is with only one user and it isn't the user's networking components, then you start troubleshooting the user's resource access to determine why the user is being denied access.

If a user's inability to access a shared resource is due to the user's configuration, there are a number of factors that can cause this problem. For example:

- The user doesn't have the necessary share permissions.
- If the shared resource is a folder or file, the user might have NTFS permissions that prevent access. (Remember, users receive the most restrictive permissions when both NTFS and share permissions are applied to a folder.)
- If the problem occurs when a user attempts to save a file he has modified, someone has configured the file with the Read Only attribute.

There are a number of techniques you can use to research the potential causes of a user being denied access.

Moving versus copying

When troubleshooting folder access, you need to keep in mind some basic rules about NTFS permissions and copying and moving files and folders.

- Copied files inherit the permissions from the new location.
- Moved files keep their original permissions.

File attributes

Files can have various attributes assigned to them. File attributes tell the operating system and applications how files should be used. You can assign the attributes described in the following table.

Attribute	Description
Read-only	Prevents inadvertent changes in a file. MS-DOS commands don't allow you to change a read-only file. Some Windows applications allow it, although they might prompt you first, letting you know that you're changing a read-only file.
Hidden	Hides the file from view in the default list display of the MS-DOS `dir` command and in Windows Explorer.
System	Indicates that the file is used by the operating system and shouldn't be altered or removed.
Archive	Indicates whether the file has been modified since a backup.

System files and folders are hidden by default in Windows, but you can use Folder Options to display them.

The Effective Permissions tool

One of the tools you can use to troubleshoot an access-denied error is the Effective Permissions tool. You use it to determine a given user's effective NTFS permissions for a particular folder or file. Note, however, that the Effective Permissions tool does *not* consider share permissions when performing its calculations; it considers only NTFS permissions. Therefore, after using this tool, you'll have additional footwork to do if you want to determine the user's effective share permissions.

The nice thing about the Effective Permissions tool is that it considers all *inherited* permissions as well as NTFS permissions explicitly assigned to groups of which the user is a member. So it does give you an accurate picture of a user's NTFS permissions.

To determine a user's NTFS permissions:

1. Access the computer that contains the shared file or folder the user is attempting to access. Open Windows Explorer.
2. Right-click the file or folder and choose Properties.
3. Select the Security tab and click Advanced to open the Advanced Security Settings dialog box.
4. Activate the Effective Permissions tab.
5. Next to the "Group or user name" box, click Select. Use the Select User, Computer, or Group dialog box to define the user or group for which you want to determine effective permissions. Click OK when you're done.
6. Review the selected checkboxes in the Effective permissions list, as shown in Exhibit 12-9. These checkboxes represent the user's effective NTFS permissions for the folder or file.
7. Write down the user's effective permissions. If the user does not have any effective permissions, you must determine how the user is being denied access; to do so, examine the NTFS permissions assignments on that folder or file.

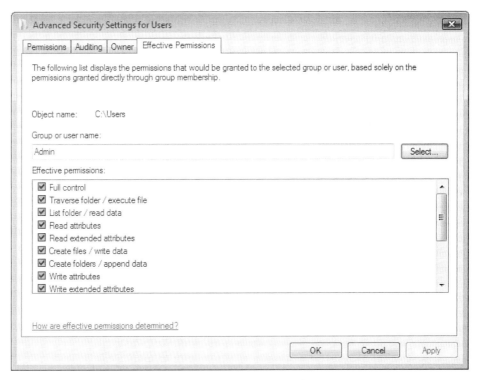

Exhibit 12-9: The Effective Permissions tool in Windows Vista

Shared Folders in Computer Management

The Shared Folders node in Computer Management enables you to view a list of shares and their permissions on the selected computer, including both local shares and administrative shares. (Administrative shares are folders that are shared by default by the operating system when it's installed.) By examining the share permissions, you can determine whether a user is being denied access as a result of NTFS permissions, share permissions, or both.

To use Computer Management to review the share permissions for a shared folder, follow these steps:

1 Click Start. Right-click Computer and choose Manage. Click Continue.
2 In the console tree, under System Tools, expand Shared Folders, and then select the Shares folder. You now see a list of all shares on the computer, including the hidden administrative shares. (You can hide any share by adding $ at the end of the share name.)
3 Right-click the folder you want to examine and choose Properties.
4 Activate the Share Permissions tab. Review the permissions assignments, as shown in Exhibit 12-10. Keep in mind that you might see permissions assigned directly to the user or to a group of which the user is a member.

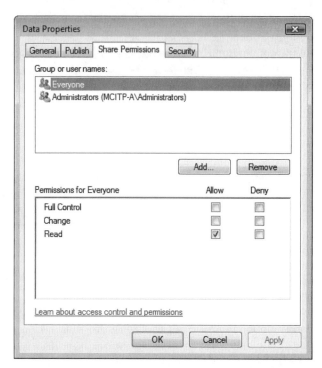

Exhibit 12-10: Reviewing the share permissions for a folder

Calculating effective permissions

As you just saw, you can use the Effective Permissions tool to determine a user's effective NTFS permissions, and use Computer Management to access the Share Permissions tab for a shared folder. You need the information you gain from both of these tools to determine the user's true effective permissions. By "true effective permissions," we mean what exactly the user can do when accessing the shared folder across the network.

Here are the steps to determine a user's total effective permissions:

1. Use the Effective Permissions tool to determine the user's effective NTFS permissions for a folder. Keep in mind that these permissions represent the combination of:
    - NTFS permissions assigned directly to the user (if any).
    - NTFS permissions assigned to a group of which the user is a member.
    - Inherited permissions, which occur when the user has NTFS permissions granted—either directly or to a group the user belongs to—for a folder that is higher in the folder hierarchy.

    The only situation in which permissions are *not* cumulative occurs when an administrator explicitly denies the user (or a group the user belongs to) access to the folder. In this scenario, the Deny permission overrides all other permission assignments, and the user is denied access.

2. Review the share permissions for the folder. As with NTFS permissions, share permissions represent the combination of:
    - Share permissions assigned directly to the user (if any).
    - Share permissions assigned to a group of which the user is a member.
    - Inherited permissions, which occur when the user has share permissions granted—either directly or to a group the user belongs to—for a folder that is higher in the folder hierarchy.

    And just as with NTFS permissions, the only time that share permissions are *not* cumulative occurs when an administrator explicitly denies the user (or a group the user belongs to) share permissions for the folder.

3. Calculate the user's effective permissions by comparing the user's effective NTFS permissions to the user's share permissions. When the user connects to the share, Windows grants the user whichever permissions are the most restrictive.

4. If you calculate the user's effective permissions and determine that the user *should* be able to modify a file but is getting the "Access Denied" message, your next step is to check the file's attributes.

Let's look at an example. Say that you have a folder named AcctgData on your server. You assign the NTFS permission of Allow Modify to the Accounting security group, of which user FSmith is a member. You remove all other default permission assignments from the folder, except for the Allow Full Control permission assignment to the built-in Administrators group. At this point, user FSmith's effective NTFS permissions are Allow Modify, which means that he can create, modify, and delete files in the folder.

Next, you share this folder as AcctgData without changing its default share permissions. The key default share permissions are:

- Administrators: Allow Full Control
- Users: Allow Read

Because FSmith is a member of the Users group by default, he gets the share permission of Allow Read. Now that we know that FSmith's NTFS permissions are Allow Modify and his share permissions are Allow Read, Smith's effective permissions when he connects to the AcctgData share are Allow Read. This is because the share permissions assignment is more restrictive than the NTFS permissions.

At this point, you can see that this user will get an "Access Denied" error if he tries to create or modify files in the AcctgData share. As a desktop support technician, you need to know how to troubleshoot such errors by determining a user's true effective permissions.

Do it!

B-6: Determining effective permissions

Here's how	Here's why
1 On your C: drive, create a folder named **SalesData**	
2 If you attempt to share the folder, what are the default share permissions?	*The default share permissions will be your PAADMIN## account with Owner permissions.*
3 Right-click **SalesData** and select **Properties**	To open the folder's Properties dialog box.
Activate the Security tab	To view the default NTFS permissions assigned to the folder.
4 What are the default NTFS permissions assigned to the Users group for the C:\SalesData folder?	*Allow Read, List folder contents, and Read & execute.*
5 What are the default NTFS permissions assigned to the Administrators group for the SalesData folder?	*Allow Full Control.*
6 Your user, PAADMIN##, is a member of the Administrators group. What will your true effective permissions be when you access the SalesData share from another computer?	
PAADMIN## is a member of the Administrators, Users, and Everyone groups. Although your user account has effective NTFS permissions of Allow Full Control, the share permissions assigned to the Everyone group are Allow Read. Your user account's effective permissions are based on the more restrictive of the NTFS and share permissions. Therefore, because the Everyone group's share permissions are Read, even you, as a member of Administrators, cannot do more than read files in this folder when connecting across the network.	
7 On the Security tab, click **Advanced**	To open the Advanced Security Settings dialog box.
Activate the Effective Permissions tab	

8	Next to the "Group or user name" box, click **Select**	
	Type **Anne** and click **OK**	To determine Anne's effective permissions.
9	Observe the list	Anne has a full range of permissions, but she doesn't have Full Control permissions.
10	Determine the effective permissions for your PAADMIN## account	
11	What set of permissions do you have? Why?	*As a member of the Administrators group, you have Full Control permissions.*
12	Close all open windows	

The Windows Security Center

Explanation

The Windows Security Center, shown in Exhibit 12-11, is a collection of utilities designed to help you view your computer's security settings in one convenient location. To configure the individual security components displayed in the Security Center, you must use the Control Panel Links within the Windows Security Center.

The Security Center provides access to the following utilities:

- Firewall
- Automatic updates
- Malware protection
- Other security settings

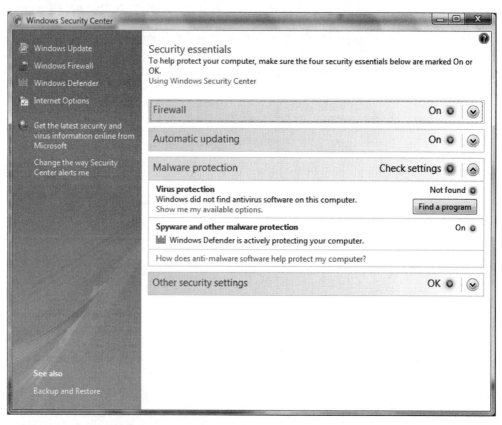

Exhibit 12-11: The Windows Security Center

Firewalls

If your computer has an Internet connection, it is vulnerable to hackers, viruses, worms, and other destructive intrusions. Windows Vista provides a firewall to help protect your computer from these problems. A *firewall* is a system that prevents access to your computer by unauthorized Internet or network users. It can be in the form of software or hardware. Windows Firewall, shown in Exhibit 12-12, is a software firewall.

To view the status of Windows Firewall:
1. Open the Control Panel.
2. Click Security.
3. Click Windows Firewall.

Exhibit 12-12: The Control Panel displays the status of Windows Firewall

Do it!

B-7: Displaying the status of Windows Firewall

Here's how	Here's why
1 Open the Control Panel	
2 Click **Security**	
3 Click **Windows Firewall**	
4 Observe the status of the firewall	It should be turned on.

Firewall configuration

Explanation

By default, Windows Firewall is turned on. Unless your computer is protected by another firewall, you should leave Windows Firewall enabled. You can check with the network administrator about the need for Windows Firewall inside a corporate network, but threats can come from other computers inside your network, not just computers on the Internet.

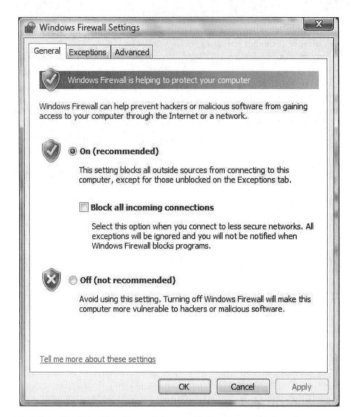

Exhibit 12-13: Windows Firewall Settings dialog box

Windows Firewall is automatically configured to block most rogue programs and to pass requests by legitimate programs. You probably won't have to change many settings. However, you might need to allow a specific type of communication to pass through the firewall, or you might need to turn the firewall on or off, depending on where you're connecting to the Internet. For example, you might want a more secure connection if you're connected to the Internet through a hotspot at an airport or through a hotel network.

To configure Windows Firewall:
1. Open the Control Panel.
2. Click Security and then click Windows Firewall.
3. Click Change Settings to open the Windows Firewall Settings dialog box.
4. When prompted, either enter the administrator's password and click OK, or click Continue (if you're logged on as an administrator).

    On the General tab, turn the firewall on or off. You can also block all incoming programs for an even more secure connection.

    On the Exceptions tab, specify firewall exceptions.

    On the Advanced tab, control which network connections are protected by the firewall.
5. Click OK.

Exceptions

To configure an exception for a specific program, select the program in the list of exceptions. If the program isn't listed on the Exceptions tab, click Add Program, select the program you want to add to the list, and click OK.

Some applications might require that you open a numbered port, which is a specific channel through which the application communicates, using TCP/IP. For example, Web page communication through HTTP uses port 80. To create an exception for a specific port, activate the Exceptions tab and click Add port. Enter the name and port number, and specify whether it's the TCP or UDP protocol. (You can obtain protocol information from the program's documentation or from a network administrator.)

Troubleshooting

Remember, when you're troubleshooting a network connection, it's important to check the status of the firewall and the list of exceptions. You might find that you can't connect to a shared resource or a program isn't functioning properly because of a missing or incorrectly configured firewall exception.

Do it!

B-8: Creating firewall exceptions

The Windows Firewall window is open.

Here's how	Here's why
1 Click **Change settings**	In the Windows Firewall window.
Click **Continue**	To open the Windows Firewall Settings dialog box.
2 Activate the Exceptions tab	
3 Click **Add program**	You're going to add a program to the list of exceptions.
Select **Windows Photo Gallery** and click **OK**	To add it to the list of exceptions.
4 Observe Windows Photo Gallery in the list	It was added and checked.
5 Click **Add port**	
Observe the Add a Port dialog box	You can use this dialog box to add an exception for a specific port and protocol.
6 In the Name box, type **FTP**	
In the Port number box, type **20**	
Verify that TCP is selected, and click **OK**	
7 Observe FTP in the list	The exception has been added and enabled. You can disable it by clearing the checkbox.
8 Click **OK**	To close the Windows Firewall dialog box.
9 Close all open windows	

Encrypting File System

Explanation

Windows Vista enables users to encrypt any files (except for operating system files) that are stored on an NTFS partition. This encryption capability is referred to as the *Encrypting File System (EFS)*. When a user encrypts a file, Windows Vista permits only that user to open the file. Microsoft designed EFS to give organizations an extra tool for protecting the hard disks in laptops. All editions of Windows Vista support EFS, except for Windows Vista Starter, Windows Vista Home Basic, and Windows Vista Home Premium.

In the past, if a laptop was stolen, a hacker could gain access to the user's files by booting the computer with another operating system or even installing an additional operating system on the computer. EFS enables users to protect their files even if their computers are stolen.

Folder encryption

You encrypt a folder or an individual file in Windows Explorer. To enable encryption:

1. Right-click the folder or file you want to encrypt and choose Properties.
2. On the General tab, click Advanced.
3. In the Advanced Attributes dialog box, check "Encrypt contents to secure data," as shown in Exhibit 12-14.
4. Click OK to close the Advanced Attributes dialog box, and then click OK to close the folder or file Properties dialog box.
5. If you enabled encryption on a folder: In the Confirm Attribute Changes dialog box, specify whether you want to encrypt only the files in the folder, or the folder, its subfolders, and all files contained in them. Click OK.

   If you enabled encryption on a file: In the Encryption Warning dialog box, specify whether you want to encrypt the file and its parent folder, or only the file. Microsoft recommends that you always encrypt the folder and not just the file because it's possible that Windows Vista might store an unencrypted temporary version of the file when you open it. Click OK.

You can identify encrypted folders and files by color. Windows Explorer displays the encrypted files and folders in green instead of the default black.

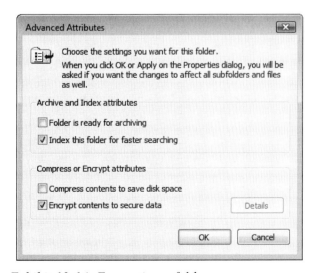

Exhibit 12-14: Encrypting a folder

BitLocker Drive Encryption

Like EFS, BitLocker enables you to implement encryption on a Windows Vista Enterprise or Windows Vista Ultimate computer. Unlike EFS, however, BitLocker encrypts the entire system drive—not just a folder or file. Other differences between BitLocker and EFS include the following:

- You can use BitLocker to encrypt the entire system drive, including all user data and settings, along with the operating system files themselves. You can't use EFS to encrypt the Windows Vista system files.
- BitLocker is designed to protect the computer, not an individual user. As a result, you might find that you need to use EFS in addition to BitLocker in order to protect specific files for individual users of the computer.
- BitLocker protects the operating system from the moment you turn the computer on. This strategy helps prevent attackers from installing malware such as rootkits.
- At the time of this writing, you can use BitLocker on only the system drive. If you have other drives (or partitions or volumes), you can't use BitLocker to protect them. You'll have to use EFS instead. The newer version of BitLocker included with Windows Server 2008 does support encrypting multiple volumes, so Microsoft will probably introduce this same feature for the Windows Vista version of BitLocker.
- If BitLocker detects a problem that could indicate a security problem, it locks the computer's drive. To resume normal operation of the computer, you must enter the BitLocker recovery password.

Hardware requirements for BitLocker

The optimal configuration of BitLocker requires computers to have *Trusted Platform Module (TPM)* chips because BitLocker stores its encryption keys on each computer's TPM chip. The advantage of implementing BitLocker in conjunction with TPM is that doing so makes BitLocker and the encryption of the C drive completely transparent to users.

When you log on to a computer on which BitLocker is enabled, BitLocker retrieves its keys from the TPM chip and then unlocks the computer's hard drive (drive C). You might find that a computer contains a TPM chip that isn't enabled in the computer's BIOS. Before you can enable BitLocker, you must enable the TPM chip by using the computer's CMOS setup utility.

BitLocker automatically initializes the TPM chip for you. If you later want to administer the TPM chip, you can do so by opening an MMC and adding the TPM Management snap-in. **Note:** After you enable the TPM chip and BitLocker initializes it, you can disable the chip only by using the TPM Management snap-in.

If your organization's computers don't have TPM chips, you can still implement BitLocker by configuring it to store its keys on a *USB flash drive (UFD)*. The disadvantage of using a UFD instead of a TPM chip is that you must make sure the drive is inserted each time you boot the computer. In addition, BitLocker requires access to the UFD, with its keys, each time the computer resumes after hibernation, standby mode, or sleep mode. Finally, if a user loses the UFD that contains the BitLocker keys (or the UFD fails), the user won't be able to access the C drive on his computer.

You can circumvent the TPM requirement in BitLocker through a group policy. To do so, select the Computer Configuration\Administrative Templates\Windows

Components\BitLocker Drive Encryption node in the MMC. Then double-click the "Control Panel Setup: Enable advanced startup options" policy setting. Select Enabled and leave all other settings configured with their default values. If you want to enforce this setting immediately, force a group policy refresh.

Do it!

B-9: Encrypting a folder

Here's how	Here's why
1 Open **Computer**	
2 Right-click the **C:\SalesData** folder and choose **Properties**	To open the SalesData Properties dialog box.
3 Click **Advanced**	To open the Advanced Attributes dialog box.
4 Check **Encrypt contents to secure data**	To enable encryption in the SalesData folder.
5 Click **OK**	To save your changes.
6 Click **OK**	To close the SalesData Properties dialog box.
7 Observe the SalesData folder	Windows displays all encrypted files in green.
8 Access the C:\SalesData folder	
9 Create a new file in the folder	Windows Vista automatically encrypts any new files you create in an encrypted folder. It also encrypts any files you copy or move to this folder.
10 Close the window	

Unit summary: Security

Topic A In this topic, you learned about **common security threats**. You learned about the areas of weakness that can give rise to security threats, and you learned about viruses, Trojan horses, worms, and social engineering. You also learned how to combat these problems by installing **antivirus software** and scanning your computer with **Windows Defender**.

Topic B In this topic, you managed **user authentication** by creating user accounts and assigning passwords. You also learned how to implement some basic security solutions and how to **troubleshoot** issues, such as "access denied" errors. In addition, you learned about User Account Control, and you learned how to determine a user's effective NTFS and share permissions for a file or folder. Finally, you learned about the Windows Security Center, Windows Firewall, Encrypting File System, and BitLocker.

Review questions

1 List some of the items that a dumpster diver looks for.

Internal phone directories, organizational charts, policy manuals, calendars, outdated hardware, systems manuals, network diagrams, and other technical information sources.

2 What kind of program poses as something else, causing the user to "willingly" inflict the attack on himself or herself?

A Trojan horse

3 List at least three primary causes of compromised security.

Technology weaknesses, configuration weaknesses, policy weaknesses, and human error or malice.

4 How does antivirus software recognize new viruses and worms?

Updated virus definitions are downloaded.

5 What is the Windows Vista built-in spyware protection function called?

Windows Defender

6 Name the components of the Windows Security Center.

Windows Firewall, Automatic updates, Malware protection (virus protection monitoring, spyware protection monitoring), and Other security settings (general security monitoring).

7 _____ is a term used to describe any type of malicious software.

Malware

8 A(n) _____ account is a collection of settings and privileges associated with a person.

User

9 A firewall is hardware or software that:

Prevents access to your computer by unauthorized Internet users.

10 True or false? The two types of user accounts are computer administrator and standard user.

True

11 Why might you set a firewall exception?

To enable a program, such as Windows Meeting Space, to communicate with your computer when that program's communications would typically be blocked.

12 The _____ security feature prompts you to click Continue or enter administrative credentials to perform some administrative tasks.

UAC

13 True or false? Passwords for Windows user accounts aren't case sensitive.

False

14 True or false? Spyware is a computer program designed to destroy data, damage your computer's operations, and distribute itself without your involvement.

False. That's the definition of a virus. Spyware is a program that gathers information about you and your Internet activities. Typically, spyware gathers this information so that you can be shown more targeted advertising.

15 What is the name of the anti-spyware program included with Windows Vista?

Windows Defender

16 Which console provides a central location for a variety of administrative tools?

Computer Management

17 True or false? You must manually update spyware signatures.

False. Windows Defender downloads and installs new spyware signatures automatically (although you can turn off that feature).

18 Which console can you use to configure security settings on a computer?

Local Security Policy

19 What is a quarantined program?

A quarantined program is a spyware application that Windows Defender has disabled or removed from your system.

Independent practice activity

During this activity, you will research different types of malware, their symptoms, and how to resolve them.

1 Use your favorite search engine to find multiple virus encyclopedias. Bookmark them in your browser.

2 Use these resources to investigate the latest security threats. Document the names, the symptoms, and how to resolve the threats if you encounter them.

Appendix A
Binary, octal, and hexadecimal numbering

This appendix covers these additional topics:

A Understanding the binary, octal, and hexadecimal numbering systems.

Topic A: Count like a computer

Explanation

As a computer support technician, you'll sometimes need to interact with the computer by using numbers or symbols that the computer can understand. To do so, you'll sometimes need to enter numerical values using a numbering system that the computer can interpret.

Numbering systems

An understanding of the "base and places" concepts is critical to understanding the other numbering systems.

Don't assume that students are familiar with these concepts in the base-10 numbering system.

A numbering system is a method of recording numbers. It follows a particular paradigm for recognizing and manipulating numerical values.

Numbering systems define a limited set of symbols with which you can represent the individual digits of a number. Numbering systems also define the concept of positions or places, which are the means by which you can construct numbers larger than the base.

The numbering system's *base* is the number of digits available. For example, in the *decimal* or base-10 numbering system, there are ten digits with which we can construct any number.

To construct numbers larger than ten digits allow, you must add digits. All the digits of a number are written next to each other, with the position or place of each digit representing the base raised to the digit position minus one.

Base-10 numbering

Any number raised to the zero power equals 1.

Any number raised to the first power equals that number.

For example, in the decimal system, the first place (the rightmost) represents multiples of 10 raised to the zero power. These are the single-digit values. The second place represents multiples of 10 raised to the first power, or multiples of 10.

In the base-10 system, the places are:

..., 1000 (or 10^3), 100 (or 10^2), 10 (or 10^1), 1 (or 10^0)

The number 23 is thus represented by two tens plus three ones.

$2 * 10^1 + 3 * 10^0 = 20 + 3 = 23$

Other numbering systems use different bases and places.

The following table provides a quick overview of how numbers larger than a single digit are constructed from powers of 10. The powers of 10 are sometimes called "places," as in "the ones place" or "the tens place."

Number	1000 (or 10^3)	100 (or 10^2)	10 (or 10^1)	1 (or 10^0)
8	0	0	0	8
23	0	0	2	3
287	0	2	8	7

The binary numbering system

The *binary* numbering system is a base-2 system. It uses just two digits—0 and 1—to represent any number. Places in this system represent powers of 2. The following table illustrates how some numbers can be constructed in the binary system.

Number	16 (or 2^4)	8 (or 2^3)	4 (or 2^2)	2 (or 2^1)	1 (or 2^0)
0	0	0	0	0	0
1	0	0	0	0	1
14	0	1	1	1	0
31	1	1	1	1	1

As you can see, many places are required to represent even small numbers when using the binary system.

Computers are constructed of millions of tiny switches. These switches can be either on or off. Thus, the binary system is well-suited for computers. In fact, everything that a computer works with or does has a representation as a binary digit.

Binary notation

Often, context makes it clear whether you're working with binary or decimal numbers. Sometimes, though, you must take extra care to be clear which you're using.

One binary notation style includes a subscript 2 following the number. Thus, you would be able to know that 10_2 is the binary number representing two, not the decimal number 10.

Another notation style involves writing the decimal digits in groups of four or eight digits, with zeros added as needed on the left to make equal groups. For example, you would write the binary number 10000000000 (1024 in base 10) as 00000100 00000000.

Conversion from base 10

A useful trick for converting base-10 numbers to binary is to construct a table like the following one. Write the base-10 number on the left. Then, starting with the leftmost binary place, put a 1 in each column if that value divides equally into the number; otherwise, put a 0 in the column.

# to convert	1024	512	256	128	64	32	16	8	4	2	1

Binary math

You can add, subtract, multiply, and divide binary numbers. You add the value at each place, carrying the remainder to the next higher place. For example, binary 10 (2) plus binary 01 (1) is binary 11 (3).

Just as with decimal numbers, the value of each place can never exceed the base minus one. In other words, binary 10 (2) plus binary 10 (2) cannot equal 20. Instead, you must add a new place to the left, putting a 1 in it. The correct answer is thus 100 (4).

Do it!

A-1: Exploring the binary numbering system

Questions and answers	
1 What's 256 in binary?	*100000000*
2 What's 1110101 minus 110110?	*This is the equivalent of 234 minus 54, which equals 180 or 10110100.*
3 Convert 1537 into binary	*11000000001*
4 Memory and storage are measured in units like kilobytes. A kilobyte is 1024 bits, not 1000 bits. Why?	*1024 is 10000000000 in binary. 1000 is 1111101000. Therefore, 1024 is a "whole" number in the binary system and is thus a logical number to use as a unit of measure.*

The octal numbering system

Explanation

The *octal* numbering system, also called base-8 numbering, uses eight digits—0, 1, 2, 3, 4, 5, 6, and 7. Thus, its base is 8 and each place represents a power of 8, as shown in the following table.

Use this table to demonstrate how the places concept enables students to convert a decimal number to its octal equivalent.

Number	4096 (or 8^4)	512 (or 8^3)	64 (or 8^2)	8 (or 8^1)	1 (or 8^0)
7	0	0	0	0	7
9	0	0	0	1	1
793	0	1	4	3	1
1024	0	2	0	0	0

Octal numbering is no longer commonly used, though at one time it was commonly used in some computer applications. Each octal digit compactly represents three binary digits.

Octal notation

As with binary numbers, you need to know whether a number is in decimal, binary, or octal notation. Of course, if the number includes digits greater than 7, you know that it can't be in octal notation.

Matching the binary notation style, you can include a subscript 8 following the number to indicate that it is an octal number. For example, you might write 1431_8 to represent decimal 793 as an octal number.

Another common technique is to precede the number with a zero. Thus, the octal equivalent of decimal 793 would be written 01431. This is the technique used by many programming languages to distinguish between decimal and octal values.

Do it!

A-2: Exploring the octal numbering system

Questions and answers	
1 Convert decimal 423 to octal	*0647*
2 Convert 123_8 to decimal	*083*

The hexadecimal numbering system

Explanation

The *hexadecimal* numbering system, also called *hex* or base-16 numbering, uses 16 digits—0, 1, 2, 3, 4, 5, 6, 7, 8 , 9, A, B, C, D, E, and F. The letter "digits" represent the decimal-equivalent values 10, 11, 12, 13, 14, and 15. For example, to represent the number 10 in hex, you write A.

In hex, the base is 16 and each place represents a power of 16, as shown in the following table.

Number	4096 (or 16^3)	256 (or 16^2)	16 (or 16^1)	1 (or 16^0)
7	0	0	0	7
15	0	0	0	F
17	0	0	1	1
453	0	1	C	5
1024	0	4	0	0
62331	F	3	7	B

Even very large numbers can be represented with just a few hexadecimal digits.

Hex numbering is often used with computers because each hex digit compactly represents four binary digits. Thus, instead of writing 11111111 to represent the number 255, you can simply write FF.

Hex notation

When you see a number containing the letters A through F, it should be obvious that you're looking at a hexadecimal number. For numbers that don't include letters, you need to include a clue that you're representing a hex value.

Matching the other notations, you can include a subscript 16 following the number to indicate that it is a hexadecimal number. For example, you might write 11_{16} to represent decimal 17 in hex.

The more common technique is to precede the number with a zero and a lowercase x. Thus, the hex equivalent of decimal 1024 would be written 0x400.

Do it! ### A-3: Exploring the hexadecimal numbering system

Questions and answers	
1 Convert 1600 to hexadecimal	**0x640**
2 Convert 23F to decimal	**575**
3 What's the sum of F plus A?	**0x19 (or 25 decimal)**
4 With the rest of the class, describe an application of hexadecimal numbering that you might have encountered	**Students familiar with Web page programming or graphics manipulation might be familiar with the RGB color notation that uses three two-digit hex numbers. For example, black is 000000, white is FFFFFF, and pure red is FF0000.**

Appendix B
CompTIA A+ acronyms

This appendix covers the following information:

A Acronyms appearing on the CompTIA A+ exams covering 2009 objectives.

Topic A: Acronym list

Explanation

The following is a list of acronyms that appear on the CompTIA A+ exams covering 2009 objectives. Candidates are encouraged to review the complete list and attain a working knowledge of all listed acronyms as a part of a comprehensive exam preparation program. Relevant exams include:

- CompTIA A+ Essentials, 220-701
- CompTIA A+ Certification: Practical Application, 2009 Edition, 220-702

CompTIA A+ Acronyms. Copyright © 2008 by CompTIA. All rights reserved.

Acronym	Spelled out
AC	alternating current
ACL	access control list
ACPI	advanced configuration and power interface
ACT	activity
ADSL	asymmetrical digital subscriber line
AGP	accelerated graphics port
AMD	advanced micro devices
APIPA	automatic private internet protocol addressing
APM	advanced power management
ARP	address resolution protocol
ASR	automated system recovery
AT	advanced technology
ATA	advanced technology attachment
ATAPI	advanced technology attachment packet interface
ATM	asynchronous transfer mode
ATX	advanced technology extended
BIOS	basic input/output system
BNC	Bayonet-Neill-Concelman or British Naval Connector
BTX	balanced technology extended
CD	compact disc

Acronym	Spelled out
CD-ROM	compact disc-read-only memory
CD-RW	compact disc-rewritable
CDFS	compact disc file system
CFS	Central File System, Common File System, Command File System
CMOS	complementary metal-oxide semiconductor
COMx	communication port (x=port number)
CPU	central processing unit
CRT	cathode-ray tube
DAC	discretionary access control
DB-25	serial communications D-shell connector, 25 pins
DB-9	9 pin D shell connector
DC	direct current
DDOS	distributed denial of service
DDR	double data-rate
DDR RAM	double data-rate random access memory
DDR SDRAM	double data-rate synchronous dynamic random access memory
DFS	distributed file system
DHCP	dynamic host configuration protocol
DIMM	dual inline memory module
DIN	Deutsche Industrie Norm
DIP	dual inline package
DLT	digital linear tape
DLP	digital light processing
DMA	direct memory access
DMZ	demilitarized zone
DNS	domain name service or domain name server
DOS	denial of service

Acronym	Spelled out
DPMS	display power management signaling
DRAM	dynamic random access memory
DSL	digital subscriber line
DVD	digital video disc or digital versatile disc
DVD-RAM	digital video disc-random access memory
DVD-ROM	digital video disc-read only memory
DVD-R	digital video disc-recordable
DVD-RW	digital video disc-rewritable
DVI	digital visual interface
ECC	error correction code
ECP	extended capabilities port
EEPROM	electrically erasable programmable read-only memory
EFS	encrypting file system
EIDE	enhanced integrated drive electronics
EMI	electromagnetic interference
EMP	electromagnetic pulse
EPROM	erasable programmable read-only memory
EPP	enhanced parallel port
ERD	emergency repair disk
ESD	electrostatic discharge
EVGA	extended video graphics adapter/array
EVDO	evolution data optimized or evolution data only
FAT	file allocation table
FAT12	12-bit file allocation table
FAT16	16-bit file allocation table
FAT32	32-bit file allocation table
FDD	floppy disk drive

Acronym	Spelled out
Fn	Function (referring to the function key on a laptop)
FPM	fast page-mode
FRU	field replaceable unit
FSB	Front Side Bus
FTP	file transfer protocol
FQDN	fully qualified domain name
Gb	gigabit
GB	gigabyte
GDI	graphics device interface
GHz	gigahertz
GUI	graphical user interface
GPS	global positioning system
GSM	global system for mobile communications
HAL	hardware abstraction layer
HCL	hardware compatibility list
HDD	hard disk drive
HDMi	high definition media interface
HPFS	high performance file system
HTML	hypertext markup language
HTTP	hypertext transfer protocol
HTTPS	hypertext transfer protocol over secure sockets layer
I/O	input/output
ICMP	internet control message protocol
ICR	intelligent character recognition
IDE	integrated drive electronics
IDS	Intrusion Detection System
IEEE	Institute of Electrical and Electronics Engineers

Acronym	Spelled out
IIS	Internet Information Services
IMAP	internet mail access protocol
IP	internet protocol
IPCONFIG	internet protocol configuration
IPP	internet printing protocol
IPSEC	internet protocol security
IPX	internetwork packet exchange
IPX/SPX	internetwork packet exchange/sequenced packet exchange
IR	infrared
IrDA	Infrared Data Association
IRQ	interrupt request
ISA	industry standard architecture
ISDN	integrated services digital network
ISO	Industry Standards Organization
ISP	internet service provider
JBOD	just a bunch of disks
Kb	kilobit
KB	kilobyte
LAN	local area network
LBA	logical block addressing
LC	Lucent connector
LCD	liquid crystal display
LDAP	lightweight directory access protocol
LED	light emitting diode
Li-on	lithium-ion
LPD/LPR	line printer daemon / line printer remote
LPT	line printer terminal

Acronym	Spelled out
LPT1	line printer terminal 1
LVD	low voltage differential
MAC	media access control / mandatory access control
MAPI	messaging application programming interface
MAU	media access unit, media attachment unit
Mb	megabit
MB	megabyte
MBR	master boot record
MBSA	Microsoft Baseline Security Analyzer
MFD	multi-function device
MFP	multi-function product
MHz	megahertz
MicroDIMM	micro dual inline memory module
MIDI	musical instrument digital interface
MIME	multipurpose internet mail extension
MLI	multiple link interface
MMC	Microsoft management console
MMX	multimedia extensions
MP3	Moving Picture Experts Group Layer 3 Audio
MP4	Moving Picture Experts Group Layer 4 Audio
MPEG	Moving Picture Experts Group
MSCONFIG	Microsoft configuration
MSDS	material safety data sheet
MUI	multilingual user interface
NAC	network access control
NAS	network-attached storage

Acronym	Spelled out
NAT	network address translation
NetBIOS	networked basic input/output system
NetBEUI	networked basic input/output system extended user interface
NFS	network file system
NIC	network interface card
NiCd	nickel cadmium
NiMH	nickel metal hydride
NLX	new low-profile extended
NNTP	network news transfer protocol
NTFS	new technology file system
NTLDR	new technology loader
NTP	Network Time Protocol
OCR	optical character recognition
OEM	original equipment manufacturer
OS	operating system
OSR	original equipment manufacturer service release
PAN	personal area network
PATA	parallel advanced technology attachment
PC	personal computer
PCI	peripheral component interconnect
PCIe	peripheral component interconnect express
PCIX	peripheral component interconnect extended
PCL	printer control language
PCMCIA	Personal Computer Memory Card International Association
PDA	personal digital assistant
PGA	pin grid array
PGA2	pin grid array 2

Acronym	Spelled out
PIN	personal identification number
PKI	public key infrastructure
PnP	plug and play
POP3	post office protocol 3
POST	power-on self test
PPP	point-to-point protocol
PPTP	point-to-point tunneling protocol
PRI	primary rate interface
PROM	programmable read-only memory
PS/2	Personal System/2 connector
PSTN	public switched telephone network
PSU	power supply unit
PVC	permanent virtual circuit
PXE	preboot execution environment
QoS	quality of service
RAID	redundant array of independent (or inexpensive) discs
RAM	random access memory
RAS	remote access service
RDRAM	RAMBUS® dynamic random access memory
RDP	Remote Desktop Protocol
RF	radio frequency
RFI	radio frequency interference
RGB	red green blue
RIMM	RAMBUS® inline memory module
RIP	routing information protocol
RIS	remote installation service
RISC	reduced instruction set computer

Acronym	Spelled out
RJ	registered jack
RJ-11	registered jack function 11
RJ-45	registered jack function 45
RMA	returned materials authorization
ROM	read only memory
RS-232 or RS-232C	recommended standard 232
RTC	real-time clock
SAN	storage area network
SATA	serial advanced technology attachment
SC	subscription channel
SCP	secure copy protection
SCSI	small computer system interface
SCSI ID	small computer system interface identifier
SD card	secure digital card
SDRAM	synchronous dynamic random access memory
SEC	single edge connector
SFC	system file checker
SGRAM	synchronous graphics random access memory
SIMM	single inline memory module
SLI	scalable link interface or system level integration or scanline interleave mode
S.M.A.R.T.	self-monitoring, analysis, and reporting technology
SMB	server message block or small to midsize business
SMTP	simple mail transport protocol
SNMP	simple network management protocol
SoDIMM	small outline dual inline memory module
SOHO	small office/home office

Acronym	Spelled out
SP	service pack
SP1	service pack 1
SP2	service pack 2
SP3	service pack 3
SP4	service pack 4
SPDIF	Sony-Philips digital interface format
SPGA	staggered pin grid array
SPX	sequenced package exchange
SRAM	static random access memory
SSH	secure shell
SSID	service set identifier
SSL	secure sockets layer
ST	straight tip
STP	shielded twisted pair
SVGA	super video graphics array
SXGA	super extended graphics array
TB	terabyte
TCP	transmission control protocol
TCP/IP	transmission control protocol/internet protocol
TDR	time domain reflectometer
TFTP	trivial file transfer protocol
TPM	trusted platform module
UAC	user account control
UART	universal asynchronous receiver transmitter
UDF	user defined functions or universal disk format or universal data format
UDMA	ultra direct memory access
UDP	user datagram protocol

Acronym	Spelled out
UNC	universal naming convention
UPS	uninterruptible power supply
URL	uniform resource locator
USB	universal serial bus
USMT	user state migration tool
UTP	unshielded twisted pair
UXGA	ultra extended graphics array
VESA	Video Electronics Standards Association
VFAT	virtual file allocation table
VGA	video graphics array
VoIP	voice over internet protocol
VPN	virtual private network
VRAM	video random access memory
WAN	wide area network
WAP	wireless application protocol
WEP	wired equivalent privacy
WIFI	wireless fidelity
WINS	windows internet name service
WLAN	wireless local area network
WPA	wireless protected access
WUXGA	wide ultra extended graphics array
XGA	extended graphics array
ZIF	zero-insertion-force
ZIP	zigzag inline package

Appendix C
Certification exam objectives map

This appendix covers these additional topics:

A CompTIA A+ 220-702 (2009 Edition) exam objectives with references to corresponding coverage in this course manual.

Topic A: Comprehensive exam objectives

Explanation

This section lists all CompTIA A+ 220-702 (2009 Edition) exam objectives and indicates where each objective is covered in conceptual explanations, activities, or both.

1.0 Hardware

Objective	Conceptual information	Supporting activities
1.1 — Given a scenario, install, configure, and maintain personal computer components		
• Storage devices		
– HDD	Unit 5, Topic A	A-1
• SATA	Unit 5, Topic A	A-1
• PATA	Unit 5, Topic A	A-1
• Solid state	Unit 5, Topic A	
– FDD	Unit 5, Topic C	C-2
– Optical drives	Unit 5, Topic B	B-1
• CD / DVD / RW / Blu-ray	Unit 5, Topic B	B-1
– Removable	Unit 5, Topic C	C-1
– External	Unit 5, Topic C	C-1
• Motherboards		
– Jumper settings	Unit 2, Topic A	A-5
– CMOS battery	Unit 2, Topic B	B-1
– Advanced BIOS settings	Unit 2, Topic A	A-1
– Bus speeds	Unit 2, Topic A	A-4, A-5
– Chipsets	Unit 2, Topic A	A-4
– Firmware updates	Unit 2, Topic A	A-1
– Socket types	Unit 2, Topic A	A-2, A-4
– Expansion slots	Unit 2, Topic A	A-5
– Memory slots	Unit 2, Topic A	A-5
– Front panel connectors	Unit 2, Topic A	A-5
– I/O ports	Unit 2, Topic A	
• Sound, video, USB 1.1, USB 2.0, serial, IEEE 1394 / FireWire, parallel, NIC, modem, PS/2	Unit 2, Topic A	A-5

Objective	Conceptual information	Supporting activities
• Power supplies		
– Wattages and capacity	Unit 1, Topic A	A-1, A-3
– Connector types and quantity	Unit 1, Topic A	A-3
– Output voltage	Unit 1, Topic A	A-1, A-3
• Processors		
– Socket types	Unit 2, Topic A	A-2
– Speed	Unit 2, Topic A	A-4
– Number of cores	Unit 2, Topic A	A-4
– Power consumption	Unit 2, Topic A	A-4
– Cache	Unit 2, Topic A	A-4
– Front side bus	Unit 2, Topic A	A-4
– 32bit vs. 64bit	Unit 2, Topic A	A-4
• Memory	Unit 3, Topic A	A-1–A-4
• Adapter cards		
– Graphic cards	Unit 4, Topic B	B-1
– Sound cards	Unit 4, Topic B	B-2
– Storage controllers	Unit 4, Topic B	B-3
• RAID cards (RAID array – levels 0, 1, 5)	Unit 5, Topic A	A-3
• eSATA cards	Unit 4, Topic B	B-3
– I/O cards		
• FireWire	Unit 4, Topic B	B-3
• USB	Unit 4, Topic B	B-3
• Parallel	Unit 4, Topic B	B-3
• Serial	Unit 4, Topic B	B-3
– Wired and wireless network cards	Unit 4, Topic B	B-3
– Capture cards (TV, video)	Unit 4, Topic B	B-3
– Media reader	Unit 4, Topic B	B-3
• Cooling systems		
– Heat sinks	Unit 2, Topic A	
– Thermal compound	Unit 2, Topic A	
– CPU fans	Unit 2, Topic A	A-3
– Case fans	Unit 2, Topic A	

Objective	Conceptual information	Supporting activities
1.2 — Given a scenario, detect problems, troubleshoot, and repair/replace personal computer components		
• Storage devices		
– HDD	Unit 5, Topic D	D-4
• SATA	Unit 5, Topic D	D-4
• PATA	Unit 5, Topic D	D-4
• Solid state	Unit 5, Topic D	
– FDD	Unit 5, Topic D	D-4
– Optical drives	Unit 5, Topic D	D-4
• CD / DVD / RW / Blu-ray	Unit 5, Topic D	D-4
– Removable	Unit 5, Topic D	D-4
– External	Unit 5, Topic D	D-4
• Motherboards		
– Jumper settings	Unit 2, Topic B	B-3
– CMOS battery	Unit 2, Topic B	B-3
– Advanced BIOS settings	Unit 2, Topic B	B-3
– Bus speeds	Unit 2, Topic B	B-3
– Chipsets	Unit 2, Topic B	B-3
– Firmware updates	Unit 2, Topic B	B-3
– Socket types	Unit 2, Topic B	B-3
– Expansion slots	Unit 2, Topic B	B-3
– Memory slots	Unit 2, Topic B	B-3
– Front panel connectors	Unit 2, Topic B	B-3
– I/O ports		
• Sound, video, USB 1.1, USB 2.0, serial, IEEE 1394 / FireWire, parallel, NIC, modem, PS/2	Unit 2, Topic B	B-3
• Power supplies		
– Wattages and capacity	Unit 1, Topic B	B-1, B-2
– Connector types and quantity	Unit 1, Topic B	B-2
– Output voltage	Unit 1, Topic B	B-1, B-2

Objective	Conceptual information	Supporting activities
• Processors		
– Socket types	Unit 2, Topic B	B-3
– Speed	Unit 2, Topic B	B-3
– Number of cores	Unit 2, Topic B	B-3
– Power consumption	Unit 2, Topic B	B-3
– Cache	Unit 2, Topic B	B-3
– Front side bus	Unit 2, Topic B	B-3
– 32bit vs. 64bit	Unit 2, Topic B	B-3
• Memory	Unit 3, Topic B	B-1, B-2
• Adapter cards		
– Graphic cards - memory	Unit 4, Topic C	C-2
– Sound cards	Unit 4, Topic C	C-2
– Storage controllers	Unit 4, Topic C	C-2
• RAID cards	Unit 4, Topic C	C-2
• eSATA cards	Unit 4, Topic C	C-2
– I/O cards		
• FireWire	Unit 4, Topic D	D-2
• USB	Unit 4, Topic D	D-2
• Parallel	Unit 4, Topic D	D-2
• Serial	Unit 4, Topic D	D-2
– Wired and wireless network cards	Unit 4, Topic C	C-2
– Capture cards (TV, video)	Unit 4, Topic C	C-2
– Media reader	Unit 4, Topic C	C-2
• Cooling systems		
– Heat sinks	Unit 2, Topic A	
– Thermal compound	Unit 2, Topic A	
– CPU fans	Unit 2, Topic A	A-3
– Case fans	Unit 2, Topic A	

Objective	Conceptual information	Supporting activities
1.3 — Given a scenario, install, configure, detect problems, troubleshoot, and repair/replace laptop components		
• Components of the LCD, including inverter, screen, and video card	Unit 7, Topic B	B-2
• Hard drive and memory	Unit 7, Topic B	B-2
• Disassembly processes for proper re-assembly		
– Document and label cable and screw locations	Unit 7, Topic B	B-2
– Organize parts	Unit 7, Topic B	B-2
– Refer to manufacturer documentation	Unit 7, Topic B	B-2
– Use appropriate hand tools	Unit 7, Topic B	B-2
• Recognize internal laptop expansion slot types	Unit 7, Topic B	B-2
• Upgrade wireless cards and video card	Unit 7, Topic B	B-1, B-2
• Replace keyboard, processor, plastics, pointer devices, heat sinks, fans, system board, CMOS battery, speakers	Unit 7, Topic B	B-2
1.4 — Given a scenario, select and use the following tools		
• Multimeter	Unit 1, Topic B	B-1
• Power supply tester	Unit 1, Topic B	B-2
• Specialty hardware / tools	Unit 6, Topic A Unit 6, Topic B	A-1 B-1
	Unit 11, Topic A Unit 11, Topic B	A-1 B-1
• Cable tester	Unit 11, Topic B	B-1
• Loopback plugs	Unit 4, Topic D	D-1
• Antistatic pad and wrist strap	Unit 1, Topic A	A-2, A-3
• Extension magnet	Unit 6, Topic A	A-1

Objective	Conceptual information	Supporting activities
1.5 — Given a scenario, detect and resolve common printer issues		
• Symptoms		
– Paper jams	Unit 6, Topic B	B-1
– Blank paper	Unit 6, Topic B	B-1
– Error codes	Unit 6, Topic B	B-1
– Out-of-memory error	Unit 6, Topic B	B-1
– Lines and smearing	Unit 6, Topic B	B-1
– Garbage printout	Unit 6, Topic B	B-1
– Ghosted image	Unit 6, Topic B	B-1
– No connectivity	Unit 6, Topic B	B-1
• Issue resolution		
– Replace fuser	Unit 6, Topic B	B-1
– Replace drum	Unit 6, Topic B	B-1
– Clear paper jam	Unit 6, Topic B	B-1
– Power cycle	Unit 6, Topic B	B-1
– Install maintenance kit (reset page count)	Unit 6, Topic A Unit 6, Topic B	A-1 B-1
– Set IP on printer	Unit 6, Topic B	B-1
– Clean printer	Unit 6, Topic A Unit 6, Topic B	A-1 B-1

2.0 Operating Systems

Unless otherwise noted, operating systems referred to within include Microsoft Windows 2000; Windows XP Professional, XP Home, and XP Media Center; Windows Vista Home Basic, Home Premium, Business, and Ultimate.

Objective	Conceptual information	Supporting activities
2.1 — Select the appropriate commands and options to troubleshoot and resolve problems		
• MSCONFIG	Unit 9, Topic C	D-3
• DIR	Unit 8, Topic A	A-2
• CHKDSK (/f /r)	Unit 5, Topic D	D-2
• EDIT	Unit 8, Topic A	A-7
• COPY (/a /v /y)	Unit 8, Topic A	A-4
• XCOPY	Unit 8, Topic A	A-4
• FORMAT	Unit 5, Topic A	
• IPCONFIG (/all /release /renew)	Unit 11, Topic B	B-4
• PING (-t –l)	Unit 11, Topic B	B-5
• MD / CD / RD	Unit 8, Topic A	A-2, A-3, A-5
• NET	Unit 8, Topic B	B-2
• TRACERT	Unit 11, Topic B	B-6
• NSLOOKUP	Unit 11, Topic B	B-6
• [command name] /?	Unit 8, Topic A	A-1
• SFC	Unit 9, Topic D	D-5
2.2 — Differentiate between Windows operating system directory structures (Windows 2000, XP, and Vista)		
• User file locations	Unit 8, Topic A	
• System file locations	Unit 8, Topic A	A-2
• Fonts	Unit 8, Topic A	
• Temporary files	Unit 8, Topic A	
• Program files	Unit 8, Topic A	
• Offline files and folders	Unit 8, Topic A	

Objective	Conceptual information	Supporting activities
2.3 — Given a scenario, select and use system utilities / tools and evaluate the results		
• Disk management tools		
– DEFRAG	Unit 5, Topic D	D-1
– NTBACKUP	Unit 9, Topic B	B-1, B-2
– Check Disk	Unit 5, Topic D	D-2
• Disk Manager		
– Active, primary, extended, and logical partitions	Unit 5, Topic A	A-2
– Mount points	Unit 8, Topic A	A-8
– Mounting a drive	Unit 8, Topic A	A-8
– FAT32 and NTFS	Unit 5, Topic A	A-2
– Drive status		
• Foreign drive	Unit 5, Topic A Unit 5, Topic D	A-2 D-4
• Healthy	Unit 5, Topic A Unit 5, Topic D	A-2 D-4
• Formatting	Unit 5, Topic A Unit 5, Topic D	A-2 D-4
• Active unallocated	Unit 5, Topic A Unit 5, Topic D	A-2 D-4
• Failed	Unit 5, Topic A Unit 5, Topic D	A-2 D-4
• Dynamic	Unit 5, Topic A Unit 5, Topic D	A-2 D-4
• Offline	Unit 5, Topic A Unit 5, Topic D	A-2 D-4
• Online	Unit 5, Topic A Unit 5, Topic D	A-2 D-4
• System monitor	Unit 9, Topic A	A-2
• Administrative tools		
– Event Viewer	Unit 9, Topic A	A-9
– Computer Management	Unit 5, Topic A Unit 9, Topic A	A-2 A-1
– Services	Unit 8, Topic B	B-1
– Performance Monitor	Unit 9, Topic A	A-2, A-3

Objective	Conceptual information	Supporting activities
• Device Manager		
– Enable	Unit 4, Topic A	
– Disable	Unit 4, Topic A	
– Warnings	Unit 4, Topic A	
– Indicators	Unit 4, Topic A	A-2, A-3, A-4
• Task Manager		
– Process list	Unit 9, Topic A	A-6
– Resource usage	Unit 3, Topic A	A-4
	Unit 9, Topic A	
– Process priority	Unit 9, Topic A	A-6
– Termination	Unit 9, Topic A	A-5, A-6
• System Information	Unit 9, Topic D	D-4
• System restore	Unit 9, Topic B	B-3, B-4
• Remote Desktop Protocol (Remote Desktop / Remote Assistance)	Unit 8, Topic C	C-1–C-4
• Task Scheduler	Unit 9, Topic C	C-1, C-2
• Regional settings and language settings	Unit 8, Topic B	B-4
2.4 — Evaluate and resolve common issues		
• Operational problems		
– Windows-specific printing problems	Unit 6, Topic B	B-1
• Print spool stalled	Unit 6, Topic B	B-1
• Incorrect / incompatible driver / form printing	Unit 6, Topic B	B-1
– Auto-restart errors	Unit 9, Topic D	D-1
– Bluescreen errors	Unit 9, Topic D	D-1
– System lockup	Unit 9, Topic D	D-1
– Device driver failure (input / output devices)	Unit 9, Topic D	D-1
– Application, install, start, or load failure	Unit 9, Topic D	D-1
– Service fails to start	Unit 9, Topic D	D-1

Objective	Conceptual information	Supporting activities
• Error messages and conditions		
– Boot		
• Invalid boot disk	Unit 9, Topic D	D-1
• Inaccessible boot drive	Unit 9, Topic D	D-1
• Missing NTLDR	Unit 9, Topic D	D-1
– Startup		
• Device / service failed to start	Unit 9, Topic D	D-1
• Device / program in registry not found	Unit 9, Topic D	D-1
– Event Viewer (errors in the event log)	Unit 9, Topic A	A-9
– System performance and optimization		
• Aero settings	Unit 8, Topic B	B-7
• Indexing settings	Unit 8, Topic B	B-5
• UAC	Unit 12, Topic B	B-5
• Sidebar settings	Unit 8, Topic B	B-8
• Startup file maintenance	Unit 8, Topic B	B-3
• Background processes	Unit 9, Topic A	A-6

3.0 Networking

Objective	Conceptual information	Supporting activities
3.1 — Troubleshoot client-side connectivity issues, using appropriate tools		
• TCP/IP settings		
– Gateway	Unit 11, Topic B	B-4
– Subnet mask	Unit 11, Topic B	B-4
– DNS	Unit 11, Topic B	B-4
– DHCP (dynamic vs. static)	Unit 11, Topic B	B-4
– NAT (private and public)	Unit 11, Topic B	B-8
• Characteristics of TCP/IP		
– Loopback addresses	Unit 11, Topic B	B-5
– Automatic IP addressing	Unit 11, Topic B	B-4
• Mail protocol settings		
– SMTP	Unit 11, Topic B	B-8
– IMAP	Unit 11, Topic B	B-8
– POP	Unit 11, Topic B	B-8
• FTP settings		
– Ports	Unit 11, Topic B	B-7, B-8
– IP addresses	Unit 11, Topic B	B-8
– Exceptions	Unit 11, Topic B	B-8
– Programs	Unit 11, Topic B	B-8
• Proxy settings		
– Ports	Unit 11, Topic B	B-7, B-8
– IP addresses	Unit 11, Topic B	B-8
– Exceptions	Unit 11, Topic B	B-8
– Programs	Unit 11, Topic B	B-8

Objective	Conceptual information	Supporting activities
• Tools (use and interpret results)		
– Ping	Unit 11, Topic B	B-5
– Tracert	Unit 11, Topic B	B-6
– Nslookup	Unit 11, Topic B	B-6
– Netstat	Unit 11, Topic B	
– Net use	Unit 8, Topic B	B-2
– Net /?	Unit 8, Topic B	B-2
– Ipconfig	Unit 11, Topic B	B-4
– telnet	Unit 11, Topic B	
– SSH	Unit 11, Topic B	
• Secure connection protocols		
– SSH	Unit 11, Topic B	B-4
– HTTPS	Unit 11, Topic B	B-4
• Firewall settings		
– Open and closed ports	Unit 11, Topic B Unit 12, Topic B	B-4 B-7, B-8
– Program filters	Unit 11, Topic B Unit 12, Topic B	B-4 B-7, B-8
3.2 — Install and configure a small office / home office (SOHO) network		
• Connection types		
– Dial-up	Unit 10, Topic A	A-1
– Broadband		
• DSL	Unit 10, Topic A	A-1
• Cable	Unit 10, Topic A	A-1
• Satellite	Unit 10, Topic A	A-1
• ISDN	Unit 10, Topic A	A-1
– Wireless		
• All 802.11	Unit 10, Topic A	A-4
• WEP	Unit 10, Topic A	A-5
• WPA	Unit 10, Topic A	A-5
• SSID	Unit 10, Topic A	A-5
• MAC filtering	Unit 10, Topic A	A-5
• DHCP settings	Unit 10, Topic B	A-5

Objective	Conceptual information	Supporting activities
– Routers / Access Points		
• Disable DHCP	Unit 10, Topic B	B-1
• Use static IP	Unit 10, Topic B	B-1
• Change SSID from default	Unit 10, Topic B	B-1
• Disable SSID broadcast	Unit 10, Topic B	B-1
• MAC filtering	Unit 10, Topic B	B-1
• Change default username and password	Unit 10, Topic B	B-1
• Update firmware	Unit 10, Topic B	B-1
• Firewall	Unit 10, Topic A	A-1
– LAN (10/100/1000BaseT, Speeds)	Unit 10, Topic A	A-2
– Bluetooth (1.0 vs. 2.0)	Unit 10, Topic A	A-4
– Cellular	Unit 10, Topic A	A-1
• Basics of hardware and software firewall configuration		
– Port assignment / setting up rules (exceptions)	Unit 12, Topic B	B-8
– Port forwarding / port triggering	Unit 12, Topic B	
• Physical installation		
– Wireless router placement	Unit 10, Topic A	A-3
– Cable length	Unit 10, Topic A	A-2

4.0 Security

Objective	Conceptual information	Supporting activities
4.1 — Given a scenario, prevent, troubleshoot, and remove viruses and malware		
• Use antivirus software	Unit 12, Topic A	A-3
• Identify malware symptoms	Unit 12, Topic A	
• Quarantine infected systems	Unit 12, Topic A	A-5
• Research malware types, symptoms, and solutions (virus encyclopedias)	Unit 12, Topic A	Unit 12 IPA
• Remediate infected systems	Unit 12, Topic A	A-5
• Update antivirus software, educate end user	Unit 12, Topic A	A-2
– Signature and engine updates	Unit 12, Topic A	A-3, A-4
– Automatic vs. manual	Unit 12, Topic A	A-3, A-4
• Schedule scans	Unit 12, Topic A	A-3, A-4
• Repair boot blocks	Unit 2, Topic B	
• Scan and removal techniques		
– Safe mode	Unit 9, Topic D Unit 12, Topic A	D-2
– Boot environment	Unit 9, Topic D Unit 12, Topic A	D-2
4.2 — Implement security and troubleshoot common issues		
• Operating systems		
– Local users and groups: Administrator, Power Users, Guest, Users	Unit 12, Topic B	B-1–B-4
– Vista User Access Control (UAC)	Unit 12, Topic B	B-5
– NTFS vs. Share permissions	Unit 12, Topic B	B-6
• Allow vs. deny	Unit 12, Topic B	B-6
• Differentiate between moving and copying folders and files	Unit 12, Topic B	
• File attributes	Unit 12, Topic B	
– Shared files and folders		
• Administrative shares vs. local shares	Unit 12, Topic B	B-6
• Permission propagation	Unit 12, Topic B	B-6
• Inheritance	Unit 12, Topic B	B-6
– System files and folders	Unit 12, Topic B	

Objective	Conceptual information	Supporting activities
– Encryption (BitLocker, EFS)	Unit 12, Topic B	B-9
– User authentication	Unit 12, Topic B	B-1, B-2, B-3, B-5
• System		
– BIOS security	Unit 2, Topic A Unit 12, Topic A	
• Drive lock	Unit 2, Topic A	A-1
• Passwords	Unit 2, Topic A	A-1
• Intrusion detection	Unit 2, Topic A	A-1
• TPM	Unit 12, Topic B	

Course summary

This summary contains information to help you bring the course to a successful conclusion. Using this information, you will be able to:

A Use the summary text to reinforce what students have learned in class.

B Direct students to the next courses in this series, if any, and to any other resources that might help students continue to learn about supporting PCs.

Topic A: Course summary

At the end of the class, use the following summary text to reinforce what students have learned. It is intended not as a script, but rather as a starting point.

Unit summaries

Unit 1

In this unit, students measured characteristics of **electricity** while following safe practices, examined **power supplies**, and installed a new power supply in a PC. Students also compared types of **power conditioning** equipment and troubleshot faulty power supplies.

Unit 2

In this unit, students examined the features, functions, and characteristics of **CPUs** and installed a CPU. Students also looked at **cooling devices** and learned how to configure the BIOS. They investigated **motherboards** and the typical components they contain, and installed a motherboard. Students also troubleshot motherboard- and CPU-related problems.

Unit 3

In this unit, students examined computer **memory**, installed RAM into a system, and troubleshot memory problems.

Unit 4

In this unit, students used **Device Manager** to examine the interrupt, IRQ, I/O address, DMA, and base memory address assignments in their PCs, as well as those of common devices. Students also installed **expansion adapters**, including video and sound cards. Students then learned how to update hardware device drivers, **troubleshoot** expansion cards, and troubleshoot ports, connectors, and cables.

Unit 5

In this unit, students learned about file systems, partitions, the Disk Management utility, and RAID levels. Students also installed **hard**, **optical**, and **floppy drives**. Students then troubleshot drive-related problems and performed drive maintenance procedures, such as **defragging**.

Unit 6

In this unit, students performed **routine maintenance tasks** on inkjet and laser **printers**. Students also learned how to troubleshoot common problems that affect printing, including problems with software, the operating system, and the printer itself. They then learned how to troubleshoot problems with scanners, fax machines, and multifunction devices.

Unit 7

In this unit, students learned how to configure a notebook computer by using the **Windows Mobility Center**, and they learned how to set **power options**. Then students replaced hot-swappable **components** and internal components in a notebook computer. Finally, students learned how to troubleshoot components of a notebook computer.

Unit 8

In this unit, students **managed directories and files** by using the command prompt and Windows Explorer. Students also learned how to manage **Windows services** and startup programs. Students then configured regional and language settings, indexing, Windows Aero, and the Windows Sidebar. Finally, students learned to how manage and troubleshoot problems remotely by using the **Remote Desktop** and **Remote Assistance** features.

Unit 9

In this unit, students maintained Windows by **monitoring performance** in Task Manager, looking for errors in **Event Viewer**, **backing up** and restoring data, working with restore points, and **scheduling tasks**. Students also learned how to use startup modes and the **System Configuration utility** to troubleshoot common Windows problems.

Unit 10

In this unit, students learned about **networking basics**, including hardware components, **protocols**, and wired and wireless **communication standards** used in SOHO networks. Then students implemented a wireless network and learned about methods to keep it secure.

Unit 11

In this unit, students learned how to assemble hardware and software **toolkits** that they can use to troubleshoot **network problems**. Then students used common troubleshooting techniques to test the **physical network**, wireless networks, and the **logical network**, including TCP/IP and other client-side connectivity issues.

Unit 12

In this unit, students learned about **common security threats**, including viruses, Trojan horses, worms, and social engineering, and they secured their computers by using antivirus software and Windows Defender. Next, students managed user **authentication** and implemented and troubleshot some basic security solutions.

Topic B: Continued learning after class

Point out to your students that it's impossible to learn to use any technology effectively in a single class. To get the most out of this class, students should begin working with computer hardware to perform real tasks as soon as possible. Axzo Press also offers resources for continued learning.

Next courses in this series

This course covers the material that students need to know in order to pass the CompTIA A+ 220-702 exam. This is the last course in the A+ series.

Other resources

For more information, visit www.axzopress.com.

Glossary

Active Directory
Microsoft's directory service, included with Windows servers, that provides a single point of administration and storage for user, group, and computer objects.

Active matrix
Flat-panel monitor technology that uses TFT to produce sharp images.

AGP (Advanced Graphics Port)
A video port used with Pentium-based computers.

Alternating current (AC)
Current that flows repeatedly back and forth through the circuit at a constantly varying voltage level.

Amp (ampere)
The unit of measure of amperage (the strength of a current of electricity).

AppleTalk
A suite of OSI upper-layer protocols from Apple Computer, used for connecting Macintosh computers and peripherals.

Application layer
Top layer of the OSI model. The layer in which applications on a network node (computer) access network services, such as file transfers, e-mail, and database access.

Authentication
The process by which your identity is validated against a database that contains your account. Typically, you present a set of credentials such as a user name and password.

Backbone
The main network cable to which other network segments connect.

Bandwidth
The amount of data that can travel over a communication line or wireless connection in a given amount of time.

Bank
A group of memory slots. You must fill all of the slots within a bank when installing memory. Typically, you must also use the same type and speed of memory within a bank.

Base memory addresses
A range of addresses that designate an area of memory in which extensions to the BIOS are stored.

Basic partition
A standard, or classic, partition. Compare to *dynamic partition*.

Basic Rate Interface (BRI)
An ISDN configuration intended for home-office and small-business users.

Baud
A measure of signal changes per second. The baud rate is analogous to the frequency of an analog wave.

Binary
The base-2 numbering system.

BIOS (Basic Input/Output System)
The computer's firmware—a set of software instructions that are stored on a chip on the motherboard and that enable basic computer functions, such as getting input from the keyboard and mouse.

Bluetooth
A standard for short-range wireless communication and data synchronization between devices.

Bus
A communication pathway within a computer. A typical PC has four buses: the address, data, expansion, and video buses.

Cable modem
A device that connects a LAN to an ISP via the cable television connection.

Card Information Structure (CIS)
One of the software layers in the PC Card specification. It provides a method of data organization and data-recording-format compatibility for a variety of PC Cards.

Card Services
An API that enables the sharing of device drivers and other software by PC Cards and sockets.

CardBus
A PC Card bus that provides 32-bit bus mastering.

Central gateway
A connection device between a LAN and the Internet.

Chipset
One or more chips, packaged into a single unit and sold together, that perform a set of functions in a computer.

Circuit
A path from the electrical source through intervening components and back to ground.

Clusters
Logical collections of one or more sectors. Data storage is managed at the cluster level, rather than the sector level.

CMOS
Complementary metal oxide semiconductor, a type of computer chip manufacturing technology. CMOS is an area of memory that's backed up by a battery and stores BIOS configuration data.

Coaxial cable
A round cable composed of a central electrically conducive wire, surrounded by an insulating layer, then a mesh layer, and finally the outer insulation layer.

COM ports
Serial ports, which are named COM1, COM2, and so forth.

Compact Flash
A flash memory card used in portable devices, especially digital cameras. Roughly the size of a book of matches.

Compression
The use of an algorithm to make data take up less space.

Conductor
A material that permits the flow of electricity.

Controller
The adapter board that plugs into a PC's expansion slot and is used to interface with a hard drive or other storage device.

Cooling fins
Metal protrusions that dissipate heat through convection.

CPU (central processing unit)
A computer chip that processes instructions, manipulates data, and controls the interactions of the other circuits in the computer. Also called the processor.

Crosstalk
Interference that occurs when two wires are running parallel to each other, and one wire carries a signal intended for the other wire.

Current
A measure of the flow of electrons past a given point; measured in amps, or amperes.

Cylinder
The logical collection of all of the tracks at a given distance from the axis.

CYMK
Cyan, yellow, magenta, and black; the colors used in inkjet printers.

Daughter board
A circuit board that connects to another circuit board (sometimes a motherboard) to provide additional functions or assist with its functions.

Decimal
The "normal" base-10 numbering system.

Defragging
Defragmenting a disk, optimizing file access speeds by relocating the clusters that make up a file to contiguous locations on the disk.

Demodulation
The process by which a modem electronically subtracts the carrier analog wave, revealing the digital signal it carries.

DHCP (Dynamic Host Configuration Protocol)
A method of automatically assigning IP addresses to nodes on a LAN.

Digital Video Interface (DVI)
A display interface that enables the use of analog and digital monitors. Data is sent from the PC to the monitor via TMDS (Transition Minimized Differential Signaling).

DIP switches
Small, typically rocker-style switches that were used with older hardware components to configure various options.

Direct current (DC)
Current that flows in a single direction at a constant voltage.

DMA (direct memory access)
A system by which a support chip manages memory access by hardware components so that the CPU doesn't have to.

DNS
A part of the TCP/IP protocol suite that translates domain names into their corresponding IP addresses. DNS is used to refer to both the Domain Name Service and the Domain Name System.

Domain name
A unique name assigned to a network and registered with ICANN.

DRAM
Dynamic RAM, which is RAM that must have its contents refreshed regularly, or those contents will fade and become unreadable.

Drive array
A collection of two or more drives that work in unison to provide a single point of data storage. A drive array appears to the operating system to be a single drive.

Driver
A form of software that interacts with a hardware device to enable that device's functionality.

DSL (Digital Subscriber Line)
A high-speed data and voice transmission line that uses telephone wires, but carries the digital data at frequencies well above those used for voice transmission.

Dual-link cable
A DVI cable that uses two TDMS 165 MHz transmitters.

DVI-D
A DVI connector that implements only digital signals.

DVI-I
A DVI connector that implements both digital and analog signals.

Dynamic partition
An enhanced type of partition that enables you to change your partitions and the volumes they contain without restarting the operating system.

ECC (error correcting code)
A technology that permits a computer not only to detect that an error has occurred, but also to correct that error. Various ECC schemes are used in telecommunications, memory storage, and data storage.

Electrophotographic
The process used by laser printers to produce images.

EMI (electromagnetic interference)
Interference in communications that is caused by crosstalk or other noise on the line and that causes problems with data transmission.

ESD (electrostatic discharge)
The discharge of static electricity, which can damage sensitive electronic components.

Ethernet
The most common form of LAN architecture. It uses bus or star topology and employs CSMA/CD to manage the flow of data on the network.

eXecute In Place (XIP)
The ability to run commands directly from code stored on a PC Card without using system RAM.

Expansion bus
The bus to which add-on adapter cards are connected to enhance the functionality of a PC.

Extended partitions
Partitions that contain one or more logical drives, which the operating system accesses for file storage.

Fiber optic cable
Cable that carries light-based data through strands of glass or plastic no thicker than a human hair.

Firewall
Hardware or software that controls the data entering or leaving a computer system. Used to maintain the security of the system.

FireWire
Apple Computer's proprietary name for the IEEE 1394 peripheral interconnection bus.

Firmware
Software written permanently or semi-permanently to a computer chip.

Flashing
The process of updating the BIOS in a PC by using a special program provided by the motherboard's or PC's manufacturer.

Flat-panel monitor
An LCD monitor that uses TFT technology.

Form factor
A description or label denoting the size and shape of a computer component. The term is used most often with cases, motherboards, and power supplies.

Fusing assembly
The set of components in a laser printer that heat the toner to melt it into the paper.

Hardware
Any physical component of a computer or peripheral device.

HBA
Host bus adapter; a SCSI drive controller.

Heat pipes
Small tubes, typically built into cooling fins, filled with a small amount of fluid. Heat vaporizes the fluid, and the vapor expands and rises to a different area of the piping. There, it transfers away its heat, condenses, and flows back to the heat source.

Heat sink
A cooling mechanism that absorbs and transfers heat better than its surroundings.

Hertz
A count of cycles per second. Hertz is used to note how many times per second alternating current switches directions (polarities).

Hex
Shorthand notation for hexadecimal numbers or the hexadecimal numbering system.

Hexadecimal
The base-16 numbering system.

Host
A computer on a network.

Hot-swapping
Changing a drive in an array, or adding or removing a device, without shutting down and powering off the system.

HTTP (Hypertext Transfer Protocol)
Protocol used to send and receive Web pages over the Internet.

Hub
A device that connects nodes on a LAN and broadcasts data received from any node to all other nodes.

HVPS
A high-voltage power supply in laser printers that creates the high voltages required in the printing process.

IEEE 1394
A high-speed peripheral interconnection bus, better known as FireWire.

Impedance
The force that opposes the flow of AC through a conductor. Analogous to resistance.

Infrared
A wireless transmission technique that uses pulses of infrared light to transmit signals between devices.

Infrared port
A line-of-sight wireless technology for connecting computing devices. It sends infrared light, which is invisible to human eyes.

Instruction
A low-level, hardware-specific command to be acted upon by a processor.

Insulator
A material that inhibits the flow of electricity.

Interface
A communications standard that defines how data flows to and from the disk drive. In practice, an interface is implemented as a circuit board attached to the drive unit.

Interrupt
A signal sent by a device to the CPU to gain its attention.

Inverter
A device that converts DC to AC.

I/O address
A section of memory shared between the CPU and a device and through which those components can transfer data.

IPCONFIG
A TCP/IP utility that displays the computer's adapter address, IP address, subnet mask, and default gateway, and allows the DHCP lease to be renewed or released by the user.

IPX (Internet Packet eXchange)
An OSI Network-layer protocol that handles moving information over the network. It is a connectionless protocol.

IPX/SPX protocol suite
The protocol suite used by Novell NetWare networks.

IRQ
Interrupt request line, a channel over which interrupt signals are transmitted.

ISA bus
Industry Standard Architecture bus; the 16-bit expansion bus of the IBM PC/AT computers and clones.

ISDN (Integrated Services Digital Network)
A technology that uses a telephone line to transmit digital data at a high speed.

Jumpers
Plastic and metal covers that slide over metal pins, used to configure older hardware components.

Laser scanning assembly
A component that contains the laser which is used to write the image to the drum in a laser printer.

Lithium ion (Li-Ion)
A lightweight battery used in portable computing devices.

Local accounts
User accounts stored in the computer's local security database and available only on the computer on which they were created.

Local area network (LAN)
A regionally confined network consisting of computers that communicate and share data and services.

Low-level formatting
The preparation step that divides the disk into tracks and divides each track into sectors. With hard drives, this step is performed at the factory.

LPT ports
Line printer (parallel) ports, which are named LPT1, LPT2, and so forth.

MBR (master boot record)
The first sector on the bootable hard disk. It contains partition information and other information used by the computer after the POST has finished.

Memory card
Solid-state flash memory in a card format.

Memory effect
A process by which batteries can gradually lose power because they "remember" how full they were the last time they were charged and then don't charge past that point when recharged.

Memory Stick
A flash memory card developed by Sony and used in portable devices, especially digital still and video cameras. Roughly the size of a pack of gum.

Metaformat
See *Card Information Structure*.

MICRODIMM
A memory standard for notebooks that uses CSP architecture, grid ball array, or other technologies.

Microprocessor
A CPU contained on a single chip. Most CPUs are microprocessors.

Mini PCI card
A card that provides the same functionality as a desktop PCI card, but in a smaller format for portable computing devices.

MIPS
Millions of instructions per second; a measure of CPU processing speed.

Modems
Devices that convert a digital signal into an analog one through a process called modulation. Modems enable you to connect your computer to another computer through a phone line.

Modulation
The process through which a modem converts a digital signal into an analog one. The digital signal is layered over the analog wave to produce a composite analog wave that encodes the digital signal.

Motherboard
The main circuit board in a personal computer.

Multimeter
A meter that can be used to measure various electrical properties.

NAT (Network Address Translation)
A service that allows multiple computers to access the Internet by sharing a single public IP address.

NetBEUI
Network BIOS Extended User Interface. A non-routable, proprietary Microsoft protocol commonly used for LANs.

NetBIOS
An OSI Session-layer protocol that provides name resolution and session management between computers.

Network interface card (NIC)
A device for connecting a node to a network.

Network layer
The layer of the OSI model that addresses data messages, translates logical addresses into actual physical addresses, and routes data to addresses on the network.

Nickel cadmium (NiCad)
A type of battery used for portable computing devices. Suffers from the *memory effect*.

Nickel metal-hydride (NiMH)
An environmentally friendly battery used for portable computing devices.

nm
Nanometer; a measurement of visible light wavelength. An nm is 1×10^{-9} meters (one millionth of a millimeter).

Node
A computer or other device connected to a LAN by a NIC.

Non-volatile memory
Memory that retains its contents even when power is removed.

Octal system
The base-8 numbering system.

OSI (Open Systems Interconnect) model
A standard means of describing a network operating system by defining it as a series of layers, each with a specific input and output.

Package
A case made from plastic, ceramic, glass, metal, or other material, plus the wires and connectors that bridge the microscopic connections on the die with the external circuitry. A package might also include support function chips, memory, and cooling-related components.

Page file
A file that is used to temporarily store active data that doesn't fit in the RAM installed on the computer.

Paper control and transport assembly
The components in a laser printer that move the paper through the printer.

Parallel transmission
A technique by which the 8 bits in a byte are transmitted simultaneously, with each bit traveling over its own path in the transmission medium.

Parity
An error detection scheme, used in telecommunications, memory storage, and data storage.

Partition
A portion of a disk that contains a volume.

Partitioning
Dividing a disk into one or more logical drives, which are also called volumes.

Patch panel
A device consisting of a row or block of jacks, used for connecting all components on a network.

PC Card
An expansion card for portable computers; approximately the size of a credit card.

PCI bus
Peripheral Component Interconnect bus, a 32- or 64-bit expansion bus used in Pentium-based and other modern PCs.

PCMCIA
Personal Computer Memory Card International Association, the group responsible for establishing the standards for expansion cards for portable computing devices.

PDA (personal digital assistant)
Handheld computing device. Most often used for organizing address books, schedules, and notes.

Peer-to-peer network
A network in which computers can act as either workstations or servers.

Peripherals
External computer components, such as printers, keyboards, and mice.

Ping
A TCP/IP utility that enables a user at one computer to determine if that node can communicate with another computer on the network.

Pixels
Picture elements; the smallest addressable area on the screen.

Plug and Play (PnP)
A system through which devices in a PC are discovered automatically and configured to use system resources without causing conflicts. PnP requires cooperation between hardware and software (operating system) components.

Port
A connector into which you can plug cables from external devices, or in some cases, plug in the devices themselves.

POST
The power-on self test, a simple set of hardware tests performed by the computer when you turn it on.

POTS (plain old telephone service)
The analog phone service used in most homes; can be used for dial-up Internet connections.

Power supply
The internal component that converts wall voltage (110 V or 220 V) to the various DC voltages used by the computer's other components.

Primary partition
A partition that is directly accessed by the operating system as a volume.

Primary Service Interface (PRI)
An ISDN configuration intended for large organizations.

Protocol
A set of rules and standards that a network uses to communicate among its nodes.

Protocol suite
A group of protocols that work together to provide services.

RAID (redundant array of independent disks)
A set of standards for lengthening disk life, preventing data loss, and enabling relatively uninterrupted access to data.

RAM (random access memory)
The hardware component that stores data as the CPU works with it.

Resistance
The force that opposes the flow of DC through a conductor. Analogous to impedance.

Resolution
The number of pixels across and down contained in an image or displayed on a monitor.

RG-58
Coaxial cable used for Ethernet networks. Also known as Thinnet.

RG-59
Coaxial cable used for cable television transmission.

RG-6
Coaxial cable used for long-distance cable television transmission.

RG-8
Coaxial cable used for Ethernet networks. Also known as Thicknet.

Riser card
A circuit board that connects to a motherboard to provide additional expansion slots or sockets.

RJ-11 connectors
Square, 6-pin connectors used with phone, modem, and LocalTalk connections.

RJ-45
A terminating 8-pin connector on a twisted-pair cable used for network connections.

Root directory
The highest-level folder on the disk.

Routable protocol
A protocol that allows data to be sent to interconnected networks on the Internet.

Router
A device that connects two or more networks and directs the data traffic passing between them.

SDRAM
Synchronous DRAM; memory that is synchronized to the system clock.

Sectors
Divisions of tracks in which data is written.

Secure Digital
A flash memory card used in portable devices, especially digital cameras.

Security Accounts Manager (SAM) database
The local security and account database on a Windows server.

Serial transmission
A transmission technique in which bits of data are sent one at a time across the medium.

Server
A computer or device that provides network services or manages network resources.

Service set identifier (SSID)
The network name for a wireless LAN.

Shadowing
The process of copying the contents of the BIOS into RAM for faster access.

SmartMedia
A flash memory card developed by Toshiba and used in portable devices, especially digital cameras.

Socket Services
BIOS-level software that manages PC Cards and detects their insertion and removal.

SODIMM (small outline dual inline memory module)
A memory standard, with 144-pin dual inline memory, used in notebook computers.

Software
A set of instructions processed by the central processing chip in the computer.

SPX (Sequenced Packet eXchange)
The OSI Transport-layer protocol that provides guaranteed delivery of packets.

Static electricity
A phenomenon that occurs when the charges on separate objects are unequal and the charge imbalance creates an electrical field that can cause objects to attract or repel each other.

STP
Shielded twisted-pair cable used for LANs.

Striping
A RAID implementation in which data is divided into blocks and the blocks are distributed across the drives in the array.

Stylus
A pointing device used to interact with touch-screen devices.

Subnet mask
A string of 32 bits that is used to define which portion of an IP address is the host ID and which part is the network ID.

Subpixels
Components of a pixel. Each pixel on an LCD monitor is composed of three subpixels, each covered by a red, blue, or green filter.

Surge protector
A device that protects computers and other equipment from electrical surges and spikes.

Switch
A device used in a LAN to direct data traffic among the nodes.

TCP/IP
A protocol suite composed of Transmission Control Protocol (TCP) and Internet Protocol (IP). The most common protocol used to connect networks.

Telnet
A TCP/IP utility that allows a user in one location to access a computer in a remote location as if the user were physically sitting in front of the remote machine.

Termination
The process of adding terminators to the bus. Both ends of a SCSI bus must be terminated. You cannot have terminators in the middle of the bus.

Terminators
Devices, basically electrical resistors, that serve to absorb signals that reach the end of the SCSI bus.

TFT (thin-film transistor)
A type of active matrix LCD monitor containing metallic contacts composed of thin film, a layer of semiconductive material, and a layer of insulating material.

Thinnet
Another name for RG-58 Ethernet cables.

Toner
Fine particles composed of carbon, polyester, and iron oxide, held in a cartridge and used in laser printers to produce images.

Toner cartridge
A container filled with toner, an EP drum, a blade to remove used toner from the drum, and a corona charging assembly used to apply a static charge to the drum after the image has printed.

Touch screen
A display in which users interact with the application by touching the display with a finger or stylus.

Tracert
A TCP/IP utility that shows the complete path that data packets are taking from the computer to reach any given destination.

Tracks
On the disk medium, concentric or spiral rings that are divided into sectors, which store data.

Transfer corona assembly
The components in a laser printer that transfer the image from the drum to the paper.

Twisted-pair wiring
A set of two wires twisted around one another in a specific manner to improve data transmission in a high-speed cable.

Type I PC Card
A PC Card, 3.3 mm thick, most often used for memory.

Type II PC Card
A PC Card, 5 mm thick, most often used for network adapters, modems, and other communications channels, such as SCSI, USB, or FireWire.

Type III PC Card
A PC Card, 10.5 mm thick, most often used for additional storage.

UDF (universal disk format)
An ISO 13346 standard implementation used for flash media, REV discs, and rewritable CD and DVD discs.

Universal data connector (UDC)
A connector used on token ring networks to connect the computer to the network.

UPS (uninterruptible power supply)
A device that protects computers and other equipment from brownouts and blackouts.

USB (Universal Serial Bus)
A peripheral specification developed by a consortium of companies. It defines a bus architecture to which you can connect one or more expansion devices.

UTP
Unshielded twisted-pair, a type of wiring that is used for LANs and does not contain any shielding.

VESA local bus (VLB)
The Video Electronics Standard Association video bus developed for 80486-based computers.

Video bus
The bus that transmits display information between the CPU and the video circuitry.

Volatile memory
Memory that loses its contents when power is removed.

Volt
The unit of measure of voltage. Officially abbreviated with an uppercase V, but often written with a lowercase v.

Voltage
The force of electricity caused by a difference in charge, or electrical potential, at two locations.

VRM (voltage regulator module)
The internal component that receives power from the power supply and sends the correct voltages to the CPU.

War driving
The act of driving around in a car and using a laptop with a wireless network card to see which networks can be connected to.

Watt
The measure of electrical power. Power is a derived quantity: 1 watt = 1 volt × 1 amp.

WEP (Wired Equivalent Privacy)
A protocol, built into the 802.11 standards, that governs how data can be encrypted while in transit on the wireless network.

Wide area network (WAN)
A network covering large geographic areas, such as counties, states, or countries, or the world.

Wi-Fi (Wireless Fidelity)
The IEEE 802.11b wireless standard with an 11 Mbps transmission rate.

WiMAX
The IEEE 802.16 Air Interface Standard, an emerging wireless standard for metropolitan area networks. It offers a range of up to 31 miles.

Windows print processes
The processes involved in getting the print request from the user to the printer.

WinModem
A Windows-based combination of simple hardware (basically, just physical components to interface with the motherboard and phone lines) and modem-function emulation software.

WINS (Windows Internet Naming Service)
A service used to resolve NetBIOS names to IP addresses and to store NetBIOS service information.

Wireless access point (WAP)
A device that wireless computing devices use to communicate and connect with network services.

Wireless router
A device to which nodes in a wireless LAN can connect, using radio waves.

Workgroup
A logical group of computers characterized by a decentralized security and administration model.

Workstation
A computer connected to a network.

WPA (Wi-Fi Protected Access)
A wireless communication protocol that is replacing WEP. It uses a shared key for security.

xD-Picture Card
A flash memory card developed by Olympus and Fujifilm and used in portable devices, especially digital cameras.

Zinc air batteries
Batteries that use a carbon membrane to absorb oxygen, contain a zinc plate, and use potassium hydroxide electrolyte. Used in portable computing devices.

Zoomed Video (ZV)
A technology that provides direct communication between the PC card and the video controller.

Index

A

AC signals, 1-14
Access control, 10-21
Access control list (ACL), 12-39
Access Denied errors, troubleshooting, 12-39
Address bus, 2-12
Advanced startup options, 9-50
Adware, 12-13
AGP slots, 4-15
Alternating current, 1-3
Analog-to-digital converter, 4-18
Antivirus software, 12-10
AppleTalk, 10-18
Applications
    Adding to Startup group, 8-28
    Managing in Task Manager, 9-15
ATA drives, identifying, 5-3
Attenuation, 11-8
Authentication on WLANs, 10-21, 10-30

B

Backups, scheduling, 9-28
Banking requirements, 3-2
Base 10 numbering, A-2
Base memory address, 4-3, 4-9
Battery backups, 1-15
Berg connector, 1-6
Binary notation, A-3
BIOS, 2-3
    Configuring, 2-5
    Troubleshooting, 2-32
    Update failures, 2-34
    Updating, 2-32, 12-20
BitLocker Drive Encryption, 12-52
Bluetooth, 10-7, 10-19
Blu-ray discs, 5-19
Boot error messages, 9-44
Boot logging, 9-50
Bottlenecks, identifying, 9-5
Branch prediction, 2-12
Buses
    Address, 2-12
    Connections for PC Cards, 7-10
    Data, 2-12
    Front-side, 2-13
    Internal, 2-12
    PCI Express, 7-10
    Types of, 4-2

C

Cable modems, 10-4
Cable testing devices, 11-8
Caches, 2-13
Card Services, 7-10
CardBus, 7-10
Carriage locks, 6-19
CD drives, 5-18
    Installing, 5-19
    Troubleshooting, 5-39
Cell-phone Internet access, 10-6
Checksum verification, 5-14
Chipsets, 2-7
Clock speed, 2-13
CMOS, 2-3
    Configuring, 3-3
    Replacing battery for, 2-30
    Troubleshooting, 2-36
Command Prompt, running as administrator, 8-26
Command-line utility (command.com), 8-2
Commands
    Chdir/cd, 8-6
    Chkdsk, 5-32
    Command/cmd, 8-3
    Copy, 8-11
    Defrag, 5-30
    Deltree, 8-14
    Dir, 8-4
    Edit, 8-16, 8-18
    Getting help on, 8-6
    IPCONFIG, 11-17
    Mkdir/md, 8-9
    Net, 8-26
    NSLookup, 11-23
    Ping, 11-20
    Rmdir/rd, 8-14
    Spaces in, 8-9
    Tracert, 11-23
    Ver, 9-57
    Xcopy, 8-12
Configuration weaknesses, 12-3
Connectors
    Floppy drives, 5-26
    Optical drives, 5-20
    Power, drives, 1-6
    Power, motherboard, 1-8
Continuous UPS, 1-15
CPUs
    Cooling, 2-21
    Factors affecting performance of, 2-12

Installing, 2-24
Package types, 2-8
Troubleshooting, 2-37
Crosstalk, 11-7
Current
    DC vs. AC, 1-3
    Measuring, 1-21

D

Data
    Backing up, 9-28
    Restoring from backups, 9-32
    Restoring with System Restore, 9-36
Data bus, 2-12
Debugging mode, 9-50
Decimals, A-2
Deleted files, recovering, 5-37
Deltree command, 8-14
Device Manager, 4-5
Digital signal processor, 4-18
Digital-to-analog converter, 4-18
DIMMs, 3-4
Dir command, 8-4
Direct current, 1-3
Directories
    Copying, 8-11
    Creating, 8-9
    Removing, 8-14
Directory structures, 8-3
Disk Cleanup utility, 5-35
Disk duplexing, 5-13
Disk Management utility, 5-7, 5-9
Disk mirroring, 5-13, 5-15
Disks
    Checking, 5-32
    Defragmenting, 5-29
DMA channels, 4-3, 4-9
DoS attacks, 12-4
Drivers, 4-13, 5-20
    Updating, 4-21
DSL, 10-3
Dual Independent Bus, 2-13
Dumpster diving, 12-7
DVD drives, 5-19
    Troubleshooting, 5-40

E

Edit command, 8-16, 8-18
Effective permissions, 12-39
Effective Permissions
    Determining, 12-40
Electricity
    Characteristics of, 1-2
    Safety precautions for, 1-10
    Static, 1-8
Elevation prompts, 12-33
Encrypting File System, 12-51
Encryption, 10-21

Ethernet types and speeds, 10-10
Event Viewer, 9-20
Events
    Filtering, 9-25
    Grouping, 9-24
    Sorting, 9-24
    Types of, 9-21
Execute in Place (XIP), 7-10
Expansion buses, 4-2
Expansion cards
    Handling, 4-13
    Installing, 4-14
Extended partitions, 5-7

F

Fax problems, troubleshooting, 6-22
Fdisk command, 5-7
File attributes, 12-40
File systems, 5-8
Firewalls, 10-7
Firmware, 2-3
Flash drives, 5-23
Floppy drives
    Cables for, 5-26
    Controllers for, 5-26
    Troubleshooting, 5-37
Folders, encrypting, 12-51
Format command, 5-9
Formatting
    High-level, 5-8
    Low-level, 5-6
Front-side bus, 2-13
FTP, 11-28

G

Gadgets, 8-38
Generators, 1-17

H

Handheld devices
    Calibrating, 7-19
    Maintaining power for, 7-22
    Memory in, 3-7
Hard drives
    Encrypting, 12-52
    Formatting, 5-9
    Freeing up space on, 5-35
    In notebooks, 7-14
    Installing, 5-2
    Partitioning, 5-6
    Preparing for use, 5-6
    Troubleshooting, 5-37
Hardware toolkit, 11-2
Heat pipes, 2-22
Heat sinks, 2-21
Hexidecimals, A-5
Hibernate mode, 7-4, 7-7

Hot-swapping, 5-23, 7-9
HTTP, 11-28
Human error, security, 12-4
Hyperthreading, 2-13

I

I/O addresses, 4-3, 4-8
IEEE 1394 ports, troubleshooting, 4-28
IEEE 802.11 standards, 10-16
IMAP4, 11-29
Impedance, 1-3
Indexing settings, 8-31
Inkjet printers, maintaining, 6-3
Interference, electrical, 11-7
IPCONFIG command, 11-17
IPX/SPX, 10-18
IRQ assignments, 4-6
ISDN, 10-3

L

Laser printers, maintaining, 6-4
Last Known Good Configuration, 9-50
Latency sensitivity, 11-11
LCD monitors, 7-17
Local Security Policy console, 12-34
Logic bombs, 12-10
Logical drives, 5-6
Loopback adapters, 4-30
Low-level formatting, 5-6

M

Malware, disabling and removing, 12-16
MBR, 5-7
Memory
   Handling, 3-3
   In handheld devices, 3-7
   In notebooks, 3-6, 7-13
   Installing, 3-2
   Monitoring usage of, 3-8
   Package types, 3-4
   Shared video, 3-6, 7-13
   Testing, 3-12
   Troubleshooting, 3-13
Memory leaks, 9-5
MICRODIMMs, 3-4
Mini PCI cards, 7-13
Mkdir/md command, 8-9
MMX, 2-13
Molex connector, 1-6
Motherboards
   Components of, 2-26
   Installing, 2-27
   Power connectors, 1-8
   Sockets and slots on, 2-11
   Troubleshooting, 2-37
Msconfig.exe, 9-53
Multimedia ports, troubleshooting, 4-29

Multimeters, 1-19
Multiprocessing, 2-13

N

Net command, 8-26
NetBEUI, 10-18
Network address translation (NAT), 10-7
Network analyzers, 11-9
Network isolation, 10-22
Network noise, 11-7
Network utilization, monitoring, 9-18
Networks
   3G and 4G, 10-6
   Protocols, 10-18
   Troubleshooting, 11-7
NICs, wireless, 10-14
Northbridge chips, 2-7
Notebooks
   Configuring with Windows Mobility Center, 7-2
   Hard drives, 7-14
   LCD monitors, 7-17
   Memory, 3-6, 7-13
   Network adapters, 7-15
   Ports for peripherals, 7-16
   Power problems, 7-22
   Replacing components in, 7-8
   Sleeping and hibernating, 7-7
   Troubleshooting, 7-17
   Using PC Cards in, 7-9
NSLookup, 11-23
NTFS permissions, 12-41

O

Octal notation, A-4
Online attacks, 12-7
Operating-system load errors, 9-48
Optical drives, installing, 5-19
Out-of-order completion, 2-13
Overclocking, 2-13

P

Packet filtering, 10-8
Page files, 3-11
Parallel ports, troubleshooting, 4-26
Partitions
   Creating, 5-7
   Primary vs. extended, 5-7
Passwords, 12-25
   Requiring, 12-29
PC Cards, 7-9
   Installing, 7-11
PCI bus, 4-2
PCI slots, 4-15
PCIe cards, 4-16
Peltier coolers, 2-22
Performance Monitor, 9-4
   Configuring, 9-9

Performance tab, Task Manager, 3-8
Ping command, 11-20
Pipelining, 2-13
Pixelation, 7-18
Plug and Play, 4-6
Port addresses, 11-25
POST troubleshooting, 2-35
POTS/PSTN, 10-3
Power conditioning, 1-15
Power supplies
   Installing, 1-12
   Selecting, 1-5
   Troubleshooting, 1-23
Power_Good signal, 1-23
Power-saving modes, 7-4
Printers
   Maintaining, 6-2
   Troubleshooting, 6-10
Processes
   Monitoring, 9-17
   Viewing, 4-4
Processors
   Specifications of, 2-14
   Using multiple, 2-14
Protocols
   AppleTalk, 10-18
   Bluetooth, 10-7, 10-19
   FTP, 11-28
   HTTP, 11-28
   IEEE 802.11a, 10-19
   IMAP4, 11-29
   IPX/SPX, 10-18
   NetBEUI, 10-18
   POP3, 11-29
   SMTP, 11-29
   SSH, 11-28
   SSL, 11-28
   TCP/IP, 10-18
   Wi-Fi, 10-19
   WiMAX, 10-19
Proxy servers, 10-8, 11-29
PS/2 ports, troubleshooting, 4-27

Q

QoS mechanisms, 11-11

R

RADIUS, 10-21, 10-23
RAID
   Level 0, 5-15
   Level 1, 5-15
   Level 5, 5-16
   Levels, 5-13
   Software vs. hardware, 5-16
RAM
   Addressable, 2-12
   Package types, 3-4
Register renaming, 2-13

Reliability and Performance Monitor, 9-2
Reliability Monitor, 9-12
Remote Assistance, 8-43
Remote Desktop, 8-46
Resistance, 1-3
   Measuring, 1-20
Resource Overview, 9-2
Resources, monitoring, real-time, 9-6
Restore points, creating, 9-34
RIMMs, 3-4
Rmdir/rd command, 8-14
Root directory, 5-8, 8-3

S

Safe mode, 9-50
SATA connector, 1-6
Satellite Internet access, 10-5
Scanners
   Maintaining, 6-8
   Troubleshooting, 6-19
SCSI drives, identifying, 5-3
Secure Shell (SSH), 11-28
Secure Sockets Layer (SSL), 11-28
Security log, 9-20
Security threats, types of, 12-2
Serial ports, troubleshooting, 4-26
Services console, 8-22
Shadowing, 2-3
Share permissions, 12-41
Shared video memory, 3-6
Shoulder surfing, 12-6
SIMD, 2-13
SIMMs, 3-4
Sleep mode, 7-4, 7-7
SMTP, 11-29
Social engineering, 12-6
   Countermeasures, 12-8
Socket Services, 7-10
Socket types, 2-11
SODIMMs, 3-4
Software toolkits, 11-4
Solid-state drives, 5-4
Sound cards, 4-18
   Troubleshooting, 4-24
Southbridge chips, 2-7
Speculative execution, 2-14
Spyware, 12-13
Stability Index, 9-13
Standby mode, 7-4
Standby UPS, 1-15
Startup errors, 9-44, 9-47
Startup group, 8-28
Startup program group, 8-28
Static electricity, 1-8
Striping, 5-13
Superpipelining, 2-14
Superscalar, 2-14
Surge protectors, 1-15

System Configuration utility, 9-53
System File Checker, 9-60
System Information window, 9-56
System resources
    For serial and parallel ports, 4-10
    Viewing, 4-5
System Restore utility, 9-34
System state, backing up, 9-28

T

Task Manager, 3-8, 4-4, 9-14
    Applications tab, 9-15
    Networking tab, 9-18
    Processes tab, 9-17
    Users tab, 9-18
Task Scheduler, 9-39
TCP/IP, 10-18
Technology weaknesses, 12-3
Text files
    Creating, 8-16
    Editing, 8-18
Throttling, 2-14
TMP chips, 12-52
Tracert command, 11-23
Transmission Control Protocol (TCP), 11-25
Trojan horses, 12-10
Troubleshooting
    Access Denied errors, 12-39
    BIOS, 2-32
    Boot errors, 9-44
    CD drives, 5-39
    CMOS, 2-36
    DVD drives, 5-40
    Faxes, 6-22
    Hard and floppy drives, 5-37
    IEEE 1394 connections, 4-28
    Memory, 3-13
    Motherboard and CPU, 2-37
    Multimedia ports, 4-29
    Networks, wired, 11-7
    Networks, wireless, 11-12
    Notebooks, 7-17, 7-22
    Operating-system load errors, 9-48
    Parallel connections, 4-26
    POST, 2-35
    Power supplies, 1-23
    Printers, 6-10
    PS/2 connections, 4-27
    Scanners, 6-19
    Serial connections, 4-26
    Sound cards, 4-24
    Startup errors, 9-47
    TCP/IP problems, 11-15
    Tools for, 11-2
    USB connections, 4-27
    Video cards, 4-23
    Windows Aero, 8-37
    Wireless connections, 4-29, 11-13

U

UPSs, 1-15
USB flash drives, 5-23
USB ports, troubleshooting, 4-27
User Account Control (UAC), 12-32
    Working with, 12-34
User accounts, 12-22
    Creating, 12-24
    Deleting, 12-31
    Disabling, 12-31
User Datagram Protocol (UDP), 11-25
Users, viewing in Task Manager, 9-18

V

Ver command, 9-57
Video adapters, 4-15
    Troubleshooting, 4-23
VoIP, 10-4
Voltage, 1-2
    Core vs. I/O, 2-18
    Measuring, 1-21
    Setting on power supply, 1-12
Voltage regulator modules, 2-18
Volumes, 5-6
    Mounting, 8-19

W

War driving, 10-20
Water pumps, 2-22
Watts, 1-3
WEP, 10-23
Wi-Fi protocol, 10-19
WiMAX protocol, 10-19
Windows
    Activation, 2-28
    Advanced startup options, 9-50
    Appearance settings, 8-33
    Indexing settings, 8-31
    Region and language settings, 8-29
Windows Backup utility, 9-28
Windows Defender, 12-13
    Configuring, 12-16
Windows Diagnostics, 9-56
Windows File Protection, 9-60
Windows Firewall, 12-46
    Configuring, 12-48
Windows Network Diagnostics, 11-31
Windows Security Center, 12-46
Windows Vista
    Aero interface, 8-33
    Aero, troubleshooting, 8-37
    Grouping and filtering events, 9-24
    Remote Assistance, 8-43
    Remote Desktop, 8-46
    Sidebar, 8-38
    Windows Mobility Center, 7-2

Wireless access points, 10-14
    Configuring, 10-26
Wireless Auto Configuration, 10-30
Wireless connections, troubleshooting, 4-29, 11-13
Wireless Internet access, 10-6
Wireless LANs
    Client/AP isolation, 10-22
    Encryption methods for, 10-22
    IEEE 802.11 standards, 10-16
    Security risks for, 10-20
    Troubleshooting, 11-12

Wireless Zero Configuration, 10-30
Worms, 12-10
WPA, 10-23

X

Xcopy command, 8-12

Z

Zoomed Video, 7-10